Beginner's Guide to Modeling, Shading, and Lighting in 3ds Max® 2016

Raavi O'Connor

3ds Max is the registered trademarks of Autodesk Inc.

Book Code: VO12C

ISBN: 978-1523705313

http://raavidesign.blogspot.co.uk

Contents

Acknowledgements

About the Author

Preface

Unit MH1: Hands-on Exercises [Modeling] MH1-1

This page intentionally left blank

Photoshop is not just about retouching images or manipulating photos; it can be used for creating custom textures. While there are some powerful 3D paint tools such as Mari that provides fluid and flexible way to paint directly onto the 3D models, Photoshop is still used by a vast majority digital artists and designers across the globe. This book presents a foundation of techniques to help you build custom textures and designs.

This book is written using Photoshop CC 2014. It is aimed at creative professionals who wants to create creative designs, textures, maps, and backgrounds in Photoshop. This book is specifically dedicated to those design and texturing artists who regularly use textures to add realism to their models/artwork.

The internet is full of resources that you can use in your 3D project. However, there is every chance that you would like to create custom textures for your models. Photoshop offers endless opportunities when it comes to creating textures (creating unique textures).

You will learn how to use the tools and techniques available in Photoshop to create custom textures for your models and designs. The examples in this book show readers step-by-step the key techniques for creating textures, maps, and backgrounds in Photoshop CC 2014, and how to effectively use filters and commands to create cool artwork. Each filter and command is explained so that you can relate them with the outcome you are seeing on the screen.

In addition to the creating backgrounds, you will learn techniques to create bump, specular, reflection, displacement, and normal maps that you can use to give life to your 3D models. Also, you will learn to create seamless high-res textures.

The commands and tools are explained with examples and related screen captures. Additional tips, guidance, and advice is provided in from of Tips, Notes, and Warnings. You will gain skills by completing the examples provided in the book.

More info: http://bit.ly/textures-cc

Acknowledgements

Thanks to:

Sarah O'Connor for the cover art and other promotional material.
Alex for formatting the book.
Everyone at Autodesk [www.autodesk.com].

Thanks to all great digital artists who inspire us with their innovative VFX, gaming, animation, and motion graphics content.

And a very special thanks to everyone who helped me along the way in my life and carrier.

Finally, thank you for picking up the book.

This page intentionally left blank

About the Author

Raavi Design, founded by Raavi O'Connor, is a group of like-minded professionals and freelancers who are specialized in advertising, graphic design, web design/development, digital marketing, multimedia, exhibition, print design, branding, and CG content creation.

At Raavi Design we strive to share the enthusiasm and ideas with other digital artists and provide quality CG content to the aspiring artists and students. Our books are written in an easy to understand language so that the users learn the complex concepts quickly.

The main features of our books are as follows:

- Nicely formatted content in books
- Less theory more practical approach saves you hours of struggle and pain
- Content written in easy to understand language
- Exercises/Labs for practice
- Free updates and exclusive bonus content
- Video tutorials
- Free textures, background design, and 3D files

Here's the list of training books that Raavi has put together:

- The Tutorial Bank: 3D, VFX, & Motion Graphics
- Build Studio Light Setup using 3ds Max and VRay
- Exploring Standard Materials in 3ds Max 2015
- Exploring Standard Materials in 3ds Max 2016
- Create Backgrounds, Textures, and Maps in Photoshop: Using Photoshop CC 2014
- Beginner's Guide To Mental Ray and Autodesk Materials In 3ds Max 2016
- Beginner's Guide For Creating 3D Models In 3ds Max 2016
- Beginner's Guide to Shading and Texturing in 3ds Max 2016
- Beginner's Guide to Modeling, Shading, and Lighting in 3ds Max 2016

You can follow Raavi O'Conner on Twitter @raavidesign. You can also contact the author using the following email id: raavioc@gmail.com.

This page intentionally left blank

Preface

Why this Book?

The **Beginner's Guide to Modeling, Shading, and Lighting in 3ds Max 2016** offers a hands-on exercises based strategy for all those digital artists [no experience required] who have just started working on the 3ds Max and interested in learning modeling, shading, texturing, and lighting in 3ds Max. This brilliant guide takes you step-by-step through the whole process of modeling, shading, and texturing. All tools, features, and concepts are discussed in detail.

In this book, the author has covered polygon and spline modeling techniques, modeling processes using **Ribbon**, material editors, **Autodesk Materials**, standard materials/maps, and **mental ray's Arch & Design** material. A better understanding of materials and maps gives you ability to add realism to your artwork. Also, the author has covered standard, photometric, and mental ray lights. The concepts you will learn using this book will immensely help you in creating realistic looking models.

What You Will Learn?

- Navigating the workspace
- Customizing the interface and understanding various UI components
- Working with the file management commands
- Understanding workspaces
- Understanding the enhanced menu system
- Using the navigational gizmos
- Polygon modeling techniques
- Modeling and painting processes using the **Ribbon**
- Spline modeling techniques
- Effecting use of modifiers
- Working with the useful but less talked about tools
- Efficiently use **Compact** and **Slate** material editors
- Create shading networks using material editors
- Quickly apply shading to models using the **Autodesk Materials**
- Create variety of shading models using **mental ray's Arch & Design** material

- Learn the mental ray's features such as **Global Illumination**, **Final Gather**, and **Caustics**
- Work with UVs using **UV Editor**
- Standard, photometric, and mental ray lights

What you need?

To complete the examples and hands-on exercises in this book, you need v2016 of Autodesk 3ds Max. To know more about 3ds Max, visit the following links:

http://www.autodesk.com/products/3ds-max/overview

If you are an educator or student, you can access free Autodesk software from the **Autodesk Education Community**. The **Autodesk Education Community** is an online resource with more than five million members that lets educators and students to download free Autodesk software. In addition, you can connect with millions of other digital artists to know about latest and greatest in the CG industry.

What are the main features of the book?

- Content written using 3ds Max 2016 in an easy to understand language
- 46 Hands-on exercises to hone your skills
- Detailed coverage of tools and features
- Additional tips, guidance, and advice are provided
- Important terms are in bold face so that you never miss them
- Support for technical aspect of the book
- Free textures, background design, and 3ds max files available for download from the accompanying website

How This Book Is Structured?

This book is divided into following units:

Unit M1 - Introduction to 3ds Max - I

- Navigating the workspace
- Customizing the interface
- Understanding various UI components
- Working with the file management commands
- Setting preferences for 3ds Max
- Understanding workspaces
- Understanding the enhanced menu system
- Working with viewports
- Setting preferences for the viewports
- Creating objects in the scene
- Selecting objects
- Using the navigational gizmos

- Moving, rotating, and scaling objects
- Getting help

Unit M2 - Introduction to 3ds Max - II
- Working with templates
- Creating clones and duplicates
- Understanding hierarchies
- Working with the **Scene** and **Layer** Explorers
- Understanding the **Mirror** tool, the **Select and Place** tool, and the **Select and Manipulate** tool
- Working with the **Align** tool and the **Array** tool
- Working with precision and drawing aids
- Understanding modifiers, and normals

Unit M3 - Working with Geometric Primitives and Architectural Objects
- Creating and modifying **Standard** Primitives
- Creating and modifying **Extended** Primitives
- Working with the **Architectural** objects
- Setting the project folder
- Using the **Align** and **Mirror** tools
- Creating clones
- Using the **Scene Explorer**
- Creating a group
- Setting grid spacings
- Using **Transform Type-In** dialog
- Using **Array** dialog
- Specifying units for the scene

Unit M4 - Working with Polygons
- Working with the polygon modeling tools
- Using the polygon modeling techniques
- Selecting polygon sub-object
- Transforming sub-objects
- Soft selecting sub-objects

Unit M5 - Graphite Modeling Tools
- Working with the **Graphite Modeling Tools**
- Selecting sub-objects
- Creating models using the tools available in the **Ribbon**
-

Unit M6 - Working with Shapes
- Generate planar and 3d surfaces
- Paths and shapes for the loft components
- Generate extrusions

- Generate revolved surfaces
- Define motion path for animations

Unit M7 - Modifiers
- Using modifiers
- Stack display
- Object-space modifiers vs World-space modifiers
- How transform affects modifiers

Unit MH1 - Hands-on Exercises [Modeling]
This unit contains 18 hands-on exercises that allow you to enhance the knowledge that you gained from Unit M1 to Unit M7.

Unit S1 - Material Editors
- **Compact Material Editor**
- **Slate Material Editor**

Unit S2 - Standard Materials and Maps
- Standard materials
- Standard maps

Unit S3 - Mental Ray and Autodesk Materials
- Global Illumination
- Final Gather
- Caustics
- Autodesk Materials
- Arch & Design Material

Unit SH1 - Hands-on Exercises [Shading - I]
Unit SH2 - Hands-on Exercises [Shading - II]
Unit SH3 - Hands-on Exercises [Shading - III]
These three units contain 25 hands-on exercises on texturing and shading in 3ds Max 2016.

Unit L1 - Standard Lighting
- Basic Lighting Concepts
- Creating and placing objects
- 3ds Max Lights
- Light Linking
- Shadows
- Lighting Effects

This unit contains 3 hands-on exercises that allow you to enhance the knowledge that you gained from Unit L1 to Unit L3.

Resources

This book is sold via multiple sales channels. If you don't have access to the resources used in this book, you can place a request for the resources by visiting the following link: *http://bit.ly/rd-contact*. Please mention **"Resources - VO12C"** in the subject line.

Customer Support

At **Raavi Design**, our technical team is always ready to take care of your technical queries. If you are facing any problem with the technical aspect of the book, navigate to *http://bit.ly/rd-contact* and let us know about your query. Please mention **"Technical Query - VO12C"** in the subject line. We will do our best to resolve your queries.

Reader Feedback

Your feedback is always welcome. Your feedback is critical to our efforts at **Raavi Design** and it will help us in developing quality titles in the future. To send the feedback, visit *http://bit.ly/rd-contact*. Please mention **"Feedback - VO12C"** in the subject line.

Errata

We take every precaution while preparing the content of the book but mistakes do happen. If you find any mistake in this book general or technical, we would be happy that you report it to us so that we can mention it in the errata section of the book's online page. If you find any errata, please report them by visiting the following link: *http://bit.ly/rd-contact*. Please mention "Errata - VO12C" in the subject line. This will help the other readers from frustration. Once your errata is verified, it will appear in the errata section of the book's online page.

Stay Connected

Stay connected with us through Twitter (**@raavidesign**) to know the latest updates about our products, information about books, and other related information.

Unit M1: Introducing 3ds Max - I

Welcome to the latest version of **3ds Max**. In any 3D computer graphics application, the first thing you encounter is interface. Interface is where you view and work with your scene. The 3ds Max's interface is intuitive and highly customizable. You can make changes to the interface and then save multiple 3ds Max User Interface [UI] settings using the **Workspaces** feature. You can create multiple workspaces and switch between them easily.

In this unit, I'll describe the following:

- Navigating the workspace
- Customizing the interface
- Understanding various UI components
- Working with the file management commands
- Setting preferences for 3ds Max
- Understanding workspaces
- Understanding the enhanced menu system
- Working with viewports
- Setting preferences for the viewports
- Creating objects in the scene
- Selecting objects
- Using the navigational gizmos
- Moving, rotating, and scaling objects
- Getting help

Note: Interface Customization

By default, 3ds Max starts with a dark theme [white text on the dark gray background]. This is good for those digital artists who spend hours working on 3ds Max, however, the default theme is not good for printing. I have customized the theme so that the captures appear fine when book is printed. You can easily switch between the custom color themes from the **Choose initial settings for tool options and UI layout** *dialog. To open this dialog, choose* **Custom UI and Default Switcher** *from the* **Customize** *menu. If you are coming from a previous version of 3ds Max, most of the interface is same.*

When you first time open the 3ds Max application, you will see the default workspace with the **Welcome Screen** [see Figure 1]. There are three panels available in the **Welcome Screen**: **Learn**, **Start**, and **Extend**.

The content of the **Start** panel appears by default in the **Welcome Screen**. From the **RECENT FILES** section of this panel, you can open the recent files you have worked on. Also, you can look for files on your storage device by clicking the **Browse** button. On the right of the **Start** panel, you will see some templates in the **START-UP TEMPLATES** section and a link to open the **Template Manager**. You can use the **Template Manager** to inspect and edit existing templates.

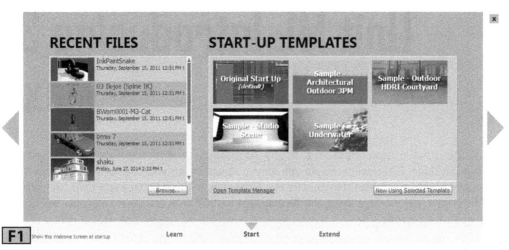

To create a new scene, choose a template and then click **New Using Selected Template**. A new scene will be created with the settings specified by that template. I will explain templates in details in the **Unit 2**. The **Learn** panel [see Figure 2] contains list of **1-Minute Startup Movies** that you can view to learn the basics of some 3ds Max features. When you select a movie from the list, you are taken to a web page where the movie is being played. In the **More Learning Resources** section, there are four links for navigating to 3ds Max Learning Channel, what's new page, learning path page, and downloading the sample content.

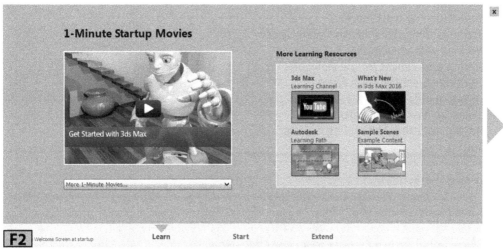

The **Extend** panel [see Figure 3] features ways to extend capabilities of 3ds Max. This panel displays featured apps from the **Autodesk Exchange Store**. It also contains list of useful Autodesk resources.

Note: Welcome Screen
*If you don't want to see the **Welcome Screen** when next time you open 3ds Max, turn off **Show this Welcome Screen at startup**. You can bring back the screen anytime by choosing **Welcome Screen** from the **Help** menu.*

Close the **Welcome Screen** to view the default UI of 3ds Max [refer Figure 4].

Notice, I have marked different components of the UI with numbers to make the learning process easier. In 3ds Max, commands and tools are arranged in groups so that you can find them easily. For example, all viewport navigation tools are grouped together on the bottom-right corner of the interface [marked as 12 in Figure 4]. The 3ds Max interface can be divided into 12 sections. I have marked those sections in Figure 4. Table 1 summarizes the numbers and the sections of the UI they represent.

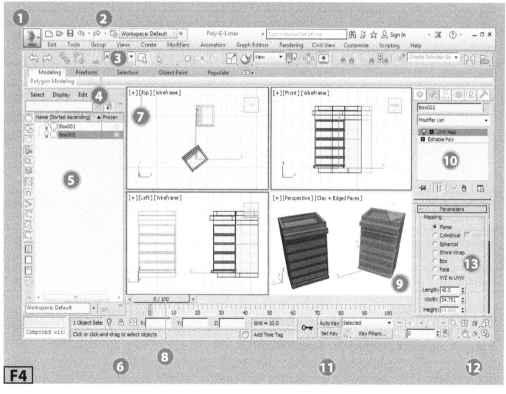

No.	Item	Description
	Table 1: 3ds Max interface overview	
1	Application Button	On clicking this button, the Application menu appears. This menu contains file management commands.
2	Quick Access Toolbar	This toolbar gives access to the file handling and undo/redo commands. It also contains a drop-down that lets you switch among different workspaces.
3	Main Toolbar	This toolbar provides many commonly used tools.
4	The Ribbon	The **Ribbon** contains many tools for modeling and painting in the scene. Also, here you will find tools for adding people to populate a scene.
5	Scene Explorer	The **Scene Explorer** lets you view, sort, filter, and select objects in a scene. You can also use it to rename, delete, hide, and freeze objects. It is also used to create and amend object hierarchies.
6	Status Bar Controls	The **Status Bar** contains the prompt and status information about the scene. The Coordinate Transform Type-In boxes in the **Status Bar** let you transform the objects manually.
7	Viewport Label Menus	These menus let you change the shading style for the viewport. They also contain other viewport related commands and features.
8	Time Slider	Allows you to navigate along the timeline.
9	Viewports	Viewports let you view your scene from multiple angles. They also allow you to preview lighting, shading, shadows, and other effects.
10	Command Panel	The **Command Panel** is the nerve center of 3ds Max. It contains six panels that you can use to create and modify objects in 3ds Max.
11	Create and Play Back Animation	These controls affect the animation. This area also contains buttons to playback animation in the viewports.
12	Viewport Navigation	These buttons allow you to navigate your scene [Active Viewport].
13	Rollout	Rollouts are used to change properties of the object in 3ds Max.

There are some other elements of the interface that are not visible in the default UI. These elements appear when you run a command from the **Main** toolbar or menu, or choose an option from the RMB click menu. Here's is the quick rundown to those elements:

■ **Floating Toolbars**: There are quite a few floating toolbars available in 3ds Max. To access these toolbar, RMB click on a gray area on the toolbar to open a popup menu [see Figure 5] containing the options for invoking the floating toolbars. The popup menu shown in Figure 5 displayed when I RMB clicked on the gray area below the **Names Selection Sets** drop-down on the **Main** toolbar. The area is marked with an arrow in Figure 5. When I chose **MassFx Toolbar** from the popup menu, the floating **Mass FX Toolbar** appeared [see Figure 6].

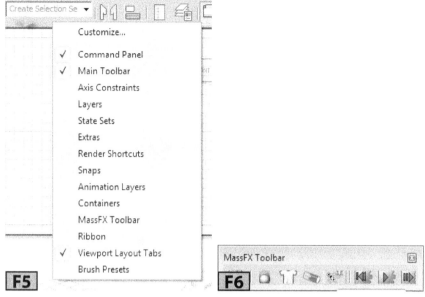

■ **Quad Menus**: Whenever you RMB click in an active viewport [except on a viewport label], 3ds Max opens a **Quad** menu at the location of the mouse pointer. The **Quad** menu can display up to four quadrants [see Figure 7] with various commands and allows you to work efficiently as the commands in the menu are context-sensitive. The **Quad** menu is the quickest way to find commands. Figure 7 shows a **Quad** menu which appeared when I RMB clicked on an **Editable Poly** object in the viewport.

■ **Caddy Controls**: A caddy control in 3ds Max can be described as **"in-canvas"** interface that comprises a dynamic label and an array of buttons superimposed over a viewport. You can use the standard mouse operations such as clicking and dragging to change the values in the spinners. The changes you made are immediately updated in the viewport. The **Chamfer** caddy control shown in Figure 8 appeared when I selected edges of a box and then clicked **Chamfer's Settings** button on the **Command Panel**.

■ **Dialogs, Windows, and Editors**: Some of the commands in 3ds Max opens dialogs, editors, and windows. Some of these elements have their own menu bars and toolbars. Figure 9 shows the **Slate Material Editor**. You can use the **M** hotkey to open this editor.

Note: Spinners

*Spinners are found everywhere in 3ds Max [I have marked **U** and **V** spinners with orange highlight in Figure 9]. Spinners are controllers that you will touch on regular basis. They allow you to quickly amend numerical values with ease. To change the value in a spinner, click the up or down arrow on the right of the spinner. To change values quickly, click and drag the arrows. You can also type a value directly in the spinner's field.*

Tip: Fast and slow scroll rate in a spinner

*Press and hold **Alt** and then click–drag the spinner's up or down arrow for a slower numerical scroll rate. Hold **Ctrl** for the faster scroll rate. RMB click on a spinner to set it to its default value.*

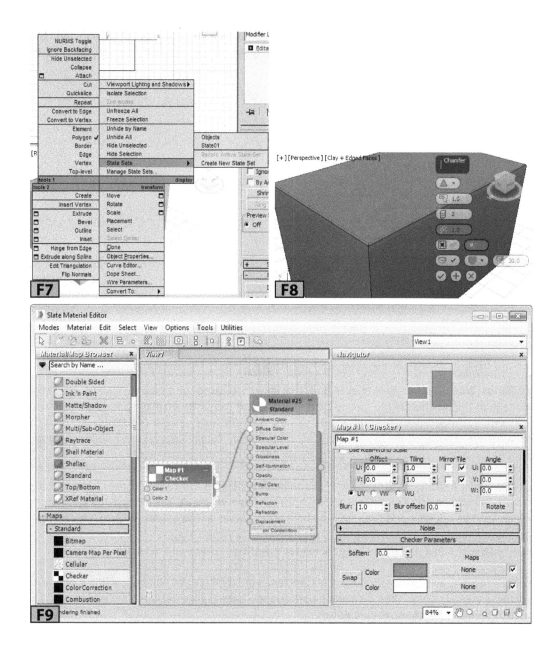

Note: Numerical Expression Evaluator

*If the type cursor is located inside a spinner and you press **Ctrl+N**, the **Numerical Expression Evaluator** appears [see Figure 10]. This evaluator lets you calculate the value for the spinner using an expression.*

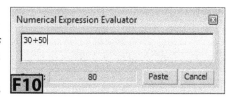

*For example, if you type **30+50** in this evaluator's field and click **Paste**, 80 appears in the associated spinner.*

Note: Modeless dialogs, controls, windows, and editors

*Quite a few dialogs in 3ds Max are **modeless** meaning the dialog doesn't need to be closed in order to work on other elements of the interface. A good example of modeless dialog is the **Slate Material Editor** [see Figure 9]. You can minimize the editor and continue working on the scene. Other modeless dialogs that you would frequently use are **Transform Type-In** dialogs, **Caddy** controls, **Render Scene** dialog, and so forth.*

Tip: Toggling the visibility of all open dialogs
*You can toggle visibility of all open dialogs by using the **Ctrl+~** hotkeys.*

UI Components

The following section presents what you need to know about 3ds Max UI.

Caption Bar

The **Caption** bar is another name for the **Title** bar. It is the topmost element in the 3ds Max UI [see Figure 11].

The **Title** bar hosts the **Application** button, **Quick Access Toolbar**, **Workspaces** drop-down, and **InfoCenter**. It also displays the name of the current 3dsMax file.

Quick Access Toolbar

This toolbar provides most commonly used file-management commands as well as commands for **Undo** and **Redo**. It also contains a drop-down that allows you to switch between different workspaces. Table 2 summarizes the interface of the **Quick Access Toolbar**.

Table 2: The **Quick Access Toolbar** interface		
Item	**Icon**	**Description**
New Scene		Click to create a new scene.
Open File		Click to open a saved file from the storage.
Save File		Click to save file to the disk.
Undo Scene Operation		Click to undo the previous operation. Click the arrow on the right of the button to open a list of previous operations performed in the scene. Hotkeys: **Ctrl+Z**.
Redo Scene Operation		Click to redo the previous operation. Hotkeys: **Ctrl+Y**.
Project Folder		Click to open the **Browse For Folder** dialog to set a project folder for the scene.
Workspaces drop-down list	Workspace: Default	Click to open the options available for managing and switching workspaces.

Quick Access toolbar drop-down		Click to display options to manage the **Quick Access Toolbar**.

Q. Can I remove a button from the Quick Access Toolbar?

Yes. RMB click on the toolbar and then choose **Remove from Quick Access Toolbar** [see Figure 12]. You can also add any button from the **Ribbon** to the **Quick Access Toolbar** by RMB clicking on the button and then choosing **Add To Quick Access Toolbar** [see Figure 13].

Q. Is there any place in the UI from where I can access file management commands?

Yes. You can access file management commands from the **Application** menu. To open the menu, click the **Application** button. You can also open the menu using the **Alt+F** hotkeys. When you press **Alt+F**, 3ds Max superimposes hotkeys on the corresponding **Application** menu items [see Figure 14].

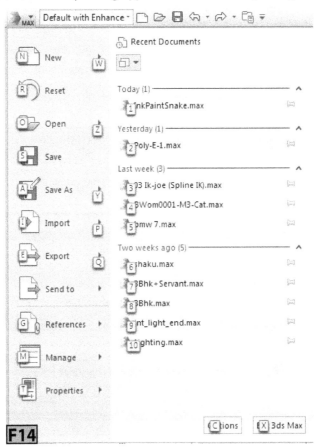

Now, for example, if you want to reset the scene, press **Atl+F+R**. To open the **Preferences** dialog, press **Alt+F+C**. To exit 3ds Max, press **Alt+F+X**.

Q. What's the function of the Reset command?

This command clears all data as well resets 3ds Max settings such as viewport configuration, snap settings, **Material Editor**, background image, and so forth. If you have done some customization during the current session of the 3ds Max, and you execute the **Reset** command, all startup defaults will be restored according to the setting stored in the **maxstrat.max** file.

Q. How can I use maxstart.max?

You can use this file to make the changes you would like to see at the startup. Start 3ds Max and make the adjustments. Then, save file in the **scenes** folder with the name **maxstrat.max**.

Note: Templates
If you reset the scene, it will also affect the template that you had used to open the scene. The template will be reset back to its default settings.

Q. How can I change the undo levels?

You can change it from the **Preferences** dialog. By default, 3ds Max allows only **20** levels for the undo operations. To change it, choose **Preferences** from the **Customize** menu. On the **General** panel of the dialog, you can set **Levels** from the **Scene Undo** group.

Q. What's the use of the Preferences dialog?

The **Preferences** dialog contains options that 3ds Max offers for its operationS. 3ds Max behaves according to the options you set in the **Preferences** dialog. You have just seen an example how you can change the undo levels. If you increase the number of levels, you force 3ds Max to obey that setting. The **Preferences** dialog comprises many panels with lots of options that you can use.

Tip: The Preferences dialog
*You can also open the **Preferences** dialog by clicking **Options** from the **Application** menu.*

Q. Can I undo all commands in 3ds Max?

No. You cannot undo commands such as saving a file or using the **Collapse** utility. If you know an action cannot be done, first hold you scene by choosing **Hold** from the **Edit** menu [Hotkeys: **Ctrl+H**]. When you want to recall, choose **Fetch** from the **Edit** menu [Hotkeys: **Alt+Ctrl+F**].

Q. Why do I need a project folder?

When you work on a project, you have to deal with many scenes, texture files, third party data, rendering, material libraries, and so forth. If you don't organize the data for the project, it would be very difficult for you to manage the assets for the project. The project folder allows you to organize all your files in a folder for a particular project. You can also set a project by choosing **Manage | Set Project Folder** from the **Application** menu.

Q. What is the Workspaces feature?

This feature allows you to quickly switch between the different arrangement of panels, toolbars, menus, viewports, and other interface elements. Figure 15 shows the UI when **Default with Enhanced Menu** workspace is chosen. Choose **Reset To Default State** from the **Workspaces** drop-down to rest the workspace to the saved settings of the active workspace. On choosing the **Manage Workspaces** from the **Workspaces** drop-down, the **Manage Workspaces** dialog appears [see Figure 16] from where you can switch, add, edit, and delete workspaces.

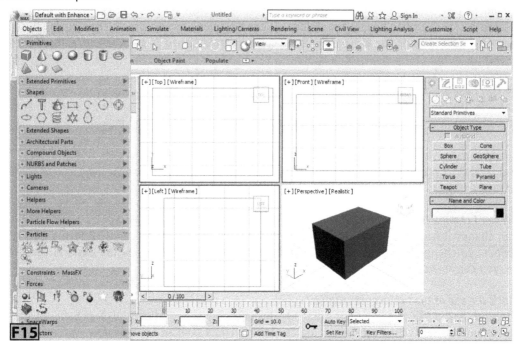

Q. What are enhanced menus?

3ds Max offers two types of menu systems for the menu bar: **Standard** menu [default] and the **Enhanced** menu. The menu bar is located directly under the main interface window's **Title** bar.

The default menu system follows the standard **Windows** conventions. When you click on a menu item on the menu bar, a pulldown menu appears. The menu in Figure 17 appeared when I clicked **Edit** on the menu bar. Notice that hotkeys are displayed next to some of the commands. You can use these hotkeys to execute the command without invoking the menu. For example, to select all objects in a scene, you can press **Ctrl+A**. Not all the commands are available all the time. These commands are context-sensitive. If a command is not available, it is grayed out in the menu, for example, see the **Fetch** command in Figure 17. If a black triangle appears [for example, see **Selection Region** command in Figure 17] on the next to a menu command, it indicates that a sub-menu exists. Place the mouse pointer on the command to view the sub-menu.

Tip: Menu hotkey
*You can use the keyboard [**Alt** key] to invoke a pulldown menu. Press **Alt**, 3ds Max displays the hotkey with an underline for the menu items. For example, to invoke the **Edit** pull-down menu, press **Alt+E**. Similarly, for the **Customize** menu, press **Alt+U**.*

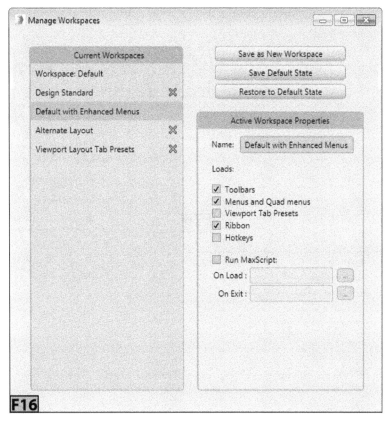

F16

Tip: Hiding menu bar

If for some reason, you want to hide the menu bar, RMB click on the menu bar then click **Show Menu Bar** *from the pop-up menu. To recover the menu back, click on the arrow located on the right of the* **Workspaces** *drop-down [see Figure 18] and then choose* **Show Menu Bar**. *You can also hide menu bar from the* **Quick Access Toolbar** *menu.*

The **Enhanced** menu system provides some additional features such as configurable display, link to relevant help topics, enhanced tooltips, and drag and drop menu categories. You can also search for the menu commands. The image at the left of Figure 19 shows standard **Rendering** menu whereas the image at the right of Figure 19 shows enhanced **Rendering** menu.

Tip: Toggling Enhanced menu

You can toggle the enhanced menu by using the **Enhanced Menu** *command. To access this command, press* **X** *to open the* **Search All Action** *dialog and then type* **enh** *in the field available in this dialog [see Figure 20]. The* **Enhanced Menus** *command appears in the list. Click it to open the enhanced menu sytem.*

Here's is a quick run down to the various functions available for the **Enhanced** menu system:

■ You can collapse or expand each panel in a menu. When collapsed, a + icon appears on the title bar. When expanded a - icon appears on the title bar [refer Figure 21]. When you position the mouse pointer on the title bar of a collapsed menu, a sub-menu appears with the content of the collapsed menu [refer Figure 21].

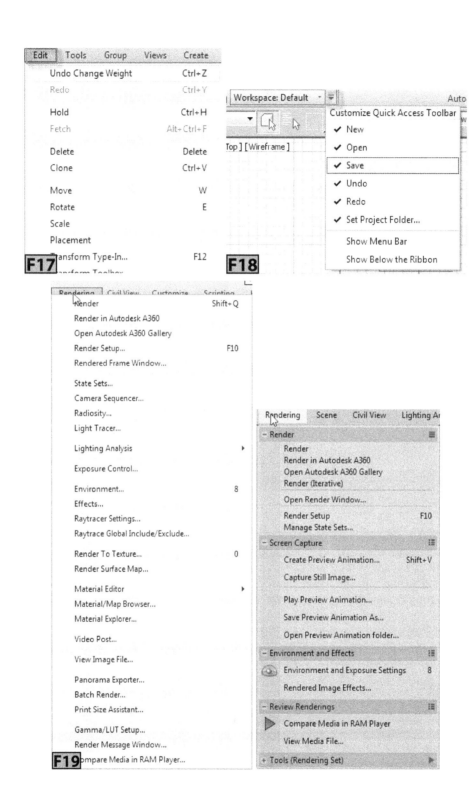

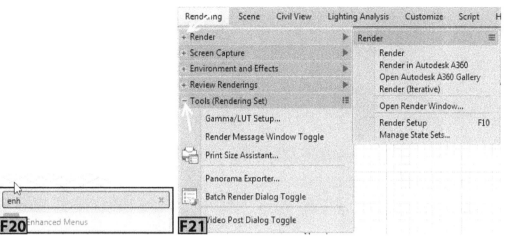

Note: Restoring menu settings
3ds Max remembers all settings of collapsed or expanded states of the menu and it restores them when you reopen 3ds Max.

■ You can view the content of a menu as icon, text, or icon+text. To toggle the view mode, click on the icon at the top-right end of the title bar [see Figure 22].

■ To view the detailed tooltip that provides a brief description of a menu command, position the mouse pointer on the menu option, a tool tip appears [see Figure 23]. If you want to see help documentation about the command under the mouse pointer, press **F1**.

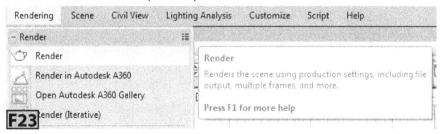

■ You can also float a menu panel or submenu. Drag the title bar of the panel away from the menu to make it a floating panel [see Figure 24].

■ You can also merge the floating panels. Drag title bar of a panel to the bottom or top of the target panel, a blue line appears [see the image at the left of Figure 25]. Release the mouse button to dock the two panels [see the image at the right of Figure 25].

■ You can also search a menu command from the menu. Type the name of the command when the menu is active. A text box appears at top of the menu when you start typing. As you type, menu shows the command matching with the string you have typed [see Figure 26].

Viewports

In 3ds Max, you will be doing most of the work in viewports. Viewports are openings into 3D space you work. A viewport represents 3D space using the **Cartesian** coordinates system. The coordinate are expressed using three numbers such as **[10, 10, 20]**. These number represent points in 3D space. The origin is always at **[0, 0, 0]**. By default, 3ds Max displays a four viewport arrangement: **Top**, **Front**, **Left**, and **Perspective**. The **Top**, **Front**, and **Left** are known as orthographic views. 3ds Max provides many options to change the viewport as well as the layout. Using multiple viewports can help you visualize the scene better.

Q. What do you mean by an Orthographic View?

Most of the 3D designs created using computer relies on the 2D representation of the designs. Some examples of the 2D representations are maps, elevations, and plans. Even to create a character model, you first design it on paper [front, side, and back views] [see Figure 27] and then create 3D model using these designs.

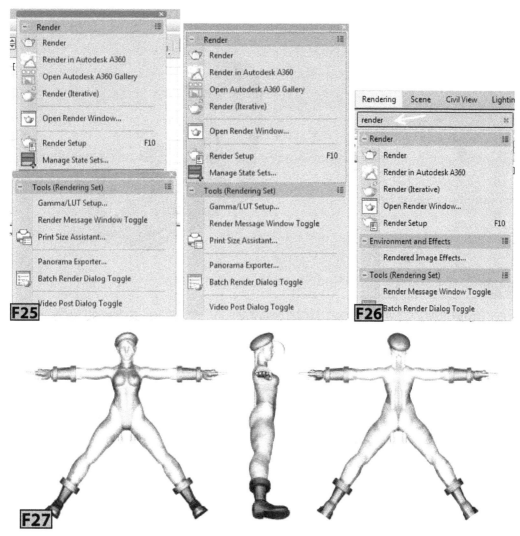

Note:
*Blueprint Courtesy: **http://www.the-blueprints.com***

In laymen terms, you can think of the orthographic views as flat, or straight on. The orthographic views are two dimensional views. Each dimension is defined by two world coordinate axes. Combination of these two axes produce three sets of orthographic views: **Top and Bottom**, **Front and Back**, and **Left and Right**. Figure 28 shows a model in three orthographic views [**Top**, **Right**, and **Left**] and in **Perspective** view.

You can change a viewport to various orthographic views using the controls available in the **Point-Of-View (POV)** viewport label menu.

The **Perspective** view on the other hand closely resembles with the human view. In 3ds Max there are three ways to create a perspective view: Perspective view, camera view, and light view.

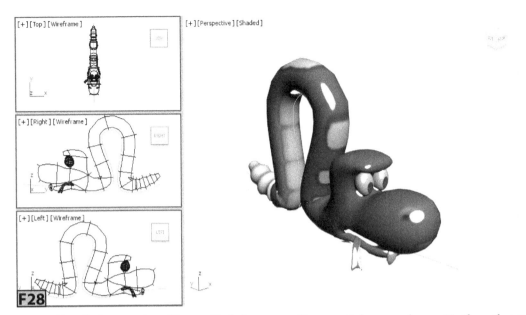

F28

Q. Can you tell me little more about Viewport Label menus and how can I change a viewport to the orthographic views?

Notice on top-left corner of a viewport, there are three labels. Figure 29 shows labels on the **Perspective** viewport. Each label is clickable [click or RMB click]. When you click on any of the labels, a popup menu appears.

F29

The left most menu is **General Viewport** label menu [marked as 1], in the middle is **Point-Of-View [POV]** viewport label menu [marked as 2], and on the right is **Shading** viewport label menu [marked as 3]. The **General Viewport** label menu comprises controls for overall viewport display or activation. It also gives you access to the **Viewport Configuration** dialog. The **POV Viewport** label menu provides options mainly for changing the viewports. To change a viewport, for example, to change the **Top** viewport to **Bottom** viewport, make sure the **Top** viewport is active and then click or RMB click on the **POV Viewport** label menu. Now, choose **Bottom** from the menu. You can also use the hotkey **B**. Table 3 summarizes the hotkeys that you can use to change the viewports.

Table 3: The hotkeys for switching the viewports	
View	**Hotkey**
Top	T
Bottom	B
Front	F
Left	L
Camera	C
Orthographic	U
Perspective	P

The **Shading Viewport** menu lets you control how objects are displayed in the viewport. I will discuss the options in this menu later in the unit.

Q. What is active viewport?

An active viewport is where all actions take place in 3ds Max. One viewport is always active in 3ds Max marked with a highlighted border. To switch the active viewport, you can use any of the three mouse buttons. It is recommended that you use the right mouse button for making a viewport active as LMB click also select objects.

When viewports are not maximized, you can press the **Windows** key and **Shift** on the keyboard to cycle the active viewport. When one of the view is maximized, pressing **Windows** key and **Shift** displays the available viewports [see Figure 30] and then you can press **Shift** repeatedly with the **Windows** key held down to cycle among viewports. When you release the keys, the chosen viewport becomes the maximized viewport.

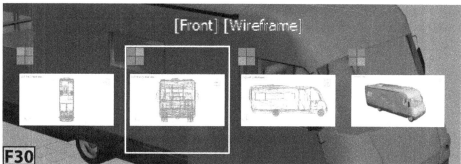

You can save an active viewport in the internal buffer and later restore it. It useful when you want to frame a shot in any view other than a camera view. One view each can be saved for the following viewports: **Top, Bottom, Left, Right, Front, Back, Orthographic,** and **Perspective.** To save an active view, activate the viewport with the zoom level you want to save and then choose **Save Active View** from the **Views** menu. To restore the view, select the viewport where you saved the view and then choose **Restore Active View** from the **Views** menu. The saved active view is saved with the scene file.

Q. How can I change the viewport configuration like the one shown in Figure 28?

The **Viewport Layouts** bar lets you quickly switch among different types of viewport layouts. This bar generally docked on the left of the viewports [see Figure 31]. If it is not visible, RMB click on the **Main** toolbar and then choose **Viewport Layout Tabs** [see Figure 32]. To change the layout, click on the arrow on the bar to open a flyout and then click on the desired layout to make it active.

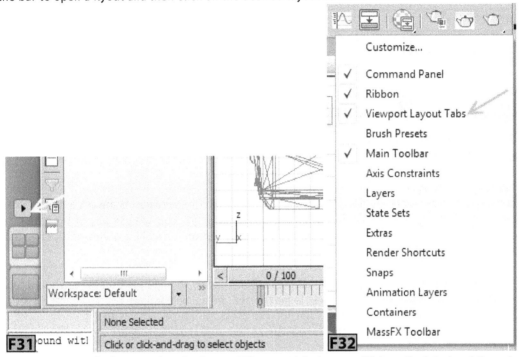

You can also change the layout using the **General Viewport** label menu. Click on the label and then choose **Configure Viewports**. The **Viewport Configuration** dialog appears [see Figure 33] with the **Layout** panel active. Choose the desired layout and then click **OK**.

Q. I can see a grid in each viewport, how can I use it?

The grid you see in each viewport is one of the three planes [along the X, Y, and Z axes] that intersect at the right angles to each other at a common point called **origin** [X=0, Y=0, and Z=0]. The three planes based on the world coordinate axes are called **home grid**. To help you easily position objects on the grid, one plane of the home grid is visible in each viewport. The grid acts as a construction plane when you create objects on it.

Tip: Turning off grid

*You can turn off the grid in the active viewport by pressing the **G** hotkey.*

Command Panel

The **Command Panel** is the nerve center of 3ds Max. It comprises of six panels that give you access to most of the modeling tools, animation features, display choices, and utilities. Table 4 summarizes the panels in the **Command Panel**.

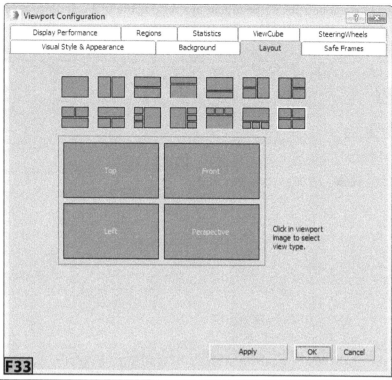

F33

Table 4: Different panels in the **Command Panel**

Panel	Description
Create	Contains controls for creating object such as geometry, lights, cameras, and so forth.
Modify	Contains controls for editing objects as well as for applying modifiers to the objects.
Hierarchy	Contains controls for managing links in the hierarchy, joints, and inverse kinematics.
Motion	Contains controls for animation controllers and trajectories.
Display	Contains controls that lets you hide/unhide objects. It also contains display options.
Utilities	Contains different utility programs.

Rollouts

Most of the controls in the **Command Panel** live inside rollouts. A rollout is a group of controls, a section of the **Command Panel** that shows parameters of the selected object. You can collapse the rollouts. When you collapse them, only the title bar of the rollout appears. Figure 34 shows the **Parameters** rollout of the **Box** primitive in the **Modify** panel of the **Command Panel**.

Once you create a box in the viewport, you can modify its parameters such as **Length** and **Width** using the **Parameters** rollout. Each rollout has a title bar that you can click to collapse or expand the rollout. You can also change the default position of the rollout by dragging the title and dropping on another place when a blue line appears [see Figure 35].

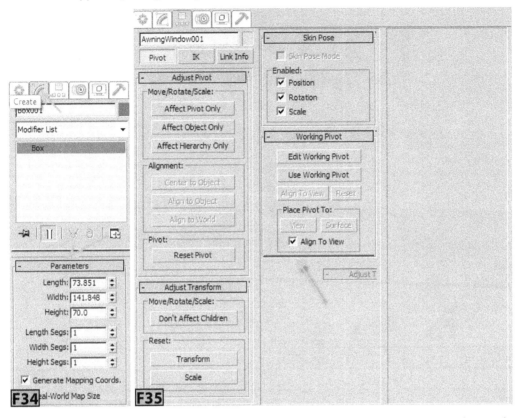

By default, the rollout occupies a single column space in UI. However, you can increase the numbers of columns by dragging the left most edge of the panel. You can create as many columns as you want [see Figure 35] as long the screen real state is available. Multiple columns are helpful when you are working with an object with which many rollouts are associated.

If you RMB click on a rollout [**on the empty gray area**], a popup menu appears [see Figure 36]. This popup allows you to open or close all rollouts at once, or close the rollout on which you RMB clicked. In the bottom section of the popup menu, you will see a list of rollouts available for the selected object. No tick appears for the collapsed rollouts.

If you have changed order of the rollouts, you can rest the order by choosing **Reset Rollout Order** from the bottom of the menu. If you have expanded the **Command Panel** to more than one column and you RMB click on a rollout, only those rollouts appear on the popup menu that are in the column [see Figure 37].

Tip: The default value for the spinners
*The nature of the spinners in 3ds Max is persistence meaning that value specified for the spinners remains set for the current spinners. For example, if you created a **Sphere** primitive with **64** segments. When you create the next sphere, the value **64** will be default for it. To reset spinners to their default values, choose **Reset** from the **Application** menu.*

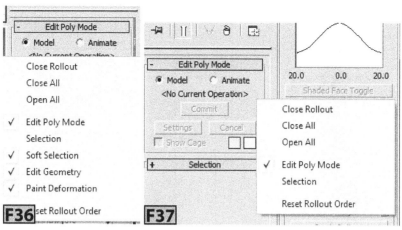

Main Toolbar

The **Main** toolbar comprises commonly used tools and dialog. Table 5 summarizes the tools available in the **Main** toolbar.

Table 5: The **Main** toolbar interface overview		
Item	**Icon**	**Description**
Undo/Redo		Undo reverses the last command. Redo reverses the last undo command.
Select and Link		Defines the hierarchical relationship [links] between two objects.
Unlink Selection		Removes the hierarchical relationship between two objects.
Bind to Space Warp		Attaches the current selection to a space warp or vice versa.
Selection Filter List		Limits the selection to specific types and combinations of objects.

Select Object		Selects objects and sub-objects. Hotkey: **Q**.
Select by Name		Allows you to select specific objects from a list of objects using the Select from Scene dialog. Hotkey: **H**.
Selection Region Fly-out		Allows you to select objects within a region using different methods. You can create different marquee shapes using the options available in this flyout.
Window/Crossing Selection Toggle		Switch between window and crossing methods for selection.
Select and Move		Selects and moves objects. Hotkey: **W**.
Select and Rotate		Selects and rotates objects. Hotkey: **E**.
Select and Scale		Selects and scales objects. Hotkey: **R** to cycle.
Select and Place Fly-out		Position an object accurately on the surface of another object.
Reference Coordinate System		Specifies the coordinate system used for a transformations (Move, Rotate, and Scale).

Use Center Flyout		Specifies geometric centers for scale and rotate transformations.
Select and Manipulate		Select objects and allows editing of the parameters for certain objects, modifiers, and controllers by dragging "manipulators" in viewports.
Keyboard Shortcut Override Toggle		Allows you to toggle between using only the "Main User Interface" hotkeys or using both the main hotkeys and hotkeys for groups such as Edit/Editable Mesh, Track View, NURBS, and so on.
2D Snap, 2.5D Snap, 3D Snap		Specify the snap types. Hotkey: **S** to cycle.
Angle Snap Toggle		Enables angle increment snap for rotation. It allows you to snap rotations to certain angles. Hotkey: **A**.
Percent Snap Toggle		Toggles increments scaling of objects by the specified percentage. Hotkeys: **Shift+Ctrl+P**.
Spinner Snap Toggle		Sets the single-click increment or the decrement value for all of the spinners in 3ds Max.
Edit Named Selection Sets		Displays the **Edit Named Selections** dialog, letting you manage named selection sets of sub-objects
Named Selection Sets	Create Selection Se	Allows you to name a selection set and recall the selection for later use.
Mirror		Enables you to move and clone selected objects while reflecting their orientation.

Align Flyout		Gives you access to six different tools for alignment. Hotkeys: Align [**Alt+A**], and Normal Align [**Alt+N**].
Toggle Scene Explorer		Toggles the **Scene Explorer**.
Toggle Layer Explorer		Toggles the **Layer Explorer**.
Toggle Ribbon		Expands or collapses the **Ribbon**.
Curve Editor (Open)		Opens the **Track View - Curve Editor**.
Schematic View (Open)		Opens the **Schematic View** window.
Material Editor flyout		Opens the **Material Editor** that provides functions to create and edit materials and maps.
Render Setup		Opens the **Render Setup** dialog. Hotkey: **F10**.
Rendered Frame Window		Opens the **Rendered Frame Window** that displays rendered output.
Render Production		Renders the scene using the current production render settings without opening the **Render Setup** dialog.
Render Iterative		Renders the scene in iterative mode without opening the **Render Setup** dialog.
ActiveShade		Creates an **ActiveShade** rendering in a floating window.
Render in Autodesk A360		Uses the **A360 Cloud** to render your scene.

Open Autodesk A360 Gallery		Opens a web page that showcases **A360 Cloud** renderings.

Docking and Floating Toolbars

3ds Max allows you to dock and float toolbars. You have already seen an example of the floating toolbar [**Mass FX Toolbar**]. By default, the **Main** toolbar is docked below the menu bar. If you want to undock it, position the mouse pointer in the double vertical lines located at the extreme left of the **Main** toolbar [also available at the extreme right]; the shape of the mouse pointer changes [see Figure 38]. Now, click and drag away and drop when the shape of the mouse pointer changes to a window icon [see Figure 39] to float the **Main** toolbar. Once the toolbar appears as a floating panel [see Figure 40], you can resize it as you resize any other panel on **Windows** operating system. You can doc the **Main** toolbar back to its last position by double clicking on the title of the floating panel. Similarly, you can float any toolbar, window, or panel [like **Command Panel**, **Scene Explorer**, and **Ribbon**] in 3ds Max.

Tip: Main toolbar visibility toggle
*You can quickly toggle the display of the **Main** toolbar by using the **Alt+6** hotkeys.*

If you RMB click on the title of a floating toolbar, window, or panel. Or, on the vertical or horizontal lines of a toolbar, window, or panel; a pop menu appears with the options to doc that element [see Figure 41].

These options allow you to doc an element on the top, bottom, left, or the right of the interface. However, you can rearrange the interface elements as per you need. For example, if you are a leftie, you would like the **Command Panel** on the left and the **Scene Explorer** on the right.

For example, to doc the **Command Panel** on the left, position the mouse pointer on the top left corner of the panel until the shape of the pointer changes [see Figure 42]. Drag the **Command Panel** to the left of the **Scene Explorer** when the shape of the cursor changes to the one shown in Figure 43 to doc the **Command Panel** on the left [see Figure 44].

Tip: Resetting Workspace
*After experimenting with the rearrangement of panels, you can reset the original positions of the elements by choosing **Reset to Default State** from the **Workspaces** drop-down.*

Note: Quick Access Toolbar
*The **Quick Access Toolbar** and **InfoCenter** toolbar cannot be undocked from the 3ds Max UI.*

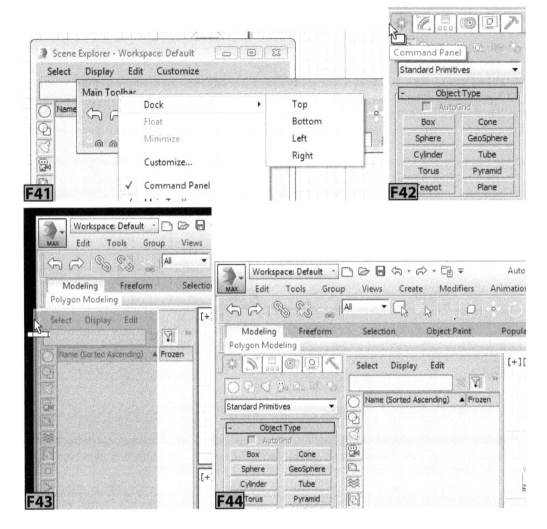

Main Toolbar Flyouts

You might have noticed a small triangle on the lower right corner of some buttons in the **Main** toolbar. Click on hold on such a button to expand a flyout with additional buttons. Figure 45 shows the **Selection Region** flyout.

Ribbon

Ribbon [see Figure 46], is available below the **Main** toolbar. The **Ribbon** appears in collapsed state by default. To expand it, double-click on it. You can toggle the display of the **Ribbon** by clicking **Toggle Ribbon** from the **Main** toolbar.

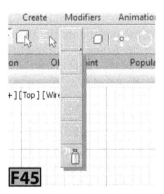

It contains many tabs. The content in the tabs is depended on the context. The items displayed may vary according to the selected sub-objects. I will cover **Ribbon** in a later unit in the book.

Most of the tools are only visible in the **Ribbon** when you are editing a poly object. You will learn about **Ribbon** and poly modeling techniques in a later unit.

Animation and Time Controls

The animation controls are found on the left of the **Viewport Navigation** controls [see Figure 47].

Two other controls that are vital to animation are **Time Slider** and **Track Bar** [see Figure 48]. These controls are available below the viewports. The **Time Slider** works with the **Track Bar** to allow you to view and edit animation. The sliders shows the current frame and the total number of frames in the range. The **Track Bar** shows the frame numbers and allows you to move, copy, and delete keys.

Table 6 summarizes the animation controls.

Table 6: The animation controls		
Item	**Icon**	**Description**
Auto Key Animation Mode, Set Key Animation Mode	Auto Key / Set Key	The Auto Key Animation Mode toggles the keyframing mode called **Auto Key**. Set Key Animation Mode allows you to create keys for selected objects individual tracks using a combination of the **Set Keys** button and **Key Filters**.
Selection List	Selected	Provides quick access to **Named Selection Sets** and track sets.
Default In/Out Tangents for New Keys		This flyout provides a quick way to set a default tangent type for new animation keys.
Key Filters	Key Filters...	Opens the **Set Key Filters** dialog where you can specify the tracks on which keys are created.
Go To Start		Moves the time slider to the first frame of the active time segment.
Previous Frame/Key		Moves the time slider back one frame.
Play/Stop		The Play button plays the animation in the active viewport. You can stop the playback by clicking on the button again.
Next Frame/Key		Moves the time slider ahead one frame.

Go To End		Moves the time slider to the last frame of the active time segment.
Current Frame (Go To Frame)		Displays the number or time of the current frame, indicating the position of the time slider.
Key Mode		Allows you jump directly between keyframes in your animation.
Time Configuration		Open the **Time Configuration** dialog that allows you to specify the settings for the animation.

Viewport Navigational Controls

The **Viewport Navigation Controls** are located at the right end of the status bar [see Figure 49].

The controls in the **Viewport Navigational Controls** depend on the type of viewport [Perspective, orthographic, camera, or light] active. Some of the buttons have a little black triangle at the right bottom corner. The arrow indicates that there are some hidden buttons exist. To view them, press and hold the LMB on the button. When a button is active, it is highlighted, to deactivate it, press **ESC**, choose another tool, or RMB click in a viewport.

Table 7 shows the controls available for all viewports. Table 8 shows the controls available for perspective and orthographic views. Table 9 shows the controls available for the camera views. Table 10 shows the controls available for the camera views.

Table 7: The viewport navigational controls available for all viewports		
Item	**Icon**	**Description**
Zoom Extents All, Zoom Extents All Selected		Allow you to zoom selected objects or all objects to their extent in the viewport.
Maximize Viewport Toggle		It switches any active viewport between its normal size and full-screen size. Hotkeys: **Alt+W**.

Table 8: The viewport navigational controls available for perspective and orthographic views		
Item	**Icon**	**Description**
Zoom		Allows you to change the magnification by dragging in a Perspective or orthographic viewport. Hotkeys: **Alt+Z**. You can also use the bracket keys, [and].
Zoom All		Allows you adjust view magnification in all Perspective and orthographic viewports at the same time.
Zoom Extents/Zoom Extents Selected		**Zoom Extents** centers all visible objects in an active Perspective or orthographic viewport until it fills the viewport. Hotkeys: **Ctrl+Alt+Z**. Zoom Extents Selected centers a selected object, or set of objects. Hotkey:**Z**.

Field-of-View Button (Perspective) or Zoom Region		**Field-of-View** adjusts the amount of the scene that is visible in a viewport. It's only available in the Perspective viewport. Hotkeys: **Ctrl+W. Zoom Region** magnifies a rectangular area you drag within a viewport.
Pan View		**Pan View** moves the view parallel to the current viewport plane. Hotkeys: **Ctrl+P.**
Walk Through		Allows you to move through a viewport by pressing arrow keys. Hotkey: **Up Arrow**.
Orbit, Orbit Selected, Orbit Sub-Object		**Orbit** rotates the viewport and uses the view center as the center of rotation. Hotkeys: **Ctrl+R. Orbit Selected** uses the center of the current selection as the center of rotation. **Orbit Sub-object** uses the center of the current sub-object selection as the center of rotation.

Table 9: The viewport navigational controls available for camera views

Item	Icon	Description
Dolly Camera, Target, or Both		This flyout replaces the **Zoom** button when the **Camera** viewport is active. Use these tools to move camera and/or its target along the camera main axis.
Perspective		It performs a combination of FOV and Dolly for target cameras and free cameras.
Roll Camera		Rotates a free camera around its local Z-axis.
Field-of-View Button		Adjusts the amount of the scene that is visible in a viewport
Truck Camera		Moves the camera parallel to the view plane.
Walk Through		Allows you move through a viewport by pressing a set of shortcut keys.
Orbit/Pan Camera		**Orbit Camera** rotates a camera about the target. **Pan Camera** rotates the target about the camera.

Table 10: The viewport navigational controls available for light views

Item	Icon	Description
Dolly Light, Target, or Both		Moves the light or its target or both along the light's main axis, toward or away from what the light is pointing at.
Light Hotspot		Allows you adjust the angle of a light's hotspot.
Roll Light		Roll Light rotates the light about its own line of sight (the light's local Z axis).

Light Falloff		Adjusts the angle of a light's falloff.
Truck Light		Moves a target light and its target parallel to the light view, and moves a free light in its XY plane.
Orbit/Pan Light		Rotates a light about the target. **Pan Light** rotates the target about the light.

Interaction Mode Preferences

If you are an **Autodesk Maya** user then it's good news for you that you can change the interaction mode to **Maya**. The **Interaction Mode** panel of the **Preferences** dialog box [see Figure 50] allows you to set the mouse and keyboard shortcut according to **3ds Max** or **Maya**. When you set **Interaction Mode** to **Maya**, most of the shortcuts and mouse operations behave as they do in **Autodesk Maya**. Here's the list:

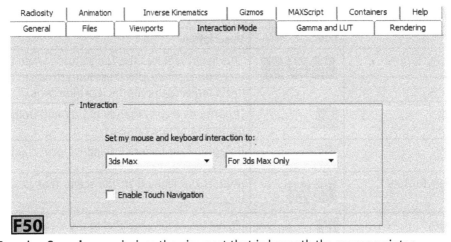

F50

- Pressing **Spacebar** maximizes the viewport that is beneath the mouse pointer.
- **Shift+Click** adds or removes from the selection. **Ctrl+Click** removes from the selection.
- The **Orbit** tools are not available in in the orthographic views.
- **Alt+Home** switches to the default perspective view.
- **Alt+LMB** drag to rotate the view. **Alt+MMB** drag to pan the view. **Alt+RMB** drag to zoom in or out in the view.

Table 11 shows a comparison between **3ds Max** and **Maya** hotkeys.

Table 11: The comparison between 3ds Max and Maya hotkeys		
Function	**3ds Max**	**Maya**
Maximize Viewport Toggle	Alt+W	Spacebar
Zoom Extents Selected	Z	F
Zoom Extents All	Shift+Ctrl+Z	A
Undo Viewport Operation	Shift+Z	Alt+Z

Redo Viewport Operation	Shift+Y	Alt+Y
Play Animation	/	Alt+V
Set Key	K	S
Group	None	Ctrl+G
Editable Poly Repeat Last Operation	;	G

Getting Around in 3ds Max

In the previous section, you have seen various components of the 3ds Max's UI. Don't get hung up on all the buttons, commands, menus, and options. It was a quick tour of the interface to get your feet wet. The more time you spent on Unit 1 and Unit 2, easier it will be for you to understand rest of the units.

Creating Objects in the Scene

You can't do much with a blank scene. You need some objects in the scene in order to work on them. 3ds Max offers a wide range of standard objects. Let's start with creating some geometry in the scene.

Start 3ds Max, if not already running. Press **Alt+F+R** to open the 3ds Max message box. Click **Yes** to reset the scene.

Notice there are several panels in the **Command Panel: Create, Modify, Hierarchy, Motion, Display,** and **Utilities**. Position the mouse pointer on a panel's icon; a tooltip appears showing the name of the panel. The **Create** panel comprises of the following basic categories: **Geometry, Shapes, Lights, Cameras, Helpers, Space Warps,** and **Systems**. Each category is farther divided into sub-categories.

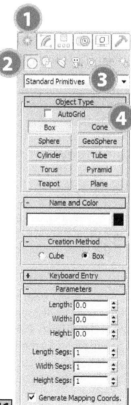

Notice in [see Figure 51] the **Create** panel [marked as 1], the **Geometry** button [marked as 2] is active. Below that button you will see a drop-down [marked as 3] that contains the **Geometry** sub-categories 3ds Max offers. Notice the **Standard Primitives** is selected in the drop-down.

Below the drop-down there is **Object Type** rollout [marked as 4]. There are ten buttons in the rollout. When you click on one of the buttons, the corresponding tool gets active and then you can create an object in the scene interactively using the mouse or by entering precise values using the keyboard.

Let's create an object from the **Standard Primitive** sub-category. Ensure you are in the **Command Panel | Create Panel | Geometry category | Standard Primitives**. Now, click on **Box** in the **Object Type** rollout.

Notice four rollouts appears in the **Create** panel: **Name and Color, Creation Method, Keyboard Entry,** and **Parameters**. The **Keyboard Entry** rollout is collapsed whereas the other two are in the expanded state.

F51

Expand the **Keyboard Entry** rollout by clicking on the title bar of the rollout. Set **Length** to **50**, **Width** to **50**, and **Height** to **10**. Click **Create**. You need to press **Enter** or **Tab** after typing the values. Congratulations, you have created your first object in 3ds Max [see Figure 52]. You have not changed values of the X, Y, and Z controls. As a result, the box is created at the origin of the home grid [0, 0, 0].

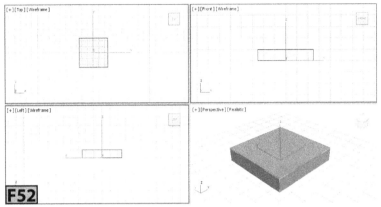

Also, notice the name of the object [**Box001**] in the **Name and Color** rollout. Every time you create an object in the scene, 3ds Max assigns it a default name.

Collapse the **Keyboard Entry** rollout. On the **Parameters** rollout, change **Length** and **Width** to **100**.

Notice the box in the scene resizes as per the new dimensions we have set for the **Length** and **Width** controls. The change occurs because still **Box** is active in the **Object Type** rollout. If you select any other tool, then you would not be able to modify values from the **Create** panel. Then, how to change the parameters? Well, once you select any other tool, you can change values for controls from the **Modify** panel [panel available on the right of the **Create** panel].

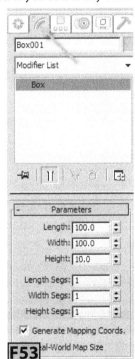

Click the **Modify** panel [see Figure 53] and notice the **Parameters** rollout appears there. Change **Height** to **20**. Change **Length Segs**, **Width Segs**, and **Height Segs** to **2** each. Notice the change is reflected on the object in the viewport.

Notice the white brackets around the box in the **Perspective** viewport. These are selection brackets that show the bounding box of the object. I am not a big fan of the selection brackets and don't find them very useful.

Press **J** to get rid of the selection brackets. In order to change values for controls of an object from the **Parameters** rollout, the object must be selected in the viewport. I will cover selection methods later in the unit. Click the **General Viewport** label in the **Perspective** viewport and choose **Configure Viewports** from the popup menu. In the **Viewport Configuration** dialog that appears, choose the **Layout** tab and then click on the layout button highlighted with white borders in Figure 54. Now, click **OK** to change the viewport layout [see Figure 55].

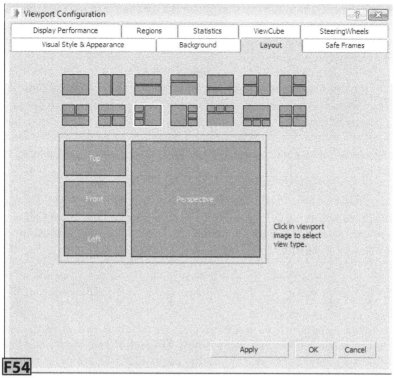

F54

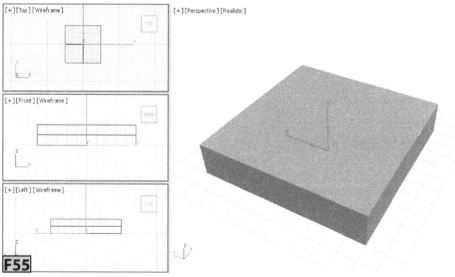

F55

You have just changed the viewport layout. The **Top, Front,** and **Left** viewports are stacked over each other on the left and on the right you will see enlarged **Perspective** viewport. I frequently change viewport layout as per my needs. In this book, especially in hands-on exercises, if you find a different viewport layout in captures, this is the place from where you can change it. I have not written this process in hands-on exercises.

MMB click on the **Left** viewport to make it active. Press **B** to change it to the **Bottom** viewport. Press **L** to change it to the **Left** viewport. As discussed earlier, the options for changing the viewport are available in the **Point-Of-View [POV]** viewport label menu. Now onward, I will refer **Point-Of-View [POV]** viewport label menu as **POV** viewport label menu.

Notice the label for the **Shading Viewport** label reads **Realistic**. Click on the **Shading Viewport** label to display the **Shading Viewport** label menu. The options in this menu allow you to define the shading style for the viewport. The default shading style is **Realistic**. **Realistic** displays textures geometry realistically. Also, the shading and lighting in the viewport is of high quality. **Shaded** smoothly shades the geometry in the viewport using the **Phong** shader. **Facets** displays faceted geometry. It ignores the smooth group settings of the geometry.

Consistent Colors shows the raw color in the viewport ignoring lighting. **Edged Faces** shows the edges of the face. Figure 56 shows the teapot in **Realistic**, **Shaded**, **Facets**, **Consistent Colors**, and **Edged Faces** shading modes, respectively. The hotkeys for **Realistic** and **Edged** Face modes are **Shift+F3** and **F4**, respectively. You can toggle these modes using **Shift+F3** and **F4** hotkeys.

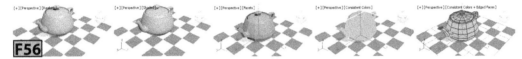

Hidden Line hides the faces and vertices whose normals are pointing away from the viewport. Shadows are unavailable in this mode. **Wireframe** displays objects in wireframe mode. The hotkey for toggling the **Wireframe** mode is **F3**. **Bounding Box** displays the edges of the bounding box of the geometry. **Clay** displays geometry in an uniform terracotta color. Figure 57 shows the teapot in the **Hidden Line**, **Wireframe**, **Bounding Box**, and **Clay** modes, respectively.

My favorite shading mode for modeling is **Clay** with **Edges Faces** and I have extensively used it in this book.

Press **Ctrl+S** to open the **Save File As** dialog and then type the name of the file in the **File name** text box and click **Save** to save the file. Now, if you want to open this file later, choose **Open** from the **Application** menu to open the **Open File** dialog. Navigate to the file and then click **Open** to open the file. If you want to save an already saved file with different name, choose **Save As** from the **Application** menu. You can also save a copy to the previous version of 3ds Max, choose **Save As** from the **Application** menu to open the **Save File As** dialog. In this dialog, choose the appropriate option from the **Save as type** drop-down [see Figure 58]. Click **Save** to save the file.

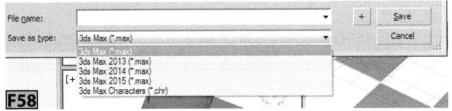

Tip: Incremental Save

*When you are working on a file, I highly recommend that you save different versions of it. If the current version gets corrupt, you can always fall back to a previous version of the file. 3ds Max allows you to save the file incrementally. In the **Save File As** dialog, click + on the left of **Save** to save the file with a name ending in a number greater than the current number displayed with the file name. For example, if the current name is **x1.max**, clicking + will save file with the name **x02.max**.*

Tip: Quick Access Toolbar

*You can also open and save files using the options available in the **Quick Access Toolbar**.*

Now, practice with the **Viewport Navigation Controls** including **ViewCube** and **StreeingWheels**.

Selecting Objects

Selecting objects is an important process before you perform any action on an object or objects. Selection in 3ds Max works on the noun-verb terminology. You first select the object (**the noun**) and then execute a command (**the verb**). 3ds Max provides a wide variety of tools for selecting objects. The **Selection** commands and functions are found in the following areas of interface:

- Main toolbar
- Edit menu
- Quad menu
- Tools menu
- Track View
- Display panel
- Modify panel
- Ribbon
- Schematic View
- Scene Explorer

Selecting Objects using Main toolbar Selection Buttons

The buttons available on the **Main** toolbar provides direct means of selection. These buttons are: **Select Object**, **Select by Name**, **Select and Move**, **Select and Rotate**, **Select and Scale**, and **Select and Manipulate**. To select an object, click on one of the selection buttons on the **Main** toolbar. Position the mouse pointer on the object that you want to select. The shape of the pointer changes to a small cross if the object is eligible for the selection. Click on the object to select it and de-select any selected object.

Note: Valid surface for selection

*The valid selection zone for the surface depends on the type of the object you are selecting and shading mode of the viewport in which you are selecting the object. In **Shaded** mode, any visible area of the surface is valid selection zone whereas in the **Wireframe** mode any edge or segment of the object is valid including the hidden lines.*

Adding and Removing Objects from the Current Selection

To extend a selection [adds objects to the existing selection], press and hold **Ctrl** while you make selections. For example, if you have selected two objects and you want to add third object to the selection, press and hold **Ctrl** and click on the third object to add it to the selection. To remove an object from selection, press and hold **Alt** and click on the object that you want to remove from the selection.

Inverting Selection

To invert the selection, choose **Select Invert** from the **Edit** menu. The hotkeys for this operation are **Ctrl+I**. For example, you have total five objects in the scene and three of them are selected. Now, to select the remaining two objects and terminating the current selection, press **Ctrl+I**.

Selecting All Objects

To select all objects, choose **Select All** from the **Edit** menu or press **Ctrl+A**.

Locking the Selection

When the selection is locked, you can click-drag mouse anywhere in the viewport without losing the selection. To lock a selection, click **Selection Lock Toggle** [see Figure 59] from the **Status Bar** or press **Spacebar**.

Deselecting an Object

To deselect an object, click on another object, or click on an empty area of the viewport. To deselect all objects in a scene, choose **Select None** from the **Edit** menu.

Selecting by Region

The region selection tools in 3ds Max allow you to select one more object by defining a selection region using mouse. By default, a rectangular region is created when you drag the mouse. You can change the region by picking a region type from the **Region** flyout [see Figure 60] **Main** toolbar.

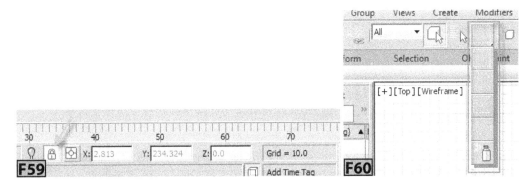

Note: Using Ctrl and Alt
*If you draw a selection region with the **Ctrl** held down, the affected objects are added to the selection. Conversely, if you hold down **Alt**, the affected objects are removed from the selection.*

Table 12 lists the types of region selection. Figure 61 shows the rectangular, circular, fence, lasso, and paint marquee selections, respectively.

Table 12: The region selection types	
Type	**Description**
Rectangular	Allows you select objects using the rectangular selection region.
Circular	Allows you select objects using the circular selection region.
Fence	Allows you to draw an irregular selection region.

Lasso	Allows you to draw an irregular selection region with single mouse operation.
Paint	Activates a brush. Paint on the objects to add them to the selection.

F61

Note: Changing the Brush Size

*You can change the brush size from the **Preferences** dialog. RMB on the **Paint Selection** type to open the dialog. In the **General panel | Scene Selection** area, you can set the brush size by specifying a value for the **Paint Selection Brush Size** control. The default value for this control is **20**.*

Specifying Region Inclusion

The button on the right of the **Region Selection** flyout is a toggle button. It allows you to specify whether to include objects touched by the region border. This button affects all region selection methods I have described above.

The default state of the button is **Crossing**. It selects all objects that are within the region and crossing the boundary of the region [see Figure 62]. The other state of the button is **Window**. It selects only those objects that are completely within the region [see Figure 63].

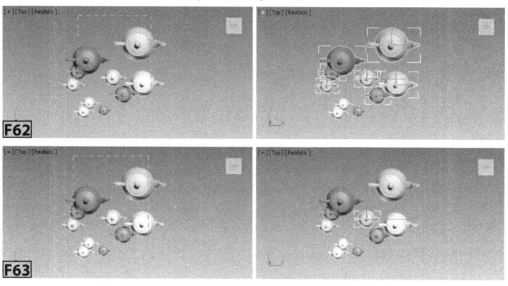

F62

F63

Select By Name

On clicking the **Select By Name** button on the **Main** toolbar, the **Select From Scene** dialog appears [see Figure 64]. It allows you to select objects by their assigned names.

To select objects by name, click **Select By Name** on the **Main** toolbar or press **H** to open the **Select From Scene** dialog. It lists all the objects in the scene. Click on the names of one or more objects to select them and then click **OK** to select the object and close the dialog and select the highlighted objects. Use **Ctrl+click** to highlight more than one entry in this dialog.

Named Selection Sets

You can name a selection in 3ds Max and then recall the selection by choosing their name from a list. To assign a name to the selection, select one or more objects or sub-objects in the scene. Click on the **Named Selection** field [see Figure 65] on the **Main** toolbar to activate a text box and then type a name for your selection set. Press **Enter** to complete the operation.

Caution: Case sensitive names
The names you enter for the selection are case-sensitive.

To retrieve a named selection set, click the **Named Selection Sets** list's arrow. Choose the desired name from the list. The corresponding objects are selected in the viewport. You can also select the selection sets from the **Named Selection Sets** dialog [see Figure 66]. To open this dialog, click **Edit Named Selection Sets** from the **Main** toolbar. Highlight the name of the set in this dialog and then click **Select Objects in Set** from the **Named Selection Sets** dialog's toolbar.

Using the Selection Filters

You can use the **Selection Filter** list [see Figure 67] to deactivate selection of all but a specific category by choosing category from this list. For example, if you select **Lights** from this list, you would be only select the light objects in the scene. To remove filtering, select **All** from this list.

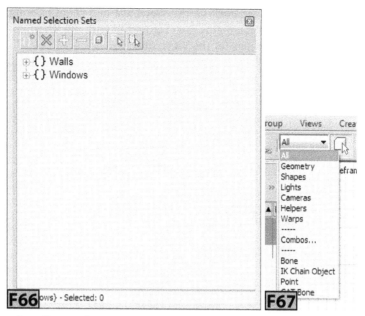

F66 ows) - Selected: 0

F67

Using the Navigation Controls

3ds Max provides two controls to navigate a viewport: **ViewCube** and **SteeringWheels**. These semitransparent controls appear on the upper right corner of a viewport and allow you to change the view without using any menu, command, or keyboard.

ViewCube

This gizmo [see Figure 68] provides a visual feedback you about the orientation of the viewport. It also lets you quickly switch between the standard and orthographic views. The **ViewCube** does not appear in the camera, light, or shape viewport as well as in the special type of views such as **ActiveShade** or **Schematic**. When the **ViewCube** is inactive, the primary function of the **ViewCube** is to show the orientation of the model based on the north direction of the model. The inactive **ViewCube** remains in the semi-transparent state. When you position the mouse pointer on it, it becomes active.

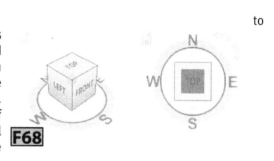

to

F68

Tip: Toggling the visibility of the ViewCube
*Press **Ctrl+Alt+V** to toggle the ViewCube's visibility.*

If you hover the mouse pointer on top of the **ViewCube**, you will notice that faces, edges, and corners of the cube are highlighted. Click on the highlighted part of the cube; 3ds Max animates the viewport and orients it according to the clicked part of the cube. Click on the home icon on the **ViewCube** to switch to the default viewport orientation. You can also click and drag the ring to spin model around its current orientation.

To change the **ViewCube's** settings, RMB click on the **ViewCube** and choose **Configure** from the popup menu to open the **Viewport Configuration** dialog [see Figure 69] with the **ViewCube** panel active. From this panel you can change various settings for the **ViewCube**.

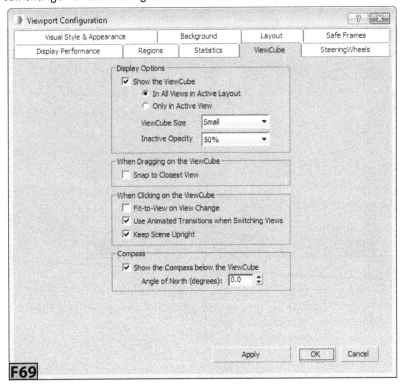

Table 13 lists the other option available in the popup menu.

Table 13: The options available for **ViewCube** in the popup menu	
Option	**Description**
Home	Restores the home view.
Orthographic	Changes the current orientation to the orthographic projection.
Perspective	Changes the current orientation to the perspective projection.
Set Current View as Home	Defines the home view based on the current orientation.
Set Current View as Front	Defines the front projection based on the current projection.
Reset Front	Resets the front projection to its default view.
Configure	Opens the **Viewport Configuration** dialog.
Help	Launches the online help system and navigate to the ViewCube documentation.

SteeringWheels

The **SteeringWheels** gizmo [see Figure 70] allows you to access different 2D and 3D navigation tools from a single tool. When you first start the **SteeringWheels** gizmo is turned off. To enable this gizmo press **Shift+W**.

When the wheel is displayed, you can activate it by clicking on one of its wedges. If you click drag a wedge, the current view changes. The navigation tools listed in Table 14 support click action.

Table 14: The navigation tools	
Tool	**Function**
Zoom	Adjust the magnification of the view.
Center	Centers the view based on the position of the mouse pointer.
Rewind	Restores the previous view.
Forward	Increases the magnification of the view.

To close a wheel, you can use one of the following methods:

1. Press **Esc**.
2. Press **Shift+W** to toggle the wheel.
3. Click the small **x** button the upper right area of the wheel.
4. RMB click on the wheel.

Tip: Changing wheel's settings
You can change the ***SteeringWheels'*** *settings from the* ***SteeringWheels*** *panel of the* ***Viewport Configuration*** *dialog box [see Figure 71].*

There are other versions of the wheels available that you can activate from the **Wheel** menu. To open the menu, click on the down arrow on the bottom-right corner of the wheel. Table 15 lists those options.

Table 15: The options available in the **Wheel** menu.	
Option	**Function**
Mini View Object Wheel	Displays the mini version of the **View Object** wheel [see the first image in Figure 72].
Mini Tour Building Wheel	Displays the mini version of the **Tour Building** wheel [see the second image in Figure 72].
Mini Full Navigation Wheel	Displays the mini version of the **Full Navigation** wheel [see the third image in Figure 72].
Full Navigation Wheel	Displays the big version of the **Full Navigation** wheel [see the fourth image in Figure 72].

Basic Wheels	Displays the big versions of the **View Object** or **Tour Building** wheel [Figure 73].
Go Home	Restores the **Home** view.
Restore Original Center	Pans the view to the origin.
Increase Walk Speed	Doubles the walk speed used by the **Walk** tool.
Decrease Walk Speed	Cuts the walk speed by half used by the **Walk** tool.
Help	Navigates you to the online documentation of the steering wheels.
Configure	Opens the **Viewport Configuration** dialog that allows you set preferences for the wheel.

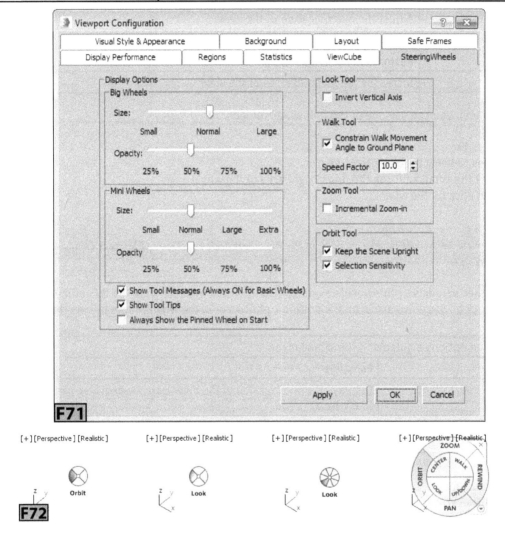

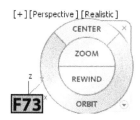
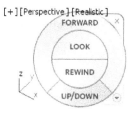

Zooming, Panning, and Orbiting Views using Mouse Scroll

To zoom in and out in the viewport, scroll the mouse wheel. It zooms in or out in steps and is equivalent to using bracket keys, **[** and **]**. If you want to gradually zoom, scroll the wheel with the **Ctrl+Alt** held down. Press and hold MMB and then drag the mouse pointer to pan the view. You can pan the viewport in any direction. To rotate the viewport press and hold **Alt+MMB** and then drag the mouse pointer.

Moving, Rotating, and Scaling Objects

The transformation tools [see Figure 74] in 3ds Max allow you to move, rotate, and scale an object[s]. A transformation is the adjustment position, orientation, and scale relative to the 3D space you are working in. 3ds Max provides four tools that allow you to transform the object: **Select and Move**, **Select and Rotate**, **Select and Scale**, and **Select and Place**. The **Select and Move**, **Select and Rotate**, and **Select and Scale** tools are generally referred as **Move**, **Rotate**, and **Scale** tools. Now onward, I will use these names.

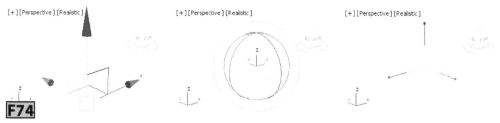

To transform an object, click the **Move**, **Rotate**, or **Scale** button from the **Main** toolbar. Position the mouse pointer on the object[s]. If the object[s] is already selected, the shape of the cursor changes to indicate transform. If object[s] is not selected, the shape of the mouse pointer changes to a crosshair. Now, drag the mouse pointer to apply the transform. You can restrict the motion to one or two axes by using the transform gizmos. The transform gizmos are the icons displayed in the viewport. Figure 74 shows the **Move**, **Rotate**, and **Scale** gizmos, respectively.

Tip: Changing size of the gizmos
You can change the size of the gizmos by using the – and = keys on the main keyboard.

When no transform tool is active and you select objects, an axis tripod appears in the viewports [see Figure 75]. Each axis tripod consists of three lines labeled as **X**, **Y**, and **Z**. The orientation of the tripod indicates the orientation of the current reference coordinate system. The point where the three lines meet indicates the current transform center and the highlighted red axis lines show the current axis constraints.

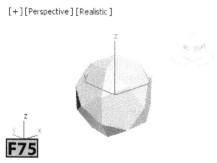

Each gizmo indicates axes by using three colors: **X** is **red**, **Y** is **green**, and **Z** is **blue**. You can use any of the axes handles to constrain transformation to that axis.

Tip: 1-minute learning movies
To more about transform tools, download the movies from the following link: http://download.autodesk.com/us/3dsmax/skillmovies/index.html.

The transform commands are also available from the **Quad** menu. To transform an object using the **Quad** menu, RMB click on the selected object[s], choose the transform command from the **Quad** menu and then drag the object to apply the transform.

Tip: Cancelling transform
To cancel a transform, RMB click while dragging the mouse.

Using the Transform Type-In dialog

You can use the **Transform Type-In** dialog to precisely enter the transformation values. To transform objects using this dialog, if the **Move**, **Rotate**, or **Scale** tool is active, press **F12** to open the dialog or choose **Transform Type-In** from the **Edit** menu to open the associated **Transform Type-In** dialog. Figure 76 shows the **Move Transform Type-In**, **Rotate Transform Type-In**, and **Scale Transform Type-In** dialogs, respectively. You can enter both the absolute and relative transformation values in this dialog.

Tip: Transform Type-In dialog
*You can also open this dialog by RMB clicking on the tool's button on the **Main** toolbar.*

The controls in this dialog are also replicated in the **Status Bar**. You can use these **Transform Type-In** boxes on the **Status Bar** to transform the object. To switch between the absolute and relative transform modes, click the **Relative/Absolute Transform Type-In** button on the **Status Bar** [see Figure 77].

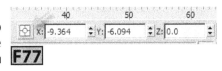

Getting Help

Autodesk provides rock solid documentation for 3ds Max. There are several places in the UI from where you can access different form of help. The help options are listed in the **Help** menu [see Figure 78]. Click **Autodesk 3ds Max Help** from the **Help** menu to open the online documentation for 3ds Max. You can also download offline help from the Autodesk website and install on your computer. If you have a slow internet connection, you can download the offline help and use it. To access offline help, download and install it on your system. Press **Alt+U+P** hotkeys to open the **Preferences** dialog [refer Figure 79].

Choose the **Help** panel from the dialog and click **Browse** to open the **Browser For Folder** dialog. In this dialog, navigate to the directory where you installed help, generally, *C:\Program Files (x86)\Autodesk\Help\3dsmax2016\en_us*. Click **OK** to close the dialog. Click **OK** from the **Preferences** dialog to close it. Now, when you press **F1**, 3ds Max will navigate you to the offline help.

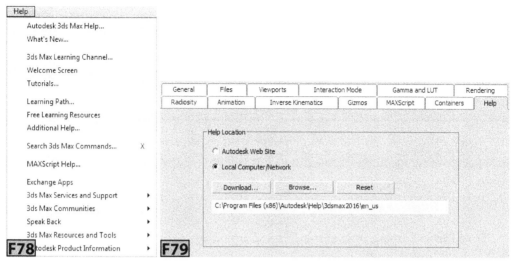

Search Command

The search command feature was introduced in 2014 version of 3ds Max. This feature helps you finding a specific command. For example, if you are looking for the **Sunlight** tool but not sure where it is on the interface. Press **X** to open the **Search Command** text box and then type **Sun**; **SunLight** System appears in a list [see Figure 80]. Click on it, 3ds Max takes you to **Systems** category of the **Create** panel in the **Command Panel**.

InfoCenter Toolbar

The **InfoCenter** is located on the right of caption bar at the top-right of the UI [see Figure 81]. This toolbar allows you to access information about 3ds Max as well as other Autodesk products.

Table 16 shows the elements of this toolbar.

Table 16: The **InfoCenter** toolbar interface overview		
Element	**Icon**	**Description**
Search field	-	The search box is marked by arrow in Figure 57. You can use this search box to lookup information in the help documentation. This field supports wildcard characters such as * and ?.
Communication Center	⬁	Takes you to the Communication Center that displays announcements about product updates and other news.
Favorites	☆	Click to view the Favorite panel.

Sign In	Sign In	Allows you to access Autodesk 360 for mobility, collaboration, and online services of the cloud.
Autodesk Exchange Apps	X	Takes you to the Autodesk Exchange Application store.
Quick Help menu	(?)	Takes you to quick help menu which is a smaller version of the Edit menu.

Hands-on Exercise

Complete the following Hands-On Exercise:

Exercise 1: *Creating Simple Model of a House*

Practical Tests

Complete the following tests:

Practical Test - 1: Coffee Table

Create the text [Love] as shown in Figure 82 using the **Box** primitive.

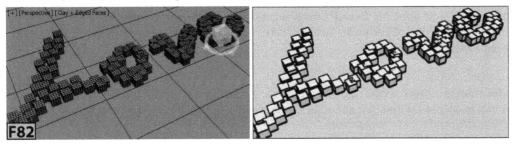

Practical Test - 2: Road Side Sign

Create a road side sign, as shown in Figure 83, using the **Box, Pyramid**, and **Box** primitives.

F83

Summary

Understanding the interface is one of the keys to be efficient in 3ds Max. The purpose of this unit was to introduce you to the 3ds Max UI. You have seen that 3ds Max offers many toolbars, menus, panels, and viewports that allow you to work with ease. In addition, you learned how to create objects and change their parameters from the Command Panel, how to select objects, and how to transform objects using the transformation tools.

The unit covered the following topics:

- Navigating the workspace
- Customizing the interface
- Understanding various UI components
- Working with the file management commands
- Setting preferences for 3ds Max
- Understanding workspaces
- Understanding the enhanced menu system
- Working with viewports
- Setting preferences for the viewports
- Creating objects in the scene
- Selecting objects
- Using the navigational gizmos
- Moving, rotating, and scaling objects
- Getting help

In next unit, I will cover some tools, aids, and explorers that you will encounter regularly in your journey of conquering 3ds Max.

Unit M2: Introducing 3ds Max - II

In the previous unit, I covered the interface as well as the tools that allow you to transform objects in the viewport. In this unit, I will cover the tools and procedures that will help you immensely during the modeling process. You will know about various explorers as well as various precision tools that 3ds Max offers. I have also covered the procedures for creating clones, and duplicates.

In this unit, I will cover the following:

- Working with templates
- Creating clones and duplicates
- Understanding hierarchies
- Working with the **Scene** and **Layer** Explorers
- Understanding the **Mirror** tool, the **Select and Place** tool, and the **Select and Manipulate** tool
- Working with the **Align** tool and the **Array** tool
- Working with precision and drawing aids
- Understanding modifiers, and normals

Working with Templates

Templates, introduced in 2016 version of 3ds Max allow you to create a base file that you can use to create new files based on a template. For example, if you regularly work on projects that consist of studio lighting, you can create a template with three point light setup, **mental ray** renderer, and HD resolution for rendering. The template will save you lot of time when you start working on a new project. The following information can be saved in templates:

- Scene and display units
- Renderer and rendering resolution
- Scene geometry, which can be animated
- The active workspace
- The order of rollouts
- The **ViewCube** settings
- Viewport layout and settings
- User paths
-

The start-up templates are available in the **Start** panel of the **Welcome Screen**. If the **Welcome Screen** is not visible, choose **Welcome Screen** from the **Help** menu. 3ds Max comes with some default templates that you can access from the **START-UP TEMPLATES** section of the **Start** panel. To start a new scene using a default template, double-click on a template preview. You can use a template by first selecting the preview icon and then clicking **New Using Selected Template**.

Click **Open Template Manager** from the **Start** panel of the **Welcome Screen** to open the **Template Manager** dialog [see Figure 1]. At the left of the dialog, you will see the preview icons of the available templates. Place the mouse pointer on the icons to view the brief description of the template. Click on an icon to see its details at the right of the dialog. Click **Set as Default** to make the selected template default for the new scenes. The array of buttons available for **Thumbnail** control allows you to set a preview icon for the template. The controls to set scene file, project folder, and workspace are available below these buttons.

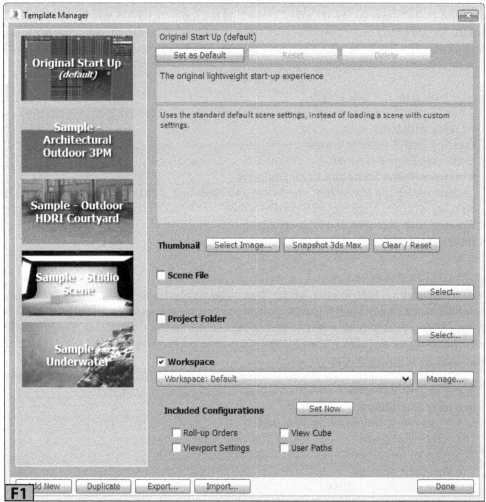

To create a new template, click **New** and then provide the required information at the right of the dialog. Click **Done** to create a new template and close the **Template Manager** dialog. To duplicate an existing template, select the template and then click **Duplicate**.

Creating Copies, Clones, and References

The general terms used for duplicating objects is **cloning**. To create a duplicate, clone, or reference, transform [move, rotate, or scale] the object with **Shift** held down. This process is generally called

Shift+Transform. There are some other tools such as the **Mirror** tool available in 3ds Max that allows you to create clones.

Q: What's is the difference between Copy, Instance, and Reference?

*There are three methods available in 3ds Max to clone the objects: **Copy**, **Instance**, and **Reference**. At geometry level, clones created using any method are identical. However, they behave differently when used with the modifiers such as **Bend** or **Twist**.*

*The **Copy** method allows you to create a completely different copy of the original object. If you modify the original object, it will have no effect on the other. The **Instance** method creates a completely interchangeable clone of the original. If you modify the original or the instance, the change will be replicated in both objects. The **Reference** method creates a clone dependent on the original upto the point when the object was created. If you apply a new modifier to the referenced object, it will affect only that object. Depending on the method used, the cloned objects are called copies, instances, or references.*

Cloning Techniques

3ds Max provides several techniques for creating clones. You can use any of these techniques on any selection. Here's the list:

- Clone
- Shift+Clone
- Snapshot
- **Array** tool
- **Mirror** tool
- **Spacing** tool
- **Clone and Align** tool
- Copy/Paste (**Scene Explorer**)

Table 1 summarizes these techniques:

Table 1: The list of cloning techniques	
Technique	**Description**
Clone	The easiest method for creating clones is to use the **Clone** command. To create clone using this command, select the object[s] that you want to clone and then choose **Clone** from the **Edit** menu or press **Ctrl+V**. The **Clone Options** dialog appears. Choose the method you want to use from the **Object** section of the dialog and then specify a name for the cloned object using **Name** text box and then click **OK** to create a clone. The clone will be superimposed on the original object at the same location. Use the **Move** tool to separate the two.
Shift+Clone	You can use this technique to clone objects while transforming them. This technique is most used technique for cloning objects. To clone and transform objects, click **Move**, **Rotate**, or **Scale** on the **Main** toolbar and then select an object, multiple objects, group, or sub-objects in a viewport. Hold down **Shift** and then drag the selection. As you drag the selection the clone is created, and transformed. Now, release **Shift** and mouse button to open the **Clone Options** dialog. Change the settings and click **OK** to create a clone.

Snapshot	You can use this feature to create an animated object over time. You can create a single clone on any frame or you can create clones on multiple frames along the animation path. The spacing between the clones is a uniform time interval.
Array	You can use the **Array** tool to create repeating design patterns for example, legs of a round coffee table, blades of a jet engine, text on the dial of a watch, and so forth. The **Array** command allows you to precisely control the transformations in 3D space.
Mirror	**Mirror** allows you to create a symmetrical copy along any combination of axes. This tool also provide an option "**No Clone**" that allows you to perform a mirror operation without creating clone.
Spacing Tool	This tool distributes objects along a path define by a spline. You can control the spacing between the objects.
Clone and Align Tool	This tool allows you to distribute the source objects to a selection of the destination objects. This tool is very useful when you work on an imported CAD file that contains lots of symbols. For example, you can replace the chair symbols in the CAD file with the actual chair geometry en masse.
Copy/Paste (Scene Explorer)	You can use the **Scene Explorer's Edit** menu command to copy paste nodes. The **Scene Explorer** should be in **Sort By Hierarchy** mode.

Working with the Mirror Tool

On clicking **Mirror** from the **Main** toolbar, the **Mirror** dialog appears [see Figure 2]. The controls in this dialog allow you to mirror the current selection about the center of the current coordinate system. You can also create a clone while mirroring a selection. To mirror an object, make a selection in a viewport. Click **Mirror** on the **Main** toolbar or choose **Mirror** from the **Tools** menu. In the **Mirror** dialog that appears, set the parameters and click **OK** [see Figure 3]. In Figure 3, I have selected the left leg of the robot and then used the **Mirror** dialog to create his right leg.

Notice in the **Mirror** dialog, there are two options at the top: **Transform** and **Geometry**. These options control how the **Mirror** tool treats the reflected geometry. **Transform** uses the legacy mirror method. This method mirrors any word-space-modifiers [**WSM**] effect. **Geometry** applies a **Mirror** modifier to the object and does not mirror any **WSM** effect.

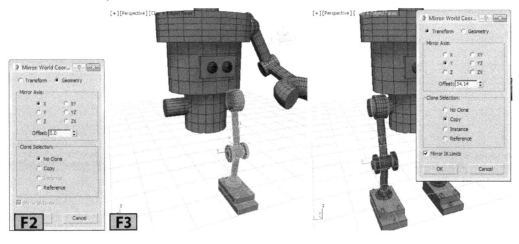

Working with the Array Tool

The **Array** tool allows you to create an array of objects based on the current selection in the viewport. The **Array** button in not visible on the **Main** toolbar by default. The **Array** button is part of the **Extras** toolbar which is not visible by default. To make it visible, RMB click on a gray area of the **Main** toolbar and then choose **Extras** from the popup menu to display the **Extras** toolbar [see Figure 4].

To understand the functioning of this tool, reset 3ds Max and create a teapot in the scene. Ensure teapot is selected in a viewport and then choose **Array** from the **Tools** menu to open the **Array** dialog. Now, click **Preview** and set other parameters as shown in Figure 5. Notice in Figure 5, 3ds Max creates **4** copies of the teapot with **60** units distance between each copy. Notice total distance is now **300** units, as shown in **Totals** section of the dialog indicating that **5** copies of the teapot are taking up **300** units space along the **X** direction.

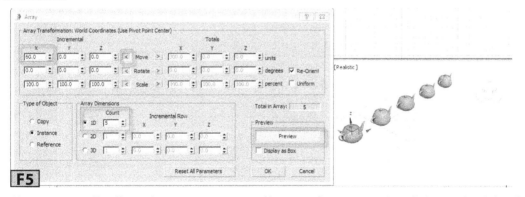

Now, if you want to distribute these teapots over a distance of say **400** units, click **>** on the right of the **Move** label and then set **X** to **400** [see Figure 6], the teapots are now spread over a distance of **400** units. Similarly, you can create an array using the **Rotate** and **Scale** transformations.

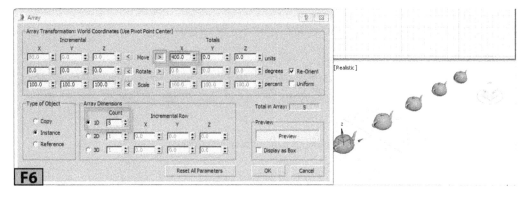

F6

Settings in Figures 7 and 8 show how you can create a 2D or 3D array, respectively, using the **Array** dialog.

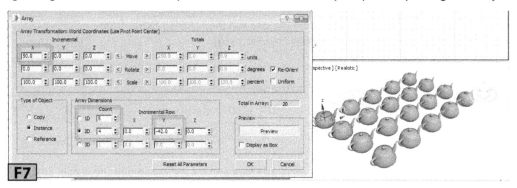

F7

You can also create a **360** degree array using the **Array** dialog. Reset 3ds Max and then create a **Teapot** primitive with radius **10** at the top edge of the grid [see Figure 9]. From the **Main toolbar | User Center flyout**, choose **Use Transform Coordinate Center** [see Figure 10]. Choose **Array** from the **Tools** menu to open the **Array** dialog. Now, specify the settings, as shown in Figure 11 to create 12 teapots in a full circle [360 degrees].

Working with the Spacing Tool

This tool allows you to distribute the selected objects along a spline or along the distance specified by two points. You can also control the spacing between two objects. This tool can be activated by choosing **Align | Spacing tool** from the menu bar or choosing **Spacing Tool** from the **Array** flyout.

To distribute objects along a path, select the objects in the scene and then activate the **Spacing Tool** to open the **Spacing Tool** dialog [see Figure 12]. This dialog gives you two methods for selecting path: **Pick Path** and **Pick Points**. If you click **Pick Path**, place a cursor on a spline in the view and click to select the spline as path.

Now, specify the number of objects you want to distribute and then choose a distribution algorithm from the drop-down available in the **Parameters** section [see Figure 13]. Turn on **Follow**, if you want to align the pivot points of the object along the tangents of the spline [see Figure 14].

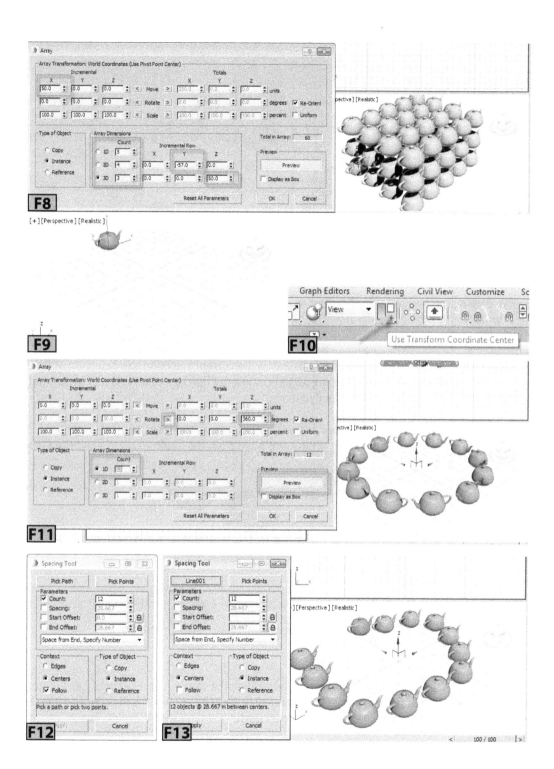

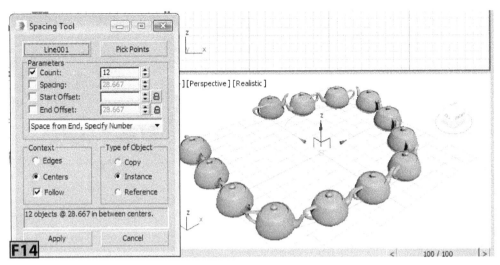
F14

If you click **Pick Points** from the **Spacing Tool** dialog, specify the path by clicking on two places in the viewport. When you are finished with the tool, 3ds Max deletes the spline.

Working with Clone and Align Tool

This tool lets you distribute the source objects based on the current selection to a selection of the target objects. You can activate this tool by choosing **Align | Clone and Align** from the **Tools** menu. Alternatively, choose **Clone and Align Tool** from the **Array** flyout.

To use the **Clone and Align** tool, create four teapots and a cone in the viewport [see Figure 15]. Select cone in a viewport and then choose **Align | Clone and Align** from the **Tools** menu to open the **Clone and Align** dialog.

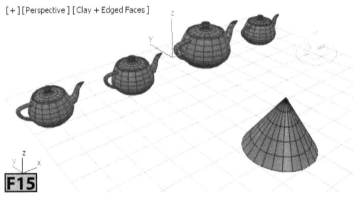
[+] [Perspective] [Clay + Edged Faces]

F15

In this dialog, click **Pick** and then click on each teapot to align the cone with the teapots [see Figure 16]. If you want to pick multiple destination objects at once, click **Pick List** to open the **Pick Destination Objects** dialog. In this dialog, select the objects and then click **Pick**.

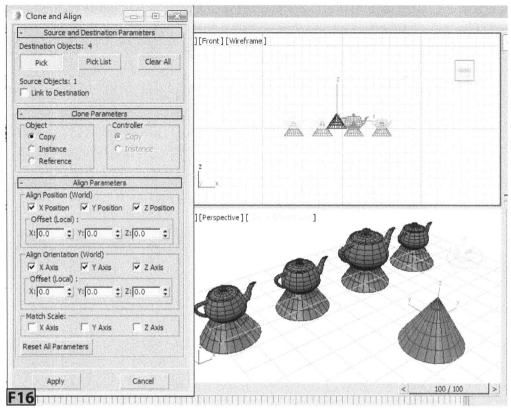

F16

Working With the Select and Place Tool

The **Select and Place** tool has been introduced in the 2015 release of 3ds Max. This tool is cousin of the **AutoGrid** option found in the **Object Type** rollout. However you can use it any time in your scene not just when you are creating an object. This tool can be activated by using one of the following four methods:

- Click the **Select and Place** icon on the **Main** toolbar.
- Choose **Placement** from the **Edit** menu.
- Press **Y** on the keyboard.
- RMB click on an object and then choose **Placement** from the **Transform** quadrant [see Figure 17].

To place an object, you don't have to select it first. Pick the **Select and Place** tool, click on the object to select it and then drag to place on another object [see Figure 18]. As you drag the object, the orientation of the object changes based on the normals of the target object and object **Up Axis** settings. The contact position of the target surface will be the object's pivot

To change the **Up Axis** settings, RMB click on the **Select and Place** tool on the **Main** toolbar to open the **Placement Settings** dialog [see Figure 19] and then select the axis from the **Object Up Axis** button array.

When **Rotate** is active on the **Placement Settings** dialog, the translation of the object is prevented and object rotates around the local axis specified with the **Object Up Axis** settings. **Use Base as Pivot** is useful in those cases when the pivot is not already located in the base of the object. **Pillow Mode** is very useful when you are trying to place an object on a target whose surface is uneven. This option prevents the intersection of the objects. When **Autoparent** is active, the placed object automatically becomes the child of the other object. This is a quick way to make parent-child relationship.

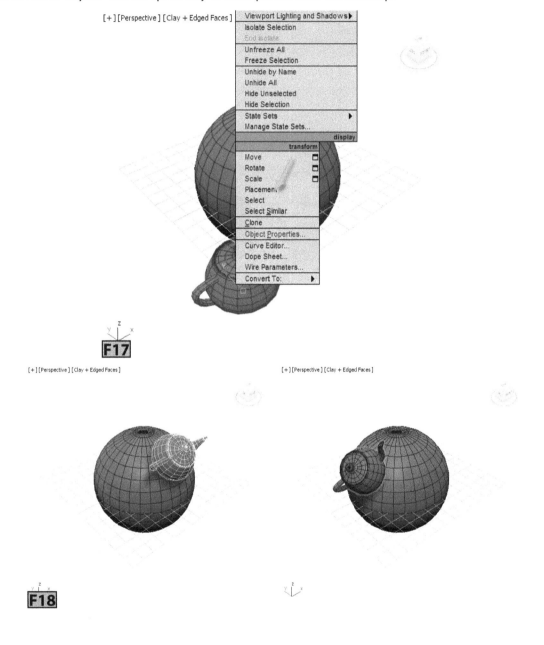

There are some more goodies associated with this tool:

- You can clone an object while dragging it by pressing **Shift**.
- Hold **Ctrl** and then drag to position an object vertically along the **Up Axis**.
- You can prevent an object from rotating while you place it by holding **Alt**.

You can also place several objects at one go. You can either select the desired objects before picking the **Select and Place** tool or you can select additional objects using **Ctrl** when this tool is active.

Each object will move according to its own pivot, unless objects are linked together.

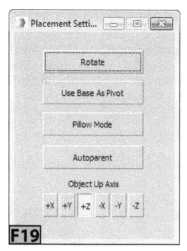

Working With the Select and Manipulate Tool

The **Select and Manipulate** tool allows you to interactively edit the parameters of certain objects by dragging the manipulators in the viewports. The state of this tool is non-exclusive. You can manipulate objects as long as any of the select mode or one of the transform mode is active but if you want to select a manipulator helper, you must deactivate the **Select and Manipulate** tool. All those primitives with a **Radius** parameter have a built-in manipulator for the radius value.
Let's see how it works:

Create a **Teapot** primitive in the scene. Pick the **Select and Manipulate** tool from the **Main** toolbar. A green ring appears beneath the teapot [see Figure 20]. Click drag the ring to interactively change the radius of the teapot. Click on **Select and Manipulate** on the **Main** toolbar to deactivate the tool. There are three types of custom manipulators available in 3ds Max: cone angle manipulator, plane angle manipulator, and slider manipulator. Let's have a look at them. The cone angle manipulator is used by a spot light's **Hotspot** and **Falloff** controls. To create a cone angle manipulator, choose **Create panel | Helpers | Manipulators** and then click **Cone Angle**. Click drag in the viewport to create the helper [see Figure 21]. To change its parameters, go to **Modify** panel and change the values.

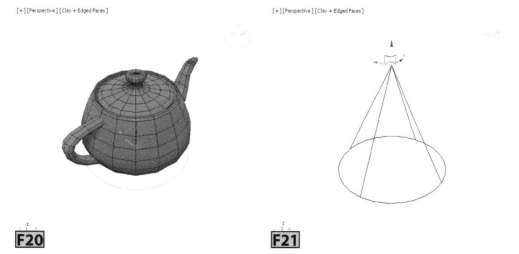

Now, let's work on a spot light to see this manipulator in action:

Create a **Teapot** primitive in the scene. Now create a spot light and place it as shown in Figure 22. Ensure the spot light is selected and then click **Select and Manipulate** from the **Main** toolbar. Two rings appear on the spot light [see Figure 23]. The inner ring controls **Hotspot** whereas the outer rings controls **Falloff**.

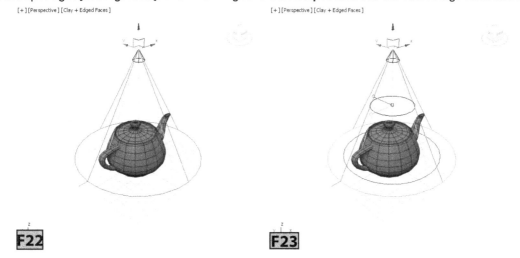

F22   F23

Click drag to interactively change these parameters. The plane angle manipulator allows you to create a lever or joystick type shape. You can use its **Angle** parameter to create a custom control. You can use this control to drive parameter of another objects.

Let's see how it works, choose **Create panel | Helpers | Manipulators** and then click **Plane Angle**. In the **Front** viewport, click drag to create a shape [see Figure 24]. The **Plane Angle** manipulator always created vertically along the Y axis of the viewport in which you are creating it. Create a teapot in the **Perspective** viewport. Ensure the **Select and Manipulate** tool is not active and manipulator is selected. Choose **Wire Parameters | Wire Parameters** from the **Animation** menu. In the popup that appears, choose **Object (Plane Angle Manipulator) | Angle** [Figure 25]. A rubber band line appears. Click on the teapot.

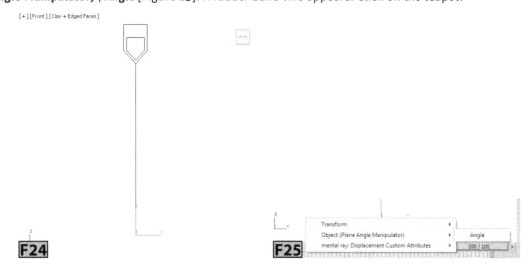

F24   F25

In the popup that appears, choose **Object (Teapot) | Radius** [see Figure 26]. In the **Parameter Wiring** dialog, click **One-way connection** button and then the **Connect** button [see Figure 27] to make the connection. Now close the dialog.

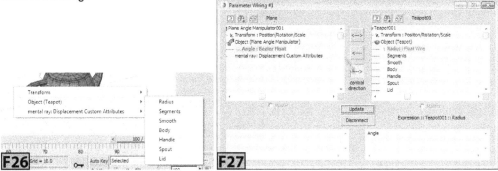

Pick the **Select and Manipulate** tool and click drag the manipulator to interactively change the radius of the teapot.

The third type of manipulator, **Slider**, creates a graphic control in the viewport. You can wire its value to a parameter of another object within the scene. Here's how:

Create a **Slider** manipulator in the **Front** viewport. Create a teapot in the **Perspective** viewport [see Figure 28].Wire the **Value** parameter to the **Radius** of the teapot as described above. Change the controls such as **Label**, **Minimum**, and **Maximum** values in the **Modify** panel [see Figure 29]. Pick the **Select and Manipulate** tool and drag the manipulator's **Adjust** control to interactively change the shape of the teapot. Figure 30 shows the components of a **Slider** control [1. Label, 2. Value, 3. Move, 4. Show/hide, 5. Slider bar, 6. Adjust value, and 7. Change width].

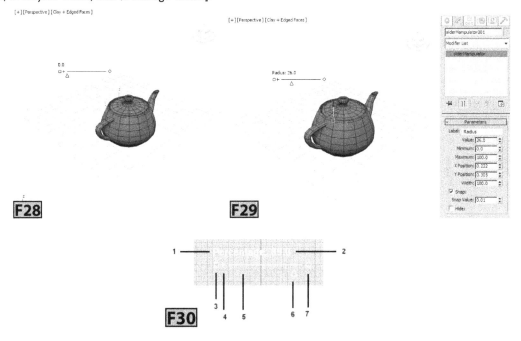

Scene Explorer

The **Scene Explorer** [see Figure 31] is a modeless dialog in 3ds Max that you can use to view, sort, filter, and select objects. In addition, you can rename, delete, hide, and freeze objects. You can also create and modify and edit object properties en masse. Each workspace in 3ds Max comes with a different **Scene Explorer** with the same name as its workspace. The **Scene Explorer** is docked to the left of the viewports.

Several explorers in 3ds Max are different versions of the **Scene Explorer**. These includes: **Layer Explorer**, **Container Explorer**, **MassFX Explorer**, and **Material Explorer**.

The **Scene Explorer** comes with many toolbars [see Figure 31]. Table 2 summarizes various toolbars available.

Table 2: The **Scene Explorer** toolbars	
Flag	**Toolbar**
1	Selection toolbar
4	View toolbar
5	Display toolbar
6	Find toolbar
7	Tools toolbar

Selection Toolbar

The **Scene Explorer** comes with two sorting modes: **Sort By Layer** mode and **Sort By Hierarchy** mode. You can use the **Sort By Layer** or **Sort by Hierarchy** button on the **Selection** toolbar [marked as 1 in Figure 31] to use these modes. The **Sort By Layer** button [marked as 2 in Figure 31] sets **Scene Explorer** to **Sort By Layer** mode. In this mode, you can use drag and drop feature for editing layers. Some other options are also available in this mode. The **Sort By Hierarchy** [marked as 3 in Figure 31] button allows you to edit hierarchies using drag and drop functionality.

If you click on an object in the **Scene Explorer**, the object is selected and the associated row in the explorer gets highlighted. To select multiple objects, click on objects with the **Ctrl** held down. Press **Ctrl+A** to select all objects, **Ctrl+I** to invert the selection, and **Ctrl+D** to deselect. These commands are also available at the right of the **Selection** toolbar [marked as 1 in Figure 31]. The **Selection Set** drop-down in the **Selection** toolbar lets you select objects using **Named Selection Sets**.

Tools Toolbar

The tools available in this toolbar are dependent on whether **Sort By Hierarchy** mode or **Sort By Layer** mode is active. When **Lock Cell Editing** is on, you cannot change any name or settings. The **Pick Parent** button is only available in the **Sort By Hierarchy** mode only. It allows you to change the parent. To make an object parent, select one or more objects and then click **Pick Parent**. Now, select the object that you want parent of the selected object. The **Create New Layer** button is available in the **Sort By Layer** mode. When you click **Create New Layer**, a new layer is created and the selection is automatically added to this layer. The new layer you create becomes the active layer and any subsequent objects you create are added to this layer automatically. If an existing layer is selected, and you click **Create New Layer**, the new layer becomes child of the selected layer. The **Add to Active Layer** is available in the **Sort By Layer** mode only. When you click on this button, all selected objects and layers are assigned to the active layer. **Select Children** allows you to select all child objects and layers of the selected items.

Tip: Selecting children
Double-clicking on a parent layer or object selects the parent and all its children.

The **Make Selected Layer Active** button is available in the **Sort By Layer** mode only. When you click on this button, 3ds Max makes the selected layer the active layer. Alternatively, click on the layer icon to make it the later active.

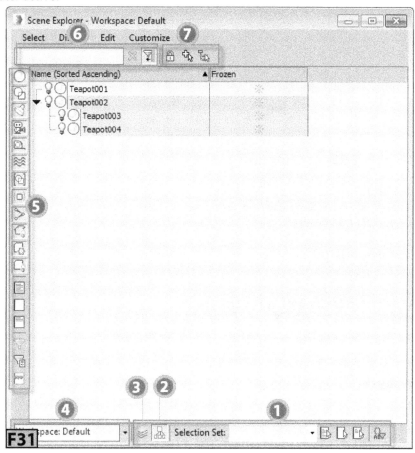

Display Toolbar

The **Display** toolbar allows you to display various categories in the **Scene Explorer**. It controls the type of objects that appear in the **Scene Explorer's** listing. You can also solo the category by clicking on one of the category button with **Alt** held down. You can also turn on or off the categories by choosing **Display | Object Types** from the **Scene Explorer's** menu bar.

View Toolbar

The **View** toolbar is located at the bottom-left corner of the **Scene Explorer**. This toolbar shows the name of the current **Scene Explorer**. When you click on the arrow located in this toolbar, a menu appears. This menu gives access to all local and global explorers.

3ds Max comes with different **Scene Explorer** configurations. These configurations are available to every scene you create in 3ds Max. Therefore, they are referred to as **Global Scene Explorers**. On the other hand the **Local Scene Explorers** live within a single scene and saved/loaded with the scene. The options to make a **Local** explorer **Global** are available in the menu located on the **View** toolbar [see Figure 32].

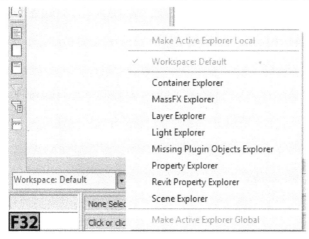

Q. How to delete objects?

*To delete one or more objects in the **Scene Explorer**, select them and then press **Delete** or RMB click on the list and then choose **Delete** from the **Quad** menu.*

Q. How to hide and show objects?

Click the light bulb icon of the layer or object to hide. The light bulb icon turns gray. Click again to reveal.

Q. How to create hierarchies in the Sort By Hierarchy mode?

*To make a parent, drag and drop the child objects' name or icon onto the object that you want to act as parent. To restore the child object to the top level, drag them to an empty area of the **Scene Explorer**. Alternatively, you can RMB click on them and then choose **Unlink** from the **Quad** menu. You can use the same techniques on the layers as well.*

Q. How to freeze objects?

*To freeze objects, click on the **Frozen** column of the object. Click again to unfreeze. If you want to freeze many objects, select them and then click on the **Frozen** column of any selected objects.*

Q. How to change object properties?

*To change the object properties, select one or more objects in the **Scene Explorer** and then RMB. Choose **Properties** from the **Quad** menu to open the **Object Properties** dialog. You can use this dialog to change the properties of the selected objects.*

Q. How to rename an object?

*Select the object and then RMB click. Choose **Rename** from the **Quad** menu and then type a new name for the object.*

Tip: Renaming objects
*Slowly double-click on the object name to rename the object if you don't want to use the **Quad** menu.*

Q. Can I add more column next to the Frozen column?

*Yes, you can. RMB click on any of the column head and then choose **Configure Columns** [see Figure 33] from the popup menu. The **Configure Column** window appears [see Figure 34]. Click on the name of the column in this window that you want to add. Figure 35 shows the **Has Material** column. A tick will appear in this column if the material has been assigned to the object.*

Q. Can I search object by names?

*Yes, you can search object by using the search text box available in the **Find** toolbar. Type the search sting and press **Enter**. For example, if you have many teapots in the scene and all have default names. Entering **tea** in the **search** field and then pressing **Enter** will select all teapots in the scene. You can also use the wild card characters **?** and ***** to create a broader search criteria.*

Working with the Precision Tools

3ds Max comes with several tools and objects that allow you to position and align objects efficiently. Two tools [**Select and Place** tool, and **Select and Manipulate** tool] I have already discussed that let you align and position objects. You have also seen the use of some helpers that are used with the **Select and Manipulate** tool.

Using Units

The units define the measurement system for the scene. The default unit system in 3ds Max is **Generic**. Besides **Generic** units, you can also use feet and inches units both decimal and fractional. The **Metric** system allows you to specify units from millimeters to kilometers. You can specify the unit system from the **Units Setup** dialog [see Figure 36]. You can open this dialog by choosing **Units Setup** from the **Customize** menu. On clicking **System Unit Setup** from this dialog, the **System Unit Setup** dialog appears from where you can specify the **System** units.

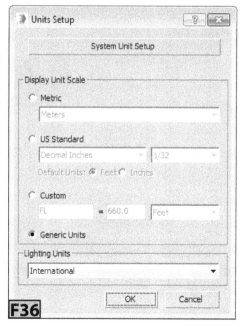

Q. What is the difference between Scene Units and System Units?

The system units only affects how geometry appears in the viewports whereas the system units control the actual scale of the geometry.

Caution: System Units

*The system units should only be changed before you create your scene or import a **unitless** file. Do not change the system units in the current scene.*

If you change units for a scene, 3ds Max automatically changes the values for the controls. For example, if you are using **Centimeters**, and value in a spinner is **30** cm, when you change units to **Decimal Inches**; 3ds Max will change the value to **11.811** inches. Now, if you type **50cm** in the spinner and press **Enter**, 3ds Max will change value to **19.685** inches. Similarly, if you type **2'** in the spinner, the value will be changed to **24.0** inches.

Using Grids

Grids are two dimensional arrays that you can use to position the objects accurately. You can use grids to visualize space, scale, and distance. You can use it as construction plane to create objects as well use it for snapping objects using the snap feature. I will discuss snap features later in this unit. 3ds Max provides two types of grids: **Home** grid and **Grid** objects.

Home Grid

The **Home** grid is defined by three intersecting planes along the world **X**, **Y**, and **Z** axes. These planes intersect at the origin defined by **0,0,0**. The **Home** grid is fixed, you cannot move or rotate it.

Tip: Home Grid

*Press **G** to toggle the visibility of the **Home** grid.*

Grid Object

The **Grid** object [see Figure 37] is a helper object that you can use to create a reference grid as per your needs. You can create as many **Grid** objects as you want in a scene. However, only one **Grid** object will be active at a time. When a **Grid** object is active, it replaces the **Home** grid in all viewports. You can rename and delete **Grid** objects like any other object. The **Grid** object is available in the **Helpers** category on the **Create** panel.

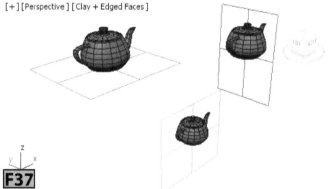

[+] [Perspective] [Clay + Edged Faces]

F37

Tip: Activating the Home grid and Grid object

*You can activate the **Home** grid by choosing **Grids and Snaps | Activate Home Grid** from the **Tools** menu. When you choose this command, it activates the **Home** grid in all viewports and deactivates the current active grid object. Similarly, you can activate a **Grid** object by choosing **Grids and Snaps | Activate Grid Object** from the **Tools** menu.*

*To align a **Grid** object with the current view, RMB click and then choose **Align Grid to View** from the **Quad** menu. You can also execute this command by choosing **Grids and Snaps | Activate Grid Object** from the **Quad** menu. The **Grid** object is aligned and will be coplanar with the current view.*

Auto Grid

The **Auto Grid** feature lets you create objects on the surface of other objects. The **Auto Grid** option is available on the **Object Type** rollout of any category. It is also available in the **Extras** toolbar. When you activate an option, and drag the cursor on the surface of an object, a construction plane is created temporarily on the surface of object.

Tip: Select and Place tool

*The **Select and Place** Tool discussed earlier provides a similar mechanism to align the objects.*

Aligning Objects

3ds Max provides six different tools for aligning the objects in a scene. These tools are available in the **Align** flyout on the **Main** toolbar.

Using with Align Tool

The **Align** tool in 3ds Max allows you to align the current selection to a target selection. You can pick the **Align** tool from the **Align** flyout on the **Main** toolbar. You can also activate this tool by choosing **Align | Align** from the **Tools** menu or by pressing **Alt+A**. Using this tool, you can align the position and orientation of the bounding box of a source object to the bounding box of a target object. A bounding box is the smallest box that encloses the extents (maximum dimensions) of an object. A bounding box appears when you set a viewport to non-wireframe mode. Figure 38 shows the extents of a teapot model.

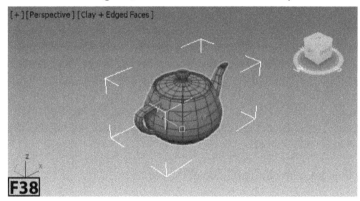

To show the bounding box, select the object and then press **J**. You can also enable display of the bounding boxes by turning on **Selection Brackets** from the **Viewport Configuration dialog | Visual Style & Appearance panel | Selection group** [see Figure 39].

Let's dive in and align some objects:

Create three boxes and assign them red, green, and blue colors [see Figure 40]. Use the following dimensions:

Red Box: Length=52, Width=61, and Height=32
Green Box: Length=35, Width=40, and Height=12
Blue Box: Length=50, Width=40, and Height=30

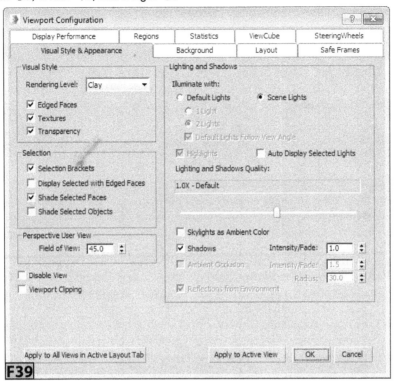

RMB click on the red box and choose **Object Properties** from the **Quad** menu. On the **General panel |
Display Properties** group, turn on **See-Through**. This will help you better see the alignment process. Now
let's center align the red and blue boxes along the **X** and **Y** axes. Make sure the red box is selected and
then pick the **Align** tool from the **Main** toolbar. Click the blue box. On the **Align Selection dialog | Align
Position (World) group**, turn on **X Position** and **Y Position**. Turn off **Z Position**. Make sure **Center** is on in
the **Current Object** and **Target Object** groups. You will see that both the objects are center aligned [see
Figure 41]. Click **OK** to accept changes.

Now, let's see how to place blue box on the top of the red box.

Select the blue box and then pick the **Align** tool from the **Main** toolbar. Click red box. We have already
performed alignment along the **X** and **Y** axes. Therefore, turn off **X Position** and **Y Position** and turn on **Z
Position**. You will see that now the blue box is at the center of the red box. Turn on **Maximum** from the
Target Object group. Notice the blue box's center is aligned to the center of the red box [see Figure 42].
Now select **Pivot Point** from the **Current Object** group. The blue box sits on the top of the red box [see
Figure 43]. Click **OK** to accept changes.

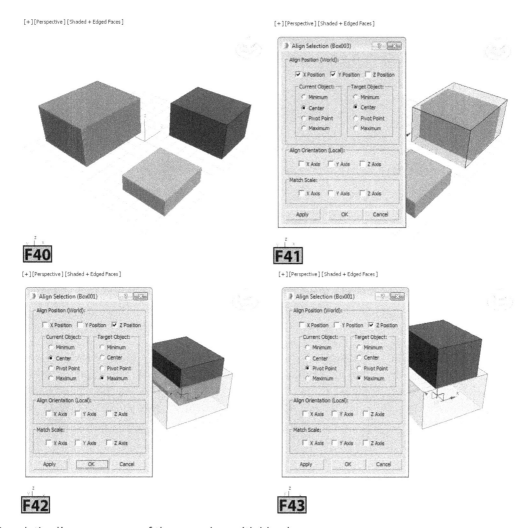

Now, let's align one corner of the green box with blue box.

Select the green box and then pick the **Align** tool from the **Main** toolbar. Click the blue box. Turn on **X Position**, **Y Position**, and **Z Position**. Turn on **Minimum** from the **Current Object** and **Target Object** groups [see Figure 44]. Click **OK** to accept changes. With the green box selected, click the blue box using the **Align** tool. Now, turn on **Z Position** and turn off **X Position** and **Y Position**. Turn on **Maximum** from the **Target Object** group and click **OK**. The boxes are now stacked over each other [see Figure 45].

Using the Quick Align Tool

The **Quick Align** tool instantly aligns an object with the target object. The hotkeys associated with this tool are **Shift+A**. To align an object, select the source object and press **Shift+A** to activate the tool. Now, click on the target object to align two objects [see Figure 46]. If the current selection contains a single object, this tool uses the pivot points of the two objects for alignment. If multiple objects are selected, the selection center of the source objects is aligned with the pivot of the target objects.

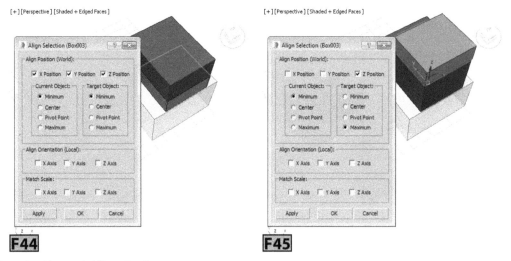

F44 **F45**

Using the Normal Align Tool

This tool allows you to align the two objects based on the directions of the normals of the selected faces. The hotkeys associated with this tool are **Alt+N**. To understand functioning of this tool, create a sphere and teapot in the scene [see Figure 47]. Select the teapot, the source object in this case. Press **Alt+N** to activate the tool and then drag across the surface of the teapot, a blue arrow indicates the location of the current normal [see Figure 48]. Keep dragging on the surface until you find the normal you are looking for. Now, click and drag on the surface of the sphere until you find the normal to which you want to align the the source object. Release the mouse button the teapot gets aligned with the sphere and the **Normal Align** dialog opens [see Figure 49]. Using the controls available in this dialog you can offset the position and orientation of the teapot.

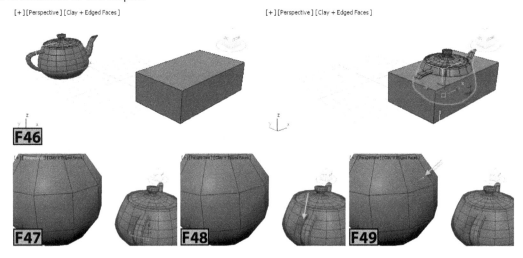

F46

F47 **F48** **F49**

Q. What are normals?

*A normal is a vector that defines the inner and outer surfaces of a face in a mesh. The direction of the vector indicates the front [outer] surface of a face or vertex. Sometimes, normals are flipped during the modeling process. To fix this issue, you can use the **Normal** modifier to flip or unify normals. Figure 50 shows the vertex and face normals, respectively.*

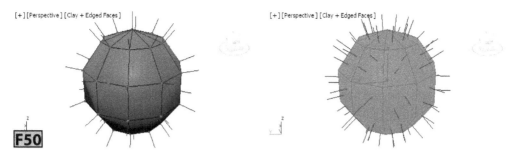

F50

Using the Place Highlight Tool

You can use this tool to align an object or light to another object so that its highlight [reflection] can be precisely positioned. To position a light to highlight a face, make sure the viewport that you want to render is active. Choose **Place Highlight** from the **Align** flyout and drag the mouse pointer on the object to place the highlight. Now, release the mouse button when the normal indicates the face on which you want to place the highlight [see Figure 51].

Note: Light type and highlights
With the omni, free spot, or directional light, 3ds Max displays face normal. With a target spotlight, 3ds Max displays target of the light and base of it's cone.

Using the Align Camera Tool

This tool lets you align the camera to a selected face normal. This tool works similar to the **Place Highlight** tool but it does not change the camera position interactively. You need to release the mouse button and then 3ds Max aligns the camera with the selected face.

Using the Align View Tool

When this tool is picked from the **Align** flyout, it opens the **Align to View** dialog that lets you align the local axis of the selection or sub-object selection with the current viewport [see Figure 52]. To use this tool, select the objects or sub-objects to align and then choose **Align to View** from the **Align** flyout. 3ds Max opens the **Align to View** dialog. Choose the options from the dialog as desired. If you want to flip the direction of alignment, turn on **Flip** on this dialog box.

F51   F52

Drawing Assistants

3ds Max provides several tools and utilities that helps you in drawing objects with precession. Let's have a look.

Measuring Distances

The **Measure Distance** tool allows you to quickly calculate distance between two points. The calculated distance appears in the **Status Bar** in Scene [display] units. To measure distance, choose **Measure Distance** from the **Tools** menu. Now, click on the point in the viewport from where you want to measure the distance. Click again in the viewport where you want to measure to. The distance between the two points is displayed in the **Status Bar**.

The **Measure** utility available in the **Utilities** panel provides the measurement of a selected object or spline. To measure an object, select the object and then on the **Utilities panel | Measure rollout**, click **Measure**. The measurements are displayed in the **Measure** rollout [see Figure 53].

There is one more utility called **Rescale World Units** that you can use to rescale the word units. You can scale entire scene or the selected objects. To rescale an object, select it and then on the **Utilities** panel click **More** to open the **Utilities** panel. Select **Rescale World Units** from the dialog and then click **OK**. The **Rescale World Units** rollout appears in the **Utilities** panel. Click **Rescale** from this rollout to open the **Rescale World Units** dialog [see Figure 54].

Set **Scale Factor** in this dialog and then turn on **Scene** or **Selection** from the **Affect** section. Click **OK** to apply the scale factor to the selected object or to entire scene. For example, you specify **Scale Factor** as **2** and turn on **Object** from the dialog, the selected object will be scaled to double of its current size.

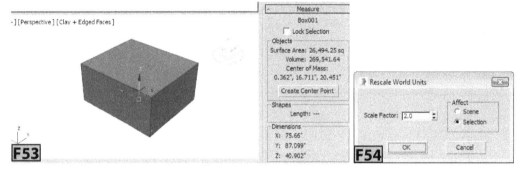

Using Snaps

The Snap tools in 3ds Max allow you to precisely control the dimensions and placement of the objects when you create them or transform them. You and invoke these tools using the **Snap** buttons available on the **Main** toolbar. You can also invoke these tools by choosing **Grids and Snaps** from the **Tools** menu.

2D Snap, 2.5 Snap, and 3D Snap

The hotkey for activating snap is **S**. The **2D Snap** tool snaps the cursor to the active construction grid including the geometry on the plane of the grid. The **Z** axis is ignored by this tool. The **2.5D Snap** tool snaps the cursor to the vertices or edges of the projection of an object onto the active grid. The **3D snap** is the default tool. It snaps the cursor directly to any geometry in the 3D space.

RMB click on snap toggle button to open the **Grid and Snap Settings** dialog [see Figure 55]. You can specify which type of snap of you want active from the **Snap** panel of this dialog box.

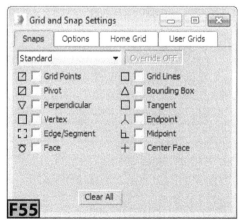

Fox example, if you want the cursor to snap to the pivot or vertices of the object, turn on **Pivot** and **Vertex** from this panel.

To see snap in action, turn on **Pivot** and **Vertex** from the **Grid and Snap Settings** dialog. Now, create a box and teapot in the viewport [see first image at the left of Figure 56]. Pick the **Move** tool from the **Main** toolbar and move the teapot to one of the vertex of the box or its pivot [see middle and right image in Figure 57].

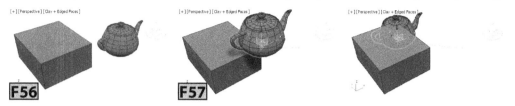

Angle Snap Toggle

You can use the **Angle Snap Toggle** to rotate an object around a given axis in the increment you set. This snap toggle also works with the **Pan/Orbit** camera controls, **FOV** and **Roll** camera settings, and **Hotspot/ Falloff** spotlight angles. The hotkey for invoking this toggle is **A**.

To rotate an object, click **Angle Snap Toggle** on the **Main** toolbar and then rotate the object using the **Rotate** tool. By default, the rotation takes place in five degree increments. You can change this default value by specifying a value for the **Angle** control in the **Options** panel of the **Grid and Snap Settings** dialog.

Percent Snap Toggle

The **Percent Snap Toggle** lets you control the increments of scaling by the specified percentage. The hotkey for invoking this toggle is **Shift+Ctrl+P**. The default percentage value is **10**. You can change this default value by specifying a value for the **Percent** control in the **Options** panel of the **Grid and Snap Settings** dialog.

Spinner Snap Toggle

This toggle allows you to set single-increment or decrement value for all the spinners in 3ds Max. The default value is **1**. To change this value, RMB click on **Spinner Snap Toggle** on the **Main** toolbar to open the **Preferences Settings** dialog. In the **Spinners** section of the **General** panel, specify a value for the **Snap** control.

Modifiers

The modifiers in 3ds Max provide a way to edit and sculpt objects. You can change shape of an object using the modifier's properties. Figure 58 shows the original box [first image] and the modified geometry after applying the **Bend**, **Twist**, and **Taper** modifiers, respectively.

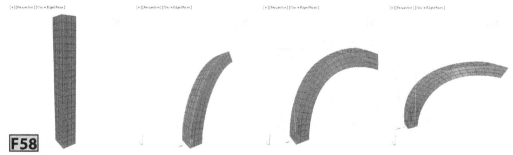

You can apply modifiers from the **Modifier** drop-down available in the **Modify** panel of **Command Panel** [see Figure 59]. The modifier you apply to an object are stored in a stack called modifier stack [see Figure 59].

Practical Test

Complete the following test:

Practical Test - 1: Robo Model

Create a robot model, as shown in Figure 60, using the **Standard** primitives.

Hints:

- The primitives used in the model shown in Figure 59 are: **Box**, **Sphere**, **Cylinder**, **Pyramid**, **Cone**, **Torus**, and **Pipe**.
- The fingers are created using **Torus** primitives. Turn on **Slice On** the **Parameters** rollout of torus to create opening in the torus.
- Use **Auto Grid** and **Select and Place** features of 3ds Max to align and place body parts.
- Create one leg and then use the **Mirror** tool to create a copy on the other side. Apply same concept on eyes and hands. Create a group before applying the **Mirror** tool.
- Create layers for different parts in the **Layer Explorer**. For example, keep all geometries that make hand in the hands layer, and so forth.
- Try to use various features of the **Scene Explorer**.

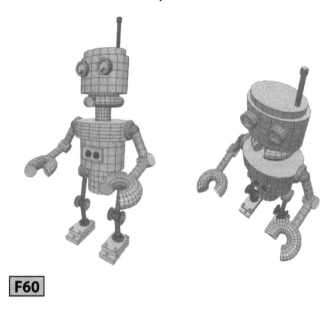

F60

Summary

In this unit, I have covered some basics of 3ds Max. It is very important that you practice all the tools and become proficient with them. The knowledge you gained in this unit will make your life easier while creating complex models in the Hands-on Exercises unit.

The unit covered the following topics:

- Working with templates
- Creating clones and duplicates, understanding hierarchies
- Working with the **Scene** and **Layer** Explorers
- Understanding the **Mirror** tool, the **Select and Place** tool, and the **Select and Manipulate** tool
- Working with the **Align** tool and the **Array** tool
- Working with precision and drawing aids
- Understanding modifiers, and normals

In the next unit, I will cover the geometric primitives. These primitives are building blocks of any model that you create in 3ds Max.

This page intentionally left blank

Unit M3: Working with Geometric Primitives and Architectural Objects

The 3D objects in the scene and the objects that are used to create them are known as geometries. Most of the 3D applications offer basic building blocks for creating geometries called geometric primitives. You can use these primitives and some modifiers to create basic models. In this unit, you will work with the **Standard** and **Extended** primitives as well as the **Architectural** objects.

In this unit, I'll describe the following:

- Creating and modifying **Standard** Primitives
- Creating and modifying **Extended** Primitives
- Working with the **Architectural** objects
- Setting the project folder
- Using the **Align** and **Mirror** tools
- Creating clones
- Using the **Scene Explorer**
- Creating a group
- Setting grid spacings
- Using **Transform Type-In** dialog
- Using **Array** dialog
- Specifying units for the scene

You can edit these geometric primitives at sub-object levels to create complex models. This process is known as surface modeling that I covered in the next unit. In this unit, I will explain **Standard** and **Extended** primitives and how you can use them to create some basic models.

The geometric primitives in 3ds Max are divided into two categories: **Standard** primitives and **Extended** primitives. Let's first start exploring the **Standard** primitives.

Standard Primitives

3ds Max offers ten standard primitives, see Figure 1. You can combine **Standard** primitives into more complex objects. You can then further refine them by using the modifiers. You can dynamically create primitives in the viewport using the mouse and most of the primitives can be generated by entering precise values using the keyboard. You can specify the parameters before creating the primitives and modify them later from the **Parameters** rollout in the **Modify** panel. Let's take a look at different **Standard** primitives.

Box

Box is the simplest of the primitives. You can use it to create rectangular as well as cubical geometries in 3ds Max [see Figure 2]. To create a **Box** primitive, on the **Create** panel, click **Geometry**, and then in the **Object Type** rollout, click **Box**. You can also choose **Box** from the **Standard** menu as well as from the **Enhanced** menu:

Standard Menu: Create menu | Standard Primitives | Box
Enhanced Menu: Objects menu | Primitives | Box

To create a box, click and drag in a viewport to specify the length and width of the box. Now, release the mouse button and drag the mouse up or down [without holding any button] to specify the height of the box and then click to complete the process.

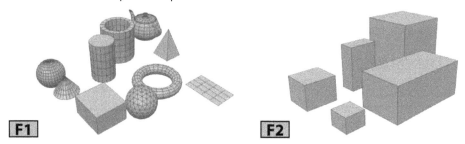

Whenever you choose a tool from the **Object Type** rollout, the **Name and Color**, **Creation Method**, **Keyboard Entry**, and **Parameters** rollouts appear on the **Command Panel**. You can use these rollouts to specify the initial properties of the objects.

Tip: Navigating between the steps
*If you are creating a primitive that requires two or more steps [for example **Cylinder** or **Torus**], you can pan and orbit the viewport between the steps. To pan the viewport, MMB drag. To orbit, hold **Alt** and then MMB drag.*

Name and Color Rollout

The controls in the **Name and Color** rollout allow you to rename the objects and change their colors. Whenever you create an object, 3ds Max assigns it a default name and color. For example, if you reset the scene and create a box in the viewport, 3ds Max assigns it the name **Box001**. To change the name of the object, type a new name in the text box available in the **Name and Color** rollout. The color swatch to the right of the text box lets you change the color of the object.

On clicking the color swatch, the **Object Color** dialog appears. You can click on one of the color swatches and then click **OK** to assign the color to the object. If you want to specify a custom color, select a color swatch for **Custom Colors** and then click **Add Custom Colors**. In the **Color Selector : Add Color** dialog that appears, specify a color and then click **Add Color** to add the chosen color to the selected swatch in **Object Color** dialog. Now, click **OK** to close the dialog and apply selected color to the object.

Tip: Scene Explorer
*As discussed in Unit 2, you can easily rename objects using the **Scene Explorer**.*

Creation Method Rollout

There are two controls available in this rollout: **Cube** and **Box**. **Box** creates a standard box primitive with different settings for length, width, and height. **Cube** creates a cube with equal width, height, and length. Creating a cube is one step operation. Click and drag the mouse pointer in the viewport to create a cube.

Parameters Rollout

The default settings in this rollout produce a box with one segment on each side. Table 1 summarizes the controls in the **Parameters** rollout.

Table 1: The controls in the **Box's Parameters** rollout	
Control	**Description**
Length, Width, Height	The **Length**, **Width**, and **Height** controls set the length, width, and height of the box, respectively. These controls also act as readouts when you interactively create a primitive.
Length Segs, Width Segs, Height Segs	The **Length Segs**, **Width Segs**, and **Height Segs** controls set the number of segments [divisions] along each axis of the object. You can set these parameters before and after the creation of the box. The default value for these parameters is **1, 1, 1**.
Generate Mapping Coords	**Generate Mapping Coords** is on by default. It generates coordinates for applying material to the box.
Real-World Map Size	**Real-World Map Size** controls the scaling method used for texture mapped material that are applied to the box. The scaling values are controlled by the settings found in the material's **Coordinate** rollout.

Note: Default values
Whatever values you specify for these controls become default for the current session.

Tip: Resolution
*If you are planning to use the modifiers such as **Bend** on a primitive, increase the values for the **Length Segs**, **Width Segs**, and **Height Segs** controls to get some extra resolution on the objects.*

Keyboard Entry Rollout

You can use the controls in this rollout to define both the size of the box as well as its position in 3D space in a single operation. The method for creating objects through keyboard is generally same for all primitives; differences might occur in the type and number of controls.

The **X**, **Y**, and **Z** controls define the position of the object. The default value is **0, 0, 0** which is center of the active grid.

Cone

You can use this primitive to create round upward or inverted cones [see Figure 3]. To create a cone, click **Cone** in the **Object Type** rollout. In the viewport, drag to define the base of the cone and then release mouse button. Now, move the mouse pointer up or down in the viewport to define the height.

The height can be negative or positive. Click to set the height. Move the mouse pointer to define the radius of the other end of the cone. If you want to create a pointed cone, set this radius to zero.

Creation Method Rollout

Two creation methods are available for the **Cone** primitive: **Edge** and **Center**. **Edge** draws a cone from edge to edge. **Center** draws from the center out.

Parameters Rollout

The default settings in this rollout produce a smooth cone with 24 sides, one cap segment and five height segments. Table 2 summarizes the controls in the **Parameters** rollout.

Control	Description
Table 2: The controls in the **Cone's Parameters** rollout	
Radius 1, Radius 2	**Radius 1** and **Radius 2** define the first and second radii of the cone. You can use these two controls to create pointed or flat-topped cones.
Height	**Height** sets the dimension of the cone along the central axis. If you set a negative value, the cone will be created below the construction plane.
Height Segments	**Height Segments** controls sets the number of divisions along the major axis of the cone.
Cap Segments	**Cap Segments** sets the number of concentric divisions in the top or bottom of the cone.
Sides	**Sides** determines the number of sides around the cone.
Smooth	**Smooth** is on by default. It blends the faces of the cone on rendering therefore producing smooth looking renders.
Slice From, Slice To	You can use the **Slice From** and **Slice To** controls to slice the cone. These two controls set the number of degrees around the local Z axis. To turn on these two controls, turn on **Slice On**.

Caution: Minimum and negative values

*If you specify negative values for **Radius 1** and **Radius 2**, these values will be converted to **0**. The minimum values for these controls is **0**.*

Note: Same value for Radius 1 and Radius 2

*If you specify a same values for **Radius 1** and **Radius 2**, a cylinder will be created. If these two values are close in size, an object is created which resembles the effect as if a **Taper** modifier is applied to a cylinder.*

Tip: Pointed cones

For improved rendering on smooth pointed cones, increase the number of height segments.

Sphere

You can use the **Sphere** primitive to create a full sphere, a hemisphere, slice of the sphere, or some part of a sphere [see Figure 4]. To create a sphere, on the **Create** panel, click **Geometry**, and then on the **Object Type** rollout, click **Sphere**.

In the viewport, drag the mouse pointer to define the radius of the sphere, release mouse button to set the radius. To create a hemisphere, create the desired sphere of the desired radius and then set **Hemisphere** to **0.5** in the **Parameters** rollout.

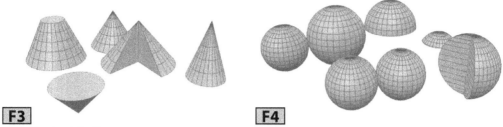

Creation Method Rollout

There are two methods available for creating a sphere: **Edge** and **Center**. **Edge** draws the sphere from edge to edge. **Center** draws a sphere from center out.

Parameters Rollout

The default values in the rollout produce a smooth sphere with **32** divisions. Table 3 summarizes the controls in the **Parameters** rollout.

Table 3: The controls in the **Sphere's** Parameters rollout	
Control	**Description**
Radius	**Radius** specifies the radius of the sphere.
Segments	**Segments** controls the number of segments for the sphere.
Hemisphere	**Hemisphere** lets you create a hemisphere. It cuts off the sphere to create a partial sphere. You can use this control to create an animation in which the sphere will be cut off starting from its base to top.
Chop, Squash	**Chop** and **Squash** determine the number of vertices and faces when you create a hemisphere. **Chop** reduces the number of vertices and faces by chopping them out whereas **Squash** maintains the number of vertices and faces by squashing the geometry toward the top of the sphere. Figure 5 shows the effect of **Chop** [left] and **Squash** [right] on a hemisphere with **16** segments.
Base To Pivot	If you turn on **Base to Pivot**, the sphere moves upward along its local Z axis and places the pivot point at its base. Figure 6 shows the pivot at the center [left], which is default, and pivot at the base of the sphere [right].

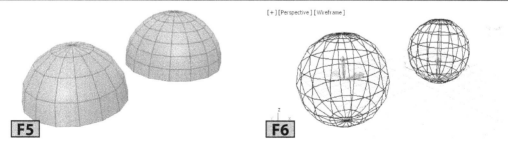

GeoSphere

You can use the **GeoSphere** primitive to create spheres and geo-hemispheres based on three classes of polyhedrons: **Tetra**, **Octa**, and **Icosa** [see Figure 7].

The **GeoSphere** primitive produces more regular shape than the **Sphere** primitive. Unlike the **Sphere** primitive, the geometry produced by the **GeoSphere** primitive has no poles which is an advantage is in certain modeling scenarios. Also, they appear slightly smoother than the standard sphere when rendered. To create a **GeoSphere**, on the **Create** panel, click **Geometry**, and then on the **Object Type** rollout, click **GeoSphere**. In the viewport, drag the mouse pointer to define the radius of the sphere, release mouse button to set the radius. To create a hemisphere, create the desired sphere of the desired radius and then check **Hemisphere** in the **Parameters** rollout.

Creation Method rollout

There are two methods available for creating a sphere: **Diameter** and **Center**. **Diameter** draws the geosphere from edge to edge whereas **Center** draws a geosphere from the center out.

Parameters Rollout

Table 4 summarizes the controls in the **Parameters** rollout.

Table 4: The controls in the **GeoSphere's Parameters** rollout	
Control	**Description**
Radius	**Radius** sets the radius of the geosphere.
Segments	**Segments** controls the number of faces in the geosphere.
Tetra, Octa, Icosa	The controls in the **Geodesic Base Type** group let you choose one of the regular polyhedrons for geosphere geometry. **Tetra** creates a four-sided tetrahedron. The facets can vary in shape and size. The geosphere can be divided into four equal segments. **Octa** creates an eight-sided tetrahedron. The facets can vary in shape and size. The geosphere can be divided into eight equal segments. **Icosa** creates a 20-sided tetrahedron. The facets are equal in size. The geosphere can be divided into any number of equal segments.

Cylinder

The **Cylinder** primitive creates a cylinder that can be sliced along its major axis [see Figure 8]. To create a cylinder, on the **Create** panel, click **Geometry**, and then on the **Object Type** rollout, click **Cylinder**. In the viewport, drag the mouse pointer to define the radius, release the mouse button to set the radius. Now, move the mouse pointer up or down to define the height, click to set it.

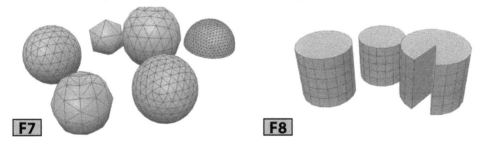

F7   F8

Parameters Rollout

The default controls in the **Parameters** rollout produce an **18** sided smooth cylinder with the five height segments, one cap segment, and the pivot point at its base. Table 5 summarizes the controls in the **Parameters** rollout.

Table 5: The controls in the **Cylinder's Parameters** rollout	
Control	**Description**
Radius	**Radius** sets the radius of the cylinder.
Height	**Height** defines the height of the cylinder along the cylinder's major axis.
Height Segments	**Height Segments** defines the number of divisions along the cylinder's major axis.
Sides	**Sides** sets the sides around the cylinder.
Cap Segments	**Cap Segments** sets the number of concentric divisions around top and bottom of the cylinder.

Tip: Resolution

*If you are going to use the cylinder with a modifier such as **Bend**, increase the number of height segments. If you are planning to modify the end of the cylinder, increase the number of cap segments.*

Tube

The **Tube** primitive produces a cylinder with a hole in it [see Figure 9]. You can use this primitive to use both round and prismatic tubes. To create a **Tube**, on the **Create** panel, click **Geometry**, and then on the **Object Type** rollout, click **Tube**. In the viewport, drag the mouse pointer to define the first radius, which can be either the inner or the outer radius of the tube, release the mouse button to set the first radius. Move the mouse pointer to create the second radius, and then click to set it. Move the pointer up or down to create the height [positive or negative] and then click to set the height of the tube.

Tip: Prismatic Tube

*To create a prismatic tube, set the number of sides to according to the type of the prismatic tube you want to create. Uncheck **Smooth** and create the tube.*

Parameters Rollout

Radius 1 and **Radius 2** are used specify the inside and outside radii of the tube. The larger among the two values defines the outside radius of the tube.

Torus

You can use the **Torus** primitive to create a doughnut like shape which is ring with the circular cross section [see Figure 10]. To create a torus, on the **Create** panel, click **Geometry**, and then on the **Object Type** rollout, click **Torus**. In the viewport, drag the mouse pointer to define a torus; the torus emerges from its center. Release the mouse button to set the radius of the torus ring. Now, move the mouse pointer to define the radius of the cross section, and click to complete the creation process.

Parameters Rollout

The default values in this rollout produce a smooth torus with **12** sides and **24** segments. The pivot point of the torus is located at the center of the torus on the plane which cuts through the center of the torus.

Rotation sets the degree of rotation. The vertices are uniformly rotated about the circle running through the center of the torus ring. **Twist** defines the degree of twist. 3ds Max twists the cross sections about the circle running through the center of the torus.

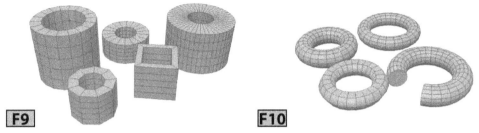

Caution: Twisting a close torus

Twisting a close torus will create a constriction in the first segment. To overcome this, you can either twist the torus in the increments of **360** *or turn on* **Slice** *and then set both* **Slice From** *and* **Slice To** *to* **0**.

The controls in the **Smooth** group control the level of smoothing. The default **All** control produces smoothing on all surfaces of the torus. **Sides** smooths the edges between the adjacent segments thus producing smooth bands which run around the torus. None turns off the smoothing and produces prism-like facets on the torus. **Segments** smooths each segment individually and produces ring-like segments.

Pyramid

The **Pyramid** primitive is used to create a pyramid like shape with the square or rectangle face and triangular sides [see Figure 11]. To create a pyramid, on the **Create** panel, click **Geometry**, and then on the **Object Type** rollout, click **Pyramid**. In the viewport, drag the mouse pointer to define the base of the pyramid. Click to set it and then drag the mouse pointer up to define the height.

Tip: Constrain the base of the pyramid to a square

To constrain the base of the pyramid to a square, drag with the **Ctrl** *key held down.*

Plane

The **Plane** primitive creates a flat plane that you can enlarge to any size [see Figure 12]. To create a **Plane**, on the **Create** panel, click **Geometry**, and then on the **Object Type** rollout, click **Plane**. In the viewport, drag the mouse pointer to create a plane.

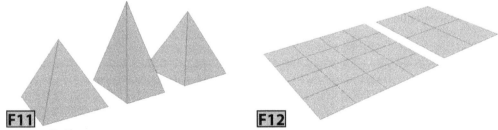

Parameters Rollout

The controls in the **Render Multipliers** group are used to set the multipliers at render time. You can use **Scale** to specify the factor by which both length and width will be multiplied at render time. **Density** specifies a factor by which the number of segments in both length and width are multiplied at the render time.

Teapot

The **Teapot** primitive is used to create a parametric teapot object [see Figure 13]. This object is comprised of a lid, body, handle, and sprout. You can create the whole teapot [which is default] or combination of the parts. You can even control which parts to display after creation. To create a **Teapot**, on the **Create** panel, click **Geometry**, and then on the **Object Type** rollout, click **Teapot**. In the viewport, click and drag to define the radius. Release the mouse button to set the radius and create teapot. You can control which part of the teapot you want to create by turning on the required controls from the **Teapot Parts** group of the **Parameters** rollout.

Extended Primitives

Extended primitives are little complex than the **Standard** Primitives. 3ds Max offers thirteen extended primitives, see Figure 14. You can combine **Extended** primitives with the **Standard** primitives and modifiers to create refined models. You can dynamically create **Extended** primitives in the viewport using the mouse and most of the primitives can be generated by entering precise values using the keyboard. You can specify the parameters before creating the **Extended** primitives and modify them later from the **Parameters** rollout in the **Modify** panel. Let's take a look at the commonly used **Extended** primitives. Experiment with the primitives that are not covered in this section. They are straight forward and you can easily understand their parameters by changing them from the **Parameters** rollout.

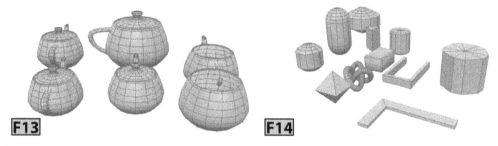

Hedra

You can use this primitive to create different type of polyhedra objects [see Figure 15].

Table 6 summarizes the controls in the **Parameters** rollout.

Table 6: The controls in the **Hedra's Parameters** rollout	
Control	**Description**
Family Group	The controls in this group allows you to choose the type of polyhedral you want to create. **Tetra** creates a tetrahedron. **Cube/Octa** creates a cubic or octahedral polyhedron. **Dodec/Icos** creates a dodecahedron or icosahedron. **Star 1** and **Star 2** create two different star-shaped polyhedron.
Family Parameters Group	The **P** and **Q** controls in this group change the geometry back and forth between the vertices and faces. In Figure 16, the left polyhedron has **P** and **Q** values set to **0** each whereas the polyhedron on the right has the **P** and **Q** values set to **0.3** each. The combined value of **P** and **Q** can be equal to or less than **1**.

Axis Scaling Group	The **P**, **Q**, and **R** controls in this group allow you to push or pull the corresponding facets in or out. The polyhedron on the left in Figure 17 is created with the default parameters. For the polyhedron on the right, I have changed **Q** and **R** values to **120** and **150**, respectively. On clicking **Reset**, the axes return to their default values.
Vertices Group	The controls in this group determine the internal geometry of each facet of the polyhedron.
Radius	Sets the radius of the polyhedron.

Note: Creating Extended primitives

*To save some space, I am not writing the process to create the **Extended** primitives. You can easily create them using the standard click drag methods as done in the **Standard Primitives** section.*

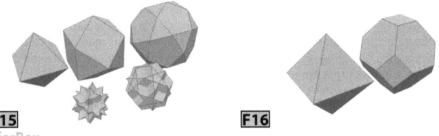

F15   **F16**

ChamferBox

You can use this primitive to create a box with beveled or round edges [see Figure 18]. Most of the controls in the **Parameters** rollout are similar to that of the **Box** primitive. Table 7 lists the controls that are unique to **ChamferBox**.

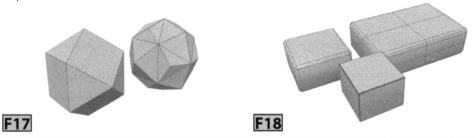

F17   **F18**

Table 7: The controls in the **ChamferBox's Parameters** rollout	
Control	**Description**
Fillet	Slices the edges of the box. Higher the value for this control, more refined fillet you will get.
Fillet Segs	Determines the number of segments in the filleted edges.
Smooth	Blends the display of faces of the box. As a result, when rendered, box appears smooth in the rendered results.

ChamferCylinder

This primitive creates a cylinder with beveled or rounded cap edges [see Figure 19].

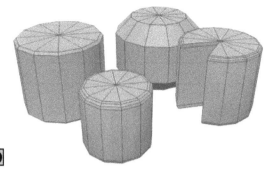

F19

Most of the controls in the **Parameters** rollout are similar to that of the **Cylinder** primitive. Table 8 lists the controls that are unique to **ChamferCylinder**.

Table 8: The controls in the **Chamfer Cylinder's Parameters** rollout	
Control	**Description**
Fillet	It chamfers the top and bottom cap edges of the cylinder. Higher the value, more refined fillet will be.
Fillet Segs	Determines the number of segments in the filleted edges of the cylinder.

Architectural Objects

3ds Max provides several architectural objects that you can use as a basic building blocks for architectural models such as home, offices, and so forth. Table 9 summaries the architectural objects that 3ds Max offers:

Table 9: The architectural objects	
Types	**Objects**
AEC Extended Objects	**Foliage, Railing,** and **Wall**
Stairs	**L-Type Stair, Spiral Stair, Straight Stair,** and **U-Type Stair**
Doors	**Pivot, Bifold,** and **Sliding**
Windows	**Awning, Casement, Fixed, Pivoted, Projected,** and **Sliding**

You can access all **AEC** objects from the **AEC Objects** sub-menu of the **Create** menu. You can also access these objects from the **Create** panel. Let's explore these objects.

Doors

The door objects allow you to quickly create a door. You can also set the door to be partially open even you can animate the opening. 3ds Max offers three types of doors. Table 10 summarizes these types.

Table 10: The door types	
Type	**Description**
Pivot	This door is hinged on one side only [see Figure 20].
Bifold	This door is hinged in the middle as well as in the side. You can use this object to model a set of double doors [see Figure 21].
Sliding	This type of door has a fixed half and a sliding half [see Figure 22].

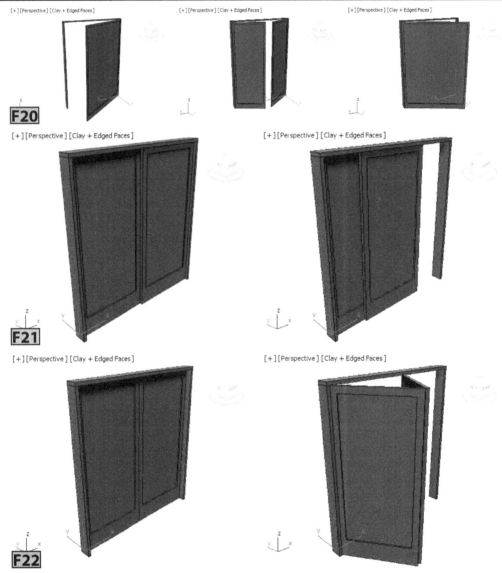

Tip: Navigating Viewport
*If while creating **AEC** objects, you need to navigate the interface between clicks, drag the **MMB** to pan the viewport, **Alt+MMB** drag to orbit the viewport, and **Alt+Ctrl+Scroll** to zoom the viewport.*

To create a door, click **Command Panel | Create panel | Geometry** and then choose **Doors** from the drop-down. In the **Object Type** rollout, choose the type of the door you want to create and then set the desired create options from the rollouts. Drag the mouse in the viewport to create first two points to define the width and angle of the base of the door. Now, release the mouse button and drag to define the depth of the door and click to set. Drag the mouse to define the height of the door and then click to finish.

Assigning Material to Doors

By default, 3ds Max assigns five different IDs to the door you create. The default **Door-Template Multi-Subobject** material is found in the **Ace Templates.mat** material library. Figure 23 shows the ID numbers and their associated parts in the door. 3ds Max does not assign a material to the door object. If you want to use the default material, you need to open the library in the **Material Editor** and then assign material to your object.

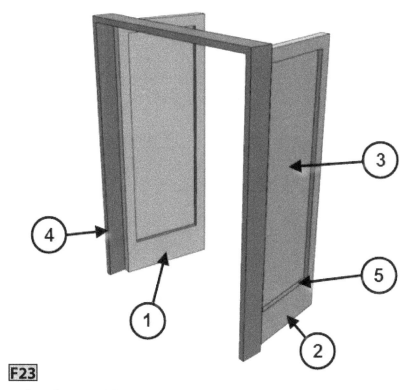

F23

Table 11 summarizes the material IDs assigned to doors.

Table 11: The material IDs	
ID	**Component**
1	Font
2	Back
3	Inner Bevel. This ID is used for glazing when you set **Panels** to **Glass** or **Beveled**.

4	Frame
5	Inner Door

Tip: The Ace Template.mat library
You can find this library at the following location: **C:\Program Files\Autodesk\3ds Max 2016\materiallibraries.**

Windows

The window objects in 3ds Max allow you to create the appearance of a window. You can also set the window to be partially open even you can animate the opening. 3ds Max offers six types of windows. Table 12 summarizes the window types.

Table 12: The window types	
Type	**Description**
Casement	Two door like sashes arrangement that can swing inward or outward [see Figure 24].
Pivoted	It pivots vertically or horizontally at the center of its sash [see Figure 25].
Projected	It has three sashes two of which open like awning in opposite directions [see Figure 26].
Sliding	It has two sashes one of which slides vertically or horizontally [see Figure 27].
Fixed	It does not open [see Figure 28].
Awning	It has a sash that is hinged at the top [see Figure 29].

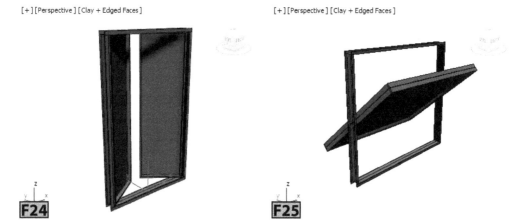

[+][Perspective][Clay + Edged Faces]   [+][Perspective][Clay + Edged Faces]

F24   F25

To create a window, click **Command Panel | Create panel | Geometry** and then choose **Windows** from the drop-down. In the **Object Type** rollout, choose the type of the window you want to create and then create the window in the viewport using click-drag operations.

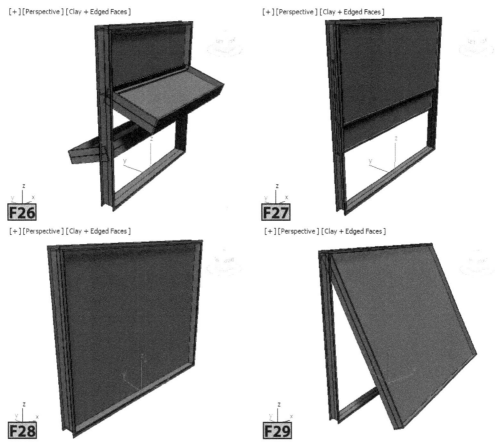

F26

F27

F28

F29

Assigning Material to Windows

By default, 3ds Max assigns five different IDs to the window you create. The default **Window-Template Multi-Subobject** material is found in the **Ace Templates.mat** material library. Figure 30 shows the ID numbers and their associated parts in the window. 3ds Max does not assign a material to the window object. If you want to use the default material, you need to open the library in the **Material Editor** and then assign material to your object.

Table 13 summarizes the material IDs assigned to windows.

Table 13: The material IDs	
ID	**Component**
1	Front Rails
2	Back Rails
3	Panels. The Opacity is set to 50%.
4	Front Frame
5	Back Frame

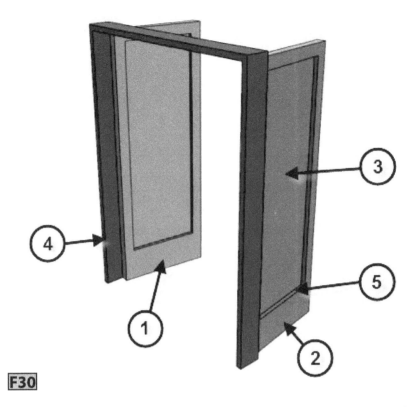

F30

3ds Max allows you to create four different types of stairs. The following table summarizes the types of stairs.

Table 14: The stairs types	
Type	**Description**
Spiral Stair	It allows you to create spiral staircase. You can specify radius, and number of revolutions. You can also add stringers, center pole, and more to the stairs [see Figure 31].
Straight Stair	It allows you to create simple straight stairs [see Figure 32].
L-Type Stair	It lets you create the L-Type stairs [see Figure 33].
U-Type Stair	It lets you create the U-Type stairs [see Figure 34].

F31

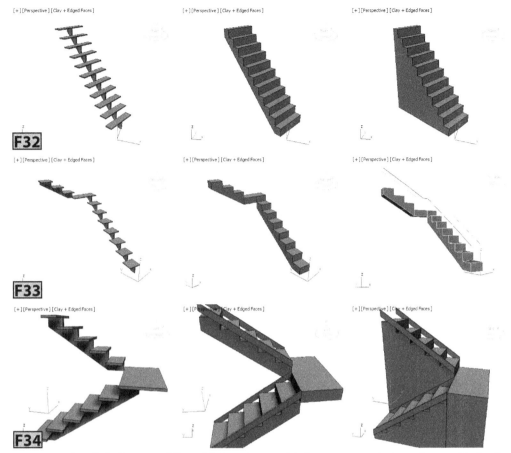

To create a stair, click **Command Panel | Create panel | Geometry** and then choose **Stairs** from the drop-down. In the **Object Type** rollout, choose the type of the stair you want to create and then create the stair in the viewport using click-drag operations.

Assigning Material to Windows

By default, 3ds Max assigns five different IDs to the stairs you create. The default **Stairs-Template Multi-Subobject** material is found in the **Ace Templates.mat** material library. 3ds Max does not assign a material to the stairs object. If you want to use the default material, you need to open the library in the **Material Editor** and then assign material to your object.

Table 15 summarizes the material IDs assigned to stairs.

Table 15: The material IDs	
ID	Component
1	Treads of the stairs.
2	Front riser of the stairs.

3	Bottom, back, and sides of the risers of the stairs.
4	Center pole of the stairs.
5	Handrails of the stairs.
6	Carriage of the stairs.
7	Stringers of the stairs.

AEC Extended Objects

AEC stands for **Architecture Engineer Construction**. These objects are designed to for use in the architectural, engineering, and construction field. To create an **AEC** object, click **Command Panel | Create panel | Geometry** and then choose **AEC Extended** from the drop-down. In the **Object Type** rollout, choose the type of the object you want to create and then create the object in the viewport using click-drag operations.

Railing

This tool allows you to create railings in a 3ds Max scene. The railing object includes rails, posts, and fencing [see Figure 35]. You can create railing by specifying the orientation and height. You can also use a spline object to create railing along it. If you edit the spline, the railing object updates to follow the path. You can use railing object with the stair object to create a complete stair.

To create a railing, click **Command Panel | Create panel | Geometry** and then choose **AEC Extended** from the drop-down. In the **Object Type** rollout, click **Railing** and then create the stair in the viewport using click-drag operations.

[+] [Perspective] [Clay + Edged Faces]

F35

Assigning Material to Railings

By default, 3ds Max assigns five different IDs to the railings you create. The default **Rail-Template Multi-Subobject** material is found in the **Ace Templates.mat** material library. 3ds Max does not assign a material to the railing objects. If you want to use the default material, you need to open the library in the **Material Editor** and then assign material to your object. Table 16 summarizes the material IDs assigned to railings.

Table 16: The material IDs	
ID	**Component**
1	Lower rails
2	Posts of the railing
3	Solid fill of the railing
4	Top of the railing
5	Pickets of the railing

Foliage

You can use this tool to place various kinds of tree species in a scene [see Figures 36 and 37]. This tool can produce good looking trees efficiently. You can define height, density, pruning, seed, canopy display, and level of detail for the **Foliage** object.

To create a tree, click **Command Panel | Create panel | Geometry** and then choose **AEC Extended** from the drop-down. In the **Object Type** rollout, click **Foliage.** In the **Favorite Plants** rollout, either drag a tree to add the scene or select the plant and then click on the viewport to place it.

Tip: Placing plants in the scene
*You can use the **Spacing** tool to place plants along a path.*

Wall

The **Wall** tool is used to create walls [see Figure 38] in 3ds Max. The wall object is made up of three sub-object types: **Vertex**, **Segment**, and **Profile** that you can use to edit it.

You can create wall in any viewport but for vertical walls you should use a **Perspective**, **Camera**, or **Top** viewport. To create a wall, set the **Width** and **Height** parameters and then click in a viewport. Now, release the mouse button and then drag to specify the length, click again.

If you want to create a single wall component, RMB, else continue clicking. To finish creating a room, click on an end segment; 3ds Max displays the **Weld Point** dialog. You can use the options in this dialog to either weld the two end vertices into a single vertex or you can keep the two end vertices distinct. **RMB** click to finish the wall.

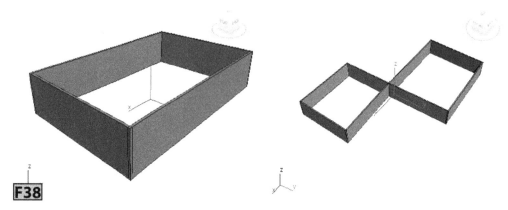

F38

Assigning Material to Walls

By default, 3ds Max assigns five different IDs to the walls you create. The default **Wall-Template Multi-Subobject** material is found in the **Ace Templates.mat** material library. 3ds Max does not assign a material to the wall object. If you want to use the default material, you need to open the library in the **Material Editor** and then assign material to your object.

Table 17 summarizes the material IDs assigned to railings.

Table 17: The material IDs	
ID	Component
1	Vertical ends of the wall.
2	Outside of the wall.
3	Inside of the wall.
4	Top of the wall, including any edges cut out of the wall.
5	Bottom of the wall.

Note: ID 2 and 3
The definitions of ID 2 and 3 is interchangeable because the inside and outside of the wall depend on your point-of-view and how you created the wall object.

Note: Inserting doors and windows in a wall
3ds Max automatically makes opening for doors and windows in a wall object. It also makes the linked doors and windows children of the wall object. To do this, directly create doors and windows on the wall by snapping to its faces, vertices, or edges.

Tip: Making opening using Boolean operations
*You can also make openings in a wall using the Boolean operations. Make the wall as **Operand A** and the other object such as box as **Operand B**. Single wall with many doors and window can slow down you system. To speed up, use multiple walls instead of a single wall. You can also collapse the stack to speed up the performance of your system.*

Hands-on Exercises

Complete the following Hands-on Exercises:

1. *Exercise - 2: Creating a Sofa*
2. *Exercise - 3: Creating a Coffee Table*
3. *Exercise - 4: Creating a foot stool*
4. *Exercise - 5: Creating a Bar Table*

Practical Tests

Complete the following tests:

Practical Test - 1: Coffee Table

Create the coffee table model [see Figure 39] using the **Box** primitive.

Dimensions:
A: Length=35.433", Width=21.654", Height=1.5"
B: Length=34.037", Width=20.8", Height=1.5"
C: Length=2", Width=2", Height=13.78"

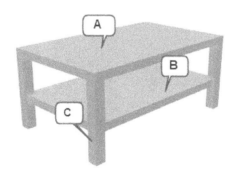

F39

Practical Test - 2: 8-Drawer Dresser

Create the 8-drawer model [see Figure 40] using the **Box** primitive. Create the knobs using the **Sphere** and **Cylinder** primitives.

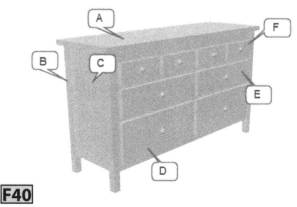

F40

Dimensions:
A: Length=65", Width=21", Height=1.5"
B: Length=2", Width=2", Height=35"
C: Length=60.76", Width=18.251", Height=30"
D: Length=27.225", Width=19.15", Height=11"
E: Length=27.225", Width=19.15", Height=7"
F: Length=12.871", Width=19.15", Height=5"

Practical Test - 3: Foot Stool

Create the foot stool model [see Figure 41] using the **ChamferCyl** and **Chamfer Box** primitives.

Dimensions 3.6.1
A: Radius=14", Height=5.91", and Fillet=0.32"
B: Radius=14", Height=7.5", and Fillet=0.74"
C: Length=1.651", Width=3.455", Height=1.496", and Fillet=0.087"

Hint
Check **Slice On** for the cylinders and set **Slice From** to **-180**. Apply the **Taper** modifier to the legs of the stool.

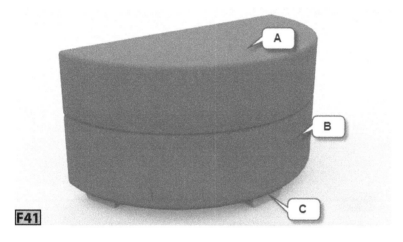

F41

Summary

In this unit, you have seen how you can quickly create models using the **Standard** and **Extended** primitives. You have also leaned about the **AEC** objects. You also got a chance to use the tools that I have covered in Unit 1 and Unit 2. Although, I have provided two exercises in this unit but you just don't stop here. Visit the **Ikea** website [*http://www.ikea.com*] and look for inspiration there. They provide the dimensions of the product along with the product features. For example, if you visit to the following link: *http://www.ikea.com/us/en/catalog/products/60128562*, you will be greeted by a **Glass-door** cabinet. Now, scroll down and choose the **Product Information** tab. Notice the dimensions [both in **inches** and **centimeters**] are mentioned under the **Product dimensions** area of the tab.

The unit covered the following topics:

- Creating and modifying **Standard** Primitives
- Creating and modifying **Extended** Primitives

- Working with the **Architectural** objects.
- Setting the project folder
- Using the **Align** and **Mirror** tools
- Creating clones
- Using the **Scene Explorer**
- Creating a group
- Setting grid spacings
- Using **Transform Type-In** dialog
- Using **Array** dialog
- Specifying units for the scene

In the next unit, I will describe surface modeling using polygons.

This page intentionally left blank

Unit M4: Working with Polygons

In unit 3, you have modeled objects using the **parametric** modeling techniques. In parametric modeling, you create primitives from the **Create** panel and modify their shapes using the creation parameters. Then, you transform the primitives using the transformation tools to create shape of the models. **Parametric** modeling is powerful and easy but it has some limitations when it comes to creating complex models. **Surface** modeling on the other hand is more flexible and allows you to create any object that you can imagine. Once you convert an object to an editable object such as an editable poly, editable mesh, editable patch, or NURBS object; 3ds Max provides specialized toolset to create the models. In this unit, I will explain the editable poly object.

In this unit, I'll describe the following:

- Working with the polygon modeling tools
- Using the polygon modeling techniques
- Selecting polygon sub-object
- Transforming sub-objects
- Soft selecting sub-objects

Editable Poly Object

The editable poly object is an editable object with five sub-object levels: **Vertex**, **Edge**, **Border**, **Polygon**, and **Element**. Sub-objects such as vertices and edges are the basic building blocks of an object. Vertices are points in 3D space. They define the structure for other sub-objects such as edges and polygons. An edge is a line connecting two vertices. The connection forms one side of the polygon. An edge cannot be shared by more than two polygons. Also, normals of the two polygons should be adjacent. When three or more edges combine together, they form a polygon. **Elements** are groups of contiguous polygons. A border can be described as the edge of a hole in the object. Figure 1 shows various sub-object levels available for the editable poly object.

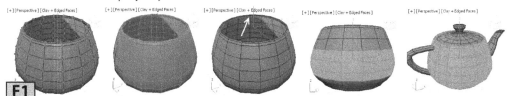

Note: The editable poly objects vs editable mesh objects
*The editable poly object is similar to the edit mesh object with the only difference is that the edit mesh object comprises of **triangular** faces whereas the editable poly object comprises of polygons with any number of vertices.*

You can convert an object to an editable poly object by using one of the following methods:

1. Select an object in a viewport and then go to the **Modify** panel. Next, RMB click on the object entry in the stack display and then choose **Convert To: Editable Poly** from the pop up menu displayed [see Figure 2].
2. Select the object in a viewport and then RMB click. Choose **transform | Convert To: | Convert to Editable Poly** [see Figure 3].
3. Apply a modifier to a parametric object that makes the object a poly object. For example, the **Turn to Poly** modifier.
4. Apply the **Edit Poly** modifier.

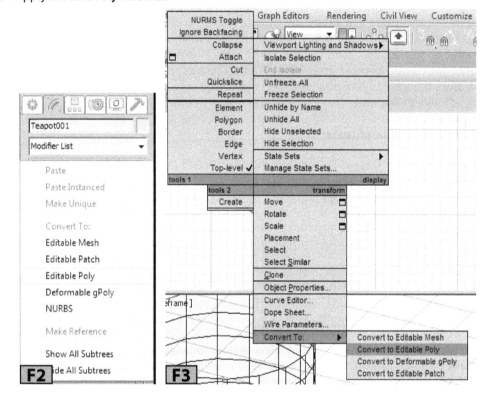

Tip: Exiting a Command
You can exit most of the poly editing commands by RMB clicking in a viewport.

Caution: Preserving the parametric nature of a primitive
*When you convert an object to an editable poly object, you lose all of its creation parameters. If you want to retain the creation parameters, use the **Edit Poly** modifier.*

Caution: Limitations of the Edit Poly modifier
*The **Edit Poly** modifier offers most of the capabilities of the **Editable Poly** object except the **Vertex Color Information**, **Subdivision Surface** rollout, **Weight** and **Crease** settings, and **Subdivision Displacement** rollout.*

*The option to convert an editable poly is also available in the **Graphite Modeling Tools**. You will learn about these tools in a later unit.*

Selecting Sub-objects

You can select sub-objects using one of the following ways:

1. Expand the object's hierarchy [by clicking the plus icon] from the stack display and then choose a sub-object level [see Figure 4]. The select sub-object will be highlighted in the stack display.
2. Click a selection button from the **Selection** rollout [see Figure 5].
3. RMB click on an object in a viewport and then choose the sub-object level from the upper left quadrant of the **Quad** menu displayed [see Figure 6].
4. Choose a selection or transform tool and then click on the sub-objects in a viewport using the standard selection techniques.

Note: Adding and removing from the selection
*To select a vertex, edge, polygon, or element, click it. To add to the sub-object selection, press and hold **Ctrl** and click. You can also drag a selection region to select a group of sub-objects. To subtract from the sub-object selection, press and hold **Alt** and click. You can also drag a selection region to deselect a group of sub-objects.*

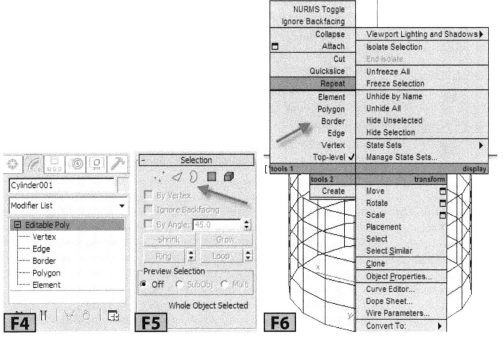

Tip: Locking selection
*Once you make the sub-object selection, you can lock the selection by pressing **Spacebar**. Locking the selection helps in unintentionally selecting other sub-objects. To release the lock press **Spacebar** again.*

*You can use the numeric keys from **1** to **5** to activate the **Vertex**, **Edge**, **Border**, **Polygon**, and **Element** sub-object levels, respectively. Press **6** to return to the **Object** level.*

Creating and Modifying Selections

The controls available in the **Selection** and **Soft Selection** rollouts let you access different sub-object levels as well as they give you ability to create and modify selections. Let's have a look at the tools available in these two rollouts.

Selection Rollout

There are five buttons at the top of the **Selection** rollout. These buttons allow you to select the sub-object levels. Table 1 summarizes function of these buttons:

Table 1: The sub-object buttons		
Button	**Interface**	**Description**
Vertex		Activates the **Vertex** sub-object level. Allows you to select the vertex beneath the mouse pointer. Draw a region selection to select the vertices within the region.
Edge		Activates the **Edge** sub-object level. Allows you to select the edge beneath the mouse pointer. Draw a region selection to select the edges within the region.
Border		Activates the **Border** sub-object level. Allows you to select a set of edges that borders a hole in the geometry. In other words, you can select the edges that are on the border.
Polygon		Activates the **Polygon** sub-object level. Allows you to select the polygon beneath the mouse pointer. Draw a region selection to select the polygons within the region.
Element		Activates the **Element** sub-object level. Allows you to select all contiguous polygons. Draw a region selection to select multiple elements within the region.

Note: Border edges

*If the concept of border edges is not clear to you, I would recommend a simple exercise. Create a **Cylinder** primitive in the scene and then convert it to **Editable Poly**. Select the **Polygon** sub-object level and then click on the top face of the cylinder to select it. Press **Delete** to delete the top face. Now, activate the **Border** sub-object level, and click on the border to select the border element [see Figure 7]. There is now only one border edge in the geometry that borders a hole in the cylinder.*

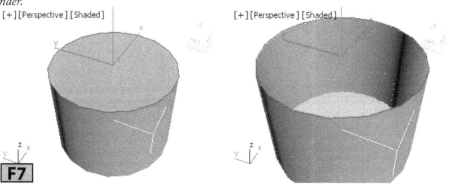

The **Named Selection Sets** list allows you to name a selection set [both at the object level as well as at the sub-object level] that you can recall later during the modeling process. For example, if you are modeling a face, you might want to select different sub-objects for various parts of the face. In such a case, you can create a selection set for a particular area of the face [nose, for example] and recall it later. It will save you lot of time as you do not have to recreate the selection later during the modeling process.

Caution: Names

The selection set names are case-sensitive.

Keep the following in mind while working with the named selection sets:

- You can transfer sub-objects selection from one modifier to another. You can also transfer the sub-object selection from one level to another in the modifier stack.
- You can transfer named selection sets only between the same types of sub-objects. For example, you cannot transfer a **Vertex** selection to a **Face** selection.
- You are only allowed to transfer selection sets between the modifiers that work on the same geometry type. For example, you cannot transfer a selection set from an **Edit Spline** modifier to **Edit Poly** modifier.
- You can copy and paste selection sets between two modifiers assigned to two different objects. However, both modifiers should handle the same types of geometry.

Caution: Changing Topology

If you modify the topology of the object, you might get unpredictable results when you use the named selection set.

To create a named selection set, select the objects or sub-objects that you want part of the set and then type the name of the selection set in the **Named Selection Sets** field [see Figure 8] of **Main** toolbar. Press **Enter** to create the selection set.

To recall a selection, select the name from the **Named Selection Sets** list. If you want to select more than one selection set from the list, press **Ctrl** while selecting names. To remove name from the selection, press and hold **Alt** and then click the name in the list.

Once you make a sub-object selection, you perform the following tasks:

- You can move, rotate, and scale sub-objects using standard transformation tools.
- You can apply the object-space modifiers.
- You can bind a space warp to the selection.
- If you have made the polygon selection, you can use the **Align**, **Normal Align**, and **Align To View** tools from the **Align** flyout of the **Main** toolbar.

If you are working with an editable object such as mesh, poly, patch, or spline, you can directly manipulate the selection using the transformations tools. However, if you are using a selection modifier such as **Mesh Select** or **Spline Select**, you need to use an **XFrom Modifier** to transform the selection.

Here's how it works:

1. Create a polygon primitive such as **Box** and then convert to an **Editable Poly** object.
2. Make a sub-object selection and move it using the **Select and Move** tool. You will notice that you can easily move the selection [see Figure 9]. Press **Ctrl+Z** to undo the last operation. Now, deselect everything. You can also press **6** on the main keyboard.
3. Apply the **Mesh Select** modifier [see Figure 10] and then make a selection. Notice that the transformation tools are inactive on the **Main** toolbar.
4. Apply the **XFrom** modifier to the object. Expand **XFrom** modifier in the stack display and select **Gizmo** [see Figure 11]. Now, you can move the selection as required.

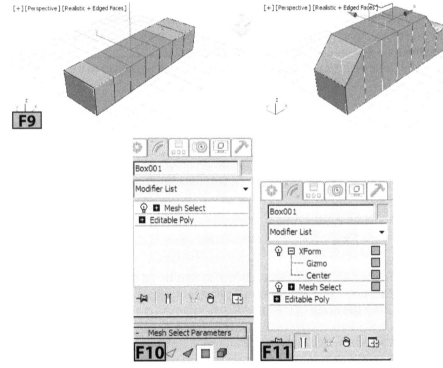

Cloning Sub-objects

When you **SHIFT+Transform** [move, scale, or rotate] a sub-object selection, the **Clone Part of Mesh** dialog appears [see Figure 12]. This dialog gives you two options: **Clone to Object** and **Clone to Element**. When you select **Clone To Object**, 3ds Max creates a separate object comprises of the selected sub-objects. If you select **Clone to Element**, the selection is cloned and it becomes an element of the current object.

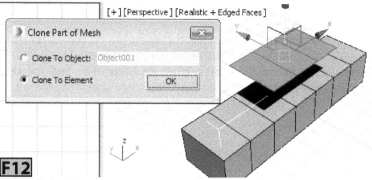

F12

Converting Sub-Object Selections

If you make a sub-object selection, for example, a vertex selection, you can convert it to a different sub-object selection such as edge or face using the **Ctrl** and **Shift** keys:

- To convert a selection to a different sub-object selection, click on the sub-object level button in the **Selection** rollout with **Ctrl** held down [see Figure 13].
- If you press **Ctrl+Shift** while clicking the sub-object level button, only those sub-objects will be selected whose source components were originally selected [see Figure 14].
- If you press **Shift** while clicking the sub-object level button, only those sub-objects will be selected that border the selection [see Figure 15].

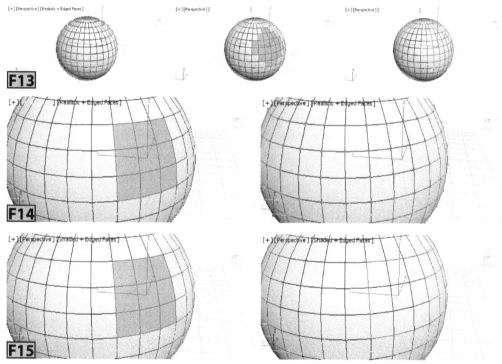

F13

F14

F15

Note: Quad Menu

*The conversion commands are also available from the **Quad** menu. To convert a selection, RMB click and then choose the desired option from the upper left quadrant of the **Quad** menu with **Ctrl**, **Shift**, or **Ctrl+Shift** held down.*

Now, let's explore the other options available in the **Selection** rollout.

When **By Vertex** is on, you can select the sub-objects that share the clicked vertex [see Figure 16]. When **Ignore Backfacing** is on, you can only select those sub-objects that are facing you. When off, you can select any sub-object beneath the mouse pointer. When **By Angle** is on and you select a polygon, all neighboring polygons are also selected based on the angle value specified by the spinner on the right of **By Angle** [see Figure 17].

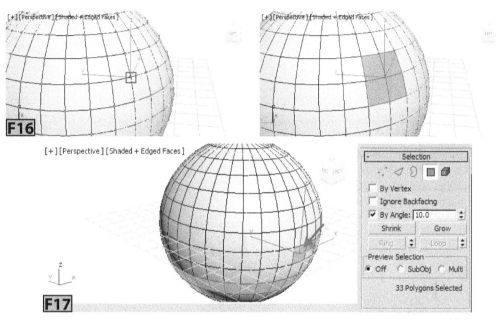

Shrink reduces the selection area by deselecting the outermost sub-objects [see Figure 18]. On the other hand, **Grow** expands the selection in all possible directions [see Figure 19].

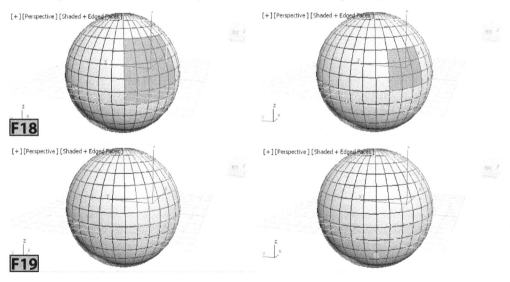

Ring lets you select an edge selection by selecting all edges parallel to the selected edges. To select an edge ring, select an edge[s] and then click **Ring** to select edges parallel to the selected edges [see Figure 20].

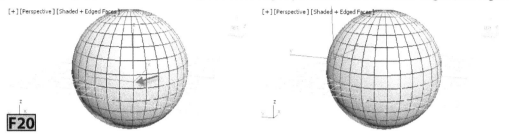

F20

Tip: Quickly selecting a ring
*Select an edge and then click on another edge in the same ring with **Shift** held down.*

The spinner next to **Ring** allows you to move the selection in the either direction to other edges in the same ring. The left image in Figure 21 shows the two edges selected. When I clicked on the up arrow of the spinner the selection moves, as shown in the right image of Figure 21. This feature works with only the **Edge** and **Border** sub-object types.

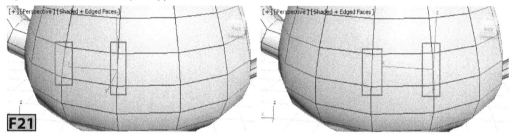

F21

Tip: Loop
If you have selected a loop, you can use the spinner to select the neighboring loop.

Loop allows you to expand edge selection as far as possible. The selection only propagates through four-way junctions. To select a loop, select and edge and then click **Loop** [see Figure 22].

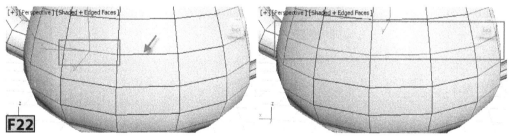

F22

Tip: Loop selection shortcut
*You can quickly select a loop by double-clicking on an edge. At **Vertex** and **Polygon** sub-levels, you can quickly select a loop by first selecting a sub-object and then **Shift** clicking another object of same type in the same loop [see Figure 23].*

The spinner on the right of **Loop** allows you to move the selection in either direction to other edges in the same loop. If you have selected a ring, it allows you to move the ring selection. This feature works with the **Edge** and **Border** sub-objects.

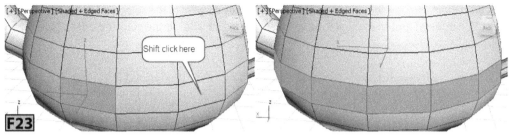

The controls in the **Preview Selection** group allow you to preview a selection before actually selecting. When **Off** is on, no preview will be available. When **SubObj** is on, you can preview the selection at the current sub-object level. The preview appears in yellow color [see Figure 24]. When **Multi** is on, you can switch between various sub-object levels.

To select multiple sub-objects at current level, press and hold **Ctrl** and move [do not click] to add highlighted sub-objects to the preview. Now, to make the selection, click. To remove sub-objects from the selection, move the mouse pointer over the selected sub-objects to highlight them in yellow. Now, press **Ctrl+Alt** and then click to deselect the sub-objects. The area below these controls displays information about the selected or highlighted polygons [see Figure 25].

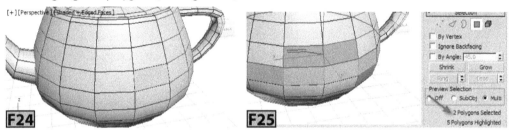

Soft Selection Rollout

The controls in the **Soft Selection** rollout let you partially select the sub-objects in the vicinity of the selected sub-objects. As you transform the sub-objects, the sub-objects in the vicinity will be transformed smoothly [see Figure 26]. The fall off appears in the viewport as a color spectrum [**ROYGB**: red, orange, yellow, green, and blue]. The sub-objects that you explicitly select coded in red color.

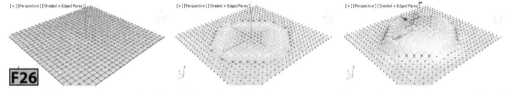

When **Edge Distance** is on, 3ds Max limits the selection to a certain number of edges specified by the spinner on right of **Edge Distance**. Figure 27 shows the selection with **Edge Distance** value set to **1** and **7**, respectively.

When **Affect Backfacing** is on, those deselected faces whose normals face in the opposite direction to the average normal of the selected sub-objects are affected by the soft-selection.

Falloff defines the distance in current units from the center to the edge of a sphere that defines the region of influence. The fall off curve appears below **Bubble**. **Pinch** affects the top point of the curve. **Bubble**

lets you expand or shrink the falloff curve along the vertical axis. Experiment with these settings to get a better understanding of how these controls affect the falloff curve.

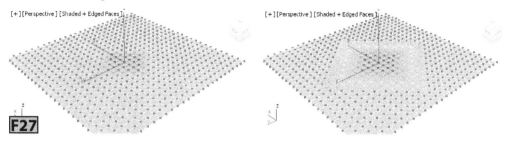

Shaded Face Toggle displays a color gradient in the viewport [see Figure 28]. The gradient represents the weight on the faces of the geometry. This feature is only available when you are working with editable poly or patch objects. **Lock Soft Selection** locks the soft selection to prevent any changes in the procedural selection.

The controls in the **Paint Soft Selection** group, let you paint soft selection on the object using a brush. Click **Paint** and then drag the mouse pointer on the surface to paint the selection. **Blur** lets you soften the edges of the selection whereas **Revert** reverses the selection.

Object Level

When no sub-object level is active, you are at the **Object** level. The controls available at the **Object** level are also available at all sub-object levels.

Edit Geometry Rollout

The **Edit Geometry** rollout provides global controls for modifying a poly object. Let's have a look at these controls:

Repeat Last

When clicked, 3ds Max repeats the most recently used command. For example, if you apply a command such as **Bevel** to some polygons and then want to apply the same settings to other set of polygons, select them and then click **Repeat Last**. The same bevel settings will be applied to the last selected polygons.

Caution: Which commands are repeated?

Repeat Last does not repeat all commands, for example, transformations. To check which command in 3ds Max will repeat, hover the mouse pointer on Repeat Last. A tooltip appears indicating which command will be repeated when you click this button [see Figure 29].

Tip: Keyboard Shortcut

You can also use the keyboard shortcuts to repeat the last command. If you are using the 3ds Max mode press semicolon (;) and if you are using the Maya mode press G.

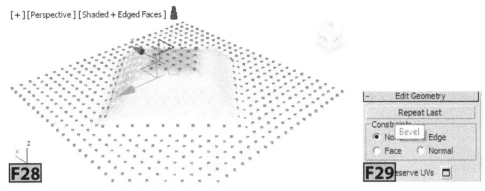

F28

F29

Constraints

The controls in this rollout let you constrain the sub-objects transformations to edges, faces, or normals of the existing geometry. Table 2 summarizes the types of constraints.

Table 2: The **Constrains** types	
Type	**Description**
None	This is the default option. No constraints will be applied.
Edge	It constrains transformations to the edge boundaries [see Figure 30].
Face	It constrains transformations to the face boundaries.
Normal	It allows the transformations along the normals.

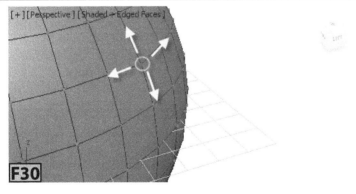

F30

Preserve UVs

When **Preserve UVs** is on, it allows you to edit the sub-objects without affecting the UV mapping [see Figure 31]. The image at the left of Figure 30 is the original vertex position. I scaled the selected vertices inward to show the function of **Preserve UVs**. The middle image shows the result when **Preserve UVs** is on. The image on at right of Figure 31 shows the result when **Preserve UVs** is off.

F31

Create

Allows you to create new geometry in the scene. The result produced by **Create** depends on which sub-object level is active. Table 3 summarizes the behavior of this command.

Table 3: Creating new geometry	
Level	**Description**
Object, Polygon, Element	Adds polygons by clicking existing or new vertices.
Vertex	Adds vertices.
Edge, Border	It adds edges between the pairs of the non-adjacent vertices on the same polygon.

To create geometry, activate a sub-object level and then click **Create**. Now, in the active viewport click to create the geometry [see Figure 32].

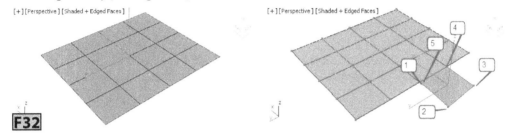

Collapse

It allows you to collapse contiguous selection of the vertices, edges, borders, or polygons by welding their vertices to a vertex. The welded vertex is placed at the center of the selection [see Figures 33 and 34].

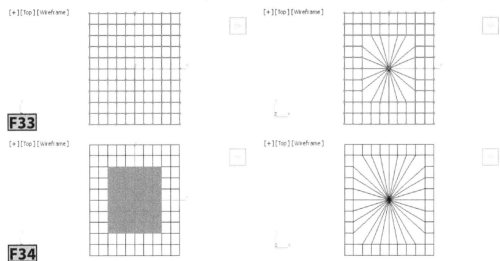

Attach

Attach allows you to attach other geometries to the selected poly object. To attach the objects, select a poly object and then click **Attach**. Now, click on the object that you want to attach; the **Attach** command remains active. If required, keep clicking on other objects to attach them to selected object. RMB click or click **Attach** again to terminate the command.

You can also attach splines, patch objects, and NURBS surfaces to a poly object. If you attach a non-mesh object it is converted to an editable format. It becomes an element of the poly object [see Figure 35].

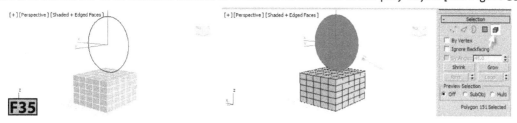

On clicking **Attach List** on the right of **Attach**, opens the **Attach List** dialog. You can use this dialog to attach multiple objects to the selected poly object.

Detach

Detach allows you to separate the selected sub-objects and corresponding polygons to an object or element. To detach sub-objects, select them and then click **Detach**. In the **Detach** dialog that appears, type the name of the object in the **Detach as** field and then click **OK**.

There are two controls in the **Detach** dialog that let you detach sub-objects as an element or a clone. These controls are **Detach To Element** and **Detach As Clone**, respectively. Turn on the required control and then click **OK**.

Slice Plane

This option is available at the sub-objects levels only. The controls in the group are known as knife tools. These tools subdivide along a poly plane [slice] or in a specific area [cut]. When you click **Slice Plane**, a gizmo appears in viewports. Also, **Slice** and **Reset Plane** controls become active in the rollout.

Transform the Gizmo in a viewport and then click **Slice** to create the edges where the gizmo intersects the edges [see Figure 36]. Click **Slice Plane** to deactivate the command. Click **Reset Plane** to reset the position of the gizmo.

If you turn on **Split**, 3ds Max creates double sets of vertices that allows you to create hole in the geometry [see Figure 37].

QuickSlice

QuickSlice allows you to quickly sub-divide a geometry without making adjustments to the gizmo. To slice a geometry, make a selection and then click **QuickSlice**. Now, drag the cursor in a viewport to create a slicing line. Release the mouse button to slice the selection [see Figure 38]. You can continue slicing the geometry or RMB click to exit the command.

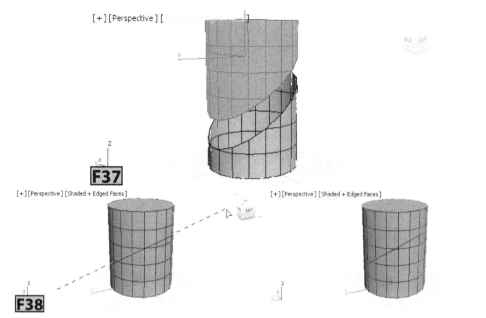

F37

F38

You can use **QuickSlice** in any viewport including perspective and camera. 3ds Max also show you the preview of the slice before you commit the command.

Caution: Polygons and Elements

*If you are at **Polygon** or **Element** level, only selected sub-objects are sliced. If you want to slice entire object, use any sub-object level other than **Polygon** and **Element**.*

Cut

Cut allows you to subdivide polygons by creating edges from one polygon to another or within the polygons. It is available at the object level as well as at all sub-object levels. To create edges, click **Cut** and then click at the start point. Move the mouse pointer and then click on another point to create connected edges [see Figure 39]. You can continue moving and clicking to create the edges. RMB click to exit the command.

Tip: Mouse pointer

The shape of the mouse pointer shows the type of sub-object it is on. Figure 40 shows the shape of the mouse pointer when you are cutting to a vertex, edge, or polygon, respectively.

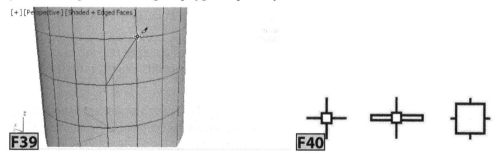

F39

F40

MSmooth

Applies smoothing to the selected area of the poly object [see Figure 41]. Click **Settings** on the right of **MSmooth** to open the **MSmooth** caddy control [see Figure 42] that allows you to adjust the settings used by the **MSmooth** command. Table 4 summarizes the **MSmooth** caddy control.

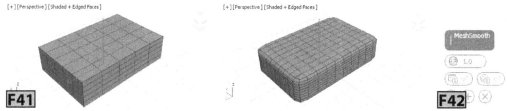

Table 4: The **MSmooth** caddy control	
Control	**Description**
Smoothness	**Smoothness** in a poly mesh is created by adding polygons to it. **Smoothness** determines how sharp the corners of the mesh are. A value of **1** adds polygons to all vertices of the mesh. If you set **Smoothness** to **0**, no polygons will be created.
Separate by Smoothing Groups	When on, the polygons are created at the edges that share atleast one smoothing group.
Separate by Materials	When on, the polygons are created at the edges that share the material IDs.

Tessellate

It subdivides the polygons based on the tessellate setting that can be accessed by clicking **Settings** on the right of **Tessellate**. Figure 43 shows the **Tessellate** caddy control. Table 5 summarizes the **Tessellate** caddy control.

Table 5: The **Tessellate** caddy control	
Control	**Description**
Type	There are two tessellation types available: **Edge** and **Face**. When **Edge** is selected, 3ds Max inserts vertices at the center of each edge and then connect them. The polygons created are the number of sides of the original polygon [see Figure 44]. On selecting the **Face** type, a vertex is created at the center of each polygon and then that vertex is connected to the original vertices. The number of polygons created are equal to the number of sides of the original polygon [see Figure 45].
Tension	It is available for only for the **Edge** type. It determines the edge tension value. A positive value pulls the edges outward whereas a negative value pulls them inward [see Figure 46].

Make Planar

Makes all selected sub-objects to be coplanar. The sub-objects are forced to be coplanar along the average surface normal of the selection [see Figure 47]. If you are at the **Object** level, all vertices of the object will be forced to be coplanar. The **X**, **Y**, and **Z** buttons let you to align the plane with the local coordinate system of the object. For example, if you click **Z**, the selection will be aligned according to the local **XY** axis [see Figure 48].

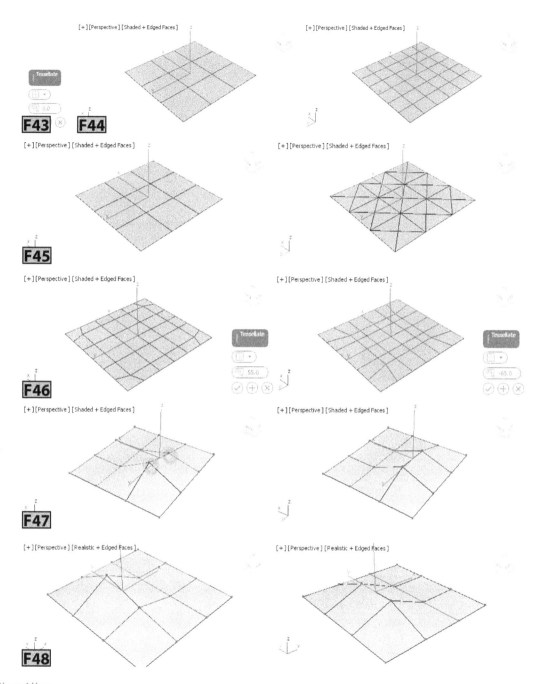

View Align

It aligns all vertices of the object to the plane of the active viewport. It affects vertices only.

Grid Align

It aligns all vertices to the construction plane of the current view. Also, it moves them to that plane. If a perspective or camera viewport is active, this command aligns vertices to the home grid [see Figure 49] otherwise the current construction plane is the active grid. For example, if you make the **Front** viewport active before clicking **Grid Align**, the **XZ** plane will be used for aligning process. If you are using a grid object, the current plane will be the active grid object.

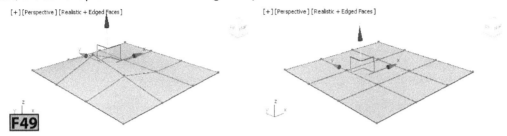

F49

Relax

It relaxes [normalizes mesh spacing] the current selection by moving each vertex towards the average location of its neighboring vertices [see Figure 50]. If you are at the **Object** level, 3ds Max applies smoothing to whole mesh otherwise the **Relax** function is applied to current sub-object selection.

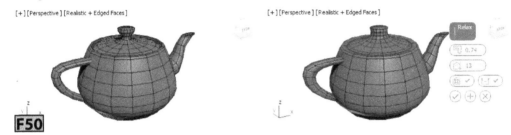

F50

The setting for the **Relax** command can be accessed by clicking **Settings** on the right of **Relax**. The **Relax** caddy control appears. Table 6 summarizes the **Relax** caddy control.

Table 6: The **Relax** caddy control	
Control	**Description**
Amount	Determines how far the vertex moves each iteration relax function. It defines a percentage of the distance from the original location to the average location of the neighbors.
Iterations	Determines how many times you want to repeat the **Relax** operation.
Hold Boundary Points	When on [default], determines whether vertices at the edges of open meshes are moved or not.
Hold Outer Points	When on, 3ds Max preserves the original position of the vertices that are farthest away from the center of the object. Figure 51 shows a mesh when **Hold Outer Points** is off.

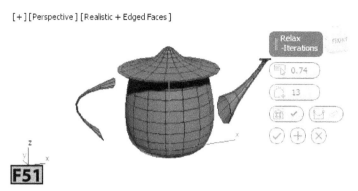

[+] [Perspective] [Realistic + Edged Faces]

Hide Selected, Unhide All, Hide Unselected

These controls are available at **Vertex**, **Polygon**, and **Element** sub-object levels. Table 7 summarizes the functions of these controls.

Table 7: The sub-object visibility	
Control	**Description**
Hide Selected	Hides the selected sub-objects.
Unhide All	Unhides the hidden sub-objects.
Hide Unselected	Hides unselected sub-objects.

Copy, Paste

These controls allow you to copy and paste named selection sets from one object to another. These commands use sub-object IDs, therefore, if there is some difference between the source and target meshes, on pasting, the selection may comprises of different sub-object selected. To understand the working of these two controls, create two **Teapot** primitives and then convert them to **Editable Poly**. Make the **Polygon** mode active and select some polygons on the source object. Type the name for the selection set in the **Named Selection Sets** drop-down. Click **Copy** to open the **Copy Names Selection** dialog, select name and then click **OK** to copy the selection set. Now, activate the **Polygon** selection level for the second teapot and click **Paste**. The polygons will be highlighted.

Delete Isolated Vertices

It is on by default. As a result, when you delete a selection of contiguous sub-objects, the isolated vertices are deleted. If off, deleting sub-object selection leaves the vertices intact.

Full Interactivity

Allows you to toggle feedback on and off for dialogs and caddies as well as for the **Quick Slice** and **Cut** controls. When on, 3ds Max updates the viewports in realtime as you use mouse in the viewport or change values numerically using keyboard.

Vertex Level

Edges and **Polygons** make a poly object. Vertices are the basic building blocks for edges and polygons. You can manipulate vertices at the **Vertex** sub-object level. The controls available for modifying the geometry at the **Vertex** level are found in the **Edit Vertices** and **Vertex Properties** rollout.

Let's discuss the controls available in this rollout.

Remove: Remove lets you delete selected vertices. The polygons that are using these vertices are combined [see the middle image of Figure 52]. The keyboard shortcut for the **Remove** function is **Backspace**.

Caution: Using Delete

*If you use the **Delete** key instead of **Backspace**, 3ds Max can create holes in the poly mesh [see the image at the right of Figure 52].*

Break: Creates a new vertex for each connected polygon to the original selection that allows you to move the corners of polygons [see Figure 53].

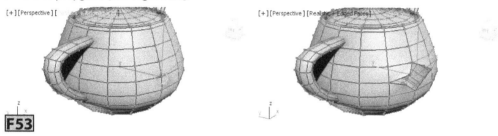

Extrude: You can use this control to extrude the vertices along a normal. 3ds Max creates new polygons that forms the sides of the extrusion [see Figure 54]. The numbers of polygons in the extrusion will be equal to the number of polygons that were associated with the selected vertex. To extrude a vertex, select it and then click **Extrude**. Drag the selected vertex vertically to set the extent of the extrusion. Drag horizontally to set the size of the base. If you have selected multiple vertices, all are affected in the same way by the **Extrude** function. RMB click to end the **Extrude** operation.

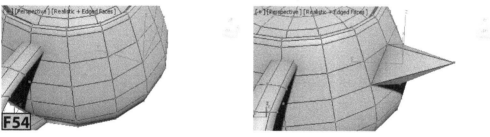

Clicking **Settings** on the right of **Extrude** opens the **Extrude** caddy control. Table 8 summarizes the **Extrude** caddy controls.

Table 8 summarizes the **Extrude** caddy control.

Table 8: The **Extrude** caddy control	
Control	**Description**
Extrusion Height	Determines the extent of the extrusion in scene units.
Extrusion Base Width	Determines the size of the base of the extrusion.

Weld: This control lets you combine the contiguous selected vertices that fall within a threshold specified using the **Weld** caddy control. To weld vertices, make a selection and then click **Settings** on the right of **Weld** to open the **Weld** caddy control. Set **Weld Threshold** and then click **OK** to weld the vertices [see Figure 55].

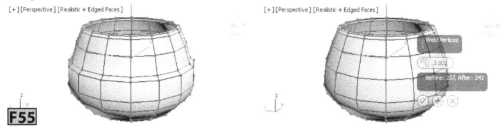

Chamfer: This control allows you to chamfer the vertices. To chamfer a vertex, select it and click **Chamfer**. Now, drag the vertex in a viewport to apply chamfering. If you have selected multiple vertices, all vertices will be chamfered identically [see middle image in Figure 56]. Clicking **Settings** on the right of **Chamfer** opens the **Chamfer** caddy control.

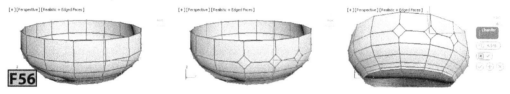

Table 9 summarizes the **Chamfer** caddy control.

Table 9: The **Chamfer** caddy control	
Control	**Description**
Vertex Chamfer Amount	Determines the extent of chamfer.
Open Chamfer	When on, you can create open space around the chamfered vertices [see right image in Figure 56]

Target Weld: This allows you to select a vertex and then weld it to a contiguous target vertex. This tool works on those vertices that are connected with a single edge. Also, this control does not allow to cross newly created edges.

To weld a vertex, select it and click **Target Weld**. When you hover the mouse pointer over the vertex, the shape of the mouse pointer changes to a plus shape. Click and drag on the vertex, a rubber band line gets attached to the mouse pointer. Now, position the mouse pointer on the neighboring vertex and when shape of the mouse changes to a plus sign, click to weld the vertices [see Figure 57].

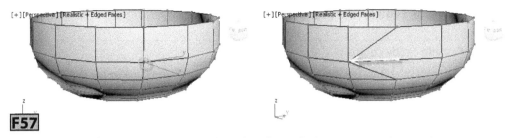

F57

Remove Isolated Vertices: It deletes all vertices that do not belong to any polygon of the selected object.

Remove Unused Map Vertices: If there are some unused map vertices that are appearing in the **Unwrap UVW** editor but cannot be used for mapping, click this control to remove them.

Weight: You can use this control to assign weight to the selected vertices. This weight is used by the **NURMS** subdivision function and the **MeshSmooth** modifier. The vertices with larger weights pulls the smoothened result towards them.

Crease: It sets the crease value for the selected vertices. This value is used by the **OpenSubdiv** and **CreaseSet** modifiers. On increasing the crease weight, 3ds Max pulls the smoothened result toward the vertices and creates a sharp point.

Vertex Properties Rollout
The controls in this rollout are only available for the **Editable Poly** object. They are unavailable for the **Edit Poly** modifier.

Edit Vertex Colors Group: The controls in this group allow you to set the color and illumination color of the selected vertices. Click the **Color** swatch to change their color. **Illumination** allows you to change the illumination color of the vertices without changing the color of the vertices. The **Alpha** control lets you set the alpha values for the vertices. These values are used when you export the data containing full RGBA set for the color values.

Select Vertices By Group: You can turn on **Color** or **Illumination** from this group to determine whether to select vertices by using the vertex color or vertex illumination values. You can also specify a custom color for selecting vertices by using the color swatch available in this group. On clicking **Select**, 3ds Max selects the vertices depending on the selection control that you had turned on. The **Range** control allow you to specify a range for the color match.

Edge Level
Edge connects two vertices. This section covers the controls available at the **Edge** sub-object level. These controls are available in the **Edit Edges** rollout.

Insert Vertex
It allows you to subdivide the edges. To insert a vertex, click **Insert Vertex** and then click on an edge [see Figure 58]. You can continue adding vertices as long as the command is active. RMB click to exit the command.

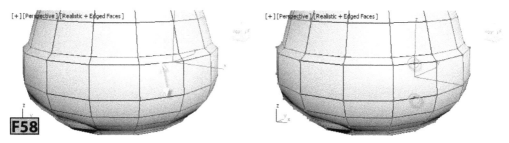

Remove: Removes the selected edges and combines the polygon [see Figure 59]. The keyboard shortcut is **Backspace**. When you remove edges, the vertices remain intact [see left image in Figure 60]. To remove the corresponding vertices, press and hold **Ctrl** when you click **Remove** [see right image in Figure 60].

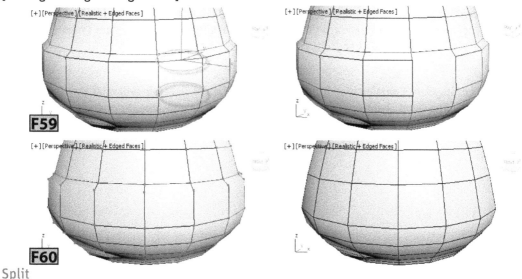

Split

It divides the mesh along the selected edges [see Figure 61].

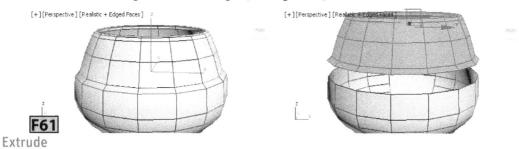

Extrude

This control allows you to extrude the edges manually or using the precise values. The precise values can be entered using the **Extrude** caddy control. The controls in the **Extrude** caddy control are similar to that of the **Extrude** caddy at **Vertex** level, refer to Table 8.

To extrude an edge, select it and then click **Extrude**. Drag the selected edge vertically to set the extent of the extrusion. Drag horizontally to set the size of the base [see Figure 62]. If you have selected multiple edges, all are affected in the same way by the **Extrude** function. RMB click to end the extrude operation.

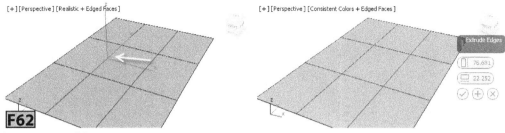

F62

Weld, Target Weld

Refer to the **Vertex Level** section for understanding the functioning of these controls. You need to select edge instead of vertex when dealing with edge welding.

Chamfer

This control allows you to chamfer an edge creating two or more edges for each chamfered edge. 3ds Max provides two types of chamfering: **Standard Chamfer** and **Quad Chamfer**. For **Standard Chamfer**, refer to the **Vertex Level** section. The **Quad Chamfer** type is discussed next.

Quad Chamfer

When you use the **Standard Chamfer** type, 3ds Max generates **quadrilaterals** and **triangles** [see middle image in Figure 63]. The **Quad Chamfer** type generates **quadrilaterals only** [see right image in Figure 63]. The area providing support to the chamfered region might contain triangles.

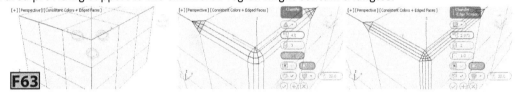

F63

When you click on **Settings** on the right of **Chamfer**, the **Chamfer** caddy control appears. Table 10 summarizes the **Chamfer** caddy control.

Table 10: The Chamfer caddy control	
Control	**Description**
Edge Chamfer Amount	Determines the amount of chamfer in scene units.
Connect Edge Segments	Adds number of polygons over the region of chamfer.
Edge Tension	Determines the angle between the new polygons. At the value of **1** all polygons will be coplanar. Figure 64 shows the chamfered edges with **Edge Tension** set to **0, 0.5**, and **1**, respectively.
Open Chamfer	Deletes the faces created after the chamfer operation.
Invert Open	This option is available for **Quad Chamfer** only. Also, **Open Chamfer** should be on. When **Invert Open** is on, 3ds Max deletes all faces except those created by the chamfering operation.
Smooth	When on, it applies smoothing groups after chamfering. Also, it enables the **Smooth Type** and **Smooth Threshold** functions.

Smooth Type	There are two types of smoothing methods available. **Smooth Entire Object** applies smoothing groups to entire object. **Smooth Chamfers** only applies smoothing groups to newly created polygons.
Smooth Threshold	If angle between the normals of two adjacent polygons is less than the value specified for the **Smooth Threshold** control, the two polygons are placed in the same smoothing group.

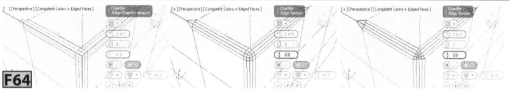

F64

Bridge

You can use the **Bridge** control to bridge the border edges to create a polygon bridge between them. Keep in mind that **Bridge** only connects the borders edges. To create bridge between the edges, select two or more border edges, and then click **Bridge**. A bridge will be created using the existing **Bridge** settings [see Figure 65]. To set **Bridge** settings, click **Settings** on the right of **Bridge**; the **Bridge** caddy control appears. Table 11 summarizes the **Bridge** caddy control;.

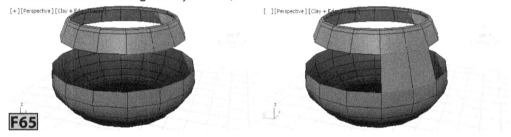

F65

Table 11: The **Bridge** caddy control	
Control	**Description**
Segments	Specifies the number of polygons along the length of the bridge.
Smooth	Sets the maximum angle for smoothing to occur.
Bridge Adjacent	Controls the minimum angle between the adjacent edges across which bridging can occur. The edges that are at less than this angle will not be bridged.
Reverse Triangulation	When you are bridging two borders edges each of which contains different numbers of the, you can use this control to define the method of triangulation. Figure 66 shows the bridge when **Reverse Triangulation** is **On** and **Off**, respectively.
Use Edge Selection	It allows you to choose between two methods. Either you can use the existing selection or you can choose the edges using caddy control. When you choose **Use Specific Edges**, the **Pick Edge 1**, **Pick Edge 2** controls become available.
Pick Edge 1, Pick Edge 2	Click **Pick Edge 1** and then click a border edge in a viewport. Select the other border edge using **Pick Edge 2**, the bridge will be created between the two border edges.

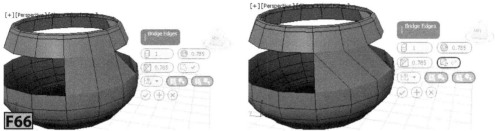

F66

Connect

Allows you to refine selected edges by creating new edges between the selected edges. To create new edges, select the edges of the active object that you want to connect and then click **Connect** [see Figure 67].

Caution: Connecting edges

*You can connect edges on the same polygon. The **Connect** command will stop the new edges to cross. For example, if you select all edges of a polygon face and apply this function, only neighboring edges are connected. The new edges will not cross each other [see Figure 68].*

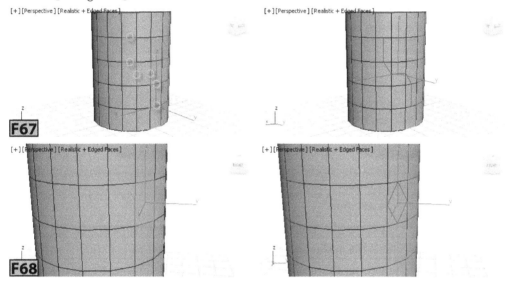

F67

F68

Clicking on the **Settings** on the right of **Connect** opens the **Connect** caddy control that allows you to change settings for the **Connect** command and also preview the changes before committing them [see Figure 69].

F69

Table 12 summarizes the **Connect** caddy control.

Table 12: The **Connect** caddy control	
Control	**Description**
Segments	Defines the number of new edges between each adjacent pair of selected edges.
Pinch	The relative spacing between the new and connecting edges.
Slide	The relative positioning of the new edges.

Create Shape from Selection

This control allows you to create a shape (spline) from the selected edges. The pivot of the shape will be created at the geometric center of the poly object. To create a shape, select the edges of the active object and then click **Create Shape from Selection** to open the **Create Shape** dialog. Type the new name in the **Curve Name** field and then choose the **Shape Type**. Next, click **OK** to create the shape [see Figure 70].

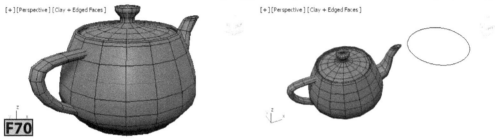

Edit Tri

This control gives you ability to modify the triangulation for the polygons. To turn on triangulation, click **Edit Tri**. The hidden edges appear on the object [see left image in Figure 71]. Now, to change the triangulation for a polygon, click a vertex; a rubber band line appears attached to the mouse pointer. Now, click on an adjacent vertex to create a new triangulation [see the right image in Figure 71].

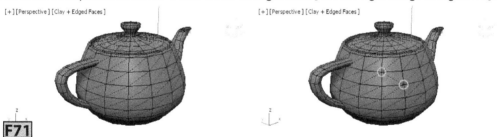

Turn

It allows you to modify polygon triangulation by clicking on the diagonals. To change triangulation, click **Turn**. The current triangulation appear on the object. Click on the diagonals to change the triangulation.

Border Level

A border can be described as the edge [boundary] of a hole. As discussed earlier, if you create a cylinder and delete its caps, the adjacent row of edges form a border. You can manipulate borders using the controls available in the **Edit Borders** rollout. Most of the controls are similar to the edge and vertex controls. Select border edges and experiment with these controls. One additional control appears in the **Edit Borders** rollout called **Cap**. It caps an entire border loop with a polygon. You can use it to fill holes in an object.

Polygon/Element Level

A polygon is formed by connecting three or more edges. Polygons form a surface that you can render. At **Polygon** sub-object level, you can select polygons and then apply various polygon modeling functions to them. At **Element** sub-object level, you can edit groups of contiguous polygons.

Tip: Highlighting polygons
*When you select a polygon, it is highlighted in red color in the viewport. You can toggle this feature on and off by pressing the **F2** key.*

You can edit polygons and elements using the controls available in the **Edit Polygons** and **Edit Elements** rollouts, respectively.

Edit Polygons Rollout

Let's first explore the tools available in the **Edit Polygons** rollout.

Insert Vertex

Allows you to subdivide a polygon manually. It also works at the **Element** sub-object level. To subdivide the polygon, click **Insert Vertex** and then click on a polygon to subdivide it. You can continue subdividing the polygons as the command remains active until you RMB click [see Figure 72].

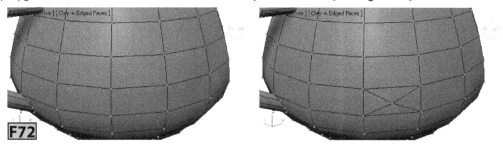

Extrude

Extruding is a process in which polygons move along a normal and new polygons are created. This command lets you extrude the polygons. To extrude the polygons, select them in a viewport and then click **Extrude**. Position the mouse pointer on the polygons. The shape of the cursor changes to the **Extrude** cursor. Drag the cursor vertically to specify the extent of extrusion and horizontally to set the base [see Figure 73].

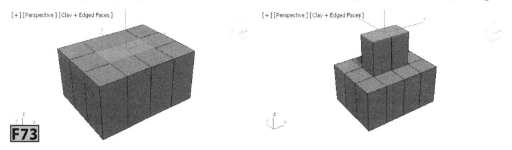

On clicking **Settings** on the right of **Extrude**, the **Extrude** caddy control appears that allows you to specify settings for extrusion.

Table 13 summarizes the **Extrude** caddy control.

Table 13: The **Extrude** caddy control	
Control	**Description**
Extrusion Type	This drop-down provides three methods for extrusion: **Group**, **Local Normal**, and **By Polygon**. On selecting **Group**, 3ds Max extrudes polygons along the average normal of each contiguous group of polygons [see left image in Figure 74]. When **Normal** is selected, the extrusion takes place along each normal of the selected polygon [see middle image in Figure 74]. On selecting **By Polygon**, each 3ds Max extrudes each polygon individually [see the right image in Figure 74].
Extrusion Height	Determines the amount of extrusion in scene units.

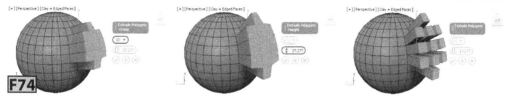

Outline

This command lets you increase or decrease the outside edge of each group of contiguous polygons. It does not scale, it just change the size of the outside edge of the selected polygons. To change the size of the outside edge of polygons, select a group of contiguous of polygons and then click **Outline**. Now, position the mouse pointer on the selected polygons and drag the pointer to outline the polygons [see Figure 75]. Notice in Figure 75 that the inner polygons are not affected by the **Outline** operation. If you want to manually specify the outline amount, then click **Settings** on the right of the **Outline** to open the **Outline** caddy control and specify the value using the **Amount** control.

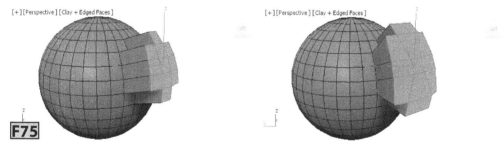

Bevel

It allows you to perform bevel function on group of contiguous selected polygons. To bevel the polygons, select them in a viewport and then click **Bevel**. Position the mouse pointer on the polygons. The shape of the cursor changes to the **Bevel** cursor. Drag the cursor vertically to define the height and horizontally to define the outline amount [see Figure 76].

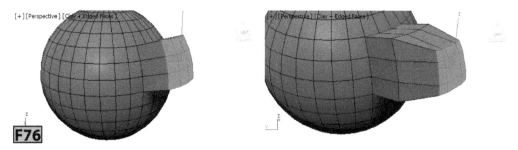

F76

On clicking **Settings** on the right of **Bevel**, the **Bevel** caddy control appears that allows you to specify settings for extrusion.

Table 14 summarizes the **Bevel** caddy control.

Table 14: The **Bevel** caddy control	
Control	**Description**
Bevel Type	This drop-down provides three methods for beveling: **Group**, **Local Normal**, and **By Polygon**. On selecting **Group**, 3ds Max bevels polygons along the average normal of each contiguous group of polygons. When **Normal** is selected, the beveling takes place along each normal of the selected polygon. On selecting **By Polygon**, each 3ds Max bevels each polygon individually.
Height	Determines the amount of extrusion in scene units.
Outline Amount	Lets you make the outer border of the selection bigger or smaller.

Inset

This command performs a bevel with no height. To inset polygons, select them and then click **Inset**, position the cursor over the polygons and the drag to define the **Inset** amount [see Figure 77].

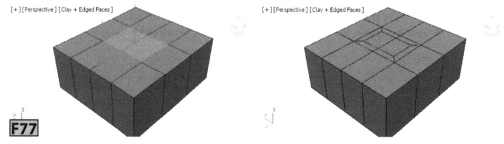

F77

On clicking **Settings** on the right of **Inset**, the **Inset** caddy control appears that allows you to specify settings for extrusion.

Table 15 summarizes the **Inset** caddy control.

Table 15: The **Inset** caddy control	
Controls	**Description**
Inset Type	This drop-down provides two methods for insetting: **Group**, and **By Polygon**. On selecting **Group**, 3ds Max insets polygons across each selection of multiple, contiguous polygons. On selecting **By Polygon**, 3ds Max insets each polygon individually.
Inset Amount	Determines the extent of inset in scene units.

Bridge

You have seen how we have applied **Bridge** function on the edges. It works similarly at the **Polygon** sub-object level. Here, you have to select polygons instead of edges [see Figure 78]. Figure 78 shows an external bridge [right] as well as internal bridge [left].

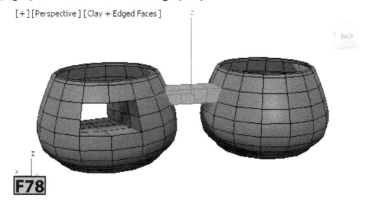

To specify settings for the **Bridge** function, click **Settings** on the right of **Bridge** to open the **Bridge** caddy control.

Table 16 summarizes the **Bridge** caddy controls.

Table 16: The **Bridge** caddy control	
Controls	**Description**
Segments	Determines the number of polygons along the length of the bridge.
Taper	Allows you to taper the bridge length towards its center. Negative values make bridge center smaller whereas the positive values makes center bigger.
Bias	Defines the location of the maximum taper amount.
Smooth	Sets the angle for smoothing.
Twist 1, Twist 2	Allow you to twist each end of the bridge.

Use Specific Borders, Use Border Selection	It allows you to choose between two methods. Either you can use the existing selection or you can choose the polygons using caddy control. When you choose **Use Specific Borders**, the **Pick Polygon 1**, **Pick Polygon 2** controls become available.
Pick Polygon 1, Pick Polygon 2	Click **Pick Polygon 1** and then click a polygon or border edge in a viewport. Select the other border edge using **Pick Polygon 2**, the bridge will be created between the two border edges.

Flip

Allows you to reverse the direction of normals on the selected polygons.

Hinge From Edge

This command allows you to perform a hinge operation in the viewport. Make a polygon selection in a viewport and then click **Hinge From Edge**. Now, drag on an edge to hinge the selection [see Figure 79].

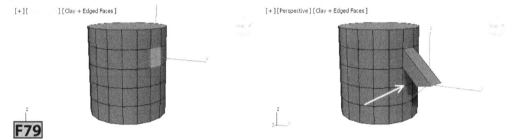

On clicking **Settings** on the right of **Hinge From Edge**, the **Hinge From Edge** caddy control appears that allows you to specify settings for extrusion.

Table 17 summarizes the **Hinge From Edge** caddy control.

Table 17: The **Hinge From Edge** caddy control	
Controls	**Description**
Angle	Sets the rotation angle around the hinge [see Figure 80].
Segments	Specifies the number of polygons along the extruded side.
Pick Hinge	Click it and then click on an edge to specify the hinge edge.

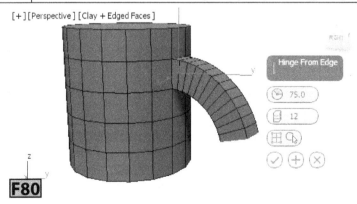

Extrude Along Spline

Allows you to extrude a selection along a spline. To extrude, create a spline and then select the polygons that you want to extrude. Click **Extrude Along Spline** and then click the spline in a viewport to extrude the polygons [see Figure 81].

On clicking **Settings** on the right of **Extrude Along Spline**, the **Extrude Along Spline** caddy control appears that allows you to specify settings for extrusion.

Table 18 summarizes the **Extrude Along Spline** caddy controls.

Table 18: The **Extrude Along Spline** caddy control	
Control	**Description**
Segments	Determines the number of polygons along the extrusion [see Figure 82].
Taper Amount	Sets the taper amount for the extrusion.
Taper Curve	Defines the rate at which tapering occurs.
Twist	Applies a twist along the length of taper.
Extrude Along Spline Align	Aligns the extrusion along the face normal [see Figure 83].
Rotation	Sets the rotation of extrusion.
Pick Spline	Allows you to pick a spline along which the extrusion will occur.

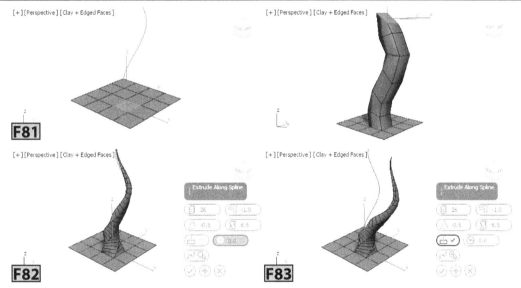

Edit Triangulation Turn

Refer to the **Edge Level** section for understanding the functioning of these controls.

Retriangulate

When clicked, 3ds Max automatically performs best triangulation on the selected polygon[s].

Edit Elements Rollout
Refer to **Edit Polygons** rollout for the controls available in this rollout.

Hands-on Exercises
Complete the following Hands-on Exercises:

1. ***Exercise – 6:*** *Creating a Serving Bowl*
2. ***Exercise – 7:*** *Creating a Kitchen Cabinet*
3. ***Exercise – 8:*** *Creating a Book*

Practical Test
Complete the following test:

Practical Test - 1: Kitchen Cabinet
Create the kitchen cabinet model [see Figure 84] using the **Box** primitive. Use dimensions of your choice.

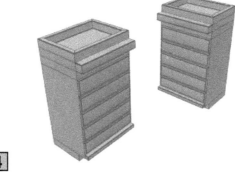

F84

Summary
This unit provided the introduction to poly modeling in 3ds Max. I have showed how to convert objects to editable poly and then create shape of the model using sub-objects and polygon editing tools.

The unit covered the following topics:

- Working with the polygon modeling tools
- Using the polygon modeling techniques
- Selecting polygon sub-object
- Transforming sub-objects
- Soft selecting sub-objects

In next unit, I will explain the tools available in the **Ribbon**.

Unit M5: Graphite Modeling Tools

In the previous unit, I covered everything you need to know about modeling with polygons. You created geometric primitives and converted them into editable poly objects and then used the tools and commands available in the **Command Panel** to create the models. 3ds Max provides another workflow for creating and editing polygons based on the **Ribbon** interface. If you have worked with any other Autodesk product such as products from the **Revit** family, you might be aware of the **Ribbon** interface. In this unit, I describe the tools available in the **Modeling** tab of the **Ribbon** interface and how you can use them to improve your modeling workflow.

In this unit, I will cover the following:

- Working with the **Graphite Modeling Tools**
- Selecting sub-objects
- Creating models using the tools available in the **Ribbon**

The Ribbon

The **Graphite Modeling Tools** are available in the **Ribbon**. These tools offer vide variety of features for editing polygons. The **Ribbon** comprises all standard **Editable Poly** tools and some additional tools for creating, selecting, and editing geometries. By default, **Ribbon** sits on top of the viewports in the collapsed state [see Figure 1].

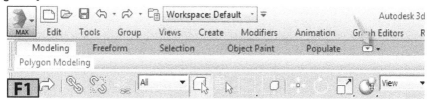

To expand **Ribbon**, either double-click on the empty gray area of the **Ribbon** or click **Show Full Ribbon** [marked with an arrow in Figure 1]. The **Ribbon** with the **Modeling** tab active will be displayed [see Figure 2].

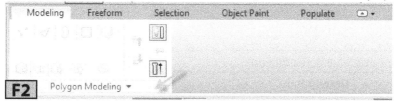

Tip: Toggling display of Ribbon
*If **Ribbon** is not visible, click **Toggle Ribbon** button on the **Main** toolbar or choose **Show UI | Show Ribbon** from the **Customize** menu.*

Each tab in **Ribbon** comprises various tabs such as the **Polygon Modeling** panel in the **Modeling** tab [marked with an arrow in Figure 2]. The display of panel in the tab is context sensitive. To view other panels in the tab, create a primitive in a viewport and then covert it to **Editable Poly**.

When you click on the arrow on the right of the panel's name, the panel expands revealing the tools and commands available in that panel. Figure 4 shows the expanded **Polygon Modeling** panel. Click on **Polygon Modeling** to collapse the panel [marked with arrow in Figure 4].

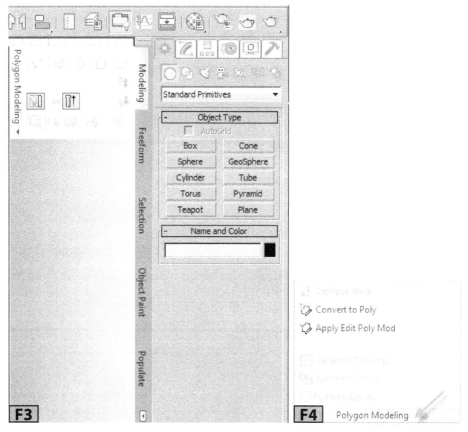

Table 1 summarizes the tabs available in the **Ribbon**.

Table 1: The tabs available in the **Ribbon**	
Tab	**Description**
Modeling	The tools in this tab are mainly used for polygon modeling. These tools are organized in different panels for easy access.
Freeform	This tab contains tools for creating and modifying geometry by painting on the surface of a geometry. You can also specify settings for paint brushes from this tab.

Selection	The special tools in this tab allow you to make sub-object selection in a unique way. For example, select sub-objects from a concave or convex area, and select sub-objects that face the viewport.
Object Paint	The tools available in this tab allow you to paint objects freehand anywhere in the scene.
Populate	This tab provides tools for adding animated pedestrians and idlers in the scene.

Tip: Tools help

*3ds Max provides extended tooltip for the tools available in the **Ribbon**. Position the mouse pointer on a tool; 3ds Max displays a smaller tooltip. If you place the mouse pointer on a tool for little longer, 3ds Max expands the tooltip and sometimes you will also see an illustration in the tooltip. Figure 5 shows an expanded tooltip when mouse pointer was placed on the **Ring** tool.*

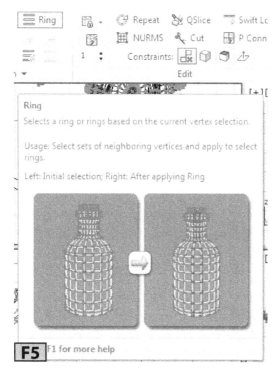

Modeling Tab

The **Modeling** tab contains the tools that you will use with the polygon models. These tools are organized in separate panels for easy access. Most of the tools in this tab are clones of the polygon editing tools found in the **Command Panel**. The best way to understand these tools is to practice them. You will use these tools in the hands-on exercises.

Freeform Tab

The **Freeform** tab [see Figure 6] provides tools for creating and modifying geometry by painting on the surface of a geometry. This tab contains three panels: **PolyDraw**, **Paint Deform**, and **Defaults**. These panels are discussed next.

PolyDraw Panel

The tools in this panel allow you to quickly sketch or edit a mesh in the main grid. You can also sketch on the surface of another object or on the object itself. This panel also provides tools for molding one object to the shape of another object. Before we explore the tools, let's understand the **Conform Options** panel which is always displayed when a conform brush tool is active.

Conform Options Panel

The options in this panel [see Figure 7] let you specify the settings for modifying tool's effects. When any conform brush tool other than the **Conform Brush** is active, the panel is named **Transform Conform Options**. Also, an additional toggle appears with the name **Offset Relative**.

Here's the quick rundown to the options available in the **Conform Options** panel.

Full Strength: Defines the size of the center area represented by a white circle in the brush [see Figure 8]. The **Strength %** setting [see Figure 7] is fully applied in this area. To adjust the brush size interactively, **Shift+drag**.

Full Strength:	192	Strength %:	100
Falloff:	372	Mirror Axis:	X Y Z
Conform:	1.200	Freeze Axis:	X Y Z
F7 Transform Conform Options		Freeze Selected Edges:	X Y Z

Falloff: **Falloff** is represented by the bigger black circle [see Figure 8]. The **Strength** in this circle decreases from full strength to zero. To adjust the brush size interactively, **Ctrl+drag**.

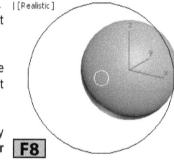

[[Realistic]

F8

Conform: It defines the rate at which the **Conform** brush deforms the painted object. Higher the values you specify for this option, instant will be the conforming effect.

Mirror: When **Mirror** is active, the tool's effect is applied equally to both sides [see Figure 9] across the mirror axis defined by the **Mirror Axis** attribute.

View/ Vertex Normal: These two options [see Figure 10] control the direction in which the **Conform** brush moves the vertices.

View pushes vertices away from the screen therefore it is dependent on the view angle of the scene. **Vertex Normal** pushes the vertices along their own normal toward the target.

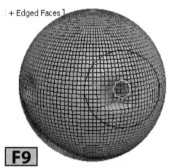

: + Edged Faces]

F9

Offset Relative: This brush is only available when you use one of the transform conform brushes. When on, it helps you in retaining the original shape of the object.

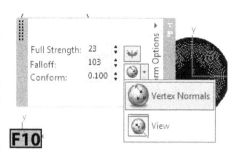

Strength %: This option defines the overall rate at which a brush deforms an object. To interactive change the value for this option, **Shift+Alt+drag**.

Use Selected Verts: When on, the deform tools only affect the selected vertices. When off, it affects all vertices of the object.

Ignore Backfacing: When on, the tools affects vertices facing you.

Mirror Axis X/Y/Z: Allow you to choose the axis across which the conform action will be mirrored.

Freeze Axis X/Y/Z: When any **Freeze Axis** button is on, the tool is prevented from moving vertices on the corresponding axis of the object.

Freeze Selected Edges X/Y/Z: When any **Freeze Selected Edges** button is on, the tool is prevented from moving edges on the corresponding axis of the object. The un-selected edges move freely.

PolyDraw Panel - Drag and Conform Tools
The tools in this panel [see Figure 11] produces different effects depending on which combination keys [**Ctrl**, **Alt**, and **Shift**] you press. Although, **PolyDraw** tools do not require you to select any sub-object level, however, it is recommended that you use these tools at the **Vertex** sub-object level for better results.

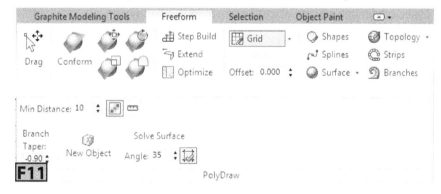

Drag: You can use the **Drag** tool to move sub-objects on the surface or grid. Table 2 summarizes the functions available with this tool.

Table 2: Functions of the **Drag** tool	
Function	**Description**
Normal	Without any modifier keys this tool move vertices by dragging them.

Shift	Moves edges.
Ctrl+Drag	Moves polygons.
Shift+Ctrl+Drag	Moves edge loops.
Shift+Ctrl+Alt+Drag	Moves elements.

You can also use this tool to move the sub-objects in screen space [perpendicular to the current view selection]. Table 3 shows these functions.

Table 3: Functions of the **Drag** tool in the screen space	
Function	**Description**
Alt+Drag	Moves vertices.
Alt+Shift+Drag	Moves edges.
Alt+Ctrl+Drag	Moves polygons.

 Conform Brush: The **Conform** brushes move the conform object's vertices towards the target. You can use these brushes in variety of modeling scenarios such as painting a road on a hilly terrain, or painting a mask on the face of a character.

To conform an object to the target object. Select the object that you want to conform. Activate the **Vertex** sub-object level for better control. Select **Draw On: Surface** from the **Draw On** drop-down [Surface ▾] on the **PolyDraw** panel. Click **Pick** and then click the target object in a viewport. The name of the object appears on the **Pick** [Pick] button. Click **Conform**, adjust brush size and strength and then drag the object toward the target using the **Conform** brush. The selected object takes shape of the target object. In Figure 12, I have conformed a **Plane** primitive to a **Sphere** primitive.

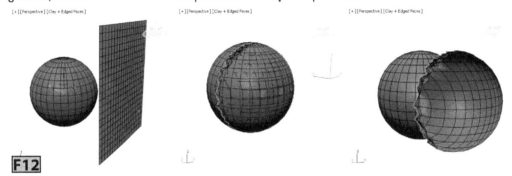

F12

Apart from the basic **Conform** brush that is described above, 3ds Max also provides four transformed based variants: **Move Conform Brush** ⟨⟩, **Rotate Conform Brush** ⟨⟩, **Scale Conform Brush** ⟨⟩, and **Relax Conform Brush** ⟨⟩. The **Relax Conform Brush** applies a relax effect to vertices within a spherical volume.

PolyDraw Panel - Add Geometry and Optimize Tools

Step Build: This tool works at the Object level as well as the sub-objects level. You can use this tool to build a surface vertex by vertex or polygon by polygon. Table 4 summarizes the functions of this tool.

Table 4: Functions of the **Step Build** tool

Function	Description
Normal	Click to place vertices on the grid or surface.
Shift+Drag	Drag over the floating vertices to fill the gaps with quad polygons.
Ctrl+Click	Click on a polygon to delete it.
Alt+Click	Click on a vertex to remove it.
Ctrl+Alt+Click	Click on an edge to remove it.
Ctrl+Shift+Click	Click to place and select vertices. You can also select the existing vertices.
Shift+Alt	Move the mouse pointer [do not drag] over the vertices to select them.
Ctrl+Shift+Alt	Drag mouse pointer to move a vertex on a grid or surface.

Caution: Vertex Ticks
*When the **Step Build** tool is active, vertex ticks are not always visible in the viewport. If you don't see the ticks at levels other than the **Vertex** level, change the display of the object to **By Object** in the object's display properties.*

Extend Tool: You can use this tool with the open edges that are on the border of the surface that have only one polygon attached. Table 5 summarizes the functions of this tool.

Table 5: Functions of the **Extend** tool

Function	Description
Normal	Drag a border vertex to create a polygon.
Shift+Drag	Drag a border edge to create a polygon.
Ctrl+Shift+Drag	Drag an edge to extend its entire loop.
Ctrl+Alt+Drag	Drag between two edges to create a polygon.
Ctrl+Click	Click to delete a polygon and associated isolated vertices.
Ctrl+Shift+Alt+Drag	Drag a vertex to move it on the surface or grid.
Alt+Drag (Screen Space)	Drag a border to create a polygon.
Alt+Shift+ Drag (Screen Space)	Drag a border edge to create a polygon.

Optimize Tool: This tool is used to remove the details from the model by drawing on it. Table 6 shows the functions of this tool.

Table 6: Functions of the **Optimize** tool

Function	Description
Normal	Click on the edges to collapse. It merges two vertices into one.
Shift+Drag	Drag from one vertex to another to weld them.

3ds Max 2016   **M5-7**

Ctrl+Drag	Drag between the vertices to connect them.
Alt+Click	Click to remove a vertex.
Shift+Ctrl+Click	Click to remove an edge loop.
Shift+Alt+Click	Click to remove a ring.
Ctrl+Alt+Click	Click on an edge to remove it.
Shift+Ctrl+Alt+Drag	Drag on a vertex to move it.

Draw On: The options in this drop-down allow you to choose the entity type on which you want to draw. The **Grid** option creates geometry on the grid of the active viewport. This option works well with the orthographic view, however, you can also use it in the **Perspective** viewport. The **Surface** option allows you to draw on another object that you specify. The **Selection** option lets you create geometry on the selected object.

Pick: This button lets you pick an object to draw on. To pick object, choose **Surface** from the **Draw On** drop-down and then click **Pick**. Now, click on the object to draw on. **Offset:** It specifies the distance that **PolyDraw** uses for creating the geometry.

PolyDraw Panel - Create Geometry Tools

Shapes: You can use this tool to draw polygons on a surface or grid. Click **Solve Surface** after creating the polygon to generate a workable mesh. The **Solve Surface** option will be displayed when you expand the **PolyDraw** panel [see Figure 13].

When **Shapes** is active, you can delete a polygon by clicking on it with the **Ctrl** held down. To move a polygon, drag the mouse pointer with **Ctrl+Shift+Alt** held down.

Topology: This tool is used to create quad polygons by drawing lines in a viewport. As you draw the quads using this tool, 3ds Max fills them with a polygon. To draw the mesh, pick **Topology** and then draw lines in a viewport. When you are done with the lines, **RMB** click to complete the operation [see Figure 14].

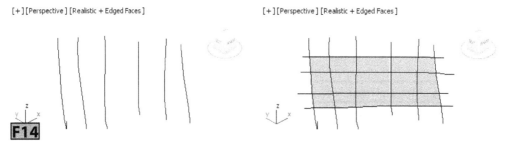

The drop-down associated with **Topology** contains an option, **Auto Weld**. When **Auto Weld** is on, 3ds Max automatically attaches the mesh to the selected object and weld their border vertices. If **Auto Weld** is off, **Topology** always creates a new mesh. The **Minimum Distance** control available in the expanded **PolyDraw** panel defines the resolution of the lines. The default value for this control is **10** which works well in most of the cases. When **Topology** is active, you can **Shift+Drag** to continue a line from the closest endpoint. To delete a line, click on it with **Ctrl** held down.

Splines: This tool draws a spline on a surface or grid. The splines created using this tool are renderable. Select the desired option from the **Draw On** drop-down and then draw to create splines. All splines are combined into single [separate] object. When **Splines** is active, you can delete a spline by clicking on it with the **Ctrl** held down. You can also move a spline to the closest splines by dragging it with **Ctrl+Shift+Alt** held down.

Strips: This tool can be used to quickly layout the topology foundation for a mesh object. It paints strips of polygons that follow the mouse drag direction [see Figure 15]. If you press **Shift** before starting the painting, 3ds Max paints from the closest existing edge. If you want to create polygon between two open edges, press **Alt** and then drag between the two open edges.

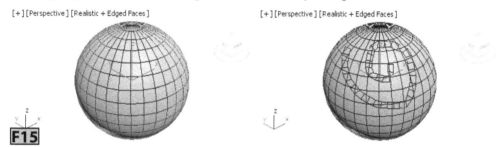

[+] [Perspective] [Realistic + Edged Faces]   [+] [Perspective] [Realistic + Edged Faces]

F15

Surface: This tool paints a surface onto an object or grid. The size of the surface polygons are controlled by the **Minimum Distance** setting available in the expanded **PolyDraw** panel. The drop-down associated with **Surface** has an option, **Quads**. When **Quads** is on, the surface is made up of quads. When off, 3ds Max create surface with triangles. To start the surface from an existing border edge, hold **Shift** before you start the drawing. It ensures that overlapping polygons are not created. To delete a polygon, click on it with the **Shift** held down; the associated isolated vertices are also deleted.

Branches: This tool creates multi-segmented extrusions from polygons [see Figure 16]. This tool works only on the selected object and **Draw On** settings does not affect it. The extent of tapering of the branches is controlled by the **Branch Taper** setting available in the expanded **PolyDraw** panel. To create branches, drag the mouse pointer on the selected object, 3ds Max creates branches from the polygons closest to the mouse pointer. Press **Shift** to draw branches from all the selected polygons. If you are at the **Polygon** level, click with **Ctrl** held down to select a polygon. You can also select/de-select additional polygons with **Shilft+Alt** held down.

Paint Deform Panel

The tools in this panel [see Figure 17] give you ability to deform mesh geometry interactively in the viewport. These tools works similarly for at the **Object** level as well at the sub-object level and are independent of any sub-object selection. To exit any tool, either click the its button or RMB click in a viewport. Let's explore various deformation tools available in 3ds Max.

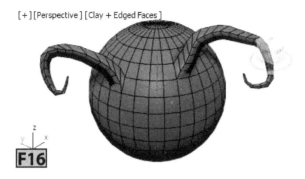

[+][Perspective][Clay + Edged Faces]

F16

 Shift/ Shift Rotate/ Shift Scale

These tools are used to move, rotate, or scale objects in the screen space [see Figure 18]. These tools are like using the standard transformation tools with soft selection. However, with these tools no initial selection is required. You can revert to previous state by using the **Revert** tool. However, this tool only works if you have used any other deform tool such as **Push/Pull**.

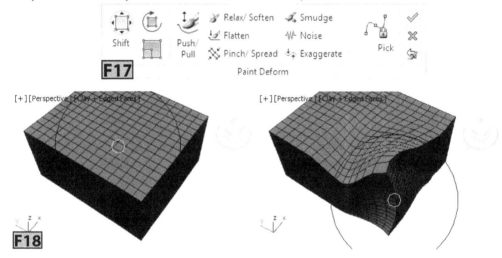

F17

[+][Perspective][Clay + Edged Faces]   [+][Perspective][Clay + Edged Faces]

F18

Push/Pull

This tool drags the vertices outward [see the left image in Figure 19]. To move vertices inward, drag with the **Alt** held down [see the right image in Figure 19]. When this tool is active you can use:

- **Ctrl** to revert to the previous saved state.
- **Shift** to relax the mesh.
- **Ctrl+Shift** to resize the brush
- **Shift+Alt** to change the strength of the brush.

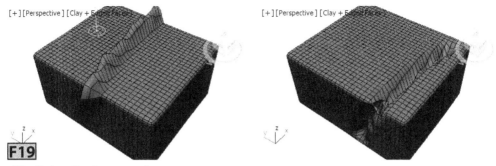

F19

Note: The Paint Options panel

*When you use any deform tool except **Shift** tools, the floating **Paint Options** panel appears [see Figure 20].*

You can use the settings from this panel to control the behavior of the deform tools.

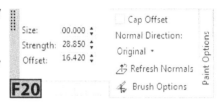

F20

Relax/Soften

This tool allows you to soften the corners [see Figure 21]. With other brushes, you can soften a geometry with **Shift** held down.

Smudge

The **Smudge** tool is used to move the vertices [see Figure 22]. It is somewhat similar to the **Shift** tool however it updates the effect continuously. Also, it does not use falloff.

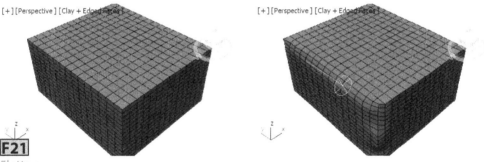

F21

Flatten

This tool lets you flatten the concave and convex areas.

Pinch/Spread

You can use this tool to move vertices together or spread them apart. To spread, drag with the **Alt** held down.

Noise

You can use this tool to add convex noise to a surface [see Figure 23]. To create concave noise, drag with **Alt** held down.

Exaggerate

This tool makes the features of the surface more pronounced by moving the convex areas outward and concave areas inward.

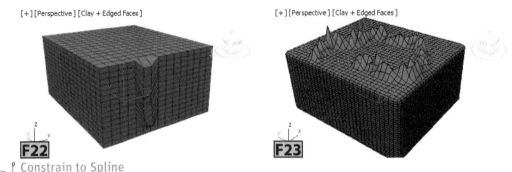

Constrain to Spline

Apart from the **Shift** tools, all other tools can use a spline as a path for mesh deformation. Create a spline and place it near the surface you want to deform [see left image in Figure 24]. Click **Pick** available below **Constrain to Spline** and then click on the spline in a viewport. Make sure **Constrain to Spline** is active then pick a deform tool such as **Noise**. Now, when you paint on the object, the deform gizmo can only be moved along the spline. Drag the mouse pointer to create the deformation [see right image in Figure 24].

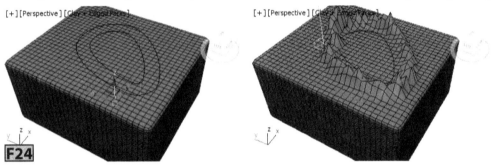

Paint Deform Panel

You can use this panel to save and load brush settings. The **Load All Brush Settings** option opens a dialog that you can use to load brush settings from an existing file. The **Save All Brush Settings** option opens a dialog that you can use to store brush settings to a file. The **Set Current Settings as Default** option saves the current brush settings as default.

Selection Tab

The **Selection** tab provides a wide array of tools that allow you to make sub-object selection such as you can select convex and concave areas, you can select the sub-object that face the camera, and so forth. Let's explore the various panels available in the **Selection** tab.

Select Panel

The tools in this panel lets you select the sub-object based on the certain topologies. Table 7 summarizes the tools available in this panel.

Table 7: The tools available in the **Select** panel		
Tool	**Icon**	**Description**
Tops		This tool selects the top of the extruded polygon. The selection depends on the active sub-object level. When the **Vertex**, **Edge**, or **Polygon** sub-object level is active, the vertices, edge outlines, or tops of the extruded polygons are selected. Figure 25 shows the top of the extruded polygons selected.
Open		This tool selects all open sub-objects [see Figure 26]. The final result depends on the active sub-object.
Hard		This tool is available at the **Edge** sub-object level. It selects all edges in a model whose faces do not share the same smoothing groups.
Non-Quads		This tool selects all non-quadrilateral polygons. This tool is available at **Polygon** sub-object level.
Patterns		This tool allows you to grow the current selection based on the pattern you select from the **Pattern** drop-down. The **Pattern 1-8** options provide different selection pattern. Make a selection in the viewport and then experiment with various patterns. **Growlines** grows the selection with gaps of unselected lines [see Figure 27]. **Checker** grows selection in from of a checker board pattern [see Figure 28]. **Dots** grows the selection such that all sub-objects have gap between them [see Figure 29]. **One Ring** grows a single polygon ring around the initial selection [see Figure 30].
By Vertex	-	When you click a vertex using this tool, all sub-objects that use the clicked vertex are selected.
By Angle	-	When on and if you select a polygon, the neighboring polygons are also selected based on the value you set in the spinner available on the right of **By Angle**.
By Material ID	-	It opens the **Material ID** dialog that you can use to set the material IDs. Also, you can select by ID and material name using this dialog.
By Smoothing Group	-	It displays a dialog that shows the current smoothing groups. To select polygon associated with a group, click the corresponding smoothing group.

[+] [Perspective] [Clay + Edged Faces]   [+] [Perspective] [Clay + Edged Faces]

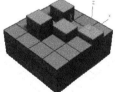

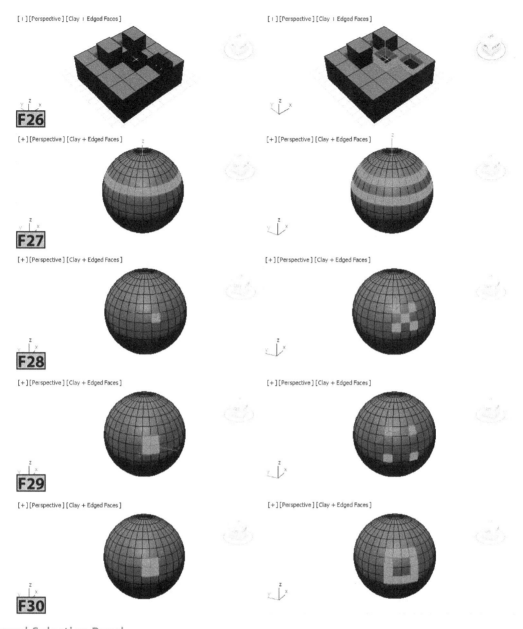

Stored Selection Panel

The options in this panel let you quickly and easily store and retrieve selections. You can also apply some basic operations between the stored selections. Table 8 summarizes the tools available in this panel.

Table 8: The tools available in the Stored Selection panel		
Tool	**Icon**	**Description**
Copy Store 1/ Copy Store 2	🗍	You can use these two buffers to place the current sub-object selection. When a buffer contains a selection, the associated button turns blue.

Paint Store 1/ Paint Store 2		These two tools restores the stored selection, clearing the existing selection. If you want to retain the current selection, click on these buttons with the **Shift** held down.
Add 1+2		It adds the two buffers and applies the selection at the current sub-object level.
Subtract 1-2		It selects non-overlapping area of **Store 1** and also clears both buffers.
Intersect		Selects the overlapping area of **Store 1** and **Store 2**.
Clear		Clears the stored selection.

Sets Panel

The tools in this panel gives you ability to copy and paste the named selection sets between objects. To use these tools, create named selection sets and then use the **Copy** and **Paste** tools from this panel to copy/paste selection from buffer.

By Surface Panel

The **Concave** /**Convex** tools allow you to select sub-objects in the concave or convex area of the mesh [see Figure 31]. The spinner located next to the drop-down allows you to specify the degree of concavity or convexity.

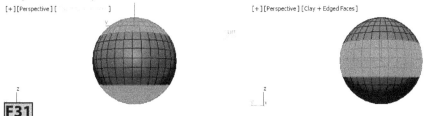

F31

By Normal Panel

The tools in this panel lets you select sub-objects based on their normal directions on the world axes. To make a selection, choose an axis and then set the value for the **Angle** control. You can invert the selection by clicking **Invert**. The selection shown in Figure 32 is created by setting **Angle** to **87** and choosing the **Z** axis.

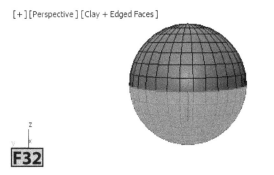

F32

By Perspective Panel

The tools in this panel let you select sub-objects based on the extent they point toward the active view. To make a selection, define an angle using the **Angle** control and then click **Select** [see left image in Figure 33]. If you click **Outline**, 3ds Max selects the outermost sub-objects [see the right image in Figure 33].

By Random Panel

The tools in this panel select sub-objects at random number or percentage. Also, you can grow or shrink the current selection randomly. To make a selection, click **Number** # or **Percent** % to enable random selection by number or percentage and then click **Select** to make the selection from the current settings. The **Select Within Current Selection** option in the **Select** drop-down selects random sub-objects within the current selection [see Figure 34]. **Random Grow** and **Random Shrink** grows or shrinks the selection randomly.

By Half Panel

These tools let you select the half of the mesh on the specified axis based on the area or volume. To select, choose an axis and then click **Select** . To toggle the selection, click **Invert Axis** .

By Pivot Distance Panel

You can use this tool to select the sub-objects based on their distance from the pivot. The **% Pivot** control defines the distance. In Figure 35, the selection is defined by setting the **% Pivot** control to **99.2%.**

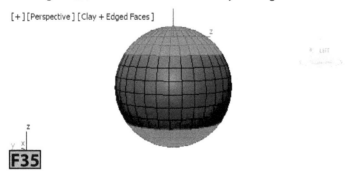

By View Panel

This feature allows you to select and grow sub-objects selection based on the current view. You can specify the distance using the **Grow From Perspective View** control.

By Symmetry Panel

You can use this feature to mirror the current sub-object selection on the specified local axis. This feature works on a symmetrical model. The center of the object is defined by the location of the pivot of the object.

By Color Panel

The options in this panel let you select vertices by color or illumination value. These options are available at only **Vertex** sub-object level. To select vertices, choose **Color** or **Illumination** from the drop-down. Then, use the color swatch to specify a color. Next, click **Select** to select the vertices.

By Numeric Panel

This feature allows you to select vertices by the number of connected edges or number of sides you specify. Figure 36 shows the panel at the **Vertex** and **Polygon** levels, respectively. The selection shown in Figure 37 shows the selection made by specifying number of **Sides** to **4** at the **Polygon** level.

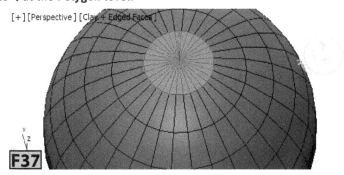

Object Paint Tab

The tools available in this tab [see Figure 38] allow you to paint objects freehand anywhere in the scene or on the target objects. You can paint multiple objects in a specific order or randomly. The objects that you add by painting are not combined with other objects. You can use the **Fill** tool to fill an edge selection with the objects.

To understand the concept, create few primitives in the viewport and then create a teapot [see the left image in Figure 39]. Ensure teapot is selected in a viewport and then click **Paint With Selected Object(s)** from the **Paint Objects** panel. Make sure **Scene** is selected from the **Paint On** drop-down. Set **Spacing** to **15** and then freehand paint on the objects in the scene [see the right image in Figure 39]. RMB click to exit the paint mode.

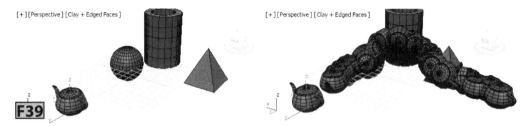

Caution: Exiting the paint mode
You can adjust stroke after painting, therefore, do not RMB click to exit the paint mode until you are satisfied with the result.

You can use the features in the **Object Paint** tab to make creative scenes. You can also use them to populate the scenes with, for example, characters or trees. I would recommend that you practice these tools and then integrate these in your workflow to create creative artwork.

Hands-on Exercises

Complete the following Hands-on Exercises:

1. ***Exercise 9:*** *Creating a Desk*
2. ***Exercise 13:*** *Creating a USB Drive–I*
3. ***Exercise 14:*** *Creating a USB Drive–II*

Summary

This unit provided the introduction to Graphite Modeling Tools in 3ds Max. I have showed how to use polygon modeling tools to efficiently create models. Also, you have leaned various sub-objects learning techniques. The unit covered the following topics:

- Working with the **Graphite Modeling Tools**
- Selecting sub-objects
- Creating models using the tools available in the **Ribbon**

In next unit, I will explain the tools 3ds Max offers for Spline modeling.

Unit M6: Working with Shapes

A shape in 3ds Max is an object consists of one or more lines. These lines which can be 2D or 3D, are used to create components for other objects. 3ds Max provides two types of shape objects **Splines** and **NURBS** curves. Most of the default shapes in 3ds Max are splines in 3ds Max.

3ds Max provides eleven basic spline objects, five extended spline objects, and two types of NURBS curves. You can use these objects in the following ways:

- Generate planar and 3d surfaces
- Paths and shapes for the loft components
- Generate extrusions
- Generate revolved surfaces
- Define motion path for animations

Apart from what mentioned above, you can also render the shape as is. When rendering is enabled for the shapes, 3ds Max renders them using a circular or rectangular cross section.

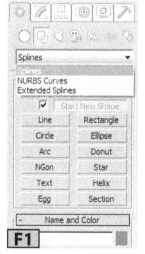

You can convert a basic spline or an extended spline to an editable spline object. This object offers a variety of controls to create less regular and complex shapes. It allows you to edit the shape at the sub-object level. However, when you convert a spline to an **Editable Spline** object, you cannot adjust the creation parameters. The editable spline object will be discussed later in this unit.

Spline and Extended Splines Primitives

You can access the shape creation tools from the **Create** panel. Go to the **Create** panel and then click **Shapes**. A drop-down appears below the **Shapes** button with three entries: **Splines**, **NURBS Curve**, and **Extended Splines** [see Figure 1]. Table 1 summarizes the available tools:

Table 1: The shapes tools available in 3ds Max	
Splines	**Line, Rectangle, Circle, Ellipse, Arc, Donut, NGon, Star, Text, Helix, Egg,** and **Section**
NURBS Curves	**Point Curve** and **CV Curve**
Extended Splines	**WRectangle, Channel, Angle, Tee,** and **Wide Flange**

You can also access these tools from the **Create** menu. If you are using the enhanced menu system, you can access shapes from the **Objects** menu.

Spline Primitives

In this section, I will explain the basic spline primitives. Let's start with the **Line** spline.

Note: AutoGrid

This option allows you to automatically create object on the surface of other objects. It creates a temporary construction plane on the face that you click. The orientation of the plane is dependent on the normals of the face.

Line Spline

A **Line** spline is a free-form spline that is made up of multiple segments. To create a line, go to the **Create** panel, click **Shapes**, and then click **Line** button on the **Object Type** rollout. Notice that various rollouts appear in the **Create** panel. Choose the creation method from the **Creation Method** rollout. Click or drag in the viewport to create the first vertex [If you click, a **Corner** vertex is created otherwise a **Bezier** vertex will be created]. Now, click or drag additional points. To finish the creation method, do one of the following: either right click to create an open spline [see Figure 2] or click on the first vertex and then choose **Yes** from the **Spline** dialog that appears [see Figure 3].

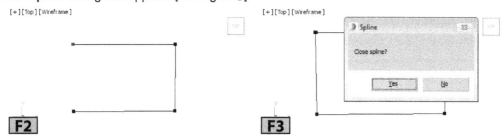

Tip: Constraining new points

*Press and hold **Shift** while creating splines to constrain new points to **90** degrees angle increments. Ensure that you use the default initial type settings.*

Tip: Constraining new points to a custom angle increment

*You can also constrain new points to a custom angle increment value. Choose **Grids And Snaps | Grid And Snap Settings** from the **Tools** menu. In the **Grid and Snap Settings** dialog that appears, choose the **Options** tab and then set a value for the **Angle** spinner. Now, press and hold **Ctrl** while creating new points to constrain them to the value specified for the **Angle** spinner.*

Tip: Panning and orbiting while creating splines

*If a spline requires two or more steps for its creation [such as **Line** or **Donut** spline], you can pan and orbit the viewport between the creation steps.*

Note: Editable Spline object

*3ds Max automatically converts a **Line** spline to an editable spline object because it has no dimensions parameters.*

Now, let's take a look at the various aspects/parameters associated with the **Line** spline. Many of them are common to most of the spline objects.

Combining Shapes While Creating Them

3ds Max allows you to combine shapes to create compound shapes. You can use this feature to create complex shapes. To create a compound shape, on the **Create** panel, turn off the box preceding the **Start**

New Shape button and then begin creating shapes. Each spline that you create added to the compound spline. You can check whether all splines are part of a compound shape or not. Go to the **Modify** panel and then click **Editable Spline** in the modifier stack. You will notice that all splines are selected in the viewport [see Figure 4].

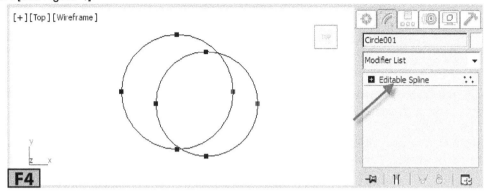

Caution: Parametric nature of splines

You cannot change creation parameters of a compound shape. For example, if you first created a circle, and then added a rectangle to create a compound shapes, you cannot switch back and change the creation parameters of the circle.

Creation Method Rollout

The controls in this rollout allow you to specify what type of vertex that will be created when you click or drag vertices in the viewport. The creation method options for the **Line** spline are different from other spline primitives.

Table 2 summarizes the controls available in the **Creation Method** rollout.

Table 2: Controls in the **Creation Method** rollout of the **Line** spline	
[Group]/Control	**Description**
[Initial Type Group]	The controls in this group set the type of vertex created when you click [not drag] a vertex location.
Corner	**Corner** creates sharp points and spline created is linear to either side of the point.
Smooth	**Smooth** creates a smooth curve through the vertex that you can adjust manually. The curvature of the spline segment is controlled by the spacing of the vertices. Figure 5 shows the splines created using the **Corner** [left image] and **Smooth** [right image] initial type options.
[Drag Type Group]	The controls in this group define the type of vertex created when you drag a vertex location.
Corner, Smooth	The **Corner** and **Smooth** controls work as discussed above.
Bezier	The **Bezier** control produces a smooth adjustable curve. The amount of curvature and direction of the curve are controlled by the dragging the mouse at each vertex. You can manually change the smoothness or curvature by manipulating the vertex handles [refer third image in Figure 6].

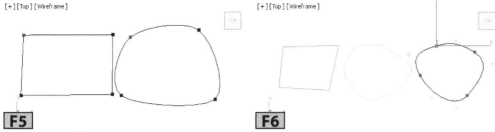

Keyboard Entry Rollout

You can use the **Keyboard Entry** rollout to precisely place vertices of a spline. To add a vertex, enter its coordinates in the **X**, **Y**, and **Z** spinners and then click **Add Point** to add a new point.

The subsequent points you insert will be added to the existing line until you click **Close** or **Finish**. **Close** closes the shape whereas **Finish** completes the line without closing it.

Rendering Rollout

The options in this rollout lets you toggle the shape renderability in the viewports as well as in the rendered output. You can also generate the mapping coordinates. You can convert the mesh displayed in the viewport to an editable mesh or editable poly object.

Table 3 summarizes the controls available in the **Rendering** rollout.

Table 3: Controls in the **Rendering** rollout of the **Line** spline	
Control	**Description**
Enable In Renderer	Turn on the **Enable In Renderer** to render the shape as 3D mesh using the **Radial** or **Rectangular** parameters set for the renderer. When on, **Renderer** gets selected in this rollout. Now, you have two options for controlling the size of the mesh: **Radial** and **Rectangular**. **Radial** renders the shape with a circular cross section whereas **Rectangular** displays the mesh of the spline as a rectangle. Figure 7 shows the spline shape with the circular cross section on rendering [**Thickness=2, Sides=12**]. Figure 8 shows the mesh with the rectangular cross section [**Length=6, Width=2**].
Enable In Viewport, Use Viewport Settings	Turn on **Enable In Viewport** to display the shape in the viewport as 3D mesh with circular or rectangular cross section [see Figures 9 and 10]. Turn on **Use Viewport Settings** to display the mesh using the **Viewport** settings. When on, **Viewport** is activated and then you can use the **Viewport** settings to control the appearance of mesh of the spline in the viewport.
Generate Mapping Coords	Turn on **Generate Mapping Coords** to apply mapping coordinates to the spline mesh. 3ds Max generates coordinates in **U** and **V** directions. The **U** coordinate wraps around the spline whereas the **V** coordinate is mapped along the length of the spline.
Real-World Map Size	The **Real-World Map Size** switch will only be available if you turn on **Generate Mapping Coords**. This control allows the scaling of textures applied to the object.

Auto Smooth	**Auto Smooth** is turned on by default. The spline is automatically smoothed using the threshold value defined by the **Threshold** spinner available below **Auto Smooth**. This value is an angle measured in degrees.

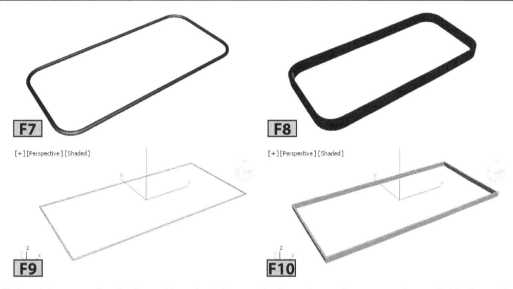

Radial and Rectangular Options: Now, let's have a look at the various controls available for radial and rectangular cross sections. Table 4 summarizes these controls.

Table 4: Various controls available for radial and rectangular cross sections

Control	Description
Thickness	Controls the diameter of the rendered spline mesh. Figure 11 shows the splines rendered with **Thickness** value set to **0.5** and **1**, respectively.
Sides	Controls the number of sides [or facets] of the mesh. Figure 12 shows the splines rendered with the **Sides** value set to **4** and **62**, respectively.
Angle	It controls the orientation of the rendered cross section. Figure 13 shows the splines rendered with the **Angle** value set to **0** and **60**, respectively.
Length	Controls the size of the cross section along the local Y-axis.
Width	Controls the size of the cross section along the local X-axis.
Aspect	It controls the aspect ratio of width to length. If the **Lock** button next to the spinner is active, adjusting length or width automatically adjusts the other to maintain the aspect ratio.

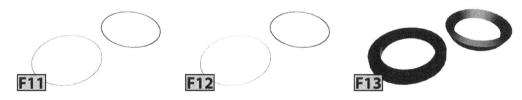

Interpolation Rollout

The controls on this rollout allow you to adjust the smoothness of a curve. Each spline segment is made up of divisions called steps. Higher the number of steps, smoother the curve will be. By default, **Optimize** is on. When on, 3ds Max removes the steps that are not necessary. When **Adaptive** is on, the **Steps** control becomes inactive. It sets the number of steps for each spline to produce smooth looking result. Figure 14 shows the wireframe view of the spline mesh created using the **Optimize** and **Adaptive** splines.

Note: Adaptive
*When **Adaptive** is on, the straight segments get zero steps.*

[+][Perspective][Wireframe]

F14

Creation Method Rollout

Many spline shapes in 3ds Max allow you to use a creation method. You have already worked on the **Line** spline's creation methods. The **Text** and **Star** splines do not have a **Creation Method** rollout. Most of the spline primitives have **Edge** and **Center** creation methods. If the **Edge** method is selected, the first click defines a point on the side or at a corner of the shape and then you drag a diameter or drag to a diagonal point. In the **Center** method, the first click defines the center of the shape and then you drag a corner point or radius.

Rectangle Spline

It creates square or rectangular splines [see Figure 15]. If you want to create a square spline, press and hold **Ctrl** while dragging in a viewport. To create a rectangular spline, first select a creation method and then drag the mouse pointer in a viewport to create a rectangle.

Table 5 summarizes the controls available in the **Parameters** rollout of the **Rectangular** spline:

Table 5: Controls in the **Parameters** rollout of the **Rectangular** spline	
Control	**Description**
Length, Width	The **Length** and **Width** controls specify the size of the rectangle along the **Y** and **X** axes, respectively.
Corner Radius	The **Corner Radius** control allows you to create rounded corners.

Circle Spline

It allows you to create close circular splines made up of four vertices [see Figure 16]. To create a circular spline, first select the creation method and then drag the mouse pointer in a viewport to draw a circle. Table 6 summarizes the controls available in the **Parameters** rollout of the **Circle** spline:

Table 6: Controls in the **Parameters** rollout of the **Circle** spline	
Control	**Description**
Radius	The **Radius** control specifies the center to edge distance of the circle.

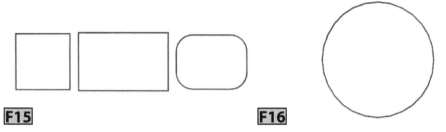

F15   F16

Ellipse Spline
You can use it to create circular or elliptical splines [see Figure 17]. If you want to create a circular spline, press and hold **Ctrl** while dragging in the viewport. To create an elliptical spline, first select the creation method and then drag the mouse pointer in the viewport to draw the ellipse.

Table 7 summarizes the controls available in the **Parameters** rollout of the **Ellipse** spline:

Table 7: Controls in the **Parameters** rollout of the **Ellipse** spline	
Control	**Description**
Length, Width	The **Length** and **Width** controls specify the size of the ellipse along the local **Y** and **Z** axes, respectively.

Arc Spline
You can use the **Arc** spline to create open and closed partial circles made up of four vertices [see Figure 18].

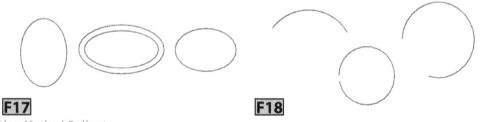

F17   F18

Creation Method Rollout
The **Arc** spline provides two methods for creating arcs: **End-End-Middle** and **Center-End-End**. To create an arc using the **End-End-Middle** method, make sure **End-End-Middle** is selected in the **Creation Method** Rollout and then drag in the viewport to define the two ends of the arc. Now, release the mouse button. Move the mouse pointer up or down to specify the third point between the two end points.

To create an arc using the **Center-End-End** method, make sure **Center-End-End** is selected in the **Creation Method** rollout and then click to set the radial center of the arc. Drag the mouse pointer and click to specify the start point of the arc. Now, move the mouse and click to specify the other end of the arc.
Table 8 summarizes the controls available in the **Parameters** rollout of the **Arc** spline:

Table 8: Controls in the **Parameters** rollout of the **Arc** spline	
Control	**Description**
Radius	**Radius** specifies the radius of the arc.
From, To	**From** specifies the location of the start point which is measured as angle from the local positive Y-axis. To specifies the location of the end point which is measured as angle from the local positive X-axis.
Pie Slice	When **Pie Slice** is on, it creates straight segments from the endpoints to the radial center which results in closed spline [see Figure 19].
Reverse	When **Reverse** is on, the direction of the **Arc** spline is reversed.

Donut Spline

It creates the donut like shape of two concentric circles [see Figure 20]. To create a **Donut** spline, first select a creation method. Drag the mouse pointer and then release the mouse button to define the first circle of the donut. Move the mouse pointer and then click to define the second concentric donut circle.

F19   F20

Table 9 summarizes the controls available in the **Parameters** rollout of the **Donut** spline:

Table 9: Controls in the **Parameters** rollout of the **Donut** spline	
Controls	**Description**
Radius 1, Radius 2	The **Radius 1** and **Radius 2** controls specify the radius of the first and second circle, respectively.

NGon Spline

It creates flat sided splines with N number of sides and vertices [see Figure 21]. To create an **NGon** spline, select a creation method and then drag the mouse pointer in a viewport. Release the mouse button to create the spline.

Table 10 summarizes the controls available in the **Parameters** rollout of the **NGon** spline:

Table 10: Controls in the **Parameters** rollout of the **NGon** spline	
Control	**Description**
Radius, Inscribed, Circumscribed	The **Radius** control specifies the distance from the radial center to the edge of the NGon. If **Inscribed** is on [default], the distance is measured from the radial center to the corners. If **Circumscribed** is on, the distance is from the radial center to the side centers.
Sides	Sides specifies the number of sides which range from **3** to **100**.
Corner Radius	**Corner Radius** controls rounding applied to the corners of the NGon.
Circular	When **Circular** is on, 3ds Max creates a circular NGon which is equivalent to a circular spline but it may contain more than four vertices. The **Circle** spline creates a circular spline object with four control vertices.

Star Spline

It creates closed star-shaped splines with any number of points [see Figure 22]. To create Star spline, drag the mouse pointer and then release the mouse button to define the first radius. Move the mouse pointer and then click to define the second radius. The second radius can be less, equal, or greater than the first radius depending on how you moved the mouse pointer.

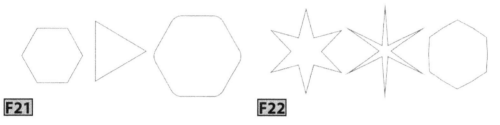

F21   F22

Table 11 summarizes the controls available in the **Parameters** rollout of the **Star** spline:

Table 11: Controls in the **Parameters** rollout of the **Star** spline	
Control	**Description**
Radius 1, Radius 2	The **Radius 1** and **Radius 2** controls specify the first set of vertices [created with the first drag] and second set of vertices, respectively.
Points	**Points** controls the number of points on the star. **Dissertation** control allows you to produce a sawtooth effect. This effect is generated by rotating the **Radius 2** vertices about the center of the star.
Fillet Radius 1, Fillet Radius 2	**Fillet Radius 1** and **Fillet Radius 2** controls let you smooth the first and second set of vertices, respectively. The rounding is created by producing two **Bezier** vertices per point.

Text Spline

It creates splines in the shape of the text [see Figure 23]. The text can be created using any **Windows** font [both **TrueType** and **OpenType**] installed on your system as well using the **Type 1 PostScript** font installed in the **Fonts** folder of the 3ds Max installation folder.

To create text, enter the text in the **Text** text box and then either click in a viewport to place the text or drag the mouse pointer to place the text in a viewport and then release the mouse button.

Table 12 summarizes the controls available in the **Parameters** rollout of the **Text** spline:

Table 12: Controls in the **Parameters** rollout of the **Text** spline	
Control	**Description**
Text Controls	From this rollout, you can choose the font, font size, alignment, kerning [distance between letters], and leading [distance between lines] for the text that you enter in the **Text** text box. The **Text** text box does not support word-wrap however you can paste multiple lines from the clipboard.

Helix Spline

It creates spiral like shapes [see Figure 24]. To create a **Helix** spline, click and drag the mouse pointer to set the starting point as well as its starting radius [**Center Creation** method] or diameter [**Edge Creation** method]. Now, move the mouse pointer vertically and then click to define the height. Move the mouse pointer and then click to define the end radius.

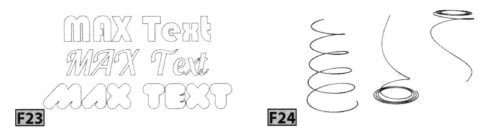

F23   **F24**

Table 13 summarizes the controls available in the **Parameters** rollout of the **Helix** spline:

Table 13: Controls in the **Parameters** rollout of the **Helix** spline	
Control	**Description**
Radius 1, Radius 2	The **Radius 1** and **Radius 2** controls specify the radius of helix start and end, respectively. **Height** controls the height of the helix.
Turns	Turns specifies the number of turns in the helix.
Bias	**Bias** forces the turns in the helix to accumulate at the one end of the helix. Figure 25 shows the rendered helix with Bias set to **-1**, **0.2**, and **1**, respectively.
CC and CCW	**CC** and **CCW** specify whether helix should turn clockwise or counterclockwise.

Egg Spline

It creates an egg shaped spline [see Figure 26]. To create an **Egg** spline, drag the mouse pointer vertically to define the initial dimension of the egg. Now, drag horizontally to change the orientation [angle] of the egg. Release the mouse button to compete the creation process.

F25   F26

Table 14 summarizes the controls available in the **Parameters** rollout of the **Egg** spline:

Table 14: Controls in the **Parameters** rollout of the **Egg** spline	
Controls	**Description**
Length, Width	The **Length** and **Width** controls specify the length and width of the egg along its long and short axes, respectively.
Outline, Thickness	When **Outline** is on, **Thickness** sets the distance between the main shape of the egg and its outline.
Angle	**Angle** specifies the angle of rotation around shape's local Z axis. When **Angle** is equal to **0**, the narrow end of the egg is at the top.

Section Spline

The **Section** spline is a special type of spline that lets you generate splines based on a cross-sectional slice through a geometry objects. To create a **Section** shape, click **Section** from the **Object Type** rollout and then drag a section plane in the viewport. Now, place and orient the plane in the viewport using transformation tools [see Figure 27]. Notice a yellow line is displayed where the section intersects the mesh. Now, on the **Section Parameters** rollout of the **Command Panel**, click **Create Shape**. In the **Name Section Shape** dialog that appears, type the name for the spline and then click **OK**. Now, select the shape in the **Scene Explorer** and then move it away using the **Move Tool** [see Figure 28].

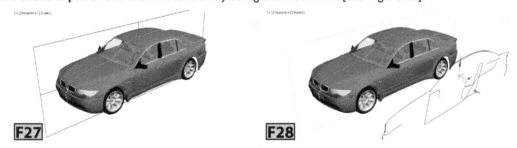

F27   F28

Table 15 summarizes the controls available in the **Section Parameters** rollout of the **Section** spline.

Table 15: Controls in the **Section Parameters** rollout of the **Section** spline	
[Group]/Control	**Description**
Create Shape	When you click this button, a shape is created based on the currently displayed intersection lines. The shape generated is an editable spline.

[Update]	The controls in this group specify when the intersection line is updated.
When Section Moves	It updates the intersection line when you move or resize the section shape.
When Section Selected	It updates the intersection line when you select the section shape. Click **Update Section** to update the intersection.
Manually	It updates the intersection line only when you click **Update Section**.
[Section Events]	These controls let you specify the extents of the cross section.
Infinite	When on, the selected plane is infinite in all directions [see Figure 29].
Section Boundary	When on, the cross section is generated only for objects that are within or touched by the boundary of the section shape [see Figure 30].
Off	No cross section is displayed or generated.
Color Swatch	You can use it to change the display color of the intersection.

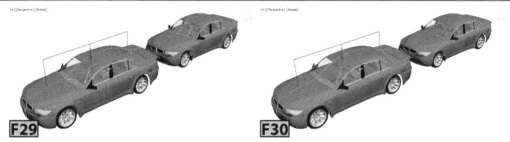

Section Size Rollout

The **Length** and **Width** controls in the **Section Size** rollout control the size of the section rectangle.

Extended Spline Primitives

In this section, I will explain the extended spline primitives. Let's start with the **WRectangle** spline.

WRectangle Spline

This **WRectangle** spline [walled rectangle] lets you create a closed shape from two concentric rectangles. Each rectangle is made up of four vertices [see Figure 31]. To create a **WRectangle** spline, drag the mouse pointer in a viewport and then release the mouse button to define the outer rectangle. Move the mouse pointer and then click to define the inner rectangle.

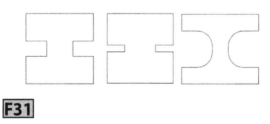

Table 16 summarizes the controls available in the **Parameters** rollout of the **WRectangle** spline.

Table 16: Controls in the **Parameters** rollout of the **WRectangle** spline	
Control	**Description**
Length, Width	These controls define the length and width of the **WRectangle** section.
Thickness	Controls the thickness of the **WRectangle** section.
Sync Corner Fillets	When on, the value specified for **Corner Radius 1** is used for both the interior and exterior corners.
Corner Radius 1	When **Sync Corner Fillets** is off, it controls the radius of the exterior corners.
Corner Radius 2	This control is only available when **Sync Corner Fillets** is off. It controls the radius of the interior corners.

Channel Spline

It creates a closed C shaped spline [see Figure 32]. To create a **Channel** spline, drag the mouse pointer in a viewport and then release the mouse button to define the outer perimeter. Move the mouse pointer and then click to define the thickness of the walls of the channel.

Table 17 summarizes the controls available in the **Parameters** rollout of the **Channel** spline.

Table 17: Controls in the **Parameters** rollout of the **Channel** spline	
Control	**Description**
Length, Width	These controls define the length and width of the channel section.
Thickness	Controls the thickness of the channel section.
Sync Corner Fillets	When on, the value specified for **Corner Radius 1** is used for both the interior and exterior corners.
Corner Radius 1	When **Sync Corner Fillets** is off, it controls the radius of the exterior corners.
Corner Radius 2	This control is only available when **Sync Corner Fillets** is off. It controls the radius of the interior corners.

Angle Spline

It creates a closed L shaped spline [see Figure 33]. To create an **Angle** spline, drag the mouse pointer in a viewport and then release the mouse button to define the initial size of the angle. Move the mouse pointer and then click to define the thickness of the walls of the angle. Table 18 summarizes the controls available in the **Parameters** rollout of the **WRectangle** spline.

F32   F33

Table 18: Controls in the **Parameters** rollout of the **Angle** spline	
Control	Description
Length, Width	These controls define the height and width of the vertical leg and horizontal legs, respectively.
Thickness	Controls the thickness of the legs of the angle.
Sync Corner Fillets	When on, the value specified for **Corner Radius 1** controls the radius for both the vertical and horizontal legs.
Corner Radius 1	When **Sync Corner Fillets** is off, it controls the exterior radius between the vertical and horizontal legs of the spline.
Corner Radius 2	This control is only available when **Sync Corner Fillets** is off. It controls the interior radius between the vertical and horizontal legs of the spline.
Edge Radii	Controls the interior radius at the outermost edges of the vertical and horizontal legs.

Tee Spline

It creates a closed T shaped spline [see Figure 34]. To create a **Tee** spline, drag the mouse pointer in a viewport and then release the mouse button to define the initial size of the tee.

Move the mouse pointer and then click to define the thickness of the walls of the tee.

Table 19 summarizes the controls available in the **Parameters** rollout of the **Tee** spline.

Table 19: Controls in the **Parameters** rollout of the **Tee** spline	
Control	Description
Length, Width	These controls define the height and width of the vertical web and flange crossing, respectively.
Thickness	Controls the thickness of the web and flange.
Corner Radius	Controls the radius of the two interior corners between the vertical web and horizontal flange.

Wide Flange Spline

It creates a closed I shaped spline [see Figure 35]. To create a **Wide Flange** spline, drag the mouse pointer in a viewport and then release the mouse button to define the initial size of the wide flange. Move the mouse pointer and then click to define the thickness of the walls of the wide flange.

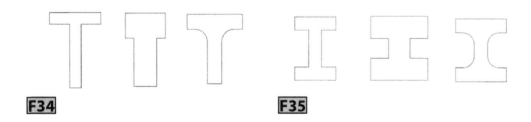

F34   F35

Table 20 summarizes the controls available in the **Parameters** rollout of the **Wide Flange** spline.

Table 20: Controls in the **Parameters** rollout of the **Tee** spline	
Controls	**Description**
Length, Width	These controls define the height and width of the vertical web and horizontal flange crossing, respectively.
Thickness	Controls the thickness of the wide flenges.
Corner Radius	Controls the radius of the two interior corners between the vertical web and horizontal flanges.

Editing Splines

You can convert a spline object to an editable spline object. The editable spline object allows you to create complex shapes using the three sub-object levels that this object provides: **Vertex**, **Spline**, and **Segment**.

The vertices define points and curve tangents. The segments connects vertices. The splines are made up of one or more connected segments.

You can convert a spline object to the editable spline object by using one of the following methods:

1. Select a spline in a viewport and then go to the **Modify** panel. Next, RMB click on the spline entry in the stack display and then choose **Convert To: Editable Spline** from the pop up menu displayed [see Figure 36].
2. Select a spline in a viewport and then RMB click. Choose **Transform [in lower right quadrant] | Convert To: | Convert to Editable Spline** [see Figure 37].
3. Select a spline in a viewport and then apply the **Edit Spline** modifier to it.
4. Import a **.shp** file to the scene.
5. Merge a shape from a 3ds Max file.

Note: Edit Spline modifier
*You can also use the **Edit Spline** modifier to convert a spline to the editable spline object. However, when you convert a spline to the editable spline object, you lose the creation parameters of the spline.*

Note: Line spline
*By default, the **Line** spline to an editable spline object because it has no dimensions parameters. Therefore, you don't need to convert a **Line** spline to the editable spline object.*

Note: Compound Shapes
A compound shape made up of two or more splines is automatically an editable spline object.

Selecting Sub-objects

You can select sub-objects using one of the following ways:

1. Expand the spline object's hierarchy from the stack display and then choose a sub-object level [see Figure 38].

2. Click a selection button from the **Selection** rollout [see Figure 38].
3. RMB click on a spline object in a viewport and then choose the sub-object level from the upper left quadrant of the **Quad** menu displayed [see Figure 39].
4. Choose a selection or transform tool and then click on the sub-objects in a viewport using the standard selection techniques.

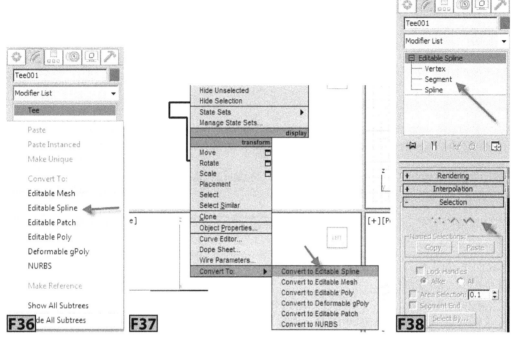

Note: Cloning sub-objects
*You can clone the sub-objects by first selecting them and then press and hold **Shift** while transforming them.*

Note: Adding and removing from the selection
*To select a segment, vertex, or spline, click it. To add to the sub-object selection, press and hold **Ctrl** and click. You can also drag a selection region to select a group of sub-objects. To subtract from the sub-object selection, press and hold **Alt** and click. You can also drag a selection region to deselect a group of sub-objects.*

Vertex Level

Vertices define points and curve tangents for a spline object. To select a vertex type, select vertex or vertices and then RMB click. Now, choose the required level from the upper left quadrant of the **Quad** menu [see Figure 40].

Table 21 shows the list of vertex types available in 3ds Max.

Table 21: The vertex types	
Type	**Description**
Corner	Creates non-adjustable vertices that generates sharp corners [see Figure 41].

Bezier	Creates adjustable vertices with locked continuous tangent handles that produces a smooth curve. The curvature is determined by the direction and magnitude of the tangent handles [see Figure 42]. You can adjust the tangent handles using the **Select and Move** and **Select and Rotate** tools.
Bezier Corner	Creates adjustable vertices with discontinuous tangent handles that produces a sharp corner [see Figure 43]. The curvature is determined by the direction and magnitude of the tangent handles. You can adjust the tangent handles using the **Select and Move** and **Select and Rotate** tools.
Smooth	Creates non-adjustable vertices that generates smooth continuous curves. The curvature is determined by the spacing between the adjacent vertices [see Figure 44].

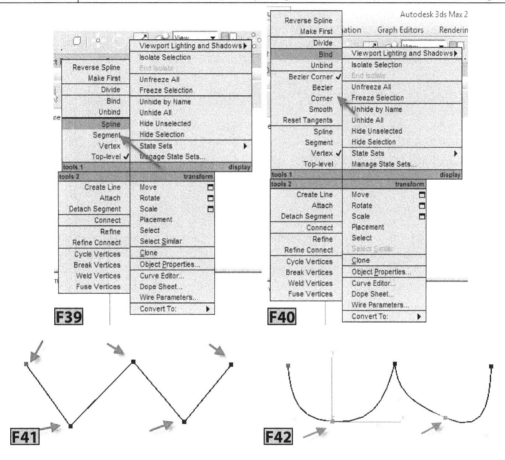

Tip: Resetting tangents

*To reset the tangent position, RMB click on the vertex or vertices and then choose **Reset Tangents** from the upper left quadrant of the **Quad** menu.*

Tip: Vertex types in the Quad menu

*If you are at **Vertex** sub-object level, the vertex types are always displayed in the **Quad** menu. The mouse pointer doesn't have to be exactly over the vertices.*

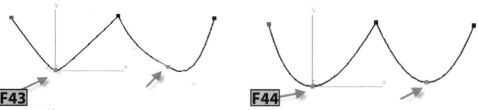

Geometry Rollout

Now, let's explore the options available for editing the editable spline object at sub-object level. These options are listed in the **Geometry** rollout.

New Vertex Type Group

The controls in this group lets you choose the type of tangency for vertices that are created when you clone segments or splines using the **Shift** key.

Caution: Scope

*These controls have no effect on the tangency of the vertices created using tools such as **Create Line**, **Refine**, and so forth. **Linear** sets linear tangency for the new vertices. **Smooth** sets smooth tangency. When on, the new overlapping vertices will be welded together. **Bezier Corner** sets the **Bezier** corner tangency.*

Note: Editable Spline - Object Level

*The following controls are also available at the editable spline object level: **New Vertex Type** group, **Create Line**, **Attach**, **Attach Mult.**, **Cross Section**, **Automatic Welding**, and **Insert**. This level is the one that is active when no sub-object level is selected.*

Create Line

Create Line adds more lines to the existing selected spline. The lines are separate splines but are part of the selected spline. To add another spline to the selected spline, select the existing spline and then create the new spline in the same way as you create the line spline.

Break

Break allows you to split a spline at the selected vertex or vertices. To split a spline, select on or more vertices and then click **Break**. Two overlapping vertices will be created at the break point. Use the **Select and Move** tool to separate the vertices [see Figure 45].

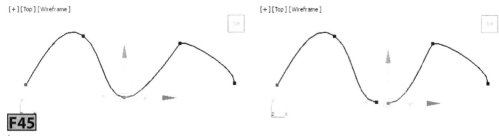

Attach

Attach attaches another spline object from the scene to the selected spline to create a compound shape. To attach a spline, select the spline and then click **Attach**. Now, hover the mouse pointer on the target spline. When the shape of the mouse pointer changes, click on the target spline to attach it to the selected spline.

When you attach shapes, the materials assigned to the two objects are combined. Here's how:

- If the target object does not have a material assigned, it inherits the material from the selected object.
- If the selected object does not have a material assigned, it inherits the material from the target object.
- If both objects have materials, the **Attach Options** dialog appears [see Figure 46]. Select the desired options from the dialog and then click **OK**. The resulting material will be a **Multi-Subobject** material.
-

Caution: Target shape's creation parameters
The target shape loses all its creation parameters. If there is any modifier stack attached to the target shape, it will be collapsed.

Attach Multiple

Attach Multiple lets you attach multiple shapes to a selected spline in a single operation. To understand this feature, select a spline object and then click **Attach Multiple**. Now, select the shapes in the **Attach Multiple** dialog that appears [see Figure 47] and click **OK** to attach the selected shapes.

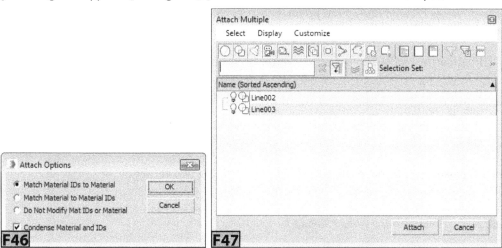

Note: Reorienting attached splines
*When **Reorient** is on, the attached splines are reoriented so that the local coordinate system of the attached splines is aligned with the selected spline.*

Cross Section

Cross Section allows you to create a spline cage out of cross sectional shapes. To create spline cage, make sure that all splines are attached. Click **Cross Section** and then click on the first spline, then second, and so forth. RMB click to complete the process and create a cage [see Figure 48].

Tip: Keeping vertices together
*If you want to edit the spline cage, turn on **Area Selection** in the **Selection** rollout before selecting the vertices otherwise you would not be able to keep their position together. In Figure 49, the vertex shown in the right is selected after turning on **Area Selection** from the **Selection** rollout.*

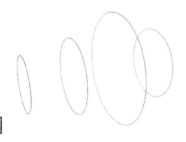 

F48

Refine

Refine adds vertices to the spline object without changing the curvature of the spline. To add vertices, click **Refine** and then hover the mouse pointer on the segments in a viewport. The shape of the mouse pointer changes on the eligible segments. Now, click to add a vertex. When you are done, click **Refine** again or press RMB.

If you click on an existing vertex, 3ds Max displays a dialog asking if you want to refine the vertex or connect to the vertex. If you choose **Connect Only**, a new vertex will not be created instead the clicked vertex will be connected to the existing vertex.

The type of vertex created during the **Refine** operation is dependent on the bordering vertices of the segment:

- If bordering vertices are smooth, a vertex of **Smooth** type is created.
- If bordering vertices are of **Corner** type, a vertex of **Corner** type is created.
- If either of the bordering vertices are of a **Corner** or **Bezier Corner** type, a vertex of **Bezier Corner** type is created.
- If the bordering vertices do not fit in the above mentioned criterion, a vertex of Bezier type is created.

Connect: It creates a new spline sub-object by connecting the two vertices.

Caution: Connecting vertices
You must turn on **Connect** *before clicking* **Refine**.

To understand functioning of **Connect**, create two straight lines in a viewport and attach them [see Figure 50]. Select **Vertex** sub-object level. Turn on **Connect**. Notice that there are some options that get activated in the **Refine** group. Now, click **Refine** and then click on the first segment. Now, click on the second segment [see Figure 51], RMB click to create to connect two vertices [see Figure 52].

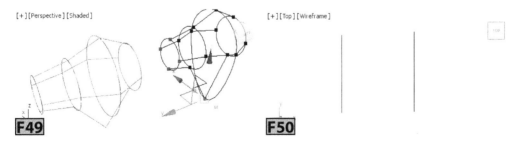

When **Linear** is on, the **Refine** operation creates straight lines using the vertices of **Corner** type. When off, the created vertices are of **Smooth** type. **Closed** allows you to create closed splines by connecting the first and last vertices [see Figure 53, the numbers show clicking order].

When **Bind first** is on, it sets the first vertex created to be bound to the center of the selected segment [see Figure 54]. **Bind last** sets the last vertex created to be bound to the center of the selected segment.

Note: Bound vertices

*To distinguish the bound vertices from the standard vertices, 3ds Max makes them black. You cannot transform a bound vertex directly. However, you can move it by shifting the connected vertices. You can also change the type of the bound vertices from the upper left quadrant of the **Quad** menu.*

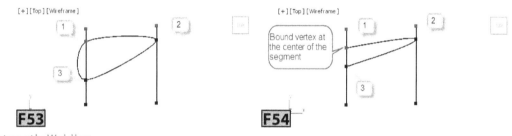

Automatic Welding

When on, the end vertices are welded together automatically, if the end vertices fall within a distance specified using **Threshold**.

Note: Automatic welding

This feature is available at the object and all sub-object levels.

Weld

Weld welds two end vertices or two adjacent vertices into a single vertex. To weld vertices, move the vertices close to each other and click **Weld**. If the vertices fall within a threshold defined by the control next to **Weld**, the selected vertices are welded to a single vertex [see Figure 55].

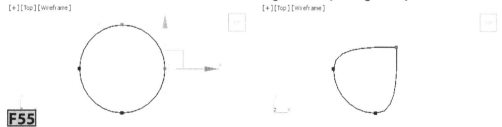

Connect

Connect connects two end vertices. To connect the vertices, click **Connect** and then drag the mouse pointer from one end vertex to another end vertex.

Insert

Insert lets you add one or more vertices creating additional segments in a spline. Click **Insert** and then click on the spline to attach the mouse pointer to the spline. Now, click to place the vertex. You can continue creating vertices. RMB click to end the operation. A single click create a corner vertex whereas dragging the mouse pointer creates a Bezier vertex.

Make First

It allows you to define which vertex in a spline is the first vertex. The first vertex in a spline is indicated by a small box around it. To make a vertex first vertex, select the vertex and then click **Make First**. If you are editing an open spline, the first vertex should be end point that is already not a first vertex. On closed spline, you can make any vertex first vertex.

The first vertex has special significance in many operations in 3ds Max. I will discuss the first vertex usages in the later units. Table 22 summarizes the importance of first vertex:

Table 22: First vertex use	
Use	**Description**
Loft Path	Indicates the start of the path [Level 0].
Loft Shape	Controls the initial skin alignment.
Path Constraint	Indicates the start of the path [indicates 0% on the location of the path].
Trajectory	Indicates the first position key.

Fuse

Fuse lets you move all selected vertices to their average center. To fuse the vertices, select them and then click **Fuse** to move the vertices to same location [see Figure 56]. Note that the **Fuse** operation does not weld the vertices, it simply moves them to same location.

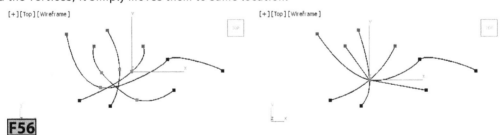

F56

Cycle

Cycle allows you to select a specific vertex from the group of coincident vertices [vertices that shares the same location]. To select a specific vertex, select one or more vertices that share the same location, and then click **Cycle** repeatedly until you select the vertex you are looking for.

CrossInsert

CrossInsert adds vertices at the intersection of two splines that are part of the same spline object. To add vertex, click **CrossInsert** and then click at the intersection of the two splines. If the distance between the splines is within the threshold defined by the control next to **CrossInsert**, the vertices are added to both splines [see Figure 57].

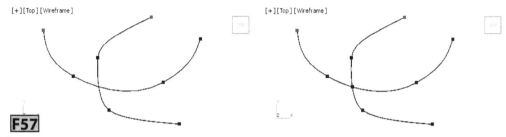

F57

Fillet

Fillet lets you create the rounded corners by adding new control vertices. You can created rounded corners by dragging the mouse pointer in a viewport or by entering precise values in the control on the right of **Fillet**. To fillet the vertices, click **Fillet** and then drag the vertices in a viewport to add rounded corners. As you drag with **Fillet**, the control on its right updated the fillet amount [see Figure 58]. You can continue dragging to add fillet to other vertices. To finish the operation, RMB click.

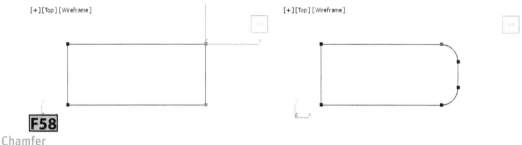

F58

Chamfer

Chamfer chops off the selected vertices by creating segments connecting new vertices [see Figure 59]. Like **Fillet** you can chamfer edges interactively or by entering precise values.

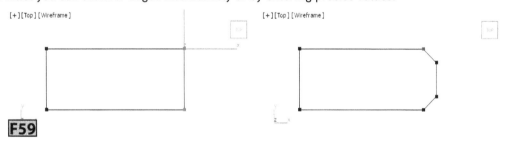

F59

Tangent

The controls available in this group let you copy paste vertex handles from one vertex to another. To copy tangent, select a vertex and then click **Copy**. Click on the tangent to copy tangent to the clipboard. Now, select another vertex, click **Paste**, and then click on the tangent of the vertex to paste the tangent [see Figure 60]. When **Paste Length** is on, the length of the handle is also copied.

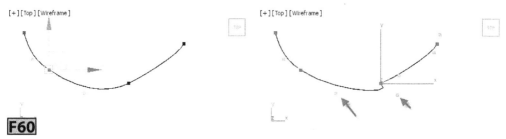

F60

Hide
Hide
It allows you to hide the selected vertices and connected segments.

Unhide All
Unhide All allows you to unhide all hidden objects.

Bind
Bind lets you create bound vertices. Refer the **Refine** section for understanding the bound vertices.

Unbind
Unbind lets you disconnect the bind vertices.

Delete
Allows you to delete the selected vertices as well as one attached segment per deleted vertex.

Show selected segs
Lets you display the selected segments in red color at the **Vertex** sub-object level [see Figure 61]. When off, the segments displayed in red only at **Segment** sub-object level.

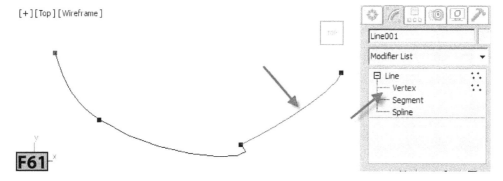

F61

Segment Level
A segment is a part of spline between two vertices of the spline. You can select one or more segments by activating the **Segment** sub-object level. Once selected, you can transform them using the transformation tools.

Most of the controls available for segments are similar to those discussed in the **Vertex Level** section. The other controls available at the segment sub-object level are discussed next.

Divide

Divide subdivides the selected segment(s) by adding a number of vertices that are specified by using the spinner available on the right of this spinner. To subdivide a segment, select segment or segments of the spline. Now, specify the number of vertices and then click **Divide** [see Figure 62]. The distance between the vertices is dependent on the curvature of the segment.

F62

Delete

Deletes the selected segments from the spline [see Figure 63].

F63

Detach

It lets you detach/copy selected segments from the spline. To detach segment or segments, select them and then click **Detach**. In the **Detach** dialog, type name in the **Detach as** text box and then click **OK**. The segment will be detached from the spline and new shape will be created [see Figure 64].

F64

There are some other controls that can be used with the detach operation. Table 23 summarizes these options.

Table 23: The Detach options	
Control	**Description**
Same Shp	When on, **Reorient** gets deactivated. The detached segment remains part of the same spline. If **Copy** is also on, the detached segment is copied at the same location.

Reorient	When on, the detached segment copies the transformation values of the spline's creation local coordinate system.
Copy	Copies the selected segment without detaching it from the spline.

Surface Properties Layout

The controls in this section allow you to apply different material IDs to spline segments. The material appears on the renderable shapes. To assign material ID to a segment or segments, select them and then enter the **ID** in the **Set ID** spinner. **Select ID** lets you select the segments corresponding to the material ID set in the spinner on the right of **Select ID**. The drop-down below **Select ID** shows the name of the sub-materials, if you have applied **Multi-Subobject** material to the object. If you have applied a material other than the **Multi-Sub-object** material, this drop-down will be inactive.

When **Clear Selection** is on, selecting a new ID or material name deselects the previously selected segments or splines.

Changing Segment Properties

You can switch the between the **Curve** or **Line type** for the selected segments. To change the type, select segments and then RMB click. Now, choose **Line** or **Curve** from the upper left quadrant of the **Quad** menu [see Figure 65]. Figure 66 shows a segment converted from the **Curve type** to **Line** type.

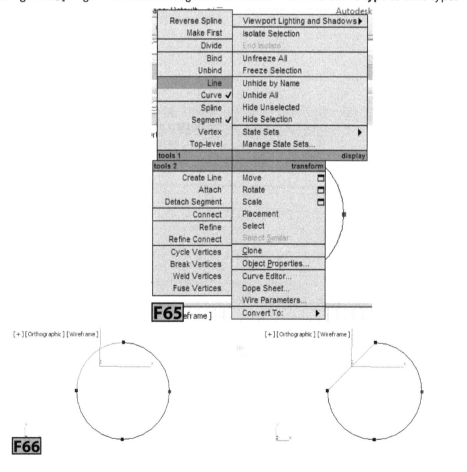

Spline Level

The **Spline** sub-object level allows you to select single spline or multiple splines in a single object. Once selected, you can transform them using the transformation tools. Most of the controls available for segments are similar to those discussed in the **Vertex Level** and **Segment Level** sections. The other controls available at the segment sub-object level are discussed next.

Geometry Rollout
Connect Copy Group

Connect Copy works when you make a clone of the spline using **Shift**. You must turn on **Connect Copy** before the cloning operation. When on, 3ds Max creates a new spline sub-object that connects the vertices of the original and cloned objects [see Figure 67]. **Threshold** defines the distance that the soft selection uses during the **Connect Copy** operation.

F67

Outline

Outline makes a copy of the spline. The copy offsets in all directions specified by the spinner on the right of **Outline**. You can also create an outline interactively by using the mouse. To create an outline, select one or more splines and then click **Outline**. Now, drag a spline to create outline [see Figure 68].

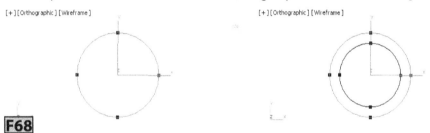

F68

Caution: Selecting splines
If there is one spline is in the scene, it is automatically selected for the outlining process. However, if you are using spinner to add outline, you must select it first.

Note: Open spline
If you are outlining an open spline, the outlining process creates a single closed spline [see Figure 69].

F69

When **Center** is on, the original spline and its outline moves away from an invisible center line by the distance specified by dragging operation or by the value specified for the spinner on the right of **Outline**.

Boolean
Boolean combines two splines. It alters the first spline you select and deletes the other one. There are three types of **Boolean** operations available. Table 24 summarizes those operations:

Table 24: The boolean operations	
Operation	**Description**
Union	Combines two overlapping splines into a single spline. The overlapping portion is removed.
Subtraction	Subtracts the overlapping portion of the second spline from the first spline.
Intersection	Leaves the overlapping portions of the two splines.

To boolean splines, make sure both splines are part of a single spline object [use **Attach** to attach them]. Select a spline and then click **Union**, **Subtraction**, or **Intersection**. Now, click **Boolean**. Hover the mouse pointer on the second spline and then click when shape of the cursor changes to complete the operation [see Figure 70].

Mirror
Mirror allows you to mirror splines horizontally, vertically, and diagonally. To mirror a spline, ensure it is selected and then click **Mirror Horizontally**, **Mirror Vertically**, or **Mirror Both**. Next, click **Mirror** to complete the operation [see Figure 71].

If **Copy** is on, 3ds Max creates a mirror copy of the spline [see Figure 72].

When **About Pivot** is on, 3ds Max mirrors the spline along its geometric center otherwise mirrors along the spline object's pivot point [see Figure 73].

F73

Trim

Trim allows you to clear the overlapping segments in a shape. The two splines must overlap each other and they should be part of the same spline object. To trim a spline, select the spline that will be used to trim the target spline. Click **Trim** and hover the cursor over the spline that you want to trim and then click when the shape of the cursor changes [see Figure 74].

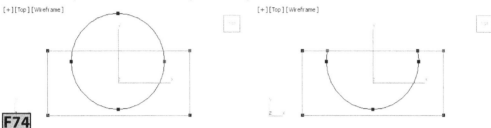

F74

Extend

Extend allows you to extend an open spline. To extend spline, you need a segment that can extend to an intersecting segment of the spline. **Extend** does not work if intersection is not possible. To understand **Extend** feature, create a circle and a line [see the left image in Figure 75]. Convert the circle to an editable spline object and then attach is with the line. Select the **Spline** sub-object mode, click **Extend**. Now, click on the each end of the line to extend it to the circle [see the right image in Figure 75].

F75

Explode

Explode breaks the segment of the selected spline and convert segments into separate splines or objects. There are two options available for the explode operation: **Splines** and **Objects**. If you choose **Objects**, the **Explode** dialog appears. Type a name in the **Object Name** text box and click **OK**. Each successive object will use a name appended with an incremented three-digit number. For example, if you type name as **myShape** and click **OK**. The name of other objects will be: **myShape001**, **myShape002**, **myShape003**, and so forth.

Note: Explode and Detach
Explode *is detach on steroids.*

Changing the Spline Type

You can change the spline type from **Curve** to **Line** and visa-versa. To change type, select the spline and RMB click. Choose **Line** or **Curve** from the upper left quadrant of the **Quad** menu. Right image in Figure 76 shows the spline object converted from **Curve** type into **Line** type.

F76

Note: Checking Self-intersecting Splines

*You can use the **Shape Check** utility to check self-intersecting splines and NURBS curves. The self-intersecting shapes may produce unpredicted results when used in loft, extrude, and lathed operations. To check intersection point, go to the **Utilities** panel and then click on **More** to open **Utilities** dialog. Select **Shape Check** from the **Utilities** list and click **OK**. The **Shape Check** rollout appears in the **Utilities** panel. Click **Pick Object** and then click the spline or NURBS curve in a viewport. The red squares appear on the intersection points [see Figure 77].*

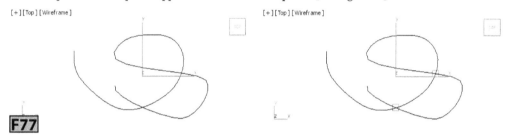

F77

Hands-on Exercises

Complete the following Hands-on Exercises:

1. **Exercise 10:** *Creating a Glass Model*
2. **Exercise 11:** *Creating a Glass Table*
3. **Exercise 12:** *Creating a Corkscrew*
4. **Exercise 15:** *Creating a Model of a Glass and Liquid*
5. **Exercise 18:** *Creating a Jug*

Practical Test
Complete the following test:

Practical Test - 1: Candle Stand
Create the candle stand model [see Figure 78] using the **Line** primitive.

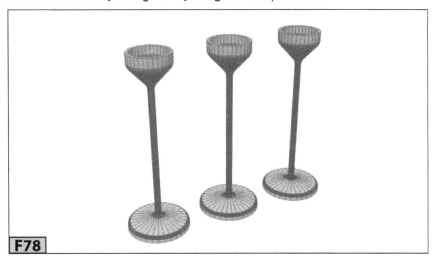

F78

Summary
In this unit, you have seen how we can make quickly make models using powerful splines. We have also created some basic models to understand functioning of splines. We will use the tools that we learned in this unit to create complex models.

The unit covered the following topics:

- Generate planar and 3d surfaces
- Paths and shapes for the loft components
- Generate extrusions
- Generate revolved surfaces
- Define motion path for animations

In the next unit, I describe about modifiers.

This page intentionally left blank

Unit M7: Modifiers

Modifiers in 3ds Max allow to sculpt or edit the objects without changing its base structure. For example, if you apply a **Taper** modifier to a cylinder, you will still able to change its parametric properties such as **Radius** and **Height**. Modifiers can change the geometry of the objects as well as their properties. In other words, modifiers add more parameters to the objects.

In this unit, I will describe the following:

- Using modifiers
- Stack display
- Object-space modifiers vs World-space modifiers
- How transform affects modifiers

Following are some points that you should remember about modifiers:

- When you apply modifiers to the objects, they are stored in a stack and displayed as a stack in the **Modify** panel. You can change the order of the modifiers in the stack to change the effect of the modifier. You can also collapse the stack to make the changes permanent.
- You can apply any number of modifiers to an object.
- When you delete a modifier, its effect on the object also vanishes.
- You can copy modifiers from one object to another.
- The order of the modifier in the stack determines the final effect. Each modifier in the stack affects the modifiers that are applied after it.
- You can apply modifiers to sub-object levels.
- You can toggle the effect of the modifiers from the stack display.

Object Space Modifiers Vs World Space Modifiers

Some modifiers that 3ds Max offers operate in the world-space. These modifiers use the world-space coordinates and are applied to the object after all object-space modifiers and transforms have been applied. You can apply the world-space modifiers like any other object-space modifier. A world-space modifier is indicated by either an asterisk of the text **WSM**.

On the other hand, the object-space modifiers affect the geometry of the object in local space. They use object's local coordinate system. The local coordinate system relates specifically to the selected object. Each object has its own local center and coordinate system. The local center and the coordinate system define the object's local space. Unlike the world coordinate system, the directions of the object's axes [X, Y, and Z] depends on the current transform of the object.

Transform

Transform [move, rotate, and scale] are the most basic manipulations of the 3d objects. Unlike most of the modifiers, transforms are independent of internal structure of an object. The transformation values are stored in a matrix called **Transformation Matrix**. This matrix is applied to the entire object. The matrix is applied after all object-space modifiers have been applied but before the word-space modifiers.

Once you create an object and apply a modifier to it, 3ds Max evaluates the flow as per the table given below:

Table 1: The Data Flow

Order	Category	Modifiers/Transform/Properties	Illustration
1	Creation Parameters	Cylinder	
2	Object Modfiers	Bend, Taper	
3	Transforms	Rotate, Position, and Scale	
4	Space Warps	Ripple	
5	Object Properties	Checker Material	

Using Modifiers

You can access modifiers from the **Modifiers** menu, the **Modifier List** from the **Modify** panel, and the applicable **Modifier Set** menu. To keep all modifiers organized, 3ds Max has grouped them in the **Modifier** menu. The following table summarizes the options available in the **Modifier** menu.

Table 2: The **Modifier** menu overview

Menu Item	Sub-menu Items
Selection Modifier	FFD Select, Mesh Select, Patch Select, Poly Select, Select By Channel, Spline Select, and Volume Select

Patch/Spline Editing	Cross Section, Delete Patch, Delete Spline, Edit Patch, Edit Spline, Fillet/Chamfer, Lathe, Normalize Spline, Renderable Spline Modifier, Surface, Sweep, and Trim/Extend
Mesh Editing	Cap Holes, Chamfer, Delete Mesh, Edit Mesh, Edit Normals, Edit Poly, Extrude, Face Extrude, MultiRes, Normal Modifier, Optimize, ProOptimizer, Quadify Mesh, Smooth, STL Check, Symmetry, Tessellate, Vertex Paint, and Vertex Weld
Conversion	Turn to Mesh, Turn to Patch, and Turn to Poly
Animation	Attribute Holder, Flex, Linked XForm, Melt, Morpher, Patch Deform, Patch Deform (WSM), Path Deform, Path Deform (WSM), Skin, Skin Morph, Skin Wrap, Skin Wrap Patch, SpineIK Control, Surf Deform, and Surf Deform (WSM)
Cloth	Cloth, Garment Maker, and Welder
Hair and Fur	Hair and Fur (WSM)
UV Coordinates	Camera Map, Camera Map (WSM), MapScaler (WSM), Projection, Unwrap UVW, UVW Wrap, UVW Mapping Add, UVW Mapping Clear, UVW and XForm
Cache Tools	Point Cache, and Point Cache (WSM)
Subdivision Surfaces	Crease, CreaseSet, HSDS Modifier, MeshSmooth, OpenSubdiv, and TurboSmooth
Free Form Deformers	FFD 2x2x2, FFD 3x3x3, FFD 4x4x4, FFD Box, and FFD Cylinder
Parametric Deformers	Affect Region, Bend, Displace, Lattice, Mirror, Noise, Physique, Push, Preserve, Relax, Ripple, Shell, Slice, Skew, Stretch, Spherify, Squeeze, Twist, Taper, Substitute, XForm, and Wave
Surface	Disp Approx, Displace Mesh (WSM), Material, and Material By Element
NURBS Editing	Displace Approx, Surf Deform, and Surface Select
Radiosity	Subdivide, and Subdivide (WSM)
Cameras	Camera Correction

Using the Modify Panel

To apply a modifier to an object, select the object in the scene and then go to the **Modify** panel. The name of the selected object appears on the top of the **Modify** panel. Apply a modifier to the object by using one of the following methods:

- Choose a modifier from the **Modifier List** available in the **Modify** panel. You can either use mouse to click on the **Modifier** or use the keyboard. For example, if you are looking for the **Mirror** modifier, type **mi**, the modifiers whose name starts with **mi** [in this case the **Mirror** modifier only] appear in the **Modifier List**. Now, you can click on the **Modifier** or press **Enter** to apply it.
- Choose a modifier from the **Modifiers** menu.
- If the **Modifier** buttons are available in the on the **Modify** panel, click one of the buttons.

Tip: Dragging a modifier to an object
*To drag a modifier form one object to another object in the scene, select an object that already has a modifier. To copy a modifier without instancing it, drag the modifier name from the stack display to the target object in the scene. If you want to create an instance, **Ctrl+drag** the modifier's name.*

Tip: Modifier Instances
*When you create an instance of a modifier, its name appears in italics in the **Modify** panel indicating that the modifier is instanced.*

Using the Configure Modifier Sets Dialog

When you click on the **Configure Modifier Sets** button in the **Modify** panel [belowmodifier stack], a menu is displayed. Choose **Show Buttons** from the menu to display the modifier buttons below the **Modifier List**. The buttons associated with the currently selected set will be displayed in the **Modify** panel. You can select various sets from the menu. Figure 1 shows the buttons associated with the **Selection Modifiers** set.

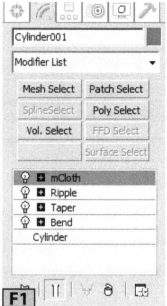

When you choose the **Configure Modifier Sets** option from the menu, the **Configure Modifier Sets** dialog appears [see Figure 2]. This dialog lets you create custom modifier and button sets for the **Modify** panel. To create a new set, set the number of desired buttons using **Total Buttons**, and then drag a modifier from the modifier list to a button.

You can also add a modifier by first highlighting the button and then double-clicking a modifier in the **Modifier List**. When you assign a modifier by double-clicking on its name, the highlight moves to the next button in the **Modifiers** group. Now, enter the name of the new set in the **Sets** edit field and then click **Save** to save the set. Click **OK** from the **Configure Modifier Sets** dialog to exit it. Similarly, you can modify an existing set.

The modifier stack [also referred to as just stack] is a list of modifiers that you apply to an object. The stack is evaluated from bottom to top. The first entry in the stack [from bottom] is always the object. The object-space modifiers appear above the object type. The world-space modifiers and space warps bound to the object are placed at the top.

You can use the stack in one of the following ways:

- Find a particular object and adjust its parameters using rollouts.
- Change the order of modifiers.
- Deactivate the effect of modifier in the stack, viewport, or both.
- Select components [such as **Gizmo** or **Center**] of a modifier.
- Delete modifiers.

The buttons at the bottom of the stack allow you to manage the stack. Table 3 summarizes the functioning of the buttons.

Table 3: The buttons found below the modifier stack		
Name	**Icon**	**Description**
Pin Stack		It locks the stack and all controls in the Modify panel to the selected object stack.
Show End Result		When active, it shows the effect of the entire stack on the selected object. When inactive, shows the result up to the currently highlighted modifier.
Make Unique		It makes an instanced object unique.
Remove Modifier		It deletes the current modifier from the stack.
Configure Modifier Sets		When this button is clicked, a menu is displayed that lets you configure the modifier button sets.

Tip: Copying and pasting modifiers
You can copy and paste modifiers between the object. RMB click on a modifier, a popup menu appears. You can use the ***Cut***, ***Copy***, ***Paste***, *and* ***Paste Instanced*** *options from the menu to edit the stack.*

Caution: World-space modifiers
While copy pasting the modifiers, ensure that you select the world-space and object-space modifiers separately. The ***Cut***, ***Copy***, *and* ***Paste*** *options are disabled in the menu if you select both types of modifiers.*

Caution: Word-space modifiers
If you paste a word-space modifier in a section of object-space modifiers, the paste occurs at the top of the world-space section.

Collapsing the Stack

You can collapse the modifier stack of an editable object to merge the cumulative effect of the collapsed modifiers. You might collapse the modifier stack in one of the following situations:

- You have finished the model and you want to keep it as is.
- You want to discard animation tracks.
- You want to save the memory by simplifying the model.

In most of the cases, collapsing the entire modifier stack or part of the stack saves memory. However, some modifiers such as **Bevel** when collapsed increases the file size as well as the memory used.

Caution: Parametric nature of the objects
Once you collapse the modifier stack, you lose access to the parametric creation parameters of the object.

Tip: Preserving the original copy
*Before you collapse a stack, choose **Save As | Save Selected** from the **Application** menu to preserve a copy of the original parametric object.*

3ds Max provides two options to collapse the stack: **Collapse To** and **Collapse All**. You can access these options by RMB clicking on the stack. The **Collapse To** option collapses the stack up to and including the chosen modifier to an editable object. You can still adjust the modifiers above the chosen modifier. The resultant object type depends on the uppermost modifier and type of geometry it outputs. For example, if the uppermost modifier is **Edit Poly**, the resultant object will be an **Editable Poly** object. If no such modifier exists in the stack, the resultant object is an editable mesh. The **Collapse All** option collapses the entire stack. It does not affect any world-space bindings.

Exploring Modifiers

As already discussed, 3ds Max offers two types of modifiers: **Word-Space Modifiers** and **Object-Space modifiers**. Let's explore these modifiers

Hair and Fur Modifier (World Space)

This modifier is the engine of the **Hair and Fur** feature in 3ds Max. You can apply this modifier to either a mesh object or a spline object. If you apply it to splines, the hair grows between the splines. When you select an object on which you have applied this modifier, hair is displayed in the viewports. You cannot select the fur itself in the viewports, however, you can select hair guides using the **Guides** sub-object level.

Note: Hair in the viewports
*The hair only renders in the **Perspective** or **Camera** viewports. If you try to render an orthographic viewport, 3ds Max presents a warning that says that the hair will not appear in the render.*

Camera Map Modifier (World Space)

This modifier is similar to the **Camera Map** modifier. It is used to apply the **UVW** mapping coordinates to the object based on a specified camera. It causes the object to blend with the background if you apply same map to the object as you apply to the scene environment.

To apply a **Camera Map** modifier, create a scene with a camera and one or more objects. Ensure that the object that you want to map is visible to the camera in the scene. Apply the **Camera Map** modifier and then click **Pick Camera** from the **Camera Mapping** rollout and click on the camera in a viewport. Now, you need to apply a map to the background. Press **8** to open the **Environment & Effects** dialog. Assign a map using the **Environment map** button. Now, open the **Material Editor** and drag the map from the **Environment and Effects** dialog to the **Material Editor**, choose **Instance** from the dialog that appears and then click **OK**. Set the tiling in the **Coordinates** rollout, if required.

Apply a material to the object in the scene and then assign the map you just created to the **Diffuse** component of the material [see Figure 3]. To create the render shown in Figure 3, I have applied a **Checker** map to both the environment and the object. Notice that the **Checker** map on the object matches the background but the shading effect of the material makes the object visible. To blend the object completely in the background, set the **Specular Level** and **Glossiness** of the material to **0**. Also, turn off the self-illumination color and set the **Self Illumination** to **100**. Now, take a render using the camera that you have assigned to the modifier [see Figure 4].

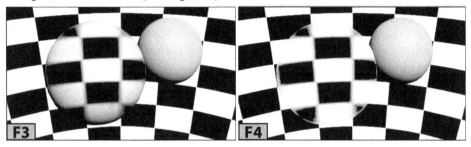

Displace Mesh Modifier (World Space)

This modifier allows you to see the effect of the **Displacement** mapping on editable mesh objects in the viewports. Also, you can see the effect of the **Displacement** mapping if you have applied a **Disp Approx** modifier to an object. This is useful when you want to visualize the effect of **Displacement** mapping in the viewports especially when you have animated the **Displacement** map or when you want to create an editable mesh from the displace geometry in the scene.

To understand the functioning of this modifier, create a **Plane** primitive with **Length**, **Width**, **Length Segs**, and **Width Segs** values set to **150**, **150**, **50**, and **50**, respectively. Apply the **Displacement** Approx modifier to the plane. Open the **Material Editor** and apply the **Standard** material to the plane. Connect the **Noise** map with the **Displacement** slot of the material. Now, add the **Displace Mesh (WSM)** modifier to the stack. The effect of the **Displacement** map appears in the viewport [see Figure 5].

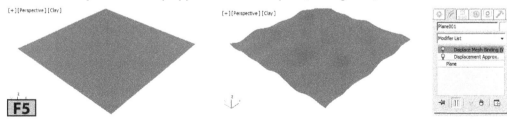

Note: The Displacement Approx modifier
If you are applying displacement to an editable mesh object, you don't need to apply this modifier in order to see the displacement effect in the viewport.

If you have changed parameters of the **Noise** map [the **Noise** map in this case], click **Update** on the **Displacement Approx** rollout to update the mesh in the viewports. When **Subdivision Displacement** is on, this modifier uses the settings that you specify on the **Subdivision Method** group of the rollout. You can also use the presets available in the **Subdivision Presets** group of the rollout. If **Subdivision Displacement** is off, this modifier applies the map by moving the vertices just as the **Displace** modifier does.

Displace NURBS Modifier (World Space)

This modifier is same as the **Displace Mesh** modifier, however, it is used with the **NURBS** objects. If a **Displacement** map is applied to a **NURBS** object, the mesh shows the effect of the **Displacement** in the viewports when you add this modifier to the stack.

MapScalar Modifier (Word Space)

This modifier is used to maintain the scale of a map that is applied to the object. In other words, it lets you resize the geometry without changing the scale of the map. Create a box and set its **Length**, **Width**, and **Height** to **70**. Create a **Standard** material with a **Checker** map connected to its **Diffuse** slot. Apply the material to the box. Add the **MapScalar** modifier to the stack. In the **Parameters** rollout of the modifier, set scale and offset values using the **Scale**, **U Offset**, and **V Offset** controls. Now, resize the box using the **Scale** tool. You will notice that the scale of the map does not change regardless of how the geometry is scaled [see Figure 6].

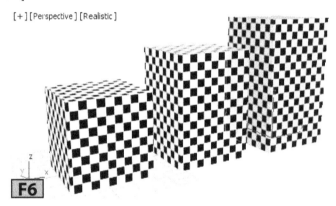

[+][Perspective][Realistic]

Note: The Scale control
*If the **Use Real-World Texture Coordinates** switch is on in the **General** panel of the **Preferences** dialog, the value **1** is displayed for the **Scale** control. If switch is off, the value **100** is displayed for the **Scale** control.*

Patch Deform Modifier (World Space)

This modifier allows you to deform an object based on the contours of a patch object.

Point Cache Modifier (World Space)

This modifier allows you to store the modifier and sub-object animation to a disk file in your HDD. This file records changes in the vertex positions. When animation is played back, this file is used instead of the modifier keyframes. This modifier is useful when computation for vertex animation slows down the system and playback. This modifier is also useful in cloth animations.

Subdivide Modifier (World Space)

This modifier is similar to the object-space **Subdivide** modifier. However, in the world-space version, the size limit is on for the mesh after it is transformed into world space coordinates.

Surface Mapper Modifier (World Space)

This modifier takes a map assigned to the **NURBS** surface and then projects it onto the modified objects. It is useful in applying a single map to a group of surface sub-objects within the same **NURBS** model. Create a **Point Surf** NURBS object and a teapot in the scene [see the left image in Figure 7]. Create a **Standard** material and connect a **Checker** map to the **Diffuse** component of the material. Apply the material to both the **NURBS** object and teapot. Select the **Teapot** in a viewport and then add the **Surface Mapper** modifier to the stack of the **Teapot**. In the **Parameters** rollout of the **Modify** panel, click **Pick NURBS Surface** and then click on the **NURBS** object in a viewport. The **NURBS** object projects the map onto the **Teapot** [see the right image in Figure 7].

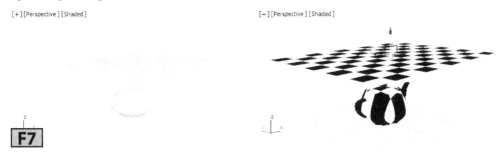

SurfDeform Modifier (World Space)

The functioning of this modifier is same as of the **PathDeform (WSM)** modifier, except that it uses a **NURBS Point** or **CV** surface instead of a curve.

Affect Region Modifier

This modifier is a surface modeling tool. It work well with at the **Vertex** sub-object level. You can use it to create a bubble or indentation in the surface. When you add this modifier to stack, it assigns an arrow like gizmo to the object that you can use in the viewport to alter the geometry. The controls in the **Parameters** rollout allow you to numerically control the shape of the deformation [see Figure 8].

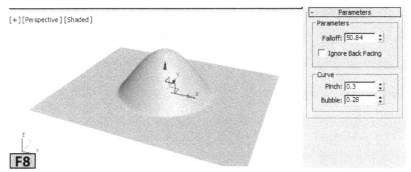

Attribute Holder Modifier

This modifier allows you to hold custom attributes for the objects in the **Modify** panel. It is an empty modifier to which you can add the custom attributes. It is a stripped down version of the **Parameter Collector** dialog that can collect only the custom attributes and appears on the **Modify** panel instead of a floating dialog.

Create a **Cylinder** primitive in the scene with the **Radius** and **Height** parameters set to **10** and **100**, respectively. Add the **Bend** modifier to the stack followed by the **Attribute Holder** modifier. Ensure that the **Attribute Holder** modifier is highlighted in the stack. Choose **Parameter Editor** from the **Animation** menu to open the **Parameter Editor** dialog. Alternatively, press **Alt+1**.

In this dialog, set **Add to Type** to **Selected Object's Current Modifier**, **Parameter Type** to **Float**, **UI Type** to **Slider**, and **Name** to **Cylinder Height** [see Figure 9]. Click **Add** from the **Attribute** Rollout, the **Cylinder Height** control appears in the **Modify Panel | Custom Attributes** rollout [see Figure 10]. Click **Add** on the **Attribute** rollout of the **Parameter Editor** dialog. Set **Add** to Type to **Selected Object's Current Modifier**, **Parameter Type** to **Integer**, **UI Type** to **Spinner**, and **Name** to **Cylinder H Segments**. In the **Integer UI Options** rollout, set **Range | From** and **Range | To** to **1** and **60**, respectively. Similarly, add two more float spinners with the name **Bend Angle**, and **Bend Direction**, respectively [see Figure 11]. Close the **Parameter Editor** dialog.

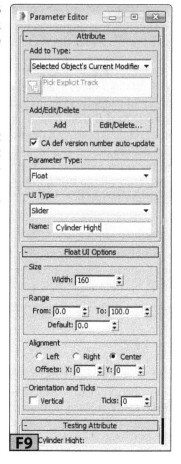

Press **Alt+5** to open the **Parameter Wiring** dialog. On the left pane of the dialog, choose **Objects | Cylinder001 | Modified Object | Cylinder (Object) | Height**. On the right pane, choose **Objects | Cylinder001 | Modified Object | Attribute Holder | Cylinder Height**. Now, click **Two-way connection** followed by **Connect** to create a connection between the selected attributes [see Figure 12]. The label on the **Connect** button changes to **Update**. Similarly, connect the **Cylinder (Object) | Height Segments**, **Bend | Angle**, and **Bend | Direction** controls from the left pane to **Cylinder H Segs**, **Bend Angle**, and **Bend Direction**, respectively, controls of the right pane [see Figure 13]. Close the **Parameter** Wiring dialog.

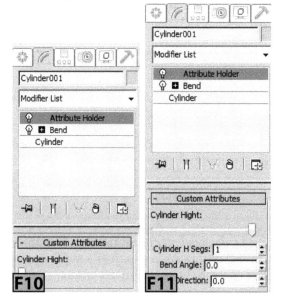

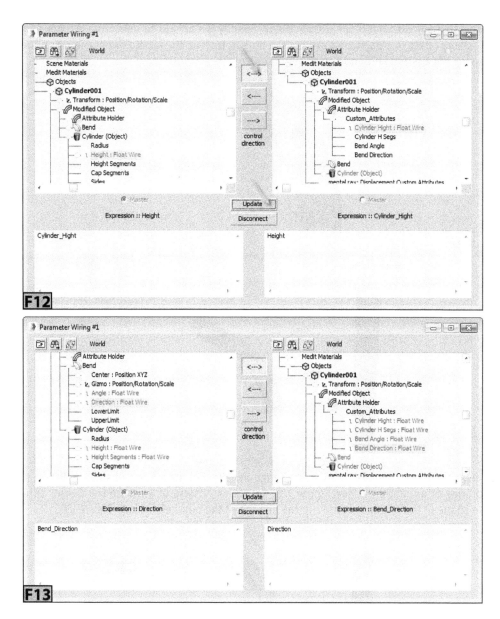

Now, experiment with the controls available in the **Modify panel | Custom Attributes rollout** of the **Attribute Holder** modifier [see Figure 14].

Bend Modifier

You can use this modifier to create a uniform 360 bend on a geometry about a single axis. You can limit bend to a section of the geometry as well as you can control the bend angle and direction.

To bend an object, add the **Bend** modifier to the stack. In the **Parameters** rollout of the modifier, set **Angle** and **Direction** in the **Bend** group to specify the angle to bend from the vertical plane and direction of the bend relative to the horizontal plane, respectively. Specify the axis to be bent from the **Bend Axis** group. To limit the bend effect to a particular area of the object, turn on the **Limit Effect** switch and then specify the limit using the **Upper Limit** and **Lower Limit** controls [see Figure 15].

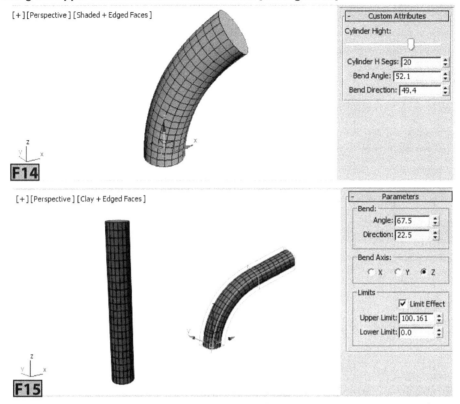

This modifier offers two sub-objects. You can change the effect of the modifier using the **Gizmo** sub-object by transforming or animating it [see Figure 16]. You can translate or animate the **Center** sub-object to change the shape of the **Gizmo** resulting in the change of the bend effect [see Figure 17].

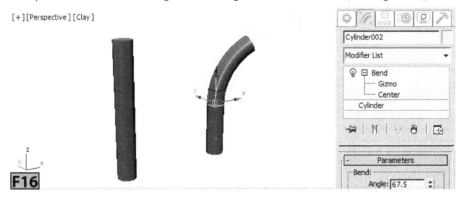

Bevel Modifier

This modifier allows you to extrude spline shapes into 3D objects and then applies a flat or round bevel on the edges. You can control the beveling from the **Bevel Values** rollout of the modifier. Create a **Text** spline and then add a **Bevel** modifier to the stack. Adjust the parameters on the **Parameters** and **Bevel Values** rollouts of the modifier [see Figure 18].

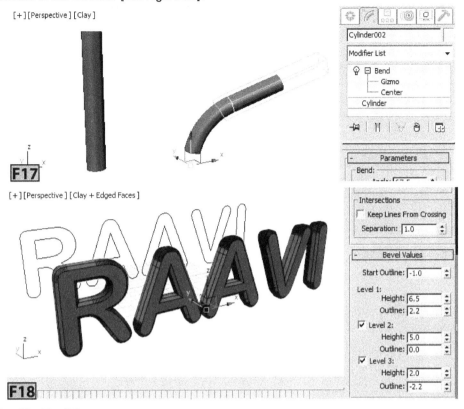

Bevel Profile Modifier

This modifier is another version of the **Bevel** modifier but it extrudes a shape using a path or profile [beveling profile]. Create a shape and profile curve and then apply the **Bevel Profile** modifier to the shape's stack.

Create a **Text** object and a **Helix** object. Select the **Text** object and add **Bevel Profile** to the stack. In the **Modify panel | Parameters rollout | Bevel Profile group**, click **Pick Profile** and then click the **Helix** object in a viewport to create bevel [see Figure 19].

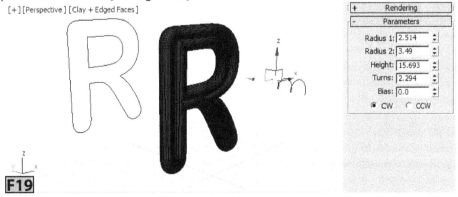

Camera Map Modifier

This modifier is the object-space version of the **Camera Map (WSM)** modifier. It assigns the planar mapping coordinates based on the current frame and specified camera. This behavior is different from the **Camera Map (WSM)** modifier which updates the coordinates at every frame.

Cap Holes Modifier

This modifier build faces on the holes in a mesh. This modifier works well with the planar holes, however, it does a reasonable job when applied to non-planar holes [see Figure 20].

[+][Perspective][Clay + Edged Faces]

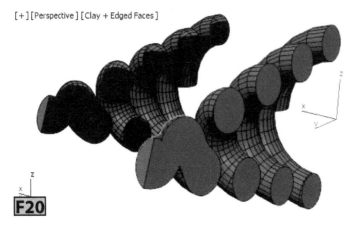

F20

Cross Section Modifier

This modifier creates a skin across multiple various shaped splines by connecting the vertices of the 3D splines. The result is another spline object to which you can apply the **Surface** modifier to create a patch surface. These two modifiers sometimes also referred to as **Surface Tools**.

Create an **Arc** object in the scene and convert it to **Editable** spline. Now, create three more copies of the Arc object and change their shape using the **Scale** tool [see the left image in Figure 21]. Attach all splines to form a single spline object. Add the **Cross Section** modifier to form a combined spline [see the middle image in Figure 21]. Now, add the **Surface** modifier to the stack to create skin [see the right image in Figure 21].

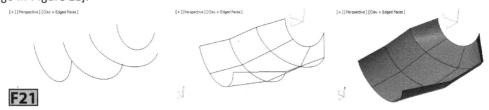

F21

Now, to change the shape, edit the combined spline at sub-objects level. The output of the **Surface** modifier is a patch surface. Therefore, you can add the **Edit Patch** modifier to the stack and edit the surface using the patch edit controls.

Delete Mesh Modifier

This modifier allows you to parametrically delete sub-object selection based on faces, vertices, edges, and objects. Create a **Teapot** object and then add the **Poly Select** modifier to the stack. Select the polygons as shown in the left image of Figure 22. Add a **Delete Mesh** modifier to delete the selected faces [see the right image in Figure 22].

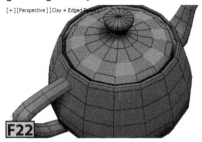 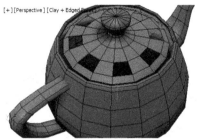

Delete Patch Modifier

It provides parametric deletion based on the patch sub-object selection. The possible choices are vertices, edges, patches, and elements.

Delete Spline Modifier

It provides parametric deletion based on the **Spline** sub-object selection. The possible choices are vertices, segments, and splines. Create a **Line** object. Add the **Spline Select** modifier to the stack and then select a segment. Now, add the **Delete Spline** modifier to the stack to delete the selected segment [see Figure 23].

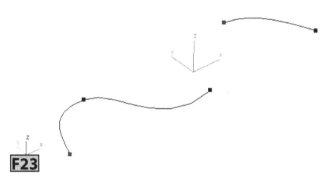

Displace Approx Modifier

See the **Displace Mesh Modifier (World Space)**.

Displace Modifier

This modifier pushes the object's geometry to reshape it using a map or bitmap texture. This modifier allows you to apply the effect using two methods:

- Apply the effect directly onto the object using the **Strength** and **Decay** values.
- Apply the effect using the grayscale values of a bitmap image.

You can use this modifier to simulate magnetic push like effect by animating its gizmos. The four gizmos provided by this modifier are: **Planar**, **Cylindrical**, **Spherical**, and **Shrink Wrap**. These gizmos are used to distribute the force specified by the **Strength** and **Decay** values.

Create a **Plane** primitive with **30** length and width segments. Add a **Displace** modifier to the stack and then set **Strength** to **-100** and **Decay** to **-0.66** in the **Parameters** rollout of the modifier. Choose **Spherical** from the **Map** group of the rollout and then select **Gizmo** sub-object from the stack. Now, use the **Move** tool to see the effect of this modifier [see the left image in Figure 24].

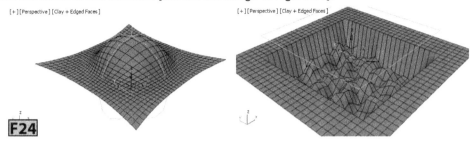

You can also use a bitmap or map to produce this effect. Click **None** associated with the **Map** control in the **Image** group to open the **Material/Map Browser**. Double-click on **Noise** to select this map. Select **Planar** from the **Map** group, the effect of the modifier is displayed in the viewport [see the right image in Figure 24].

To change the parameters of the **Noise** map, drag the **Map** button to the **Material Editor**. Choose **Instance** from the dialog box displayed. Now, double-click on the map node to view its properties. Change the properties as per need.

Edit Mesh Modifier

The **Edit Mesh** modifier has all the capabilities of the **Editable Mesh** object except that you cannot animate sub-objects.

Edit Normal Modifier

You can use this modifier to procedurally and interactively change the vertex normals of an object. This modifier is specifically used when you intend to output the meshes for the game engines and 3D rendering engines that support specified normals. The orientation of the vertex normals affects how light is reflected by the neighboring surfaces. By default in 3ds Max, rules of real-world physics are followed in which the angle of reflection is equal to the angle of incidence. However, using this modifier, you can set the angle of reflection as per your needs.

Edit Patch Modifier

The **Edit Patch** modifier has all the capabilities of the **Editable Patch** object except that you cannot animate sub-objects.

Edit Poly Modifier

The **Edit Poly** modifier has all the capabilities of the **Editable Poly** object except **Vertex Color** information, **Subdivision Surface** rollout, **Weight** and **Crease** settings, and **Subdivision Displacement** rollout. This modifier lets you animate sub-object transforms and parameters.

Edit Spline Modifier

The **Edit Spline** modifier has all the capabilities of the **Editable Spline** object. The **Rendering** and **Interpolation** rollouts are not available for this modifier. Also, you cannot create direct vertex animation using this modifier.

Extrude Modifier

This modifier allows you to add depth to a shape object. It also makes the shape object parametric. Create a **Rectangle** shape object and covert it to editable spline. Create an outline and apply **Extrude** modifier to the spline object. In the **Parameters** rollout, specify a value for the **Amount** control to set the depth of extrusion [see Figure 25]. Specify a value for the **Segments** control to set the segments that will be created for the extruded object.

You can use the **Cap Start** and **Cap End** controls to generate a flat surface over the start and end of the extruded object [see Figure 25]. The controls in the **Output** group let you choose the output mesh type when stack is collapsed. The available options are **Patch**, **Mesh**, and **NURBS**.

Face Extrude Modifier

This modifier extrudes the faces along their normals [see Figure 26]. There are many differences between the **Face Extrude** function and the **Face Extrude** modifier. The one big difference is that all parameters of this modifier are animatable.

FFD Modifiers

FFD stands for **Free-Form** deformation. You can use these modifiers in a variety of ways. You can use it to create bulge in a mesh, animate dancing cars, and so forth. When you apply a **FFD** modifier such as **FFD 2x2x2**, **FFD 3x3x3**, or **FFD 4x4x4**, it surrounds the selected geometry with a lattice. You can transform the lattice and use its control points to adjust the shape of the geometry [see Figure 27].

Each modifier provides a different lattice resolution [**2x2x2**, **3x3x3**, and **4x4x4**]. For example, a **4x4x4** resolution produces a lattice with four control points across each of its dimensions resulting in **12** points in each side of the lattice.

There are three sub-objects available with this modifier. At **Control Points** sub-object level, you can select the control points of the lattice and then change the shape of the underlying geometry by transforming them. At the **Lattice** sub-object level, you can transform the lattice box separately from the geometry. At **Set Volume** level, the color of the lattice control points turns green. You can select and manipulate the points without affecting the underlying geometry. You should use this level to set the initial state of the lattice.

*You can use the **FFD(box)** and **FFD(cyl)** modifiers to create box-shaped or cylinder-shaped FFD lattices. These modifiers are also available as space warps.*

Fillet/Chamfer Modifier

This modifier lets you fillet or chamfer corner vertices between linear segments of the shape objects. This modifier rounds corners where the segments meet by adding new control vertices. It also bevels the corners. This modifier works on the splines at the sub-object level. It does not work between two independent shape objects.

Create a **Star** shape object in the scene and add the **Fillet/Chamfer** modifier to the stack. Now, at the **Vertex** sub-object level of the modifier, select the vertices that you want to affect and then specify the desired settings in the **Edit Vertex** rollout to generate different shapes [see Figure 28].

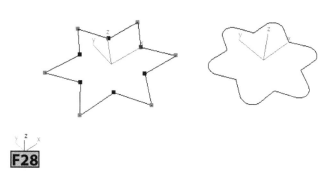

Flex Modifier

This modifier creates virtual springs between vertices of an object thus simulating a soft body dynamics behavior. You can control the stiffness and stretching of the springs. You can also control the sway of the springs that is how much the spring angle changes in relation with the movement of the springs. This modifier works with NURBS, patches, polygon and mesh objects, shapes, FFD space warps, and any plug-in-based object types that can be deformed.

HSDS Modifier

HSDS stands for **Hierarchical SubDivision Surfaces**. This modifier implements the Hierarchical SubDivision Surfaces. You can use this modifier to as a finishing tool for subdivision surfaces.

Lathe Modifier

You can use the **Lathe** modifier to rotate a shape or NURBS curve about a specified axis. Create a **Shape** object [see the left image in Figure 29] and add the **Lathe** modifier to the stack. In the **Parameters** rollout of the modifier, ensure that **Degrees** is set to **360** to create a full **360** degrees lathe. Specify the segments for the lathe object using the **Segments** control. Click **Y** in the direction group to set the **Y** axis as the axis of revolution relative to the pivot point of the object. Click **Min** from the **Align** group to align the axis of revolution to the minimum extent of the shape. The right image in Figure 29 shows the full lathe object.

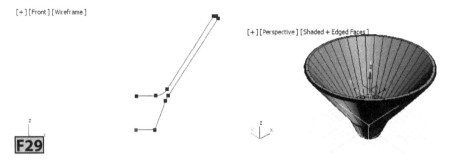

F29

You can turn on the **Weld Core** switch to weld vertices that lie on the axis of revolution. This modifiers also presents the **Axis** sub-object. At this level, you can transform and animate the axis of revolution.

Lattice Modifier

This modifier allows you to create renderable structure from a geometry. It can be thought of an alternative method to create wireframe effect. It gives you options to create joints, struts, or both. Figure 30 shows a sphere with joints, struts, and both join and struts, respectively.

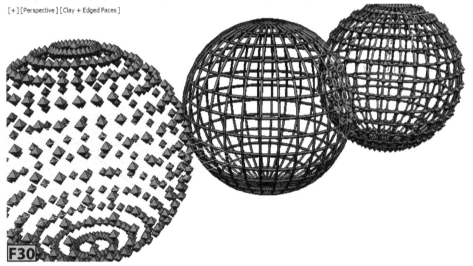

F30

Linked XForm Modifier

This modifier links the transform of any object or sub-object selection to another object. The other object is called the control object. The transforms of the control object are passed onto the object or sub-object selection.

Create a **Sphere** and a **Cone** primitive in the scene. **Cone** will be the control object. Now, select sphere and add **Linked XForm** modifier to the stack. In the **Parameters** rollout, click **Pick Control Object** and then click on cone in a viewport. Now, when you transform the cone, the sphere will also receive the transforms.

Delete the modifier from the stack and convert sphere to **Editable Poly**. At **Vertex** sub-object level, select some vertices [see left image in Figure 31]. Link **Cone** to vertices as discussed above. Now, when you move the cone, the selected vertices will also receive the transform.

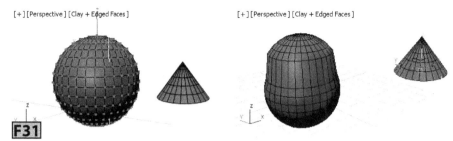

F31

MapScalar Modifier

See the **MapScalar Modifier (Word Space)** modifier.

Material Modifier

This modifier allows you to animate, or change the assignment of the existing material IDs on an object.

MaterialByElement Modifier

This modifier allows you to apply different material IDs to objects containing multiple elements. You can apply IDs at random or you can use a formula. Select **Random Distribution** from the **Parameters** rollout to assign the material IDs to different elements at random. The **ID Count** control lets you assign the minimum number of materials IDs to be assigned. Select **List Frequency** to define a percentage of each [up to eight] of the material IDs.

Melt Modifier

This modifier allows you to create realistic melting effect on all types of objects, including editable patches and NURBS object. It also works on the sub-object selections passed up the stack. Create a cylinder with enough sub-divisions and then apply the **Melt** modifier to it. In the **Melt** group of the **Parameters** rollout, specify the strength of the melt using the **Amount** control. The **% of Melt** control in the **Spread** group lets you specify the spread of the melt [see Figure 32]. The controls in the **Solidity** group determine the center of the melted object. There are several presets available in this group that you can use to specify the solidity of the object. If you want to specify a custom solidity, select **Custom** from this group.

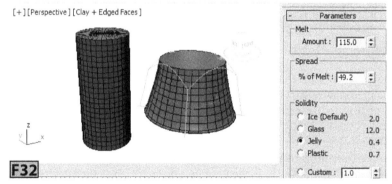

F32

This modifier has two sub-objects, **Gizmo** and **Center**. You can transform and animate these two sub-objects to change the effect of the melt.

Mesh Select Modifier

This modifier provides a superset of the selection functions available in the **Edit Mesh** modifier. It allows you to pass the sub-object selection up the stack to other subsequent modifier.

MeshSmooth Modifier

This modifier allows you to smooth the geometry by subdividing it. You can use this modifier to produce a **Non-Uniform Rational MeshSmooth** object, **NURMS** in short. A **NURMS** objects is similar to the **NURBS** object in which you set different weights for vertices [see Figure 33]. You can farther alter the geometry by modifying the edge weight.

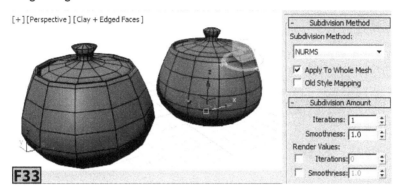

You can choose the desired method from the **Subdivision Method** drop-down of the **Subdivision Method** rollout. The available methods are: **NURMS**, **Classic**, and **Quad** Output. The **Iteration** control in the **Subdivision Amount** rollout lets you specify the number of times you want to subdivide the mesh.

Mirror Modifier

This modifier allows you to parametrically mirror an object or a sub-object selection [see Figure 34]. Apply this modifier to the stack and then select the axis or axis pair from the **Mirror Axis** group of the **Parameters** rollout. If you want to create a copy of the object, select the **Copy** switch and then specify the offset distance using the **Offset** control.

Tip: Modeling a character
*When you have created one side of a character and you want to mirror the other side, use the **Symmetry** modifier instead of the **Mirror** modifier as the **Symmetry** modifier allows you to weld the seam which results in a better looking model.*

Morpher Modifier

You can use this modifier to change the shape of the mesh, patch, or **NURBS** model. Morphing is generally used for lip-sync and facial expressions. This modifier also allows you to morph splines and world-space **FFDs**. Also, you can morph from one shape to another using this modifier.

MultiRes Modifier

This modifier reduces the number of polygons in a mesh to improve the rendering time [see Figure 35]. You can also reduce the number of vertices and polygons using the **Optimize** modifier. However, this modifier has certain advantages over the **Optimize** modifier such as it is faster and lets you specify exact percentage for reduction. You can also specify the vertex count for reductions.

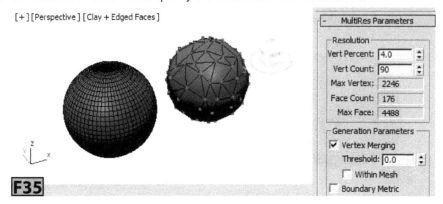

To reduce the polygons, apply this modifier to the stack. In the **Generation Parameters** group of the **MultiRes Parameters** rollout, click **Generate** to initialize the modifier. In the **Resolution** group, specify a value for the **Vert Percent** or **Vert Count** to reduce the polygons.

Noise Modifier

This modifier alters the position of the vertices of an object along any combination of three axes [see Figure 36]. You can use it to create random variations in the shape of the object. You can also animate the change in shape of the mesh. Add the modifier to the stack and then in the **Strength** group of the **Parameters** rollout, set the strength using the **X, Y,** and **X** controls. Turn on the **Fractal** switch from the **Noise** group to produce a fractal like effect [see Figure 37]. When you turn on this switch, the **Roughness** and **Iterations** controls appear in the rollout. You can use these controls to determine the extent of the fractal variation and number of iteration used by the modifier, respectively.

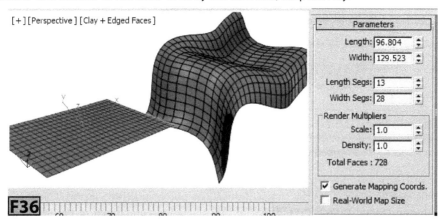

Normal Modifier

This modifier allows you to unify or flip the normals of an object without first converting it to an **Edit Mesh** modifier. Turn on the **Unify Normals** switch in the **Parameters** rollout to unify the normals so that they all point in the same direction, usually outward. Turn on the **Flip Normals** switch to reverse the direction of all surface normals.

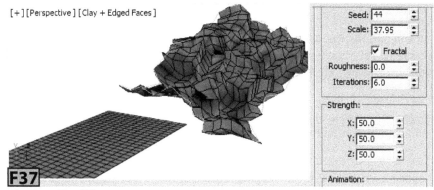

F37

Normalize Spline Modifier

You can use this modifier to add new control points at regular interval in a spline [see Figure 38]. This is useful in normalizing the spline that you will use with the motion paths. The **Set Length** control in the **Parameters** rollout lets you set the length of the spline segments. 3ds Max uses this control to set the vertices at the regular intervals. The **Accuracy** control lets you define the precision of the normalization. The range for this control is 1 to 20.

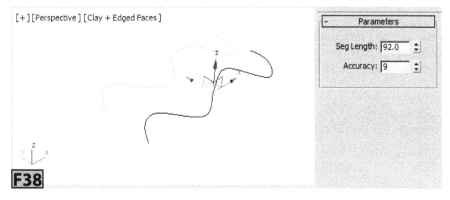

F38

Optimize Modifier
See the **MultiRes Modifier**.

Patch Select Modifier
This modifier provides a superset of selection functions available in the **Edit Patch** modifier.

Patch Deform Modifier (Object Space)
See the **PatchDeform Modifier (World Space)** modifier.

PathDeform Modifier (Object Space)
See the **PathDeform Modifier (World Space)** modifier.

Point Cache Modifier (Object Space)
See the **Point Cache Modifier (World Space)** modifier.

Poly Select Modifier

This modifier provides a superset of selection functions available in the **Edit Poly** modifier.

Preserve Modifier

When you push and pull vertices to model a surface, the edges of the mesh get stretched that results in an irregular geometry. This modifier allows you to retain [as much as possible] the original length of the edge thus producing a cleaner mesh.

Projection Modifier

This modifier is generally used for producing normal bumps maps. Apply this modifier to the low-resolution object and then pick a high resolution object as the source of the projected normals.

Projection Holder Modifier

This modifier appears when the **Project Mapping** feature of the **Projection** modifier is used. It contains data generated by the **Project Mapping** feature such as **UVW** mapping data.

ProOptimizer Modifier

This modifier allows you to interactively reduce the number of vertices in a model while preserving the original appearance/features of the model such as material, mapping, and vertex color information. When this modifier is used, the memory requirement for a model are reduced. You can optimize a model using one of the following two methods:

- You can use the **ProOptimizer** modifier to interactively optimize the model.
- You can use the **Batch ProOptimizer** utility to optimize multiple scenes at one go. When you use this utility, you can optimize the meshes before you import them to save the time.

Push Modifier

This modifier allows you to push the selected vertices inward or outward along the average vertex normals to create an inflation like effect [see Figure 39].

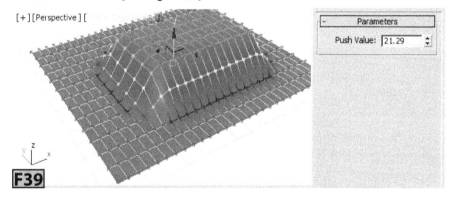

F39

Quadify Mesh Modifier

You can use this modifier to convert object structure to quadrilateral polygons using the relative size that you specify. This modifier helps you to create mesh with rounded model with help of the **Smooth** modifier.

Relax Modifier

This modifier allows you to reduce the surface tension by moving the vertices closer to or away from their neighbors. This results in smooth object, however, the model appears little smaller than the un-relaxed model.

Note: Neighboring Vertex
A neighboring vertex is the vertex that shares a visible edge with the current vertex.

Renderable Spline Modifier

This modifier makes a spline object renderable without needing to convert it to an **Editable Spline** object. It also allows you to apply same rending properties to multiple splines. This modifier is useful when you link an AutoCAD drawing.

Ripple Modifier

You can use this modifier to create a ripple effect on the geometry [see Figure 40]. You can use its **Gizmo** sub-object to change the ripple effect.

Note: The Ripple space warp
*The **Ripple** space warp has the same features as the **Ripple** modifier, however, you can apply the **Ripple** space warp to a large number of objects.*

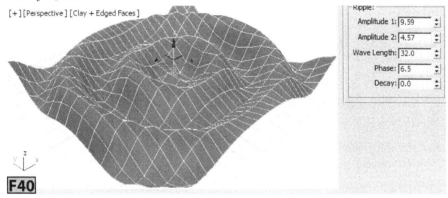

Select By Channel Modifier

This modifier is used with the **Channel Info** utility. When you save a vertex selection into a subcomponent using the **Channel Info** utility, you can use this modifier to quickly access the selection.

Shell Modifier

This modifier allows you to give thickness to an object by creating extra set of faces on the opposite direction of the existing faces [see Figure 41]. You can specify the offset distances using the **Inner Amount** and **Outer Amount** controls available in the **Parameters** rollout.

Skew Modifier

This modifier can be used to create a uniform offset in an object's geometry [see Figure 42]. You can control and direction of the skew on any of three axes. You can also limit the skew effect by turning on the **Limit Effect** switch and then using the **Upper Limit** and **Lower Limit** controls.

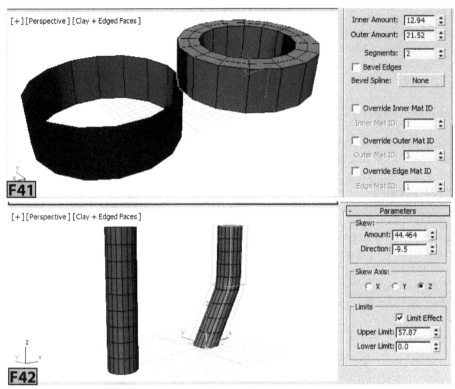

Skin Modifier

This modifier is a skeleton deformation tool that allows you to deform one object with another object. You can deform the **Mesh**, **Patch**, and **NURBS** objects using the bones, splines, and other objects.

Skin Morph Modifier

This modifier allows you to use a bone's rotation to drive the deformation of the mesh object. This modifier is used with other modifiers such as **Skin** and **Physique**.

Skin Wrap Modifier

You can use this modifier to deform an object with another object. Although, you can use this modifier in a variety of ways but its primary use is to animate a high-resolution object mesh with help of a low-resolution mesh.

Skin Wrap Patch Modifier

This modifier allows you to deform a mesh object with help of a patch object. Each point on the patch object influences a surrounding volume of points on the mesh object.

Slice Modifier

You can use this modifier to slice though selected objects or sub-objects using a cutting plane. Its functioning is similar to the **Slice** function of the **Editable Mesh** object. However, it does not require to be an **Editable Poly** or **Editable Mesh** object. You can also animate the position and rotation of the slicing plane.

Smooth Modifier

You can smooth a faceted geometry using this modifier. It eliminates the faceting by grouping the faces into smoothing groups. It smoothens the faces based on the angle of adjacent faces.

Spherify Modifier

This modifier distorts an object into a spherical shape [see Figure 43]. The end result is dependent on the topology of the object.

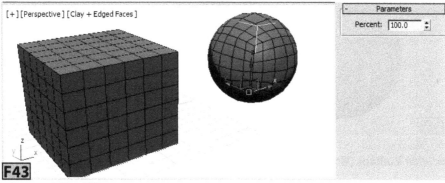

Spline IK Control Modifier

The basic use of this modifier is to prepare a spline or **NURBS** curve for use with the **Spline IK Solver**. When this modifier is applied to a spline object, you can transform its vertices without needing to access the **Vertex** sub-object level. It places knots [control points] at each vertex and then you can manipulate the knots to change the shape of the spline.

Spline Select Modifier

This modifier is a superset of the selection functions found in the **Edit Spline** modifier. It passes a sub-object selection up the stack to other modifiers.

Squeeze Modifier

The modifier lets you create a squeezing [create bulge] effect on the objects [see Figure 44]. The vertices closest to the object's pivot point move inward. The squeeze operation is applied around the **Squeeze** gizmo's local Z axis.

STL Check Modifier

This modifier checks if the object is correct for exporting to an **STL** file format. **STL** [**stereolithography**] files are used by the specialized machines to create prototype models based on the supplied **STL** file. The **STL** file must have a complete and closed surface.

Stretch Modifier

The **Stretch Modifier** allows you to create traditional squash and stretch effects that are used in animations [see Figure 45]. This modifier applies a scale effect along a specified axis and opposite scale along the two remaining minor axes.

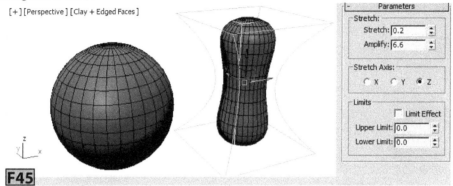

F45

Subdivide Modifier (Object Space)

See the **Subdivide Modifier (World Space)** modifier.

Substitute Modifier

This modifier allows you to replace one or more objects with other objects in a viewport or at render time. The substitute object can be instanced in the current scene or can be referenced from an external file. This modifier is useful for the designers who use 2D shapes in their AutoCAD drawings. When they link the AutoCAD drawing to 3ds Max, they want to see how the object will look like in their design. This modifier allows them to achieve that objective.

Surface Modifier

See the **Cross Section Modifier**.

Surface Select Modifier

This modifier allows you to add a **NURBS** sub-object selection in the stack. Then, you can modify the selected sub-objects. It can select any kind of NURBS sub-objects except imports.

SurfDeform Modifier (Object Space)

See the **SurfDeform Modifier (World Space)** modifier.

Sweep Modifier

You can use this modifier to extrude a cross section along an underlying spline or **NURBS** curve path. It provides a number of pre-made cross sections such as angles, channels, wide flenges, and so forth [see Figure 46]. You can also use a custom spline or NURBS curve as custom sections.

Symmetry Modifier

See the **Mirror** modifier.

Taper Modifier

This modifier creates tapered contours by scaling both ends of an object's geometry [see Figure 47]. It scales up one end and scales down the other end. You can also limit the taper effect.

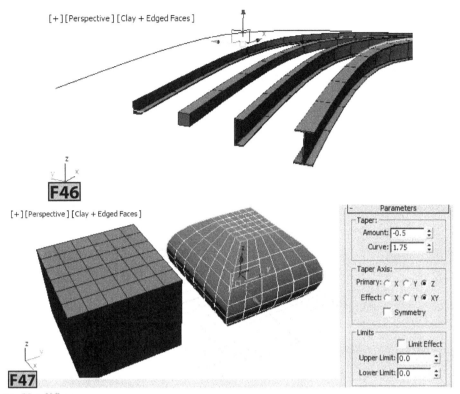

Tessellate Modifier

This modifier is used to subdivide the faces of a mesh [see Figure 48]. It is useful in smoothing the curved surface and creating additional geometry for other modifiers to act on. The **Tension** control in the **Parameters** rollout allows you to add convexity or concavity to the subdivided surface.

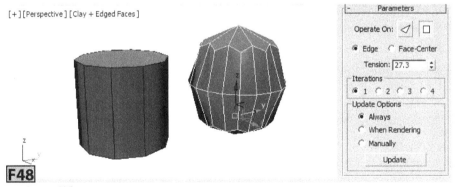

Trim/Extend Modifier

This modifier is used to clean up the overlapping or open splines in a multi-spline shape. To trim you need the intersecting splines. If the section intersects at both ends, the entire section will be deleted by this modifier up to the two intersections. To extend, you need an open spline.

TurboSmooth Modifier

This modifier is like the **MeshSmooth** modifier with the following differences:

- **TurboSmooth** is faster and memory efficient than the **MeshSmooth** modifier.
- **TurboSmooth** uses a single subdivision method, NURMS. It has no sub-object levels and outputs a triangle-mesh object.

Turn To gPoly Modifier

This modifier converts geometry to the hardware mesh format used internally by 3ds Max. This internal hardware format allows 3ds Max to speed up the performance when the mesh is edited.

Turn To Mesh Modifier/ Turn To Patch Modifier/ Turn To Poly Modifier

These modifiers allow you to apply the object conversions in the modifier stack. When you apply general purpose modifiers, these modifiers give you ability to explicitly control the output type of the object before hand.

Twist Modifier

This modifier creates a twisting effect on the surface of an object [see Figure 49]. You can control the angle of twist as well as you limit the effect of the **Twist** modifier. When you add this modifier to the stack, its gizmo is placed at the pivot point of the object and the gizmo lines up with the local axis of the object.

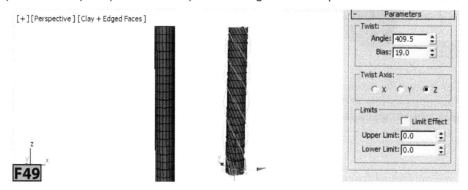

UVW Mapping Modifiers

These modifiers are used to control the texture mapping. You can use them to manage UV coordinates and to apply materials to the objects.

Vertex Weld Modifier

This modifier works similar to the **Weld** feature in an **Editable Poly** and similar objects. You can use this modifier to combine the vertices that lies within a specified distance from each other.

Vertex Paint Modifier

This modifier allows you to paint vertex colors onto an object. The amount of color that 3ds Max applies to the vertex depends on the distance of the vertex from the position of the cursor on the face. You can also paint vertex alpha and illumination values as well.

Volume Select Modifier

This modifier lets you make a sub-object selection of vertices or faces. You can use a cylinder-shaped or sphere shaped gizmo, or an object in the scene to define the volume of the selection area to which you can then apply other modifiers.

Wave Modifier

This modifiers creates a wave like effect [see Figure 50]. You can use the standard **Gizmo** and **Center** sub-objects to change the wave effect. This modifier is similar to the **Wave** space warp which is useful when you want to create a wave effect on the large number of objects.

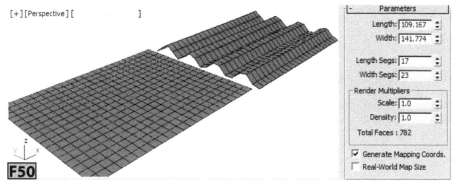

XForm Modifier

This modifier is used to apply transformations to the objects. You can use it to animate the transformations of a sub-object selection. Also, you can transform an object at any point in the stack.

Hands-on Exercises

Complete the following Hands-on Exercises:

1. *Exercise 16:* Creating a Model of a Building
2. *Exercise 17:* Creating a Model of a Paper Basket

Summary

As you have seen, modifiers are integral part of various processes in 3ds Max. 3ds Max provides two types of modifiers: object-space modifiers and world-space modifiers. The object-space modifiers works in the local space and directly affect the object's geometry. The word-space modifiers acts as the object-specific space warps. However, they use the world space rather than the object-space for applying their effects.

The unit covered the following topics:

- Using modifiers
- Stack display
- Object-space modifiers vs World-space modifiers
- How transform affects modifiers

This page intentionally left blank

Unit MH1: Hands-on Exercises [Modeling]

Before you start the exercises, let's first create a project folder for the hands-on exercises of this unit. You can proceed without creating a project folder but I highly recommend that you create one. The project folder allows you to keep your file organized.

Open the **Windows Explorer** and create a new directory with the name **3dsmax2016** in the **C** drive of your system. Start 3ds Max. From the **Application** menu, choose **Reset**. Click **Yes** from the dialog that opens.

From the **Application** menu, choose **Manage | Set Project Folder** to open the **Browse for Folder** dialog. Navigate to the **3dsmax2016** directory that you have created and then click **Make New Folder**. Create the new folder with the name **hoexm1** and click **OK** to create the project directory.

Now, if you navigate to the **\3dsmax2016\hoexm1** directory, you will see a number of sub-directories [see Figure 1].

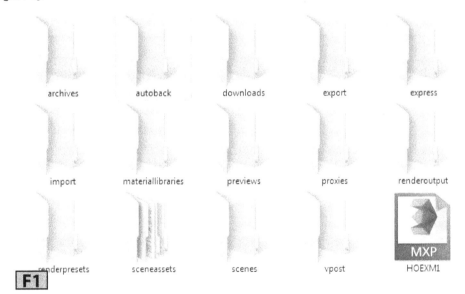

archives   autoback   downloads   export   express

import   materiallibraries   previews   proxies   renderoutput

renderpresets   sceneassets   scenes   vpost   HOEXM1

F1

What just happened?
*Here, I have set a project folder for the hands-on exercises of this unit. When you set a project folder for a scene, 3ds Max creates a series of folders such as **scenes**, **sceneassets**, and so forth. These folders are default locations for certain types of operations in 3ds Max. For example, the **scenes** folder is used when 3ds Max opens or saves scene files.*

*It is a good idea to reset the scene before you start new work because the **Open** command defaults to the folder where the previous scene was saved. After the reset operation, the **Open** command defaults to the **scenes** folder of the current project folder.*

The **hoexm1** folder will contain all the data related to the hands-on exercises of this unit.

Hands-on Exercise MH1-1: Creating Simple Model of a House

OK, now it is time to work on the first exercise of the book. In this exercise, you will create a simple model of house using the **Standard Primitives** [see Figure 2].

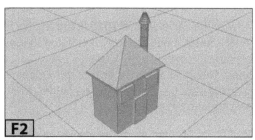 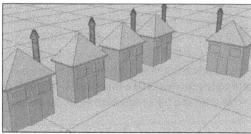

Table 1 summarizes the exercise:

Table 1 - Creating a Simple Model of a House	
In this exercise, you will learn how to	• Reset 3ds Max settings • Create objects • Use navigational controls • Align objects • Undo and redo scene views • Use navigational gizmos • Use **Transform Type-In** boxes
Skill level	Beginner
Project Folder	**hoexm1**
Time to complete	20 Minutes
Final exercise file	**hoem1-1-end.max**

Start 3ds Max. Choose **Reset** from the **Application** menu or press **Alt+F+R**. Click **Yes** on the **3ds Max** message box to reset the settings. Choose **Unit Setup** from the **Customize** menu to open the **Units Setup** dialog. Ensure that **Generic Units** in on in this dialog box and then click **OK** to close the dialog.

Click **Box** on the **Object Type** rollout in the **Command Panel** and then click-drag in the **Perspective** viewport to define the length and width of the box. Release the mouse button to define the length and width of the box. Release the LMB and then drag upward to define the height. Click to specify the height.

Press **J** to turn off the selection brackets and **F4** to turn on the **Edged Faces** mode. Now, click on the **Shading Viewport** label and choose **Clay** from the popup menu. Press **G** To turn off the grid. Press **G** again to turn it on. Drag the mouse pointer with the **MMB+Alt** held down to rotate the view. Drag the mouse pointer with the **MMB** held down to pan the view. Drag the mouse pointer with the **Ctrl+Alt+MMB** held down to zoom in or out of the view. You need to place the mouse pointer on the area for which you want to change the magnification.

Next, you will use the brackets keys to change the settings.

Place the mouse pointer on the area for which you want to change the magnification settings and then use the bracket keys **[** and **]** to change the level of magnification. MMB click on the **Perspective** viewport to make it active, if not already active. Press **Alt+W** to maximize the viewport. Click on the **Home** icon on the **ViewCube** to restore the home view. Alternatively, you can RMB click on the **ViewCube** and then choose **Home** from the **ViewCube's** menu.

Press **Alt+W** again to restore the four viewport arrangement. Click drag the compass ring of the **ViewCube** to change the orientation of the viewport. Now, click-drag edges, corners, or faces of the **ViewCube** and experiment with various possibilities that **ViewCube** offers. When done, click on the **Home** icon to restore the view.

Press **Shift+Z** repeatedly to undo the scene view changes. Press **Shift+Y** to redo the scene view changes. Click on the **ViewCube's Home** icon to restore the home view. Press **Ctrl+P** to activate the **Pan View** tool and then drag in the viewport to pan the view. Now, press **Ctr+R** to activate the **Orbit** tool and drag in the viewport to rotate the view. Press **Q** to deactivate the **Orbit** tool and activate the **Select** tool. Press **Shift+W** to activate **StreeringWheels**. Click drag the **ZOOM** wedge to change the magnification level. Similarly, experiment with other wedges of the wheel. Press **Esc** to turn off **SteeringWheels**.

Make sure **Box001** is selected in the viewport and then RMB click on the **Move** tool to open the **Move Transform Type-In** dialog. In the **Absolute:World** group of the dialog, RMB click on the spinners to set them to their default values which is **zero**. You will notice that the box is now placed at the origin in the viewports. The **Move Transform Type-In** dialog is a **modeless** dialog. You don't have to close it in order to work on the model we are creating in this exercise.

Choose the **Modify** panel in the **Command Panel**. In the **Parameters** rollout, set **Length**, **Width**, and **Height** to **80**, **50**, and **70**, respectively, to change the size of the box. Press **Ctr+Shift+Z** to zoom the box to its extents in all viewports [see Figure 3].

If you press **Z** the box will be zoomed in the active viewport only.

Now, let's create door and windows of the house.

Create another box in the **Perspective** viewport and then set its **Length**, **Width**, and **Height** to **23**, **6**, and **40**, respectively [see Figure 4]. Ensure **Box002** and the **Move** tool selected and then enter **-25**, **-2.3**, and **-0.03** in the **Transform Type-In** boxes in the **Status Bar** [see Figure 5].

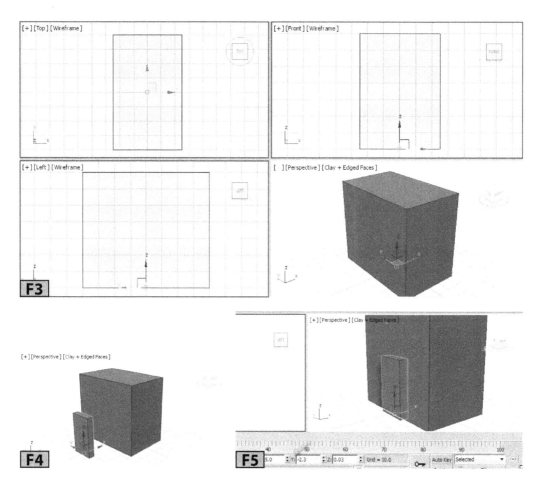

Create two windows using the **Box** primitive. Use the values **23**, **6**, and **18** for the **Length**, **Width**, and **Height** spinners, respectively. Now, align the boxes [see Figure 6]. Ensure the **Box** tool is active and then turn on **AutoGrid** from the **Object Type** rollout. Position the mouse pointer on the **Box001**, an axis tripod shows up [see Figure 7]. Create a box on the **Box001**.

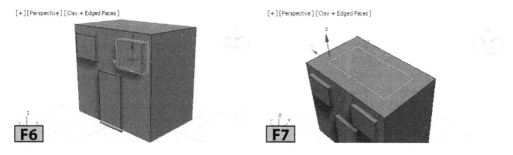

Ensure **Box005** is selected and then click **Align** on the **Main** toolbar. Now, click **Box001** in the **Perspective** viewport to open the **Align Selection** dialog. In this dialog, set the values as shown in Figure 8 and click **OK** to align the boxes.

Ensure **Box005** is selected and then choose the **Modify** panel. On the **Parameters** rollout, set **Length**, **Width**, and **Height** to 91, 60, and 2, respectively [see Figure 9]. Choose the **Create** panel and ensure **Auto Grid** is on. Click **Pyramid** on the **Object Type** rollout and then create a pyramid on **Box005**. Align **Pyramid001** with **Box005**. Ensure **Pyramid001** is selected and then in the **Modify panel | Parameters rollout**, set **Width**, **Depth**, and **Height** to **60**, **90**, and **46**, respectively [see Figure 10].

Now, let's create a chimney for the house.

On the **Create** panel, choose **Cylinder** from the **Object Type** rollout and create a cylinder in the **Perspective** viewport. In the **Modify panel | Parameters rollout**, set **Radius** and **Height** to **5** and **60**, respectively. Now, place **Cylinder001** on the roof using the **Move** tool [see Figure 11]. In the **Create** panel, choose **Cone** from the **Object Type** rollout and ensure **AutoGrid** is on. Create a cone on **Cylinder001**. Align **Cone001** and **Cylinder001**.

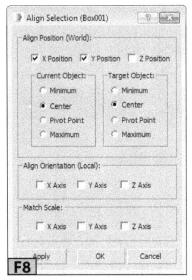

F8

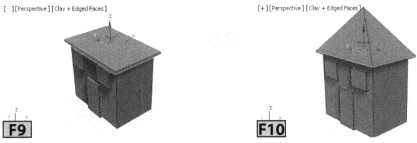

F9   F10

In the **Modify panel | Parameters rollout**, set **Radius 1**, **Radius 2**, and **Height** to **7.5**, **2**, and **13**, respectively [see Figure 12].

F11   F12

Choose **Select All** from the **Edit** menu to select all objects in the scene. Choose **Group** from the **Group** menu to open the **Group** dialog. In this dialog, type **House** in the **Group name** field and click **OK** to create a group. Press **Ctrl+S** to open the **Save File As** dialog. In this dialog, navigate to the location where you want to save the file. Type the name of the file in the **File name** text box and then click **Save** to save the file.

Hands-on Exercise MH1-2: Creating a Sofa

In this exercise, you will model a sofa using the **Box** primitive [see Figure 13]. The following table summarizes the exercise:

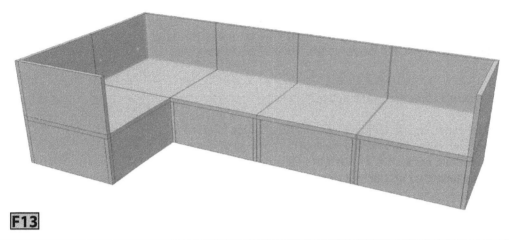

F13

Table 2: Creating Model of a Sofa	
In this exercise, you will learn how to:	• Create simple geometry • Setup units and home grid settings • Use the **Align** tool • Use the **Mirror** tool • Create clones • Use the **Scene Explorer** • Create a group • Open and close a group
Skill level	Beginner
Time to complete	30 Minutes
Topics in the section:	• Specifying the Units for the Exercise • Creating One Seat Section of the Sofa • Creating Corner Section of the Sofa
Project folder	**hoexm1**
Units	**US Standard – Decimal Inches**
Final exercise file	**hoem1-2-end.max**

Specifying the Units for the Exercise

From **Customize** menu choose **Units Setup**. In the **Units Setup** dialog that opens, select **US Standard** from the **Display Unit Scale** group. Next, choose **Decimal Inches** from the drop-down located below **US Standard** [see Figure 14] and then click **OK** to accept the change.

Here, I have set the display units for the scene. The units that you set here are used to measure geometry in the scene. You can also set the lighting units using this dialog box. Apart from the display units, you can also set the system units that 3ds Max uses for the internal mechanism. To view controls available for changing system units, click **System Unit Setup** on the **Units Setup** dialog.

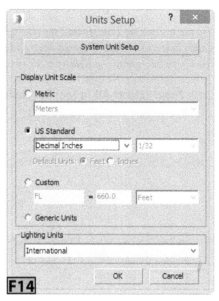

It is important to understand the difference between the system and display units. The scene units only affect how geometry is displayed in the viewports whereas the system units control the actual scale of the geometry.

Caution: System Units

*The system units should only be changed before you create your scene or import a **unitless** file. Do not change the system units in the current scene.*

RMB click on any snap toggle button on the **Main** toolbar. In **F14** the **Grid and Snap Settings** dialog that opens, choose the **Home Grid** panel and then set **Grid Spacing** to **6**, **Major Lines every Nth Grid Line** to **12**, and **Perspective View Grid Extent** to **10**.

What Just Happened?

*The home grid provides a visual reference to the user. It helps in visualizing space, scale, and distance. Here, I have set **Grid Spacing** to **6**, the size of the smallest square of the grid. In the previous step, I have set the units to inches therefore the size of one grid space is equal to **6** inches. For example, if you create a box with width set to **24** inches, it will take **4** grid boxes.*

Close the **Grid and Snap Settings** dialog. From the **Application** menu, choose **Save** to open the **Save File As** dialog. In the **File name** text box type **hoem1-2-end.max** and then click **Save** to save the file.

Note: Saving Files

*I highly recommend that you save your work at regularly by pressing **Ctrl+S**.*

Creating One Seat Section of the Sofa

On the **Create** panel, click **Geometry**, and then on the **Object Type** rollout, click **Box**. In the **Perspective** viewport, drag out a box of any size. Go to **Modify** panel, and on the **Parameters** rollout, set **Length** to **25.591**, **Width** to **25.591**, and **Height** to **1**. RMB click on the **Select and Move** tool on the **Main** toolbar to open the **Move Transform Type-In** dialog and then set **X** to **0**, **Y** to **0**, and **Z** to **11.42** in the **Absolute:World** group. Close the dialog.

What just happened?

*Here, I have set the position of the box using the **Transform Type-In** dialog [**Move Transform Type-In** dialog]. This dialog allows you to enter precise values for move, rotate, and scale transforms. To open this dialog, RMB click on **Select and Move**, **Select and Rotate**, or **Select and Scale** tool on the **Main** toolbar. You can also press **F12** while one of the aforesaid tools is active to open the dialog.*

Tip: Transform Type-In boxes

*You can also use the **Transform Type-In** boxes on the **Status Bar**. To transform objects, ensure they are selected. Type the values in the **Transform Type-In** boxes and then press **Enter**. You can toggle between the absolute transform and relative transform by clicking the **Relative/Absolute Transform Type-In** button available to the left of the transform boxes.*

Click **Zoom Extents All** to zoom on **Box001** in all viewports [see Figure 15].

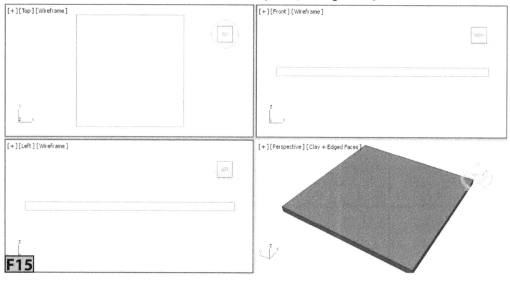

In the **Create** panel, click **Geometry**, and then in the **Object Type** rollout, click **Box**. Activate the **Top** viewport. Expand the **Keyboard Entry** rollout, and set **Length** to **25.591**, **Width** to **1**, and **Height** to **11.417**. Click **Create**. Click **Align** on the **Main** toolbar. Now, click **Box001**.

In the **Align Selection** dialog that opens, set the controls shown in Figure 16. Click **OK** to accept the changes made [see Figure 17].

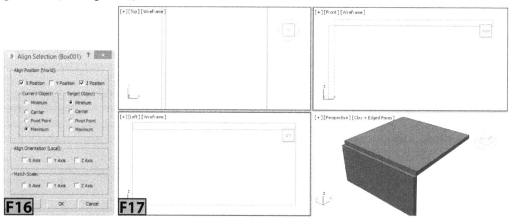

Align **Box001** and **Box002** using **Select and Move** [see Figure 18]. Click **Mirror** on the **Main** toolbar to open the **Mirror** dialog. In this dialog, make sure **X** is selected in the **Mirror Axis** group. Select **Copy** from the **Clone Selection** group and then set **Offset** to **24.591**.

MH1-8   Unit MH1: Hands-on Exercises [Modeling]

Click **OK** to accept the changes made and create a mirror copy of **Box002** [see Figure 19].

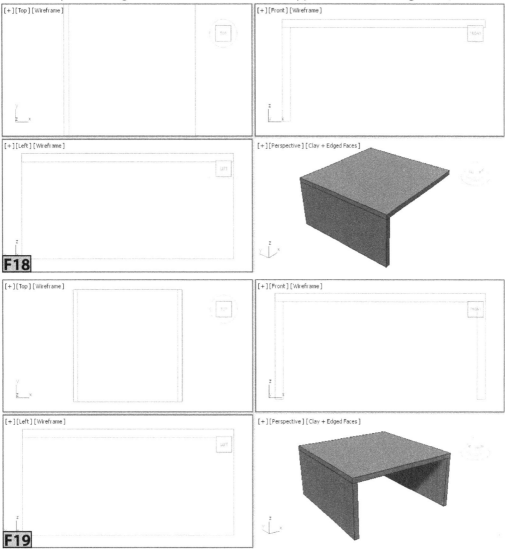

Activate the **Top** viewport. On the **Create** panel, click **Geometry,** and then in the **Object Type** rollout, click **Box**. Expand the **Keyboard Entry** rollout and then set **Length** to **1**, **Width** to **25.591**, and **Height** to **25.984**. Click **Create** to create a box with the name **Box004**. Make sure **Box004** is selected.

Activate the **Top** viewport. Click **Align** on the **Main** toolbar and then click **Box001**. In the **Align Selection** dialog that opens, set the controls shown in Figure 20 and click **OK** to align the objects [see Figure 21].

Activate the **Top** viewport. On the **Create** panel, click **Geometry,** and then on the **Object Type** rollout, click **Box**. Expand the **Keyboard Entry** rollout and then set **Length** to **1**, **Width** to **23.591**, and **Height** to **11.417**. Click **Create** to create a box with the name **Box005**. Next, align it as shown in Figure 22.

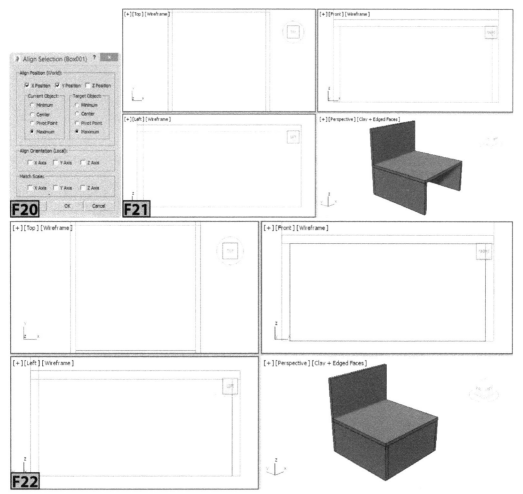

Select **Box001** to **Box005** in the **Scene Explorer**. RMB click on the selection to open a **Quad** menu. Choose **Add Selected To | New Group** from the menu. In the **Group** dialog that opens, type the group name as **oneSeat** and click **OK**.

Creating Corner Section of the Sofa

Collapse **oneSeat** in the **Scene Explorer**, if no already collapsed, RMB click on it and select **Clone** from the **Quad** menu. In the **Clone Options** dialog that opens, select **Copy** from the **Object** group. Change the **Name** to **cornerSeat** and click **OK**.

In the **Perspective** viewport, move the **cornerSeat** to the right of **oneSeat**. Select **cornerSeat** in the **Scene Explorer**, from the **Group** menu, select **Open**. Select **Box008** from the **Scene Explorer**.

Go to **Modify** panel, and on the **Parameters** rollout, set **Height** to **25.984**. From the **Group** menu, select **Close**. Figure 23 shows the **cornerSeat** and **oneSeat**. Now, make various combinations of **oneSeat** and **cornerSeat** by making copies of them [see Figure 24]. Press **CTRL+S** to save the file.

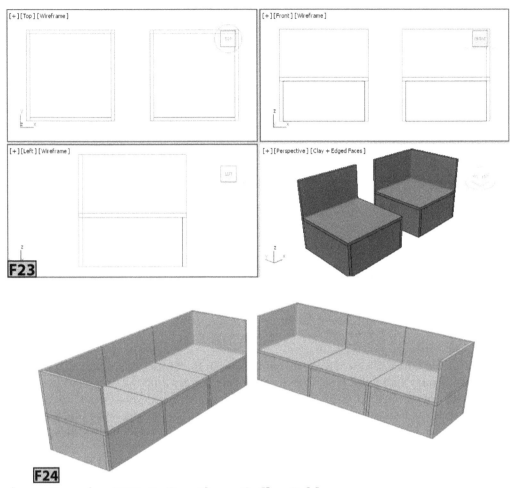

F23

F24

Hands-on Exercise MH1-3: Creating a Coffee Table

In this exercise, you will model a coffee table using the **Cylinder** and **Torus** primitives [see Figure 25]. The following Table 3 summarizes the exercise:

Table 3: Creating Model of a Coffee Table	
In this exercise, you will learn how to:	• Create simple geometry • Setup units and home grid settings • Use the **Select and Place** tool
Skill level	Beginner
Time to complete	20 Minutes
Topics in the section:	• Specifying the Units for the Exercise • Creating the Coffee Table
Project Folder	**hoexm1**

Units	Metric - Centimeters
Final exercise file	hoexm1-3-end.max

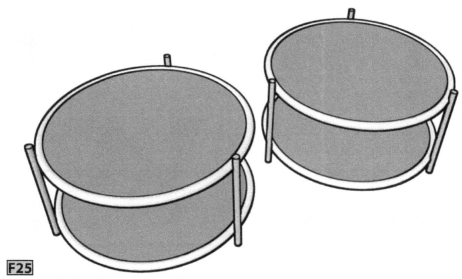

F25

Specifying the Units for the Exercise

Reset 3ds Max. From **Customize** menu choose **Units Setup**. In the **Units Setup** dialog that opens, select **Metric** from the **Display Unit Scale** group. Next, select **Centimeters** from the drop-down located below **Metric**, if already not selected. Click **OK** to accept the change. RMB click on any snap toggle button on the **Main** toolbar. In the **Grid and Snap Settings** dialog that opens, choose the **Home Grid** panel and then set **Grid Spacing** to **5**, **Major Lines every Nth Grid Line** to **10**, and **Perspective View Grid Extent** to **8**.

Close the **Grid and Snap Settings** dialog. From the **Application** menu, choose **Save** to open the **Save File As** dialog. In the **File name** text box type **hoexm1-3-end.max** and click **Save** to save the file.

Creating the Coffee Table

In the **Create** panel, click **Geometry**, and then in the **Object Type** rollout, click **Cylinder**. Activate the **Top** viewport. Expand the **Keyboard Entry** rollout, and set **Radius** to **37.5** and **Height** to **2**.

In the **Parameters** layout, set **Height Segments** to **1**, **Cap Segments** to **1**, and **Sides** to **63**. Click **Create** from the **Keyboard Entry** rollout. In the **Create** panel, click **Geometry**, and then in the **Object Type** rollout, click **Torus**. Create a torus in the **Top** viewport.

Go to **Modify** panel and then in the **Parameters** rollout set **Radius 1** to **37.5**, **Radius 2** to **1.581**, **Segments** to **100**, and **Sides** to **12**. Now, click **Select and Place** tool on the **Main** toolbar and then drag torus onto the cylinder to align the two objects [see Figure 26]. If required, use the **Move** tool to align the two objects. Place the two objects at the origin as discussed earlier.

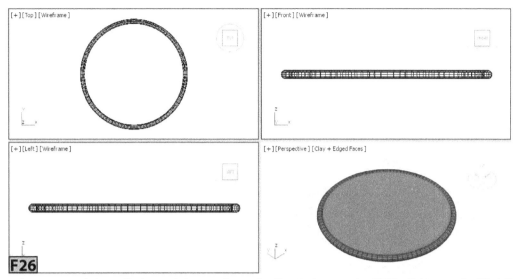

F26

Select the torus and the cylinder and then activate the **Front** viewport by MMB clicking on it. Click **Select and Move** on the **Main** toolbar and then press **Shift**, move the selection down by **30** units along the negative **Y** direction. In the **Clone Options** dialog that appears, choose **Copy** from the **Object** group and click **OK** to create a copy of the selected object [see Figure 27].

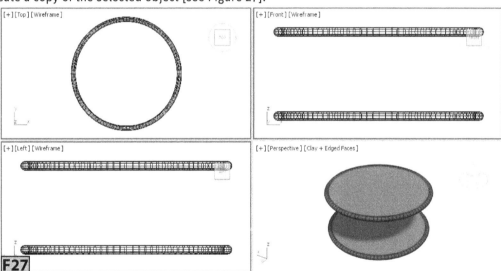

F27

In the **Create** panel, click **Geometry**, and then in the **Object Type** rollout, click **Cylinder**. Create a cylinder in the **Top** viewport. Go to **Modify** panel and then in the **Parameters** rollout set **Radius** to **1.2**, **Height** to **41**, **Height Segments** to **1**, and **Sides** to **18**. Next, make sure that **Select and Move** tool is active and then on the **Status Bar**, enter **-40.246**, **0**, and **-35.352** in the **Transform Type-In** boxes to place the cylinder [see Figure 28]. In the **Hierarchy** panel of the **Command Panel**, click **Use Working Pivot** from the **Working Pivot** rollout.

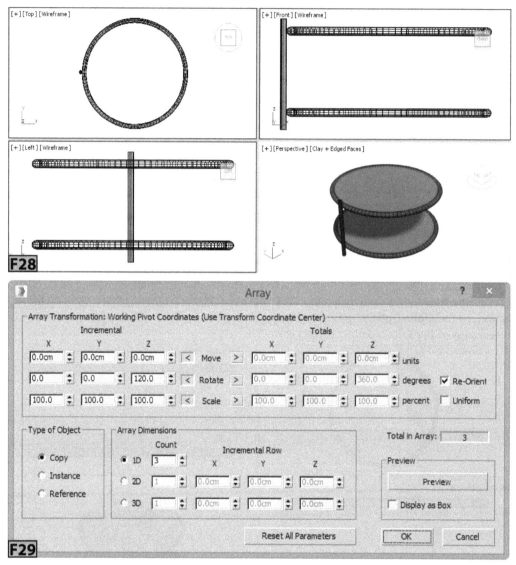

Ensure **CylinderOO3** is selected in a viewport and then choose **Array** from the **Tools** menu. Set the parameters in the **Array** dialog, as shown in Figure 29 and click **OK** to create two more copies of the cylinder [see Figure 30].

Select all objects from the **Scene Explorer** and then choose **Group** from the **Group** menu. Name the group **coffeeTable**. Press **CTRL+S** to save the file.

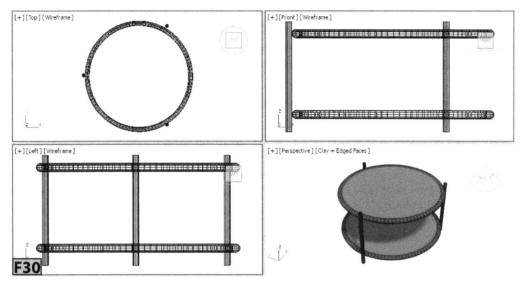

Hands-on Exercise MH1-4: Creating a foot stool

In this exercise, you will model a foot stool using the **ChamferBox** and **OilTank** extended primitives [see Figure 31]. The following table summarizes the exercise:

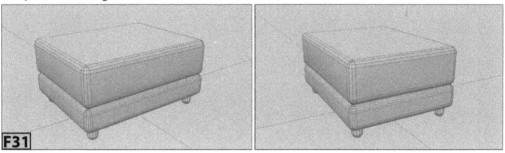

Table4: Creating a Foot Stool	
In this exercise, you will learn how to:	• Create extended primitives • Create clones
Skill level	Beginner
Time to complete	20 Minutes
Topics in the section:	• Specifying the Units for the Exercise • Creating the Stool
Project folder	**hoexm1**
Units	**US Standard – Decimal Inches**
Final exercise file	**hoexm1-4-end.max**

Specifying the Units for the Exercise

Reset 3ds Max. From **Customize** menu choose **Units Setup**. In the **Units Setup** dialog that opens, select the **US standard** option from the **Display Unit Scale** group. Next, select **Decimal Inches** from the drop-down located below the **US standard** option, if already not selected. Click **OK** to accept the change.

RMB click on any snap toggle button on the **Main** toolbar. In the **Grid and Snap Settings** dialog that opens, choose the **Home Grid** tab and then set **Grid Spacing** to **3**, **Major Lines every Nth Grid Line** to **5**, and **Perspective View Grid Extent** to **5**. Close the **Grid and Snap Settings** dialog.

Creating the Stool

In the **Create** panel, click **Geometry**, and then choose **Extended Primitives** from the drop-down located below **Geometry**. In the **Object Type** rollout, click **ChamferBox**. Create a chamfer box in the **Top** viewport. Go to **Modify** panel and then in the **Parameters** rollout set **Length** to **24.8**, **Width** to **31.5**, **Height** to **5**, **Fillet** to **1.2**, and **Fillet Segs** to **5**. Rename the chamfer box to **baseGeo**.

Click **Select and Move** in **Main** toolbar and then enter **0** in all **Transform Type-In** boxes to place the box at the origin. Press **Shift+Ctrl+Z** to zoom the chamfer box to its extents. In the **Perspective** viewport, press **Shift** and drag **baseGeo** along the **+Z** axis about **5**. In the **Clone Option** dialog that appears, make sure **Copy** is chosen from the **Object** group. Type **seatGeo** in the name text box and click **OK**. Go to **Modify** panel and then in the **Parameters** rollout set **Height** to **8**, **Fillet** to **0.72** and **Fillet Segs** to **3**. Align the boxes [see Figure 32].

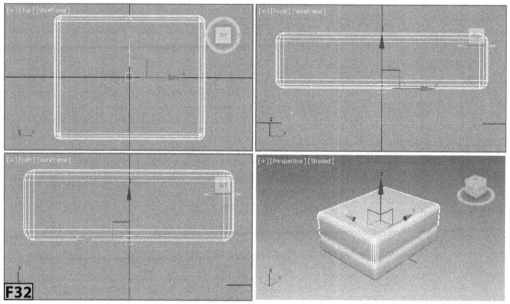

In the **Create** panel, click **Geometry**, and then choose **Extended Primitives** from the drop-down located below **Geometry**. In the **Object Type** rollout, click **OilTank**. Create an oil tank in the **Top** viewport. Go to **Modify** panel and then in the **Parameters** rollout set **Radius** to **1.1**, **Height** to **5**, **Sides** to **25**, and **Cap Height** to **9**.

Rename oil tank as **legGeo** and then align it [see Figure 33]. Create three more copies of legGeo and align it viewports [see figure 34].

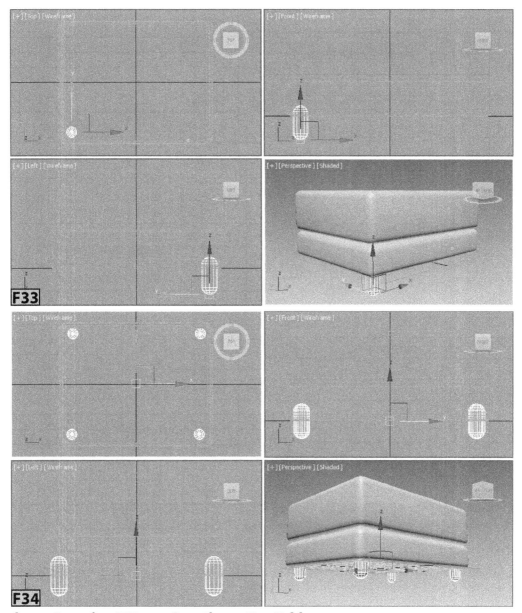

Hands-on Exercise MH1-5: Creating a Bar Table

In this exercise, you will model a bar table using the **ChamferBox** and **ChamferCyl** extended primitives [see Figure 35]. The following table summarizes the exercise:

Table 5: Creating a Bar Table	
In this exercise, you will learn how to:	• Create extended primitives • Create clones • Apply **Bend** and **Taper** modifiers • Use the working pivot

Skill level	Beginner
Time to complete	40 Minutes
Topics in the section:	• Specifying the Units for the Exercise • Creating the Bar Table
Project folder	**hoexm1**
Units	**US Standard – Decimal Inches**
Final exercise file	**hoexm1-5-end.max**

F35

Specifying the Units for the Exercise

Reset 3ds Max. From **Customize** menu choose **Units Setup**. In the **Units Setup** dialog that opens, select the **US standard** option from the **Display Unit Scale** group. Next, select **Decimal Inches** from the drop-down located below the **US Standard** option, if already not selected. Click **OK** to accept the change.

RMB click on any snap toggle button on the **Main** toolbar. In the **Grid and Snap Settings** dialog that opens, choose the **Home Grid** tab and then set **Grid Spacing** to **3**, **Major Lines every Nth Grid Line** to **5**, and **Perspective View Grid Extent** to **5**. Close the **Grid and Snap Settings** dialog.

Creating the Bar Table

In the **Create** panel, click **Geometry**, and then choose **Extended Primitives** from the drop-down located below **Geometry**. In the **Object Type** rollout, click **ChamferCyl**. Create a cylinder in the **Top** viewport. Go to **Modify** panel and then in the **Parameters** rollout set **Radius** to **13.78**, **Height** to **1.5**, **Fillet** to **0.15**, **Fillet Segs** to **5**, and **Sides** to **50**. Rename the cylinder as **topGeo**.

Click **Select and Move** in **Main** toolbar and then enter **0** in all **Transform Type-In** boxes to place **topGeo** at the origin. Create another chamfer cylinder in the **Top** viewport and rename it as **supportGeo**. Go to **Modify** panel and then in the **Parameters** rollout set **Radius** to **1.3**, **Height** to **38**, **Fillet** to **0**, **Fillet Segs** to **1**, and **Sides** to **18**. Now, align **topGeo** and **supportGeo** in viewports [see Figure 36].

In the **Create** panel, click **Geometry**, and then choose **Standard Primitives** from the drop-down located below **Geometry**. In the **Object Type** rollout, click **Tube**. Create a tube in the **Top** viewport. Place the tube at the origin. Go to **Modify** panel and then in the **Parameters** rollout set **Radius 1** to **4**, **Radius 2** to **1.3**, **Height** to **2**, and **Sides** to **50**. Rename tube as **tubeGeo** [see Figure 37].

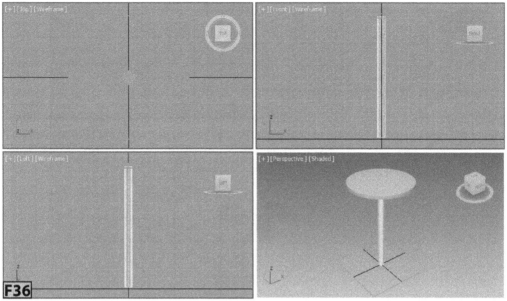

In the **Create** panel, click **Geometry**, and then choose **Extended Primitives** from the drop-down located below **Geometry**. In the **Object Type** rollout, click **ChamferBox**. Create a box in the **Top** viewport. Go to **Modify** panel and then in the **Parameters** rollout set **Length** to **2.1**, **Width** to **12.8**, **Height** to **1.6**, **Fillet** to **0.1** and **Fillet Segs** to **6**. Rename the box as **legGeo**. From the **Object-Space Modifiers** section of the **Modifier List**, select **Taper**. In the **Parameters** layout, set **Amount** to **-0.64**. Set **Primary** to **X** in the **Taper Axis** area. Now, aline **legGeo** with **tubeGeo** [see Figure 38].

Create another chamfer box in the **Top** viewport. Go to **Modify** panel and then in the **Parameters** rollout set **Length** to **1.57**, **Width** to **5.6**, **Height** to **0.64**, **Fillet** to **0.07**, **Width Segs** to **32**, and **Fillet Segs** to **3**. From the **Object-Space Modifiers** section of the **Modifier List**, select **Bend**. In the **Parameters** layout, set **Angle** to **213**. Turn on **X** in the **Bend Axis** area [see Figure 39].

Create another chamfer cylinder in the **Top** viewport. Go to **Modify** panel and then in the **Parameters** rollout set **Radius** to **1.362**, **Height** to **1.72**, **Fillet** to **0.1**, **Fillet Segs** to **5**, and **Sides** to **50**. Align the cylinder with the box and then group them with the name **grpRoller**. Align **grpRoller** with **legGeo** [see Figure 40] and then group them as **grpLeg**.

Activate the **Top** viewport. In the **Command Panel**, click **Hierarchy**, and then click **Use Working Pivot**. Click **Select and Rotate** on the **Main** toolbar. Click **Angle Snap Toggle** on the **Main** toolbar. Press **Shift** and rotate **grpLeg** clockwise by **90** degrees. In the **Clone Options** dialog that opens [see Figure 41], turn on **Reference** in the **Object** group.

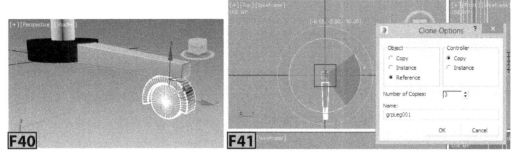

Set **Number of Copies** to **3** and click **OK** to create **3** more legs [see Figure 42]. Toggle of the working pivot by clicking **Use Working Pivot** in the **Hierarchy** panel.

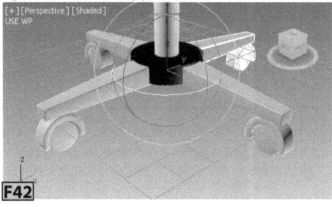

Hands-on Exercise MH1-6: Creating a Serving Bowl

In this exercise, you will create model of a bowl [see Figure 43]. Table 6 summarizes the exercise:

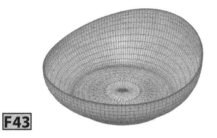 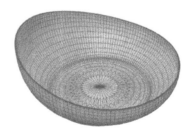

F43

Table 6: Creating A Serving Bowl	
In this exercise, you will learn how to:	• Convert a parametric primitive to an **Editable Poly** object. • Use polygon and edge selection techniques. • Remove sub-objects from an object. • Chamfer, extrude, and inset faces. • Use the **Taper** modifier's gizmo. • Use the **TurboSmooth** modifier.

Skill level	Beginner
Time to complete	20 Minutes
Topics in the section:	• Specifying the Units for the Exercise • Creating the Bowl
Project folder	**hoexm1**
Units	**Metric - Centimeters**
Final exercise file	**hoexm1-6-end.max**

Specifying the Units for the Exercise

From **Customize** menu choose **Units Setup**. In the **Units Setup** dialog that opens, turn on **Metric** from the **Display Unit Scale** group. Next, select **Centimeters** from the drop-down located below **Metric**, if already not selected. Click **OK** to accept the change.

RMB click on any snap toggle button on the **Main** toolbar. In the **Grid and Snap Settings** dialog that opens, choose the **Home Grid** panel and then set **Grid Spacing** to **5**, **Major Lines every Nth Grid Line** to **5**, and **Perspective View Grid Extent** to **10**. Close the **Grid and Snap Settings** dialog.

Creating the Bowl

On the **Create** panel, click **Geometry** and then on the **Object Type** rollout, click **Cylinder**. Create a cylinder in the **Top** viewport. Go to **Modify** panel and then on the **Parameters** rollout, set **Radius** to **25.591**, **Height** to **13**, **Sides** to **36**, and **Height Segments** to **2**.

Set the **Transform Type-In** boxes in the **Status Bar** to **0** to place the cylinder at the origin [see Figure 44]. Now, rename the cylinder as **bowlGeo**. RMB click on **bowlGeo**. In the **transform** quadrant of the **Quad** menu that appears, choose **Convert To: Convert to Editable Poly**. Click **Polygon** in the **Modify panel | Selection rollout** and then select the top polygon of **bowlGeo**. Press **Delete** to remove the polygon.

Click **Select and Uniform Scale** on the **Main** toolbar. Select the bottom set of vertices and uniformly scale them down about **70%** [see Figure 45]. You can use the **Scale Transform Type-In** dialog to precisely enter the scale value.

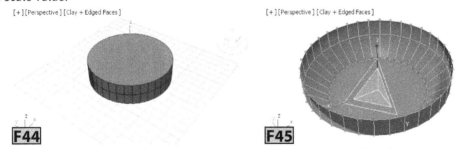

Click **Select Object** on the **Main** Toolbar. Select the bottom polygon of **bowlGeo** and then click **Settings** on the right of **Extrude** in the **Modify panel | Edit Polygons rollout**. In the **Extude's** caddy, set **Height** to **1** and click **OK** [see Figure 46]. Click **Settings** on the right of **Inset** in the **Modify panel | Edit Polygons rollout**. In the **Inset's** caddy, set **Amount** to **2** and click **Apply and Continue**. Now, set **Amount** to **7** and click **OK** [see Figure 47].

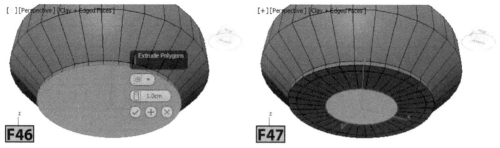

F46   F47

In the **Modify panel | Selection rollout**, **Ctrl+click Vertex**. Click **Settings** on the right of **Weld** in the **Edit Vertices** rollout. In the **Weld's** caddy, set **Weld Threshold** to **4** and click **OK**. Now, click on **Editable Poly** in the modifier stack list to exit the sub-object level. From the **Modifier List | OBJECT-SPACE MODIFIERS section**, choose **Shell**. In the **Parameters** rollout, set **Outer Amount** to **0.5**. From the **Modifier List | OBJECT-SPACE MODIFIERS** section, choose **Edit Poly**.

Click **Edge** in the **Modify panel | Selection rollout**. Select the edges [see Figure 48] and click **Loop** from the Selection rollout. Click **Settings** on the right of **Chamfer** in the **Edit Edges** rollout. In the **Chamfer's** caddy, set **Amount** to **0.1** [see Figure 49] and click **OK**.

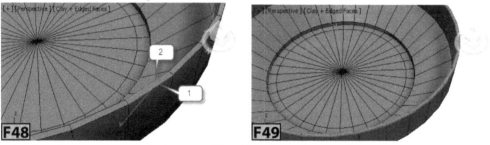

F48   F49

Similarly, chamfer the edges at the bottom of **bowlGeo** (see Figure 50). Now, click **Edit Poly** in the stack display to activate the **Object** level.

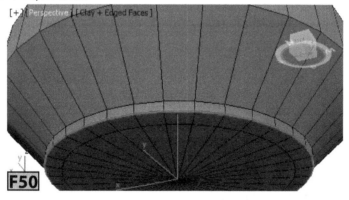

F50

From the **Modifier List | OBJECT-SPACE MODIFIERS** section, choose **Taper**. In the modifier stack display, expand **Taper** and click on **Gizmo** sub-object. Click **Select and Uniform Scale** on the **Main** toolbar and then scale down the gizmo [see Figure 51]. Exit **Taper's** sub-object level.

In the **Parameters** rollout, set **Amount** to **0.26** and **Curve** to **-0.93**. Also, set **Primary** to **X** and **Effect** to **Z** [see Figure 52].

What just happened?
*I have applied the **Taper** modifier to change the shape of the bowl. This modifier produces a tapered contour by scaling the ends of the geometry. The **Taper's** gizmo allows you to manipulate the result. **Amount** controls the extent of scaling. The controls in the **Primary** group define the central axis for taper. **Effect** determines the direction of taper.*

From the **Modifier List | OBJECT-SPACE MODIFIERS section**, choose **TurboSmooth**. In the **Modify panel | TurboSmooth** rollout set **Iterations** to **2**.

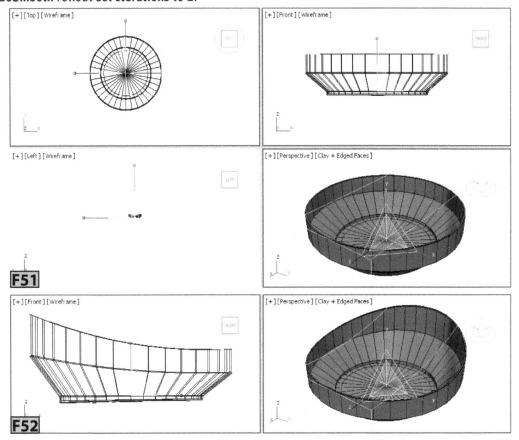

What just happened?
*The **TurboSmooth** modifier smoothes the geometry in the scene by subdividing the geometry. I have applied it to **bowlGeo** because I want to get rid of the hard outer edges. **Iterations** defines the number of times geometry is subdivided.*

Hands-on Exercise MH1-7: Creating a Kitchen Cabinet

In this exercise, you will create model of a kitchen cabinet [see Figure 53].

F53

The following table the exercise:

Table 7: Creating a Kitchen Cabinet	
In this exercise, you will learn how to:	• Convert a parametric primitive to an editable Poly object • Use polygon and edge selection techniques • Remove sub-objects from an object • Chamfer edges • Extrude and inset faces
Skill level	Beginner
Time to complete	20 Minutes
Topics in the section:	• Specifying the Units for the Exercise • Creating the Kitchen Cabinet
Project folder	**hoexm1**
Units	**Metric - Centimeters**
Final exercise file	**hoexm1-7.max**

Specifying the Units for the Exercise

From **Customize** menu choose **Units Setup**. In the **Units Setup** dialog that opens, turn on **Metric** from the **Display Unit Scale** group. Next, select **Centimeters** from the drop-down located below **Metric**, if already not selected. Click **OK** to accept the change. RMB click on any snap toggle button on the **Main** toolbar. In the **Grid and Snap Settings** dialog that opens, choose the **Home Grid** panel and then set **Grid Spacing** to **5**, **Major Lines every Nth Grid Line** to **5**, and **Perspective View Grid Extent** to **10**. Close the **Grid and Snap Settings** dialog.

Creating the Cabinet

On the **Create** panel, click **Geometry** and then on the **Object Type** rollout, click **Box**. Create a box in the **Top** viewport. Go to **Modify** panel and then on the **Parameters** rollout, set **Length** to **38**, **Width** to **45**, and **Height** to **76**. Set the **Transform Type-In** boxes in the **Status Bar** to **0** to place the box at the origin [see Figure 54].

Convert the **Box001** to the **Editable Poly** object. Select the top and bottom polygons of the box [see Figure 55] and then click **Detach** from the **Modify Panel | Edit Geometry** rollout. Click **OK** in the **Detach** dialog to create a new object from the selected polygons with the name **Object001**.

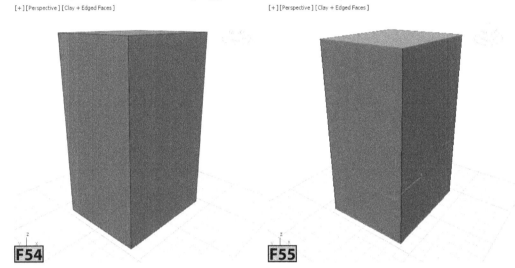

Select **Object001** from the **Scene Explorer** and activate **Polygon** sub-object level. Now, select top and bottom polygons of **Object001**. Click **Settings** on the right of **Extrude** in the **Modify panel | Edit Polygons** rollout. In the **Extude's** caddy, set **Height** to **5** and click **OK** [see Figure 56]. Select the polygon, as shown in Figure 57 and then move it by **3** units in the positive **X** direction [see Figure 58].

Select the top polygon and then click **Settings** on the right of **Extrude** in the **Modify panel | Edit Polygons** rollout. In the **Extude's** caddy, set **Height** to **5** and click **OK** [see Figure 59]. Similarly extrude the front polygon by **3** units [refer Figure 60].

F59   F60   F61

Select **Box001** from the **Scene Explorer** and then activate the **Edge** sub-object level. Select the edges, as shown in Figure 61. Click **Connect** in the **Modify panel | Edit Edges** rollout to connect the selected edges [see Figure 62].

Select the polygons as shown in Figure 63 and then click **Settings** on the right of **Inset** in the **Modify panel | Edit Polygons rollout**. In the **Inset's** caddy, set **Inset Type** to **By Polygon**, and **Amount** to 2 and then click **OK** [see Figure 64].

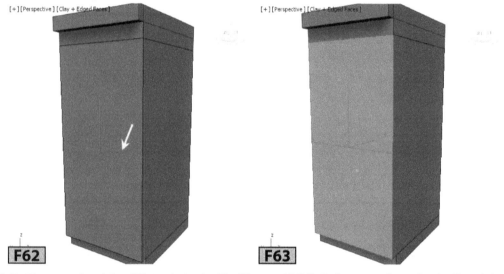

F62   F63

Click **Settings** on the right of **Extrude** in the **Modify panel | Edit Polygons** rollout. In the **Extude's** caddy, set **Extrusion Type** to **By Polygon** and **Height** to **1.5** and click **OK** [see Figure 65].

Select **Box001** from the **Scene Explorer** and then on the **Modify Panel | Edit Geometry rollout**, click **Attach**. Click on **Object001** in a viewport to attach the two objects. Now, rename the resulting mesh as **cabinetGeo**. Activate the **Edge** sub-object and then select the outside edges. Click **Settings** on the right of **Chamfer** in the **Modify panel | Edit Edges rollout**. In the **Chamfer's** caddy, set **Chamfer Type** to **Quad Chamfer**, Edge **Chamfer Amount** to **0.1**, and **Connect Edge Segments** to **1**. Click **OK** [see Figure 66].

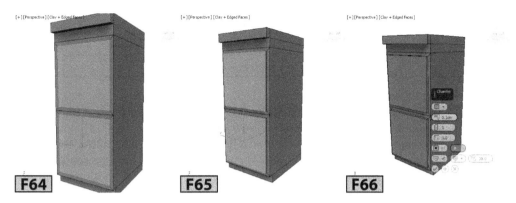

F64	F65	F66

Hands-on Exercise MH1-8: Creating a Book

In this exercise, you will create model of a book [see Figure 67].

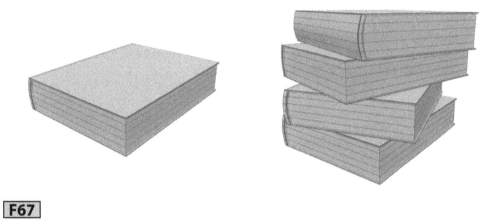

F67

Table 8 summarizes the exercise:

Table 8: Creating model of a book	
In this exercise, you will learn how to:	• Convert a parametric primitive to an editable object • Use polygon and edge selection techniques • Add segments to the objects • Chamfer edges • Extrude faces
Skill level	Beginner
Time to complete	20 Minutes
Topics in the section:	• Specifying the Units for the Exercise • Creating the Book

Project folder	**hoexm1**
Units	**US Standard – Decimal Inches**
Final exercise file	**hoexm1-8-end.max**

Specifying the Units for the Exercise

From **Customize** menu choose **Units Setup**. In the **Units Setup** dialog that opens, select **US Standard** from the **Display Unit Scale** group. Next, select **Decimal Inches** from the drop-down located below **US Standard** and then click **OK** to accept the change. RMB click on any snap toggle button on the **Main** toolbar. In the **Grid and Snap Settings** dialog that opens, choose the **Home Grid** panel and then set **Grid Spacing** to **5**, **Major Lines every Nth Grid Line** to **5**, and **Perspective View Grid Extent** to **5**. Close the **Grid and Snap Settings** dialog.

Creating the Book

On the **Create** panel, click **Geometry** and then on the **Object Type** rollout, click **Box**. Create a box in the **Top** viewport. Go to **Modify** panel, and in the **Parameters** rollout, set **Length** to **7.44**, **Width** to **9.69**, and **Height** to **2**. Set the **Transform Type-In** boxes in the **Status Bar** to **0** to place the box at the origin. Now, rename the box as **bookGeo**.

RMB click on **bookGeo**. In the **transform** quadrant of the **Quad** menu that appears, choose **Convert To: Convert to Editable Poly**. Click **Edge** in the **Modify panel | Selection rollout** and then select the edge shown in Figure 68. Click **Ring** to select the edge ring [see Figure 69].

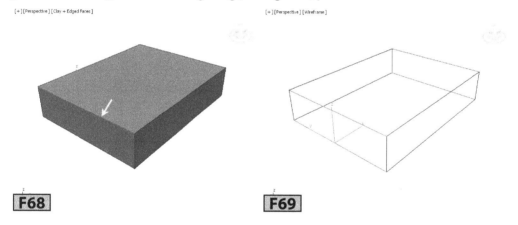

F68   F69

Click **Settings** on the right of **Connect** in the **Edit Edges** rollout. In the **Connect's** caddy, set **Slide** to **95** [see Figure 70] and then click **OK** to connect the selected edges. Similarly, add four edge loops [**Segments: 4, Slide: 0**] to the part of the book that will make up the pages [see Figure 71].

Click **Polygon** in the **Modify panel | Selection rollout** and then select the polygons shown in Figure 72. Click **Settings** on the right of **Inset** in the **Edit Polygons** rollout. In the **Inset's** caddy, set **Amount** to **0.08** [see Figure 73] and then click **OK** to inset the polygons.

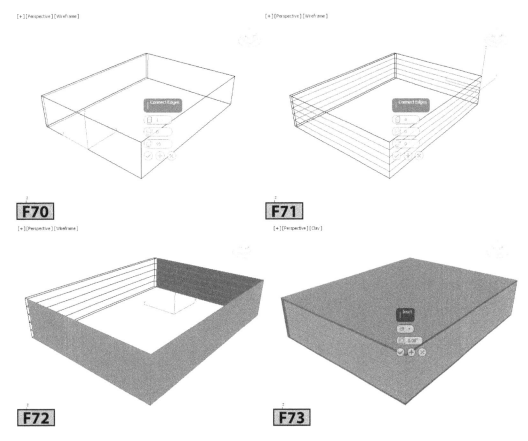

F70

F71

F72

F73

Click **Settings** on the right of **Extrude** in the **Edit Polygons** rollout. In the **Extrude's** caddy, set **Group** to **Local Normal** and **Height** to **-0.129** [see Figure 74] and then click **OK** to extrude the polygons. Click **Edge** in the **Modify panel** | **Selection rollout** and then select all outer edges of the cover shown in Figure 75.

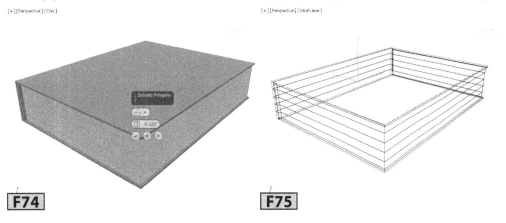

F74

F75

Click **Settings** on the right of **Chamfer** in the **Edit Edges** rollout. In the **Chamfer's** caddy, set **Edge Chamfer Amount** to **0.01** and **Connect Edge Segments** to **2** [see Figure 76] and then click **OK** to chamfer the edges. Click **Vertex** in the **Modify panel** | **Selection rollout** and then select the vertices shown in Figure 77. Click

Select and Move on the **Main** toolbar and then adjust the vertices in the **Left** viewport to modify the shape of the book [see Figure 78].

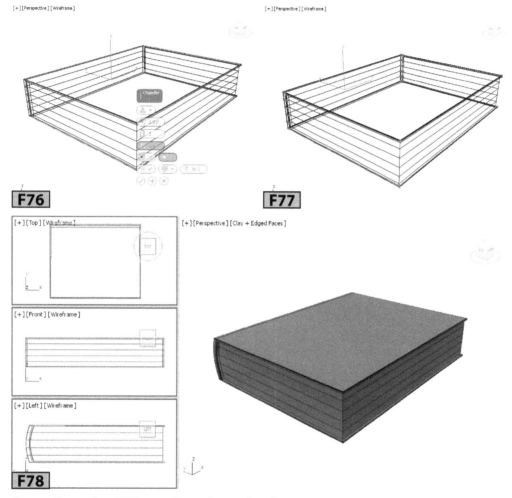

Hands-on Exercise MH1-9: Creating a Desk

In this exercise, you will model a desk [see Figure 79].

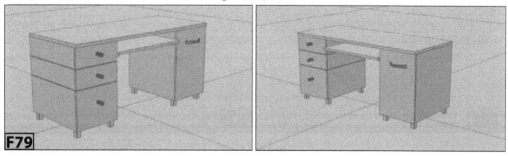

Table 9 summarizes the exercise:

Table 9: Creating a model of a desk	
In this exercise, you will learn how to:	• Convert a parametric primitive to a editable object • Use the tools in the Polygon Modeling Ribbon • Use polygon and edge selection techniques • Add segments to the object • Chamfer edges • Inset and Extrude faces • Attach, Detach, and Bridge polygons • Use the **Quick Slice** feature • Use **NURMS** smoothing
Skill level	Intermediate
Time to complete	1 Hour
Topics in the section:	• Specifying the Units for the Exercise • Creating the Desk
Project folder	**hoexm1**
Units	**Metric - Centimeters**
Final exercise file	**hoexm1-9-end.max**

Specifying the Units for the Exercise

From **Customize** menu choose **Units Setup**. In the **Units Setup** dialog that opens, select the **US Standard** option from the **Display Unit Scale** group. Next, select **Centimeters** from the drop-down located below the **Metric** option, if already not selected. Click **OK** to accept the change.

RMB click on any snap toggle button on the main toolbar. In the **Grid and Snap Settings** dialog that opens, choose the **Home Grid** tab and then set **Grid Spacing** to **10**, **Major Lines every Nth Grid Line** to **10**, and **Perspective View Grid Extent** to **5**. Close the **Grid and Snap Settings** dialog.

Creating the Desk

On the **Create** panel, activate **Geometry**, then on the **Object Type** rollout, click **Box**. Create a box in the **Top** viewport. On the **Modify** panel | **Parameters** rollout, set **Length** to **60**, **Width** to **150**, and **Height** to **2.5**. Click **Select and Move** on the **main toolbar**. Set the **Transform Type-In** boxes to **0** on the **status bar** to place the box at the **origin**. Create another box in the **Top** viewport. In the **Modify** panel | **Parameters** rollout, set **Length** to **60**, **Width** to **40**, and **Height** to **62**. Align the two boxes [see Figure 80]. Create copy the box that you have just created and then align it [see Figure 81].

Now, you will start using the tools and options available in the **Graphite Modeling Tools** ribbon to start shaping the desk. By default, the ribbon is minimized below the **Main** toolbar [see Figure 82]. Click **Show Full Ribbon** to display the full **Ribbon** [see Figure 83]. You will see that the tools in the **Polygon Modeling** panel are inactive because no polygon model exists in the scene [all objects are primitives at this stage]. To expand the **Polygon Modeling** panel and view all tools and options available in it, click **Polygon Modeling**. This expands the panel and displays the tools available in it.

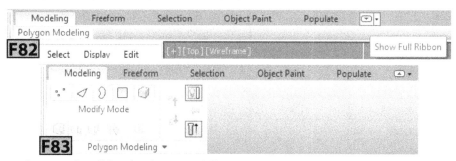

Select the top box. On the **Ribbon | Polygon Modeling** panel, click **Convert to Poly** [see Figure 84]. On the **Ribbon | Geometry (All)** panel, **Shift** click on **Attach**. In the **Attach List** dialog that appears, select **Box002** and **Box003** using **Ctrl** and then click **Attach** to attach the selected boxes to the top box. Rename the unified geometry as **deskGeo**.

Tip: Opening settings of a tool
*If you want to open settings for any tool available in the **Ribbon**, **Shift** click on the tool.*

The **Attach** tool lets you make other objects in the scene part of the selected object. To attach other object, click **Attach** and then select the objects one by one in the viewports. To exit, RMB click in the active viewport, or click the **Attach** tool again. Shift clicking on **Attach** opens the **Attach List** dialog that allows you to select objects from a list.

Note: How materials of the objects are combined
*When you attach objects to a poly object, the materials of the objects are combined. If the objects being attached have no material, they inherit the material of the poly object. If the poly object that you are attaching to doesn't have a material, it inherits material of the objects being attached. In case, when both objects have materials applied, the resulting material is a new **Muti/sub-object** material that includes the input material.*

On the **Ribbon | Polygon Modeling** panel, click **Edge**. Select the edge as shown in Figure 85 and then on the **Ribbon | Modify Selection** panel, click **Ring**. On the **Ribbon | Loops** panel, click **Connect**. An edge loop appears.

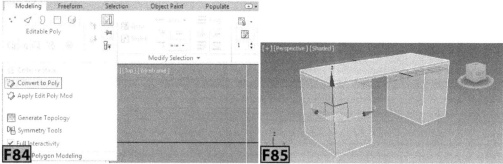

Select the edge shown in Figure 86 and then connect them as done before [see Figure 87]. Hold **Ctrl** and double-click on the edge loop that you created earlier to select it [see Figure 88]. On the **Ribbon | Edges** panel, Shift click on **Chamfer**. In the **Chamfer's** caddy, set **Edge Chamfer Amount** to **0.2** and click **OK** [see Figure 89].

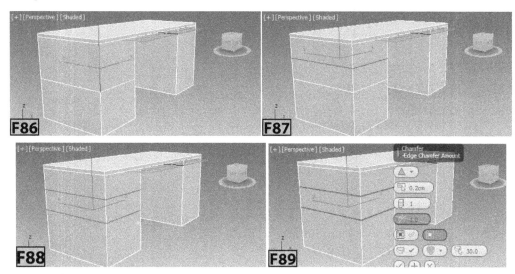

On the **Ribbon | Polygon Modeling** panel, click **Polygon**. Select the polygons [see Figure 90]. Click **Select and Move** on the **main toolbar**. In the **Perspective** viewport, press **Shift** and move the selected polygon slightly [**about 1.2**] outward in the negative Y direction. Release **Shift**. In the **Clone Part of Mesh** dialog that appears, type **drawerGeo** in the text box next to **Clone To Object** and click **OK**.

Ensure the **drawerGeo** is selected. From the **Modifier List | Object-Space Modifiers** section, choose **Shell**. On the **Parameters** rollout, set **Outer Amount** to **1.5**. Align the **drawerGeo** with the **deskGeo** [see Figure 91].

Similarly, detach the polygon shown in Figure 92. Name it as **drawerGeo1**, apply the **Shell** modifier and then align it with **deskGeo** [see Figure 93]. Hide the drawer geometries from the scene using the **Scene Explorer**. Select **deskGeo** and activate the **Front** viewport.

On the **Ribbon | Polygon Modeling** panel, click **Edge**. On the **Ribbon | Geometry (All)** panel, click **Slice Plane**. This will display a **slice plane gizmo** in the viewport and opens the **Slice Mode** panel. Adjust the position of the plane as shown in Figure 94 and then click **Slice** on **Slice Mode** panel to subdivide the geometry [see Figure 95].

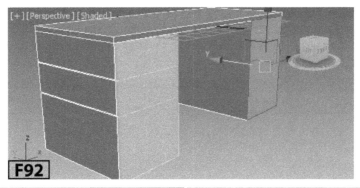

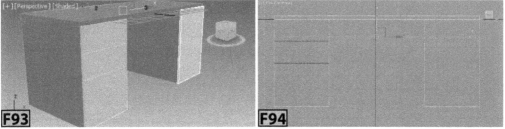

Similarly, add **two** more slices maintaining a gap of **2 units** between them [see Figure 96]. On the **Ribbon | Polygon Modeling** panel, click **Polygon**. Select the polygons, refer to Figure 97. On the **Ribbon | Polygons** panel, **Shift** click **Extrude**. In the **Extrude's** caddy, set **Height** to **4** and click **OK** [see Figure 97].

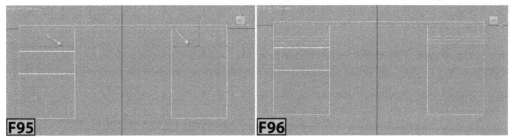

Select the polygons shown in Figure 98. On the **Ribbon | Polygons** panel, click **Bridge** to create a bridge between the selected polygons [see Figure 99].

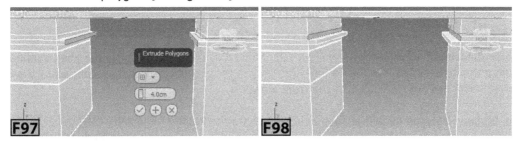

On the **Ribbon | Geometry (All)** panel, click on **Detach**. In the **Detach** dialog that appears, set **Detach as** to **sliderGeo** and click **OK**. Select **sliderGeo** and move it slightly toward the negative Y axis. From the **Modifier List | Object-Space Modifiers** section, choose **Shell**. On the **Parameters** rollout, set **Inner Amount** to **1.674** and **Outer Amount** to **0**.

What just happened?

The **Detach** tool separates the selected sub-objects and associated polygons as new object or element(s). When you click **Detach**, the **Detach** dialog appears. Type the name of the new object in the **Detach as** textbox and click **OK** to create the new object with the specified name. The selection is removed from the original object. You can turn on **Detach To Element** to make the detached sub-object selection part of the original object but it becomes a new element. Turn on **Detach as Clone** to detach the selection as copy of the original selection; the selection remains intact with the original object.

Select **deskGeo** and then select the front polygon shown in Figure 100. Move it slightly toward the negative Y axis.

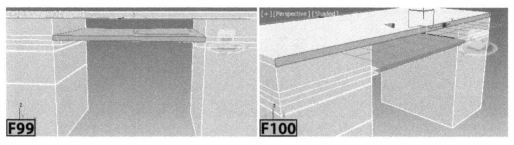

On the **Ribbon | Polygon Modeling** panel, click **Edge**. On the **Ribbon | Edit** panel, click **Swift Loop** to make it active. Press **Ctrl+Shift** and then click on the edges on the drawers that you have created using **Slice Plane**. This will remove the edges [see Figure 101].

The **SwiftLoop** tool allows you to interactively place edges. As you move the cursor over the object surface, a real-tme preview is shown indicating that where the loop will be created when you click. Following are some different features of this tool:

- **Ctrl** click to select an edge loop and activate the **Edge** sub-object level automatically.
- **Alt** drag a selected edge to slide the edge loop between its bounding loops.
- **Ctrl+Alt** drag is a same as the **Alt** drag. However, it also straighten out the edge loop, if necessary.
- **Ctrl+Shift** click on a edge loop to remove it.
- **Shift** click to insert a new loop and adjust it to the flow of the surrounding surface.

Ensure the **drawerGeo** and **drawerGeo1** are visible in the scene. On the **Ribbon | Edit** panel, click **Swift Loop** to turn it off. On the **Create** panel, activate **Geometry**, then on the **Extended Primitives | Object Type** rollout, click **ChamferCyl**. Create a cylinder in the **Top** viewport. On the **Modify** panel | **Parameters** rollout, set **Height** to **6**, **Radius** to **1.5**, and **Fillet** to **0.074**. Now, set **Height Segs** to **2**, **Fillet Segs** to **3**, and **Sides** to **18**. Align it with **drawerGeo** [see Figure 102].

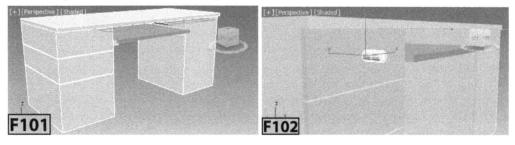

Select the cylinder. On the **Ribbon | Polygon Modeling** panel, click **Convert to Poly**. On the **Ribbon | Polygon Modeling** panel, click **Edge**. Select the edge shown in Figure 103. On the **Ribbon | Modify Selection** panel, click **Loop.** On the **Ribbon | Edges** panel, **Shift** click on **Chamfer**. In the **Chamfer's** caddy, set **Edge Chamfer Amount** to **0.05** and click **OK** [see Figure 104].

On the **Ribbon | Polygon Modeling** panel, **Ctrl** click **Polygon**. On the **Ribbon | Polgon Modeling** panel, click **Shrink** to select the polygons created using the chamfer edge operation [see Figure 105]. On the **Ribbon | Polygons** panel, **Shift** click **Inset**. In the **Inset's** caddy, set **Amount** to **0.02** and click **OK** [see Figure 106].

On the **Ribbon | Polygons** panel, **Shift** click **Extrude**. In the **Extrude's** caddy, set **Extrusion Type** to **Local Normal** and **Height** to **-0.03**. Next, click **OK**. On the **Ribbon | Edit** panel, click **Swift Loop** to make it active. Insert edge loops as shown in Figure 107. These edges will help in holding the shape of the groove when you will apply **NURMS** smoothing to the knob. Turn off **Switch Loop**. On the **Ribbon | Edit** panel, click **Use NURMS** to smooth the object [see Figure 108]. Create two more copies of knob and align them [see Figure 109].

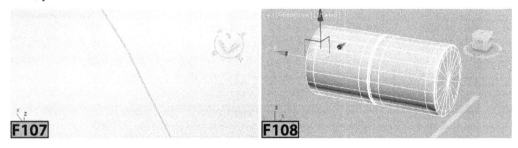

What just happened?
NURMS *stands for* **Non-Uniform Rational Mesh Smooth**. *This tool features smoothing to the objects using NURMS subdivision; the same method used by the* **MeshSmooth** *and* **TurboSmooth** *modifiers. When you click* **Use NURMS**, *the* **Use NURMS** *panel appears. The* **Iterations** *spinner in this panel specifies the number of iterations used to smooth the poly object.*

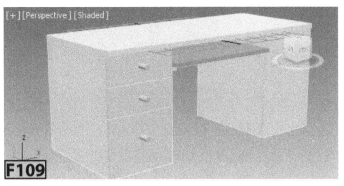

F109

Caution: Calculation Time
Specify the number of iterations carefully. It increases the number of vertices and polygons in an object. As a result, the calculation time can increase as much as four times for each iteration. The value in the **Smoothness** *spinner controls how sharp a corner must be before polygons ae added to smooth it.*

On the **Create** panel, activate **Geometry,** then on the **Extended Primitives | Object Type** rollout, click **ChamferBox**. Create a box in the **Top** viewport. On the **Modify** panel | **Parameters** rollout, set **Length** to **2**, **Width** to **26.4**, **Height** to **1.5**, and **Fillet** to **0.05**. Set **Width Segs** to **12**. From the **Modifier List | Object-Space Modifiers** section, choose **Bend**. On the **Parameters** rollout, set **Angle** to **152** and **Bend Axis** to **X**. Now, align the handle with the **drawerGeo1** [see Figure 110].

From the **Modifier List | Object-Space Modifiers** section, choose **Taper**. On the **Modify** panel | modifier stack display, expand **Taper** and click **Gizmo**. Click **Select and Uniform Scale** on the **Main** toolbar. Change the size of **gizmo** along the **x-axis** [see Figure 111]. On the **Parameters** rollout, set **Amount** to **-1.1** and **Effect** to **Y**. From the **Modifier List | Object-Space Modifiers** section, choose **TurboSmooth** to smooth the handle [see Figure 112].

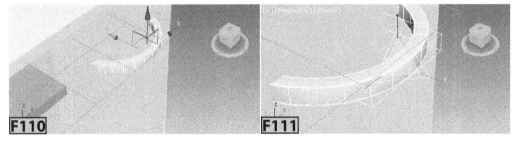

F110   **F111**

Convert **drawerGeo** and **drawerGeo1** to **Editable Poly**. Select **drawerGeo** and then on the **Ribbon | Polygon Modeling** panel, click **Edge**. Press **Ctrl+A** to select all the edges of **drawerGeo**. On the **Ribbon | Edges** panel, **Shift** click **Chamfer**. In the **Chamfer's** caddy, set **Edge Chamfer Amount** to **0.06** and click **OK**. Similarly, chamfer all edges of **drawerGeo1** and **deskGeo**. On the **Create** panel, activate **Geometry,** then on the **Extended Primitives | Object Type** rollout, click **ChamferBox**. Create a box in the **Top** viewport. On the **Modify** panel | **Parameters** rollout, set **Length** to **4**, **Width** to **4**, **Height** to **8**, and **Fillet** to **0.353**. Set **Fillet Segs** to **2**. Ensure the **Length Segs**, **Width Segs**, and **Height Segs** are set to **1**. Rename the box as **legGeo**. Align legGeo as shown in Figure 113. Create seven more copies of **legGeo** and align them as shown in Figure 114.

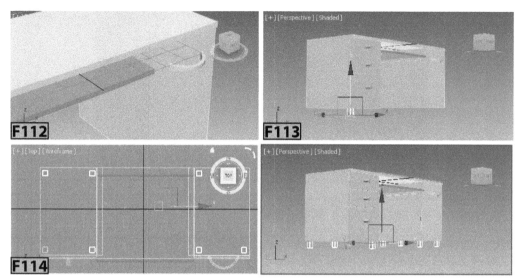

Hands-on Exercise MH1-1O: Creating a Glass Model

In this exercise, you will model a glass using the **Line** primitive and **Lathe** modifier [see Figure 115].

Table 10 summarizes the exercise:

Table 10: Creating model of a glass	
In this exercise, you will learn how to:	• Create a line using **Line** spline • Create surface using the **Lathe** modifier • Fillet vertices
Skill level	Beginner
Time to complete	15 Minutes

Topics in the section:	• Specifying the Units for the Exercise • Creating the Glass
Project folder	**hoexm1**
Units	**Generic Units**
Final exercise file	**hoexm1-10-end.max**

Specifying the Units for the Exercise

From **Customize** menu choose **Units Setup**. In the **Units Setup** dialog that opens, select the **Generic Units** option from the **Display Unit Scale** group.

Creating the Glass

Go to the **Create** panel, click **Shapes**, then click **Line**. In the **Front** viewport, create a shape [see Figure 116]. In the **Modify** panel | **Selection** rollout, click **Vextex**. Select the vertices shown in Figure 117 and then RMB click. Choose **Bezier** from the **tool1** quadrant of the quad menu.

Note: Object Level
*When you first access the **Modify** panel with an editable spline selected, you are at the **Object** level.*

Click **Select and Move** from the **Main** toolbar. Adjust the shape of the curve by moving the vertices and tangents [see Figure 118]. In the **Modify** panel | **Geometry** rollout, click **Fillet**. Click and drag over the vertices [see Figure 119] to apply fillet to them [see Figure 120].

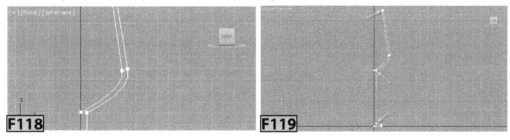

From the **Modifier List** | **Object-Space Modifiers** section, choose **Lathe**. In the **Modify** panel | **Parameters** rollout, click **Min** in the **Align** group. Set **Segments** to **22** [see Figure 121]. Now, check **Weld Core** and **Flip Normals**.

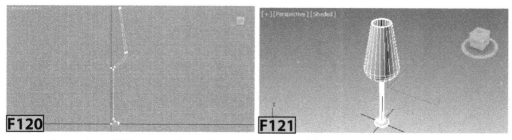

Hands-on Exercise MH1-11: Creating a Glass Table

In this exercise, you will model a glass table using the **Rectangle** spline, **ChamferCyl** primitive, and **Extrude** modifier [see Figure 122]

Table 11 summarizes the exercise:

Table 11: Creating model of a glass table	
In this exercise, you will learn how to:	• Create a rectangle using **Rectangle** spline • Extrude spline using the **Extrude** modifier
Skill level	Beginner
Time to complete	15 Minutes
Topics in the section:	• Specifying the Units for the Exercise • Creating the Glass Table
Project folder	**hoexm1**
Units	**Generic Units**
Final exercise file	**hoexm1-11-end.max**

From **Customize** menu choose **Units Setup**. In the **Units Setup** dialog that opens, select the **Generic Units** option from the **Display Unit Scale** group.

Creating the Glass Table

Go to the **Create** panel, click **Shapes**, then click **Rectangle**. In the **Front** viewport, create a shape. Click **Select and Move** on the **Main** toolbar. Set the **Transform Type-In** boxes to **O** on the **status bar** to place the rectangle at the **origin**. On the **Modify** panel | **Parameters** rollout, set **Length** to **55**, set **Width** to **149**, and **Corner Radius** to **16** [see Figure 123].

RMB click on the rectangle and then choose **Convert To: | Convert to Editable Spline** from the **transform** quadrant of the **Quad** menu. On the **Modify** panel | **Selection** rollout, click **Spline**. Click on the rectangle in a viewport to select the **Spline** sub-object level [see Figure 124]. On the **Modify** panel | **Geometry** rollout, set **Outline's** spinner to **-8** to create an outline [see Figure 125].

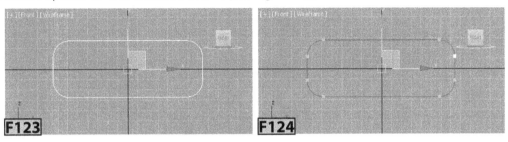

F123   F124

Apply a **Extrude** modifier to the rectangle. On the **Parameters** rollout, set **Amount** to **-100** to extrude the shape [see Figure 126]. In the **Front** viewport, **Shift** drag the spline and then create two instances of it using the **Clone Options** dialog's options [see Figure 127].

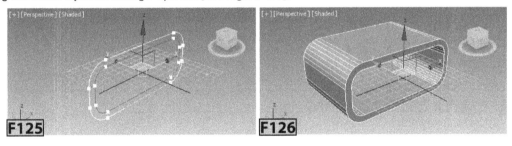

F125   F126

Go to the **Create** panel, click **Geometry | Extended Primitives**, then click the **ChamferCyl** button. In the **Top** viewport, create a cylinder. On the **Modify** panel | **Parameters** rollout, set **Radius** to **6**, **Height** to **16**, **Fillet** to **0.8**, and **Fillet Segs** to **0**. Now, align the cylinder with the table [see Figure 128]. Create three more copies of the cylinder and align them [see Figure 129].

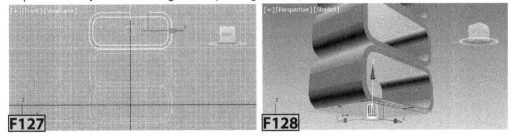

F127   F128

F129

Hands-on Exercise MH1-12: Creating a Corkscrew

In this exercise, you will model a corkscrew using the **Helix** Spline and **Loft** compound object [see Figure 130].

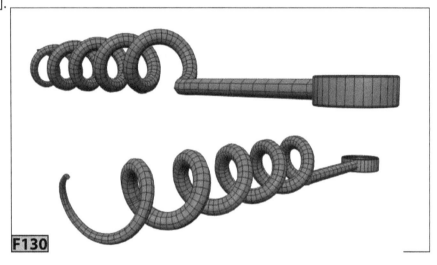

F130

Table 12 summarizes the exercise:

Table 12: Creating model of a corkscrew	
In this exercise, you will learn how to:	• Use the **Helix** spline • Create surfaces using the **Loft** compound object
Skill level	Beginner
Time to complete	15 Minutes
Topics in the section:	• Specifying the Units for the Exercise • Creating the Corkscrew
Project folder	**hoexm1**
Units	**Generic Units**
Final exercise file	**hoexm1-12-end.max**

From **Customize** menu choose **Units Setup**. In the **Units Setup** dialog that opens, select the **Generic Units** option from the **Display Unit Scale** group.

Creating the Corkscrew

Go to the **Create** panel, click **Shapes**, then click **Helix**. In the **Top** viewport, create a shape. On the **Modify** panel | **Parameters** rollout, set **Radius 1** to **8**, **Radius 2** to **8**, **Height** to **120**, and **Turns** to **5.5**. In the **Front** viewport, rotate it by **-90** degrees [see Figure 131].

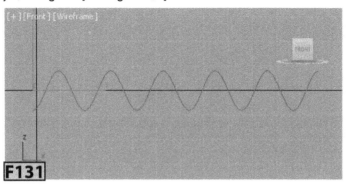

F131

RMB click on the helix and then choose **Convert To: | Convert to Editable Spline** from the **transform** quadrant of the **Quad** menu. On the **Modify** panel | **Selection** rollout, click **Vertex** and then move the **start yellow** vertex toward left about **60** units in the **Front** viewport [see Figure 132].

Apply a **Normalize Spl.** modifier to the helix. On the **Modify** panel | **Parameters** rollout, set **Seg Length** to **5**. RMB click on the helix and then choose **Convert To: | Convert to Editable Spline** from the **transform** quadrant of the **Quad** menu. Go to the **Create** panel, click **Shapes**, then click **Circle**. In the **Left** viewport, create a circle. On the **Modify** panel | **Parameters** rollout, set **Radius** to **2.5**. Select helix in a viewport. Go to the **Create** panel, click **Geometry | Compound Objects**, then click **Loft**. On the **Creation Method** rollout, click **Get Shape** and then click circle in a viewport to loft the circle along the helix [see Figure 133].

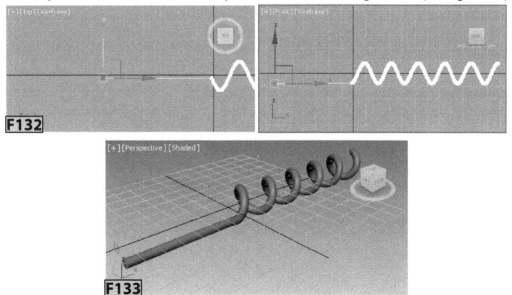

F132

F133

On the **Modify** panel | **Skin Parameters** rollout | **Options** group, set **Shape Steps** to **1** and **Path Steps** to **2**. On the **Modify** panel | **Deformations** rollout, click **Scale**. In the **Scale Deformation** dialog that opens, click **Insert Corner Point** and then add a point below the **80** mark [see Figure 134]. Now, click **Move Control Point** and move the end point downward [see Figure 135] to scale the end area of the corkscrew [see Figure 136]. Go to the **Create** panel, click **Geometry** | **Extended Primitives**, then click the **ChamferCyl** button. In the **Top** viewport, create a cylinder.

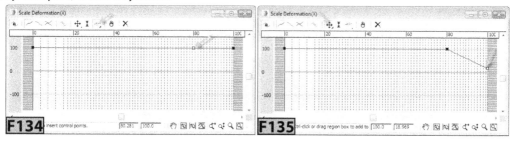

On the **Modify** panel | **Parameters** rollout, set **Radius** to **9.3**, **Height** to **6.5**, **Fillet** to **0.41**, **Sides** to **32**, and **Fillet Segs** to **3**. Now, align the cylinder with the corkscrew [see Figure 137].

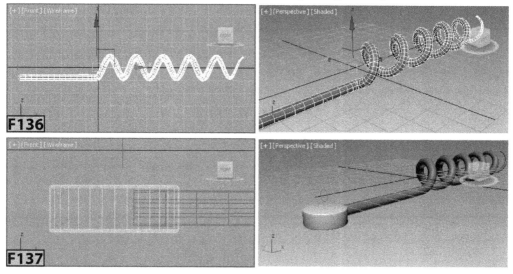

Hands-on Exercise MH1-13: Creating a USB Drive-I

In this exercise, you will model a USB connector [see Figure 138]. Table 13 summarizes the exercise:

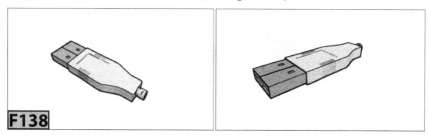

Table 13: Creating a USB drive	
In this exercise, you will learn how to:	• Use the tools from the **Ribbon** • Use the **ShiftLoop** tool
Skill level	Intermediate
Time to complete	40 Minutes
Topics in the section:	• Specifying the Units for the Exercise • Creating the USB Connector
Project folder	**hoexm1**
Units	**Metric - Millimeters**
Final exercise file	**hoexm1-13-end.max**

Specifying the Units for the Exercise

From **Customize** menu choose **Units Setup**. In the **Units Setup** dialog that opens, select the **Metric** option from the **Display Unit Scale** group. Next, select **Millimeters** from the drop-down located below the **Metric** option, if already not selected. Click **OK** to accept the change. RMB click on any snap toggle button on the main toolbar. In the **Grid and Snap Settings** dialog that opens, choose the **Home Grid** tab and then set **Grid Spacing** to **3**, **Major Lines every Nth Grid Line** to **5**, and **Perspective View Grid Extent** to **3**. Close the **Grid and Snap Settings** dialog.

Creating the USB Connector

Create a box in the **Top** viewport. On the **Modify** panel | **Parameters** rollout, set **Length** to **15**, **Width** to **30**, **Height** to **5**, and **Width Segments** to **2**. Rename the cylinder as **ucGeo**. Click **Select and Move** on the main toolbar. Set the **Transform Type-In** boxes to **0** on the **status bar** to place the cylinder at the **origin**. On the **Ribbon** | **Polygon Modeling** panel, click **Convert to Poly**. Activate **Edge** sub-object level and then on the **Ribbon** | **Edit** panel, click **SwiftLoop**. Create two loops [see Figure 139]. Slide the loops toward right using **Alt** [see Figure 139]. Deactivate **SwiftLoop**.

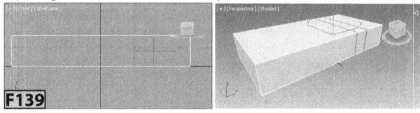

Activate **Vertex** sub-object level and then adjust the shape of the connector using **Select and Move** and **Select and Uniform Scale** [see Figure 140]. Activate **Polygon** sub-object level and then select the front polygon. On the **Ribbon** | **Polygons** panel, **Shift** click **Inset**. In the **Inset's** caddy, set **Amount** to **0.5** and then click **OK** [see Figure 141].

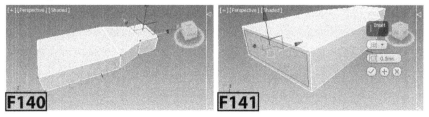

On the **Ribbon | Polygons** panel, **Shift** click **Extrude**. In the **Extrude's** caddy, set **Amount** to **-8** and then click **OK** [see Figure 142]. Activate **Edge** sub-object level and then select the edge shown in Figure 143. On the **Ribbon | Modify Selection** panel, click **Ring**. On the **Ribbon | Loops** panel, **Shift** click **Connect**. In the **Connect's** caddy, set **Segments** to **2** and **Pinch** to **62** [see Figure 144]. Click **OK**. Similarly, create two more edge loops [see Figure 145].

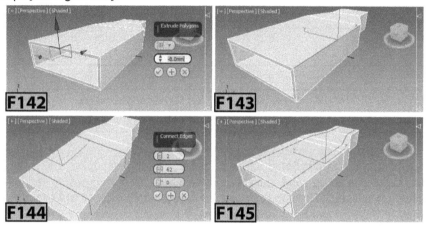

Activate **Polygon** sub-object level and then select the polygon shown in Figure 146. On the **Ribbon | Polygons** panel, **Shift** click **Inset**. In the **Inset's** caddy, set **Amount** to **0.5** and **then** click **OK**. On the **Ribbon | Polygons** panel, **Shift** click **Extrude**. In the **Extrude's** caddy, set **Amount** to **-0.3** and **then** click **OK** [see Figure 147].

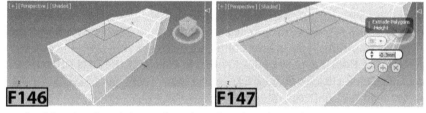

Activate **Edge** sub-object level and then select the edge ring shown in Figure 148. In the **Ribbon | Loops** panel, **Shift** click **Connect**. In the **Connect's** caddy, set **Segments** to **14** and **Pinch** to **-59**. Click **OK** [see Figure 149].

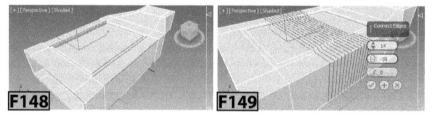

Activate **Polygon** sub-object level and then select every other polygon loop using the **Ctrl** and **Ctrl+Shift** [see Figure 150].

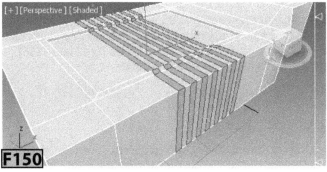

Now, in the **Top** viewport, remove the polygons from the selection using **Alt** [see Figure 151].

On the **Ribbon | Polygons** panel, **Shift** click **Inset**. In the **Inset's** caddy, set **Amount** to **0.1** and then click **OK**. On the **Ribbon | Polygons** panel, **Shift** click **Extrude**. In the **Extrude's** caddy, set **Extrusion Type** to **Local Normal** and **Amount** to **-0.2** and **then** click **OK** [see Figure 152].

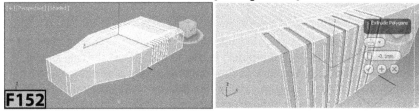

Activate **Edge** sub-object level and then on the **Ribbon | Edit** panel, click **SwiftLoop**. Create edge loops around the sharp edges of the **ucGeo** [see Figures 153 and 154].

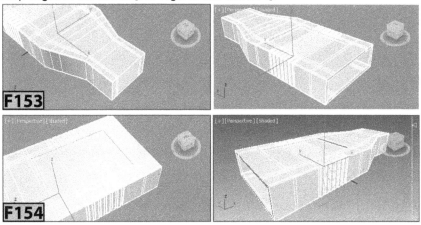

Now, insert an edge loop shown in Figure 155. On the **Ribbon | Edges** panel, **Shift** click **Chamfer**. In the **Chamfer's** caddy, set **Edge Chamfer Amount** to **0.05** and **Connect Edge Segments** to **1**. Click **OK**. Select the polygons created using the chamfer operation. On the **Ribbon | Polygons** panel, **Shift** click **Extrude**. In the **Extrude's** caddy, set **Amount** to **-0.04** and then click **OK** [see Figure 156].

Apply a **TurboSmooth** modifier to usGeo to smooth the geometry [see Figure 157]. Create a box in the **Top** viewport. On the **Modify** panel | **Parameters** rollout, set **Length** to **14**, **Width** to **20**, **Height** to **4**, and **Width Segments** to **1**. Raname the cylinder as **cGeo**.

On the **Ribbon | Polygon Modeling** panel, click **Convert to Poly**. Activate **Polygon** sub-object level and then select the front polygon. On the **Ribbon | Polygons** panel, **Shift** click **Inset**. In the **Inset's** caddy, set **Amount** to **0.5** and then click **OK** [see Figure 158].

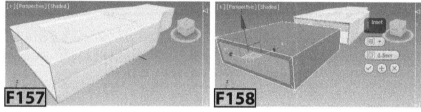

On the **Ribbon | Polygons** panel, **Shift** click **Extrude**. In the **Extrude's** caddy, set **Amount** to **-6** and then click **OK** [see Figure 159]. Activate **Edge** sub-object level and then select the ring shown in Figure 160. In the **Ribbon | Loops** panel, **Shift** click **Connect**. In the **Connect's** caddy, set **Segments** to **2** and **Pinch** to **-85**. Click **OK**. Select the newly created polygons and on the **Ribbon | Polygons** panel, **Shift** click **Extrude**. In the **Extrude's** caddy, set **Amount** to **-0.2**, type to **Local Normal** and then click **OK** [see Figure 161]. Activate **Edge** sub-object level. Insert edge loops using **SwiftLoop** as shown in Figure 162.

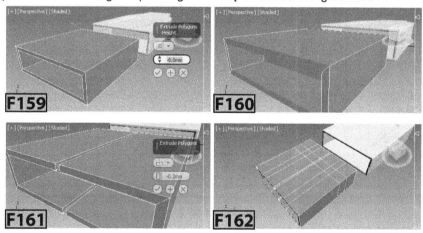

Activate **Polygon** sub-object level. Select the polygons shown in Figure 163 and delete them using **Delete**. Activate **Edge** sub-object level and select the edges shown in Figure 164. On the **Ribbon | Edges** panel, **Shift** click **Chamfer**. In the **Chamfer's** caddy, set **Edge Chamfer Amount** to **0.06** and **Connect Edge Segments** to **3**. Click **OK**.

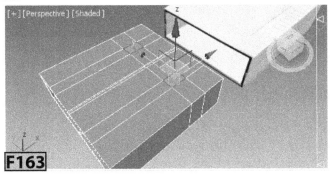

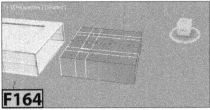

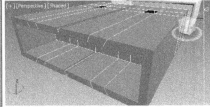

Select the edges that make up the holes and then on the **Ribbon | Edges** panel, **Shift** click **Extrude**. In the **Extrude's** caddy, set **Height** to **-0.1** and **Width** to **0** and then click **OK**. Place the metal connector inside its case. Now, create a new box primitive and then place inside the metal connector as shown in Figure 165.

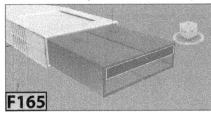

Create a cylinder in the **Top** viewport. On the **Modify** panel | **Parameters** rollout, set **Radius** to **2**, **Height** to **4.3**, and **Height Segments** to **5**. On the **Ribbon | Polygon Modeling** panel, click **Convert to Poly**. Activate **Polygon** sub-object level and then select the polygons shown in Figure 166.

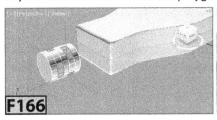

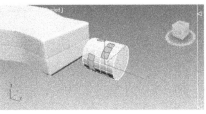

On the **Ribbon | Polygons** panel, **Shift** click **Inset**. In the **Inset's** caddy, set **Amount** to **0.2** and **then** click **OK**. On the **Ribbon | Polygons** panel, **Shift** click **Extrude**. In the **Extrude's** caddy, set **Amount** to **-0.5** and **then** click **OK.** Align the cylinder with the casing [see Figure 167].

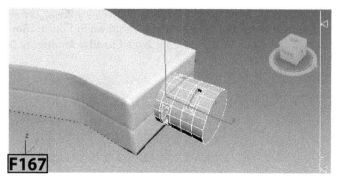

Hands-on Exercise MH1-14: Creating a USB Drive-II

In this exercise, you will model a USB drive [see Figure 168].

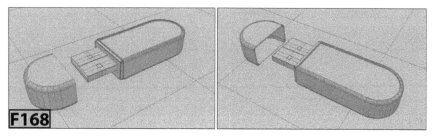

Table 14 summarizes the exercise:

Table 14: Creating model of a USB drive	
In this exercise, you will learn how to:	• Use the tools from the **Ribbon**
Skill level	Intermediate
Time to complete	1 Hour
Topics in the section:	• Specifying the Units for the Exercise • Creating the USB Drive
Project folder	**hoexm1**
Units	**Metric - Millimeters**
Final exercise file	**hoexm1-14-end.max**

Specifying the Units for the Exercise

From **Customize** menu choose **Units Setup**. In the **Units Setup** dialog that opens, select the **Metric** option from the **Display Unit Scale** group. Next, select **Millimeters** from the drop-down located below the **Metric** option, if already not selected. Click **OK** to accept the change. RMB click on any snap toggle button on the main toolbar. In the **Grid and Snap Settings** dialog that opens, choose the **Home Grid** tab and then set **Grid Spacing** to **3**, **Major Lines every Nth Grid Line** to **3**, and **Perspective View Grid Extent** to **3**. Close the **Grid and Snap Settings** dialog.

Creating the USB Drive

Create a cylinder in the **Top** viewport. On the **Modify** panel | **Parameters** rollout, set **Radius** to **7.5**, **Height** to **7**, **Height Segments** to **1**, and **Sides** to **32**. Rename the cylinder as **usbGeo**. Click **Select and Move** on the **main toolbar**. Set the **Transform Type-In** boxes to **0** on the **status bar** to place the cylinder at the **origin**. On the **Ribbon** | **Polgon Modeling** panel, click **Convert to Poly**. Activate **Vertex** sub-object level and then select the vertices in the **Front** viewport [see Figure 169].

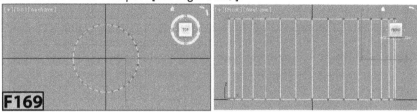

In the **Top** viewport, move the selected vertices towards right along the x-axis about **25** units [see Figure 170].

On the **Ribbon** | **Geometry (All)** panel, click **Slice Plane**. This will display a **slice plane gizmo** in the viewport and opens the **Slice Mode** panel. Adjust the position of the plane as shown in Figure 171 and then click **Slice** on **Slice Mode** panel to subdivide the geometry. On the **Ribbon** | **Geometry (All)** panel, click **Slice Plane** to deactivate the slice plane feature.

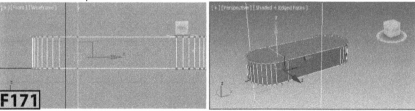

Activate **Edge** sub-object level and then in the **Front** viewport, drag a selection window to select the edges [see Figure 172]. Press **Ctrl+I** to invert the selection. **Remove** the edges from the selection that you created using **Slice Plane**. On the **Ribbon** | **Edges** panel, **Shift** click **Chamfer**. In the **Chamfer's** caddy, set **Edge Chamfer Amount** to **0.8** and **Connect Edge Segments** to **7** [see Figure 173]. Click **OK**.

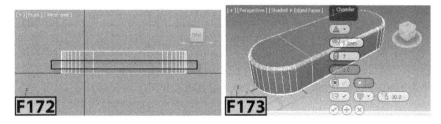

Activate **Polygon** sub-object level and then select polygons [see Figure 174].

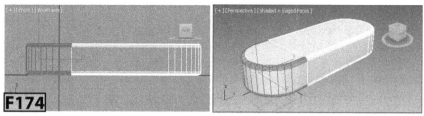

On the **Ribbon | Geometry (All)** panel, click **Detach**. In the **Detach** dialog that appears, type **capGeo** in the **Detach as** text box and then click **OK**. Move the cap slightly towards left and then apply a **Shell** modifier to it. On the **Parameters** rollout, set **Outer Amount** to **0.4**. Activate **Border** sub-object level for **usbGeo** and then make the border selection [see Figure 175]. On the **Ribbon | Geometry (All)** panel, click **Cap Poly** to create a polygon.

Activate **Polygon** sub-object level and then select the newly created polygon. On the **Ribbon | Polygons** panel, click **Shift** click **Inset**. In the **Inset's** caddy, set **Amount** to **0.5** and then click **OK**. On the **Ribbon | Polygons** panel, click **Shift** click **Extrude**. In the **Extrude's** caddy, set **Amount** to **0.8** and **then** click **OK**. Activate **Edge** sub-object level and then select the edge loops shown in Figure 176. On the **Ribbon | Edges** panel, **Shift** click **Chamfer**. In the **Chamfer's** caddy, set **Edge Chamfer Amount** to **0.1** and **Connect Edge Segments** to **4.** Click **OK**.

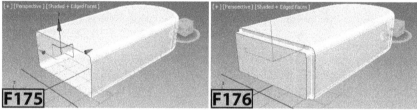

Activate **Polygon** sub-object level and then select the top polygon of the **usbGeo**.On the **Ribbon | Polygons** panel, click **Shift** click **Inset**. In the **Inset's** caddy, set **Amount** to **0.3** and **then** click **OK** [see Figure 177]. On the **Ribbon | Polygons** panel, click **Shift** click **Extrude**. In the **Extrude's** caddy, set **Amount** to **-0.4** and **then** click **OK** [see Figure 178].

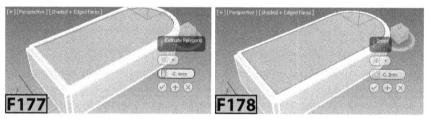

Activate **Edge** sub-object level and then select the loop shown in Figure 179. On the **Ribbon | Edges** panel, **Shift** click **Chamfer**. In the **Chamfer's** caddy, set **Edge Chamfer Amount** to **0.4** and **Connect Edge Segments** to **4.** Click **OK**.

Now, create the USB connector as done in the previous exercise.

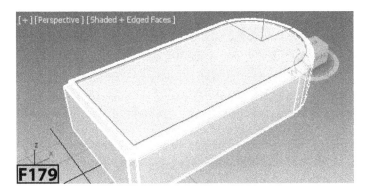

F179

Hands-on Exercise MH-15: Creating a Model of a Glass and Liquid

In this exercise, you will model a glass and liquid [see Figure 180].

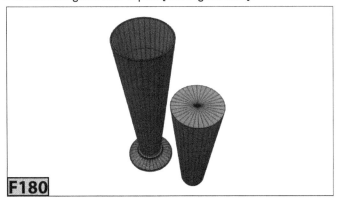

F180

Table 15 summarizes the exercise:

Table 15: Creating Model of a Glass and Liquid	
In this exercise, you will learn how to:	• Create profiles using splines • Use the **Lathe** modifier
Skill level	Intermediate
Time to complete	1 Hour
Topics in the section:	• Specifying the Units for the Exercise • Setting the Blueprint • Creating the Glass • Creating the Liquid
Project folder	**hoexm1**
Units	**Generic Units**
Final exercise file	**hoexm1-15-end.max**

Specifying the Units for the Exercise

From **Customize** menu choose **Units Setup**. In the **Units Setup** dialog that opens, select the **Generic Units** option from the **Display Unit Scale** group.

Setting the Blueprint

Go to the **Create** panel, click **Geometry**, then click **Plane**. In the **Front** viewport, create a plane. On the **Modify** panel | **Parameters** rollout, set **Length** to **100** and **Height** to **75**. Click **Material Editor** from the **Main** toolbar. Create a standard material using the **Material Editor** and apply it to the plane. Use the **glassRef. png** for the **Diffuse** map. In the **Coordinates** rollout, turn off **Use Real-World Scale** and then set **U Tiling** and **V Tiling** to **1**. Make sure the **Front** viewport is active and then press **G** to turn off the grid. Also, change display mode to **Shaded** [see Figure 181].

Creating The Glass

Go to the **Create** panel, click **Shapes**, then click **Line**. In the **Front** viewport, create a shape [see Figure 182]. In the **Modify** panel | **Selection** rollout, click **Vextex**. On the **Modify** panel | **Geometry** rollout, click **Fillet**. Click and drag over the vertices to get the shape [see Figure 183].

Make sure the **X** coordinate value for the selected vertices shown in Figure 184 is same. Hide the **plane**.

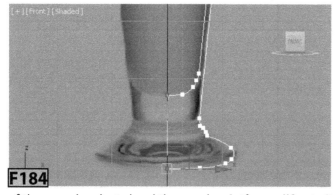

Make sure the **profile** of the curve is selected and then apply a **Lathe** modifier to it.

In the **Modify** panel | **Parameters** rollout, click **Min** in the **Align** group. Set **Segments** to **32**. Now, turn on **Weld Core** [see Figure 185]. Rename the geometry as **glassGeo**.

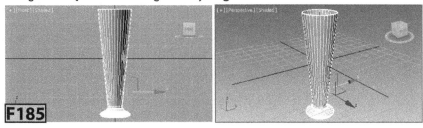

Creating The Liquid

Select **glassGeo** and then on the **Ribbon** | **Polygon Modeling** panel, click **Convert to Poly**. Activate **Edge** sub-object level and then on the **Ribbon** | **Edit** panel, click **SwiftLoop**. Insert an edge loop as shown in Figure 186. Click **SwiftLoop** again to deactivate it. Activate **Polygon** sub-object level and then select the inner polygons shown in Figure 187.

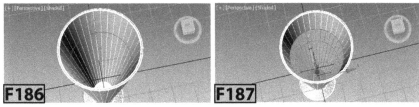

Shift drag the selected polygons to the right [see Figure 188]. In the **Clone Part of Mesh** dialog that opens, select **Clone to Object** and then type **liquidGeo** as the name of the clone, and then click **OK**. Select **liquidGeo** and then activate **Border** sub-object level. Now, select the border [see Figure 189].

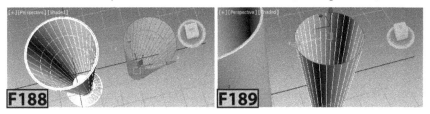

On the **Ribbon** | **Geometry (All)** panel, click **CapPoly**. Now, activate **Polygon** sub-object level and then select the cap polygon. On the **Ribbon** | **Polygons** panel, **Shift** click **Inset**. In the **Inset's** caddy, set **Amount** to **5** and **then** click **OK** [see Figure 190]. On the **Ribbon** | **Polygon Modeling** panel, **Ctrl** click **Vertex**. On the **Ribbon** | **Vertices** panel, **Shift** click **Weld**. In the **Weld's** caddy, set **Weld Threshold** to **15** and **then** click **OK** [see Figure 191] to weld the vertices.

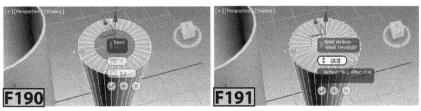

Activate **Edge** sub-object level and then select the edge loop shown in Figure 192. On the **Ribbon | Edges** panel, **Shift** click **Chamfer**. In the **Chamfer's** caddy, set **Edge Chamfer Amount** to **0.09** and **Connect Edge Segments** to **4** [see Figure 193]. Click **OK**. Align the **glassGeo** and **liquidGeo** using the align tool.

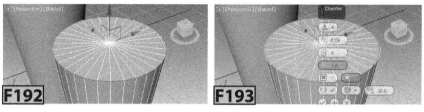

Hands-on Exercise MH1-16: Creating a Model of a Building

In this exercise, you will model a building using various modifiers [see Figures 194 through 197].

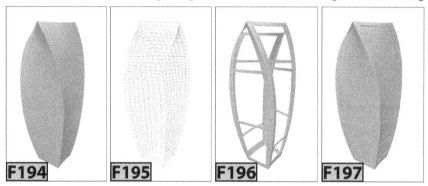

Table 16 summarizes the exercise:

Table 16: Creating Model of a Building	
In this exercise, you will learn how to:	• Use the **Twist**, **Taper**, **Lattice**, and **Blend** modifiers to change the shape of the geometry • Use polygon and edge selection techniques • Use the **Edit Poly** modifier • Chamfer edges
Skill level	Intermediate
Time to complete	45 Minutes
Topics in the section:	• Specifying the Units for the Exercise • Creating the Tower • Creating the Mullions • Creating the Outer Shell
Project folder	**hoexm1**
Units	**Metric - Meters**
Final exercise file	**hoexm1-16-end.max**

From **Customize** menu choose **Units Setup**. In the **Units Setup** dialog that opens, select the **Metric** option from the **Display Unit Scale** group. Next, select **Meters** from the drop-down located below the **Metric** option, if already not selected. Click **OK** to accept the change.

RMB click on any snap toggle button on the main toolbar. In the **Grid and Snap Settings** dialog that opens, choose the **Home Grid** tab and then set **Grid Spacing** to **10**, **Major Lines every Nth Grid Line** to **10**, and **Perspective View Grid Extent** to **7**. Close the **Grid and Snap Settings** dialog.

Creating the Tower

On the **Create** panel, click **Geometry**, and then on the **Object Type** rollout, click **Box**. In the **Perspective** viewport, drag out a box of any size. Go to **Modify** panel, and on the **Parameters** rollout, set **Length** to **80**, **Width** to **80**, and **Height** to **400**. Also, set **Length Segs** to **8**, **Width Segs** to **8**, and **Height Segs** to **50** [see Figure 198].

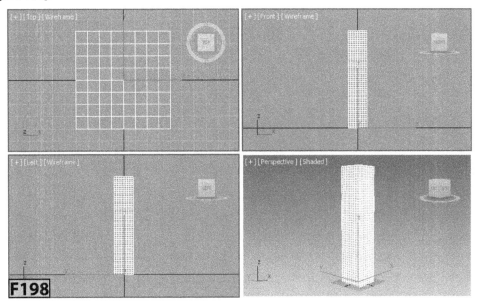

In the **Name And Color** rollout, change the name of the object to **Tower**. Now, you will apply various modifiers to create distinct building shape. From the **Object-Space Modifiers** section of the **Modifier List**, select **Taper**. In the **Taper** group of the **Parameters** rollout, set **Amount** to **0.35** and curve to **2.04**. The building bulges out [see Figure 199].

From the **Object-Space Modifiers** section of the **Modifier List**, select **Bend**. In the **Bend** group of the **Parameters** rollout, set **Angle** to **27.5** and **Bend Axis** to **Y**. The building bends along the Y axis [see Figure 200]. From the **Object-Space Modifiers** section of the **Modifier List**, select **Twist**. In the **Twist** group of the **Parameters** rollout, set **Angle** to **45.5** and **Bias** to **93.5**. The building twists along the Z axis [see Figure 201].

Creating the Mullions

Select **Tower** in the **Scene Explorer** and then RMB click on it. From the **Quad** menu that opens, choose **Clone** to open the **Clone Options** dialog. Select **Reference** from the **Object** group. Next, type **Mullions** in the **Name** text box and the click **OK**.

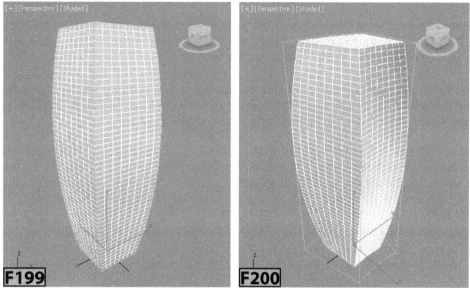

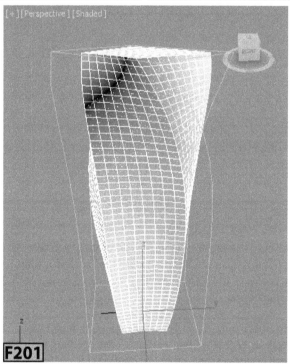

In the **Scene Explorer**, click **Tower's** bulb icon to hide it. Go to **Modify** panel and from the **Object-Space Modifiers** section of the **Modifier List**, select **Edit Poly**. In the **Selection** rollout, click **Polygon** and then select the center polygons [see Figure 202]. Click **Grow** thrice to select all top polygons of the building [see Figure 203].

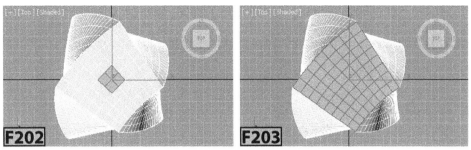

F202   F203

Delete the selected polygon by pressing **Delete**. Similarly, delete the bottom polygons. From the **Object-Space Modifiers** section of the **Modifier List**, select **Lattice**. In the **Struts** group of the **Parameters** rollout, set **Radius** to **0.5**, and **Sides** to **5**. Also, turn on **Smooth**.

Creating the Outer Shell

In the **Scene Explorer**, click the **Mullions's** bulb icon to hide it. Select **Tower** and create a clone with the name **Shell**. Make sure to select **Reference** from the **Object group** in the **Clone Options** dialog.

Make sure **Tower** and **Mullions** are not visible in the scene. Select the **top** and **bottom** polygons of **Shell** and delete them as done earlier. Also, turn off the **Twist**, **Bend**, and **Taper** modifiers.

In the **Selection** rollout, make sure **Ignore Backfacing** is turned off. In the **Front** viewport, select polygons [see Figure 204]. Press **Delete** to remove the selected polygons. Similarly, remove polygons from the other remaining two sides. Use a different pattern for these sides [see Figure 205].

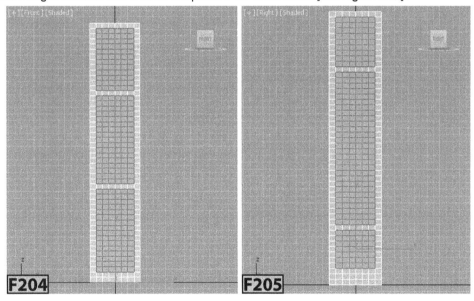

F204   F205

In the **Selection** rollout, click **Edge** and then select the four corner edges [see Figure 206]. Now, click **Loop** to select the loops [see Figure 207]. In the **Edit Edges** rollout, click **Chamfer's** settings box to open the **Chamfer** caddy controls. Set **Amount** to **1.636** and **Segments** to **5** [see Figure 208]. Click **OK**. From the **Object-Space Modifiers** section of the **Modifier List**, select **Shell**. In the **Parameters** rollout, set **Outer**

Amount to **2.0** [see Figure 209]. Now turn on the **Shell's Twist**, **Taper**, and **Bend** Modifiers. Turn on the **Tower** and **Mullions** from the **Scene Explorer**. Assign colors of your choice to **Tower, Shell,** and **Mullions** [see Figure 210]. Now, create different version of the building [see Figure 211].

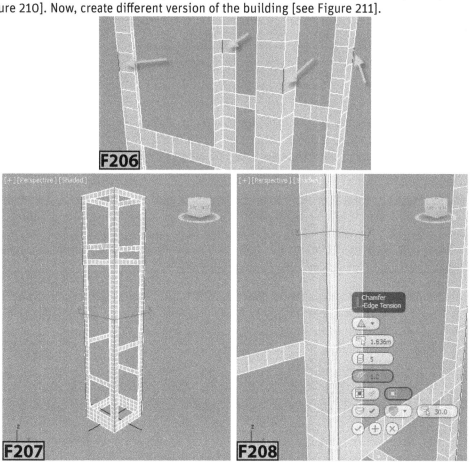

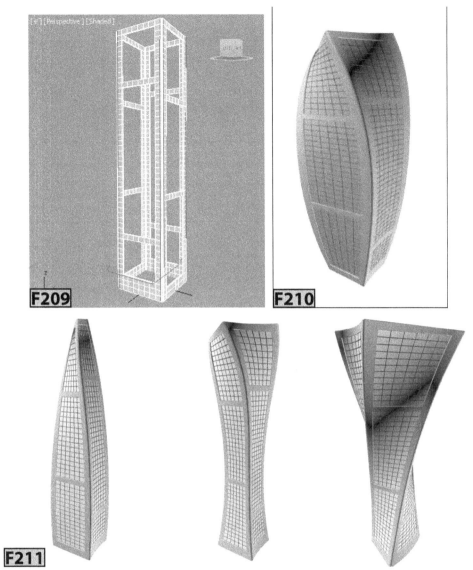

Hands-on Exercise MH1-17: Creating a Model of a Paper Basket

In this exercise, you will model a melted waste paper basket using various modifiers [see Figure 212].

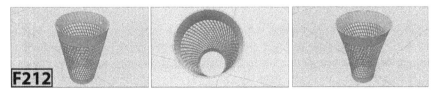

Table 17 summarizes the exercise:

Table 17: Creating model of a paper basket	
In this exercise, you will learn how to:	• Use the **Twist**, **Taper**, and **Shell** modifiers • Use polygon and edge selection techniques • Use the **Edit Poly** modifier • Inset faces
Skill level	Beginner
Time to complete	35 Minutes
Topics in the section:	• Specifying the Units for the Exercise • Creating the Basket
Project folder	**hoexm1**
Units	**Metric - Centimeters**
Final exercise file	**hoex1-17-end.max**

Specifying the Units for the Exercise

From **Customize** menu choose **Units Setup**. In the **Units Setup** dialog that opens, select the **Metric** option from the **Display Unit Scale** group. Next, select **Centimeters** from the drop-down located below the **Metric** option, if already not selected. Click **OK** to accept the change. RMB click on any snap toggle button on the main toolbar. In the **Grid and Snap Settings** dialog that opens, choose the **Home Grid** tab and then set **Grid Spacing** to **5**, **Major Lines every Nth Grid Line** to **10**, and **Perspective View Grid Extent** to **8**. Close the **Grid and Snap Settings** dialog.

Creating the Basket

On the **Create** panel, click **Geometry**, and then on the **Object Type** rollout, click **Cylinder**. In the **Perspective** viewport, drag out a cylinder of any size. Go to **Modify** panel, and on the **Parameters** rollout, set **Radius** to **14.5** and **Height** to **30**. Also, set **Height Segments** to **12** and **Sides** to **40** [see Figure 213].

From the **Object-Space Modifiers** section of the **Modifier List**, select **Edit Poly**. In the **Selection** rollout, click **Vertex** and then select **top row of vertices** of the cylinder in the **Front** viewport. RMB click on the **Select and Move** button on the **Main** toolbar.

In the **Offset:Screen** group of the Move **Transform Type-In** dialog that opens, set **Y** to **5** and then press **Enter** to move the vertices by **5** units in the **Y** direction [see Figure 214].Select all the vertices except the bottom row and move them by **6** units in the **Y** direction [see Figure 215].

In the **Selection** rollout, click **Polygon** and then select all the middle polygons [see Figure 216]. In the **Edit Polygons** rollout, click **Inset's Settings** button. In the **Inset's** caddy control, select **By Polygon** from **Group**. Now, set amount to **0.3** and click **OK** to inset the selected polygons. Delete the polygons. Select the top cap polygon and delete it as well [see Figure 217]. From the **Object-Space Modifiers** section of the **Modifier List**, select **Shell**. In the **Parameters** layout, set **Outer Amount** to **0.5**.

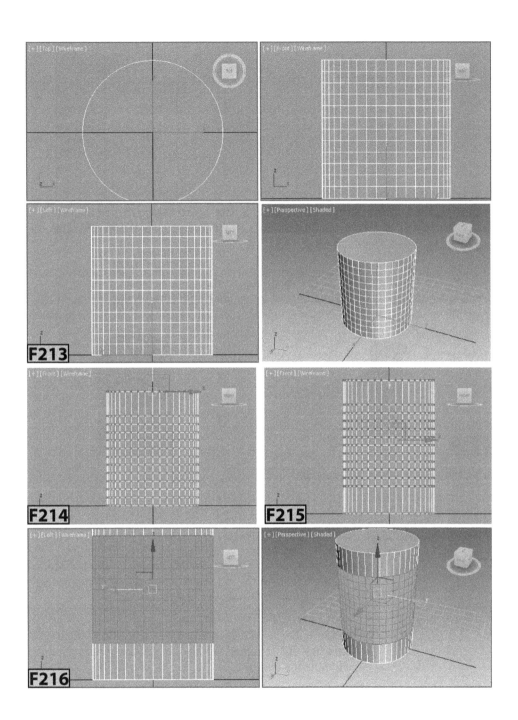

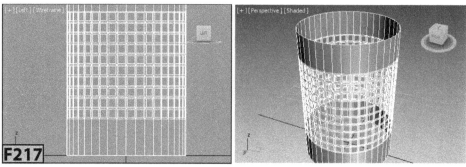

From the **Object-Space Modifiers** section of the **Modifier List**, select **Taper**. In the **Parameters** layout, set **Amount** to **0.44** and **Curve -0.7**. From the **Object-Space Modifiers** section of the **Modifier List**, select **Twist**. In the **Parameters** layout, set **Angle** to **66.5**.

Hands-on Exercise MH1-18: Creating a Jug

In this exercise, we are going to create model of a jug using spline and polygon modeling techniques [see Figure 218].

The following table summarizes the exercise.

Table 18: Creating Model of a Jug	
In this exercise, you will:	• Set units to **Centimeters** • Use the **Line** primitive to create path for **Loft** feature • Use the **NGon** primitive to create shapes for the **Loft** feature • Create handle of the jug by extruding polygons along a spline • Refine the model by adding segments to it
Topics in this section:	• Getting Ready • Creating Shape of the Jug Using Line and NGon Spline Primitive • Creating the Handle of the Jug Using Extrude Along Spline Feature • Refining the Model
Skill Level	Intermediate
Project Folder	**hoexm1**
Final Exercise File	**hoem1-18-end.max**
Time to Complete	30 Minutes

Start 3ds Max and then reset it. Ensure the project folder is set to the **hoemh2** folder. From **Customize** menu choose **Units Setup**. In the **Units Setup** dialog that opens, select **Metric** from the **Display Unit Scale** group. Next, select **Centimeters** from the drop-down located below **Metric**, if already not selected. Click **OK** to accept the change.

Creating Shape of the Jug Using Line and NGon Spline Primitive

Activate the **Front** viewport. Go to the **Create** panel, click **Shapes**, and then ensure that **Shapes** is selected in the drop-down below the **Shapes** button. On the **Object Type** rollout, click **Line**. Expand the **Keyboard Entry** rollout, and then click **Add Point** to add a point at the origin. Now, set **Y** to **30** and then click **Add Point**. This action creates a line in the **Front** viewport [see Figure 219]. This line will serve as path for the **Loft** tool. Click **Select Object** on the **Main** toolbar to deactivate the line tool.

On the **Object Type** rollout, click **NGon** and then create an **NGon** in the **Front** viewport. On the **Modify panel | Parameters rollout**, set **Radius** to **7**, and **Sides** to **26**. Turn on the **Circular** switch. Create four more copies of the **NGon**. The total number of **NGons** will be **5** [see Figure 220]. Change the radius of the three rightmost **NGons** to **4** [see Figure 221].

The last **NGon** will be the spout of the jug. Select it and then covert it to **Editable Spline** object. Activate the **Vertex** sub-object and then select the top four vertices as shown in Figure 222.

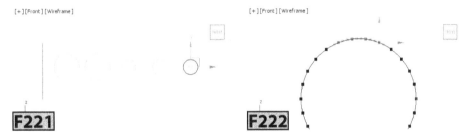

RMB click on the vertices and then choose **Corner** from the **tool1** quadrant of the **Quad** menu. Now, select the middle two vertices and move them using the **Move** tool [see Figure 223]. Ensure the vertices are still selected and them RMB click. On the **tool1** quadrant of the **Quad** menu, choose **Smooth** to make the shape of the spout [see Figure 224]. Deactivate the **Vertex** sub-object level.

Select the **Line** in the **Front** viewport. Go to the **Create** panel, click **Geometry**, and then ensure that **Compound Objects** is selected in the drop-down below the **Geometry** button. On the **Object Type** rollout, click **Loft**. On the **Path Parameters** rollout, ensure **Path** to set to **0** and click **Get Shape** button on the **Creation Method** rollout. Now, click on the **NGon** on the right of the line. Set **Path** to **1** and then click **Get**

Shape. Now, click on the second **NGon** in the Front viewport. Similarly, pick the other three **NGons** with **Path** value set to **82, 85,** and **100,** respectively. This action creates the shape of the jug in the viewport [see Figure 225].

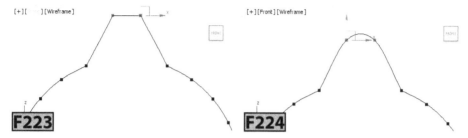

On the **Modify** panel, turn of the **Cap End** switch from the **Skin Parameters | Capping group**. On the **Options** group, set **Shape Steps** to **0** and **Path Steps** to **3**. Turn on the **Linear Interpolation** switch. Now, delete all spline objects from the scene. Add a **Shell** modifier to the stack and then set **Outer Amount** to **0.559** in the **Modify panel | Parameters rollout** [see Figure 226].

Creating the Handle of the Jug Using Extrude Along Spline Feature

Convert model to an **Editable Poly** object. Now, select the edges as shown in Figure 227. On the **Ribbon |** **Loops** panel, click **Connect** with the **Shift** held down, the **Connect Edges** caddy appears in the viewport. Set **Segments** to **4** [see Figure 228] and click **OK**. Now, select the polygons as shown in Figure 229. On the **Ribbon | Polygons panel**, click **Inset** with the **Shift** held down, the **Inset** caddy appears in the viewport. Set **Inset Amount** to **0.516** and then click **OK**. Now delete the polygons using the **Delete** key. Now, activate the **Border** sub-object. Select the two border edges that we just created by deleting the polygons and then on the **Ribbon | Geometry (All) panel**, click **Cap Poly** to fill the holes we just created.

In the **Right** viewport, create a shape as shown in Figure 230. Select the jug and then select the polygon as shown in Figure 231. On the **Ribbon | Polygon panel**, click **Extrude on Spline** with the **Shift** held down, the **Extrude Along Spline** caddy appears. Click **Pick Spline** and then click on the path in a viewport to extrude the selected polygon along the spline. Set **Segments** to **26** and click **OK**. Select the polygons as shown in Figure 232. On the **Ribbon | Polygon panel**, click **Bridge** with the **Shift** held down, the **Bridge Polygons** caddy appears. Set **Segments** to **2** and click **OK** to create a connection between the selected polygons [see Figure 233].

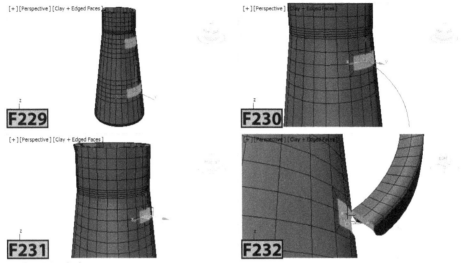

Refining the Model

Adjust the shape of the handle near the bridged polygons at **Vertex** and **Edge** sub-objects levels using **Move** and **Scale** tools [see Figure 234]. Select the top edges of the jug and then on the Ribbon | Edges panel, click Chamfer with the Shift held down, the **Chamfer** caddy appears. Set **Connect Edge Segments** to **2** and **Edge Chamfer Amount** to **0.086** and then click **OK** [see Figure 235].

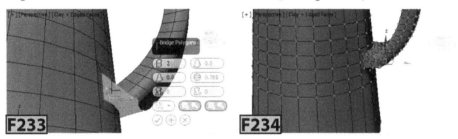

On the **Ribbon | Edit panel**, click **Shift Loop** and then add an edge loop as shown in Figure 236. Similarly, add another edge loop, as shown in Figure 237. Repeat the process for the bottom part of the handle. Now, select the edges as shown in Figure 238. On the **Ribbon | Loops panel**, click on the **Flow Connect** arrow and turn on the **Auto Ring** switch. Now, click **Flow Connect** to insert edge loops [see Figure 239]. Similarly, add edge loops for other three edges of the handle.

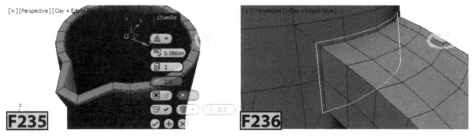

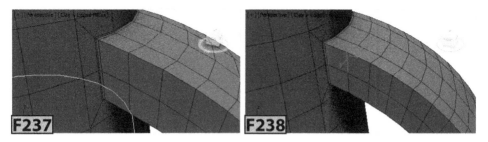

Select the bottom polygon of the jug and then on the **Ribbon | Polygons panel**, click **Inset** with the **Shift** held down. Set **Amount** to **0.5** and click **Apply and Continue**. Now, set **Amount** to **3** and click **OK** [see Figure 240].

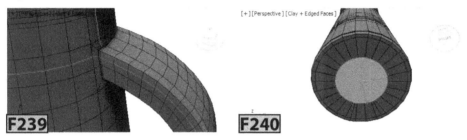

Make sure the bottom polygon is still selected and then on the **Ribbon | Polygon Modeling panel**, click **Vertex** to select all the vertices associated with the selected polygon. On **Ribbon | Vertices panel**, click **Weld** with the **Shift** held down, the **Weld Vertices** caddy appears. Set **Weld Threshold** to **5** and click **OK** to weld the vertices [see Figure 241]. Repeat the process for the inner bottom polygon of the jug [see Figure 242]. Now, apply the **Turbosmooth** modifier to the stack.

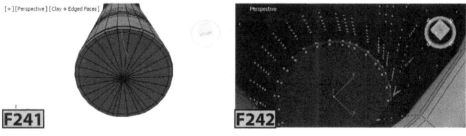

Unit S1-Material Editors

A material editor is a dialog that allows you to create, and edit materials as well as to assign them to the objects in the scene. A material in 3ds Max defines how light is reflected and transmitted by the objects in a scene.

In the unit, I will describe the following:

- **Compact Material Editor**
- **Slate Material Editor**

3ds Max offers two material editors, **Compact Material Editor** and **Slate Material Editor**. These editors offer a variety of the functions and features that allow you to design realistic looking surfaces in 3ds Max. To open an editor, choose **Compact** 🔲 or **Slate** 🔲 option from the **Material Editor** flyout on the **Main** toolbar. You can also open an editor by choosing **Compact Material Editor** or **Slate Material Editor** from the **Rendering** menu | **Material Editor** sub-menu | **Compact Material Editor/Slate Material Editor**. If you are using the enhanced menu system, these options are in the **Material** menu | **Create/Edit Materials** sub-menu.

Compact Material Editor

This was the only material editor available prior to the 2011 release of 3ds Max. It is comparatively a small dialog [see Figure 1] than the **Slate Material Editor** and allows you to quickly preview the material. If you are assigning materials that have already been designed, this material editor is the preferred choice.

Note: Additional Features
*The **Compact Material Editor** has some options such as **Video Color Check** and **Custom Sample Objects** that are not available in the **Slate Material Editor**.*

The **Compact Material Editor's** interface consists of menu bar at the top [see Figure 1], sample slots below the menu bar, and toolbars at the bottom and right of the sample slots. Now onward, I will refer to these toolbars as horizontal and vertical toolbars, respectively. The interface also contains many rollouts. The content on these rollouts depends on the active material slot and the type of material it hosts.

Note: Switching Editors
*If you want to switch to **Slate Material Editor**, choose **Slate Material Editor** from the editor's **Modes** menu.*

Sample Slots

The sample slots allow you to preview material and maps. By default, six sample slots appear in the editor. You can increase the number of slots by choosing **Cycle 3x2, 5x3, 6x4 Sample Slots** from the editor's **Options** menu. This option cycles through the 3x2, 5x3, and 6x4 slots arrangement. You can toggle these options by using the **X** hotkey. To make a sample slot active, click on the sample slot. The active sample slot appears with a white border around it.

Caution: Maximum number of sample slots
*The **Compact Material Editor** allows you to edit up to 24 material at a time. However, the scene might contain an unlimited numbers of materials. When you finish a material and apply it to the objects in the scene. You can use the slot occupied by that material to design the next material.*

By default, material appears on a sphere geometry in a sample slot. You can change the sphere to cylinder or cube by choosing the desired option from the **Sample Type** flyout. This flyout is the first entry in the editor's vertical toolbar. To view a magnified version of the sample slot in a floating window, double-click on it. You can resize the window to change the magnification level of the sample slot.

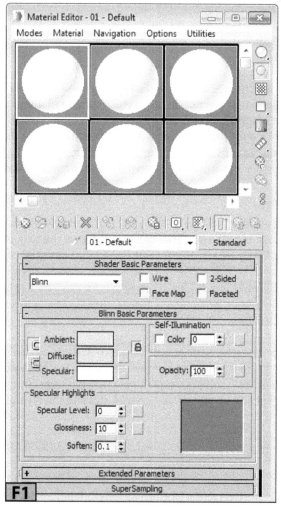

Hot and Cool Materials

A sample slot is considered to be hot if it is assigned to one or more surfaces in the scene. When you use the editor to adjust properties of a hot material the changes are reflected in the viewport at the same time. The corners of a sample slot indicates whether the material is hot or not. Here're the possibilities:

No triangle: The material is not used in the scene.

Outlined white triangle: The material is hot and the changes you make to it will change the material displayed in the scene.

Solid white triangle: The material is not only hot but it is also applied to the currently selected object in the scene.

Notice the three sample slots in Figure 2 that shows three possibilities: a hot material applied to the currently selected, a hot material is applied to the scene but not on the currently selected object, and a cool material which is active but not assigned to scene, respectively. If you want to make a hot material cool, click **Make Material Copy** from the horizontal toolbar. You can have the same material with the same name in multiple slots but only one slot can be hot. However, you can have more than one hot sample slot as long as each sample slot has a different material.

Note: Dragging a material
If you drag a material to copy it from one sample slot to another, the destination slot will be cool whereas the original slot remains hot.

When you RMB click on a sample slot, a popup menu appears. Table 1 summarizes the options available in this menu.

Table 1: Sample slot RMB click menu	
Option	Description
Drag/Copy	This is on by default. When on, dragging a sample slot copies the material from one sample slot to another.
Drag/Rotate	When you select this option, dragging the sample slot rotates the sample geometry in the slot. This is useful in visualizing the map in the slot.
Reset Rotation	Resets the sample slot's rotation.
Render Map	Opens the **Render Map** dialog that allows you to render the current map. You can create an **AVI** file if the map is animated.
Options	Opens the material editor's options.
Magnify	Generates a magnified view of the current sample slot.
Select By Material	Selects objects based on the material in the sample slot.
Highlight Assets in the ATS dialog	This option is typically used for the bitmap textures. It opens the **Asset Tracking** dialog with the assets highlighted.
Sample Windows options	You can use these options to change the number of slots displayed in the material editor.

By default, the **Standard** material is displayed when you select a sample slot. If you want to use the **Standard** material, you can choose the desired shading model from the drop-down available in the **Shader Basic Parameters** rollout of the editor and then assign colors or maps to the various components of the material. For example, if you want to assign a map to the **Diffuse** component of the material, click on the button located at the right of the **Diffuse** color swatch to open the **Material/Map Browser** which is a modeless dialog. From the browser, select the map from the **Maps | Standard** rollout and then click **OK**.

Tip: Material Map Browser
You can also double-click on a map to select it and close the browser.

For example, if you want to apply a checker map, double-click on the **Checker** map from the **Maps | Standard** rollout of the browser. Once you select the map, 3ds Max shows rollouts in the editor that you can use to edit the properties of the map. To go back to the parent level, click **Go To Parent** 🔾 from the horizontal toolbar.

You can also copy map from one component to another component. For example, you have applied a map to the **Diffuse** component of the material and you want to copy it to **Opacity** component. Drag the **Diffuse's** button onto the **Opacity's** button, the **Copy (Instance) Map** dialog appears. Select the desired option from the **Method** group and then click **OK** to create an instance, a copy, or just to swap the materials from one slot to another.

Note: Other materials
*If you want to use any other material than the **Standard** material, click on **Type** button [currently labelled as **Standard**] to open the **Material/Map Browser**. Double-click on the desired material from the **Materials | Standard** rollout; the **Replace Material** dialog appears with options to discard the old material or keep the old material as a sub-material. Choose the desired option and click **OK**. The label **Standard** on the button will be replaced by the type of the new material. For example, if you have chosen **Blend**, the **Standard** label will be replaced by the **Blend** label.*

By default, 3ds Max gives a name to each material. This appears name below the horizontal toolbar. If you want to change the name, edit the name in the field. The name field only displays 16 characters but the material name can be longer than 16 characters.

If the material you want to change is present in the scene but is not displayed in any of the sample slots, you can get it directly from the scene. To do this, select the object in the scene and click a sample slot to make it active. From the horizontal toolbar, click **Get Material** 🗙 to open the **Material/Map Browser**. Find the scene material in the **Scene Materials** rollout and then double-click on the name of the material. You can also drag the material name to the sample slot. When you get a material from the scene, it is initially a hot material.

To apply a material to the objects in the scene, drag the sample slot that contains the material to the object[s] in the scene. If there is only one object selected in the scene, the material is immediately applied to that object. If there are more than one objects in the scene, 3ds Max prompts you to choose whether to apply the material to the single object or to the whole selection. You can also apply material to the selection by clicking **Assign Material To Selection** 🔲 on the horizontal toolbar. Once you apply material to objects in the scene, click **Show Shaded Material in Viewport** 🖾 on the horizontal toolbar to view the material on the objects in the scene.

You can also save a material to the library. A material library helps you in organizing materials. You can use a material from a library in another scene, if required. To save a material to the library, on the horizontal toolbar, click **Put To Library** ▦, the **Put To Library** dialog appears. In this dialog, change the name of the material or leave as is. Click **OK** to save the material. The material is saved in the currently opened library. If no library is open, a new library is created. You can save this library as a file using the **Material/Map Browser** controls.

To get a material from the library, click **Get Material** ▦ to open the **Material/Map Browser**. Now, open a library group. In the list of the materials in the library, double-click on the name of the material that you intend to use. The material you choose from the library replaces the material in the active sample slot.

Material/Map Browser

The **Material/Map Browser** [see Figure 3] allows you to choose a material, map, or mental ray shader. When you click the Type button or any button on the Compact Material Editor, a modal version of the Material/Map Browser opens.

At the top-left corner of the browser, the **Material/Map Browser Options** button ▼ is available. When you click this button, a menu is displayed from where you can set various options for the **Material/Map Browser**. The **Search by Name** field on the right of the button allows you to filter the maps and materials in the browser. For example, if you type **grad** in the field and press enter, the maps and materials will be displayed below the field whose names start with the characters **grad** [see Figure 4].

The main part of the browser is the list of materials and maps arranged in the rollouts [groups]. You can collapse or expand these groups.

Caution: Materials and maps in the Material/Map Browser

*By default, the **Material/Map Browser** only displays those maps and materials that are compatible with the active renderer.*

Note: Material/Map Browser's contextual menu

When you RMB click on an empty area of the browser, a popup menu appears [see Figure 5]. The options in the first sections are the shortcuts to the browser's functionality. The other section contains two options that you can use to unhide or hide all child nodes in the active view. We will discuss active view little later in the unit.

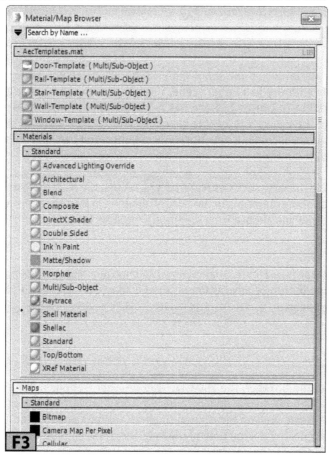

Material Explorer

The **Material Explorer** [see Figure 6] allows you to browse and manage all materials in a scene. You can open the explorer from the **Rendering** menu. If you are using the enhanced menu system, you can open it from the **Materials** menu | **Tools (Material Set)** sub-menu. You can also open it as an extended viewport. To do this, choose **Material Explorer** from the **Point-Of-View (POV) Viewport Label Menu | Extended Viewports**.

The **Compact Material Editor** lets you set the properties of the materials but there is limitations on number of materials it can display at a time. However, with the **Material Explorer**, you can browse all the materials in the scene. You can also see the objects onto which the materials are applied, you can change the material assignment, and manage materials in other ways.

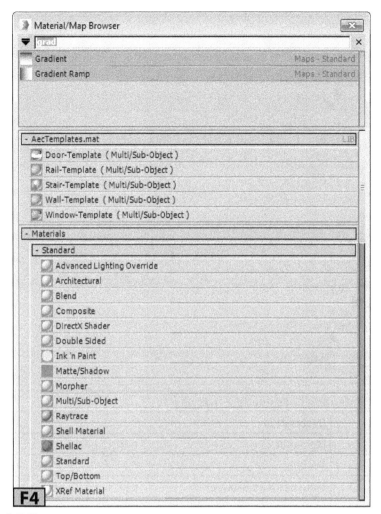

Slate Material Editor

The **Slate Material Editor** is little complex than the **Compact Material Editor**. In this editor, the entities are displayed in form of nodes that you can wire together to create material trees. If you are working on a large scene with lots of materials, this editor is the preferred choice. The powerful search function provided by this editor, lets you find materials in a complex scene easily.

I mostly used the **Slate Material Editor** as its interface [see Figure 7] is more intuitive when it comes to designing materials. I have marked various components of the interface with numbers in Figure 7. Table 2 summarizes the **Slate Material Editor's** interface.

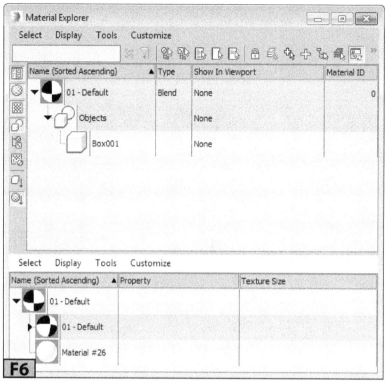

Table 2: The **Slate Material Editor's** interface overview	
Number	Description
1	Menu bar
2	Toolbar
3	Material/Map Browser
4	Status
5	Active View
6	View navigation
7	Parameter Editor
8	Navigator

There are three main visual elements of the **Slate Material Editor**: **Material/Map Browser**, **Active View**, and **Parameter Editor**. The **Active View** is the area where you create material trees and make connections between nodes using wires. The **Parameter Editor** is the area where you adjust settings of maps and materials.

You can float the components of the editor such as **Material/Map Browser**, or **Parameter Editor** [except view]. For example, to float the **Material/Map Browser**, double-click on its title. To dock it back to the editor, again double-click on its title.

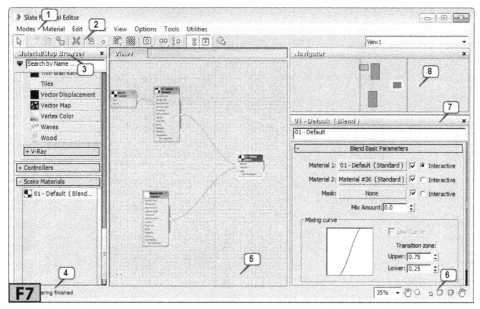

Note: Preview window

By default, each material preview window opens as a floating window. When you dock a material preview window, it docks to the upper left area of the editor.

When you add materials or maps in the **Slate Material Editor**, they appear as nodes [see left image in Figure 8] in the active view. You can then connect these nodes using wires to make material trees. A node has several components, here's is a quick rundown.

- The title bar of the node shows name of the material or map, material or map type, and a small preview icon of the material or map.
- Below the title bar the component of the material or map appear. By default, 3ds Max shows only those components that you can map.
- On the left side of each component a circular slot [marked as 1 in the right image of Figure 8] is available for input. You can use these sockets to wire maps to the node.
- On the right of the node, a circular slot [marked as 2 in the right image of Figure 8] that is used for the socket.

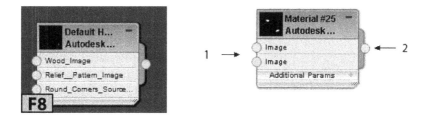

You can collapse a node to hide its slots. To do this, click on the minus sign [marked as 1 in Figure 9] available on the upper right corner of the node. To resize a node horizontally, drag the diagonal lines available on the bottom-right of the node [marked as 2 in Figure 9]. When you resize a node horizontally, it's easier to read the name of the slots. To change the preview icon size, double-click on the preview. To reduce the preview, double-click again. When a node's parameters are displayed in the **Parameter Editor**, 3ds Max shows a dashed border around the node in the active view [see Figure 10].

To create a new material, drag the material from the **Material/Map Browser** to the active view, 3ds Max places a node for the material in the active view. It is a good habit to change the name of the material immediately. It will make your life easier if you are working on a complex scene with tons of materials. To rename a material, RMB click on it and choose **Rename**. In the **Rename** dialog, change the name of the material and click **OK**. To change the properties of the material, double-click the node in the active view and then change the properties from the **Parameter Editor**.

Tip: Renaming materials
The name of a material can contain special characters, numbers, and spaces.

To get a material from the scene, click **Pick Material From Object** 🖉 from the toolbar. Now, click on the object in a viewport to get the material. To apply a material to objects in the scene, drag the output socket of the node and then drop the wire on an object in the scene. As you drag the mouse in a viewport, a tooltip appears below the mouse pointer showing the name of the object. You can apply the material even if the object is not selected. If there is only one object selected in the scene, the material is immediately applied to that object. If there are more than one objects in the scene, 3ds Max prompts you to choose whether to apply the material to the single object or to the whole selection. You can also apply material to the selection by clicking **Assign Material To Selection** 🞂 on the toolbar.

To make a copy of the material, drag the material from the **Material/Map Browser | Scene Materials** group (or any library) to the active View. The **Instance (Copy)** dialog appears. Select **Instance** or **Copy** from this dialog and click **OK**. To duplicate a node in the active view, select the node[s] that you want to duplicate and then drag the nodes with the **Shift** held down.

To select the objects onto which you have applied the same material, in the active view, RMB click on the node and then choose **Select | Select By Material** from the popup menu. 3ds Max opens the **Select Objects** dialog with the objects highlighted. Click **Select** to select the highlighted objects.

To select a node, ensure the **Select Tool** [hotkey **S**] is active, and then click on the node. To select multiple nodes, click on the nodes with the **Ctrl** held down. If you want to remove nodes from the selection, click on the nodes with **Alt** held down. To select all nodes, press **Ctrl+A**. To invert the selection, press **Ctrl+I**. To select none of the nodes, press **Ctrl+D**. To select children, press **Ctrl+C**. To select a node tree, press **Ctrl+T**. These functions are also accessible from the **Select** menu of the editor.

Note: Selected node

When a node is selected in the view, a white border appears around it. Also, the background including the title bar is darker. When node is not selected, the border appears gray and background is lighter.

Tip: Deselecting nodes
*To deselect nodes, click on the blank area of the view using the **Select Tool**.*

To move a node, drag it in the active view. To create clone of a node, drag it with the **Shift** held down. If you drag a node with **Ctrl+Shift** held down, 3ds Max clones the node and all its children. These methods also work on multiple selections.

If you want to move a node and its children, click **Move Children** from the toolbar and drag a node. You can toggle this feature temporarily without clicking **Move Children** by moving the node with **Ctrl+Alt** held down. This feature can be accessed from the editor's **Options** menu.

The layout buttons on the toolbar allow you to arrange nodes in the active view. The **Layout All - Vertical** and **Layout All - Horizontal** buttons on the toolbar allow you to arrange nodes in an automatic layout along the vertical or horizontal axis in the active view. These options are also available in the editor's **View** menu. The **Layout Children** button allows you to automatically layout the children of the selected node.

If you turn on the **Show Shaded Map In Viewport** or **Show Realistic Map In Viewport** from the toolbar for a material or map, a red diagonal shape appears on the node in the active view [see the left image in Figure 11]. The **Navigator** also shows a red diagonal shape to indicate this [see the middle image in Figure 11]. This shape also appears in the **Scene Materials** rollout of the **Material/Map Browser** [see the right image in Figure 11].

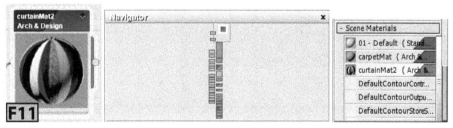

The **Preview** window [see Figure 12] of the editor allows you to visualize how material or map will appear in the scene. The main part of the window is a rendering of the material or map. You can resize this window like you resize any other window in 3ds max that is, by dragging its corners. Making a window larger helps you in visualizing the material, however, larger previews take longer to render. To open this window, RMB click on a node and then choose **Open Preview Window** from the popup menu.

To close a window, click **X** on the upper-right corner of the window. By default, a sphere is displayed as a sample geometry in the scene. If you want to change this geometry, choose **Cylinder** or **Box** from **RMB click** menu | **Preview Object Type** sub-menu. You can open any number of **Preview** windows in the editor. However, the drop-down available at the bottom of the **Preview** window allows you to switch the previews in a single window.

Caution: Preview window

*When open a new scene, the **Preview** window remains open, however, it may not correspond to any material. I recommend that you close all Preview windows before creating a new scene. The previews are not saved with the scene.*

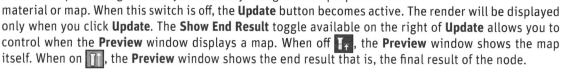

When the **Auto** switch is on in the **Preview** window, 3ds Max automatically renders the preview again when you make any changes to the properties of a material or map. When this switch is off, the **Update** button becomes active. The render will be displayed only when you click **Update**. The **Show End Result** toggle available on the right of **Update** allows you to control when the **Preview** window displays a map. When off [image], the **Preview** window shows the map itself. When on [image], the **Preview** window shows the end result that is, the final result of the node.

Wiring Nodes

As you already know, wires are used to connect material or map components. To understand the wiring process, from the **Material/Map Browser** | **Materials** rollout | **Standard** rollout, drag **Standard** to the active view to create a **Standard** material node. Similarly, drag **Checker** from the **Material/Map Browser** | **Maps** rollout | **Standard** rollout to the active view to create a **Checker** node [see left image in Figure 13]. Click-drag the **Standard** material's **Diffuse Color** socket, a wire appears. Now, drop the wire on the output socket of the **Checker** node to make a connection [see the right image in Figure 13]. You can also connect in reverse. You can connect the output socket of the **Checker** node to the **Diffuse Color** slot of the **Standard** material.

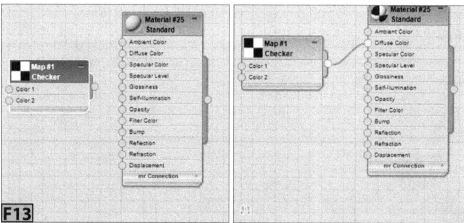

Now, drag and the **Standard** material's **Bump** socket to the blank area, a popup menu appears [see the left image in Figure 14], choose **Standard** | **Noise** from the menu to insert a **Noise** node and make connection between the **Noise** node and **Bump** socket of the **Standard** material [see the right image in Figure 14].

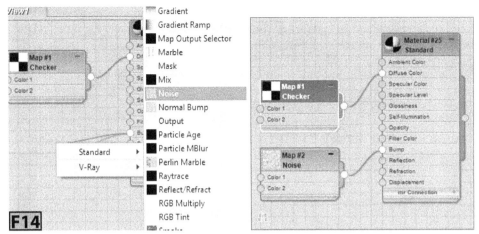

F14

You can also connect a map directly to a socket without first dragging to the active view. To do this, drag the **Falloff** map from the **Material/Map Browser | Maps** rollout | **Standard** rollout to the **Reflection** socket of the **Standard** material. When the socket turns green, release the mouse to make the connection [see Figure 15]. Another way to connect a node to a socket is that to double-click on a socket to open the **Material/Map Browser**. Now, select the desired map or material from the browser. You can also drag a wire on the title bar of a node. A popup menu appears [see Figure 16] that allows you to select component to wire.

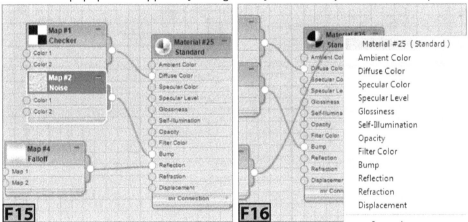

F15   F16

To delete a connection [wire], select the wire and then press **Delete**. The selected wire appears in white color. You can also drag away a wire from a socket where it has been connected to terminate the connection. To replace one map with another, drag from the new map's output socket to the output socket of the original map.

To insert a node into a connection, drag the node from the **Material/Map Browser** and then drop it on the wire. You can also drag from one of the node's input sockets to the wire to insert the node. If a node is lying on the active view and you want to insert it, drop the node on the wire with **Ctrl** held down. To disconnect an inserted node, drag the node and then press **Alt** while dragging.

When you RMB click on a wire, a popup menu appears [see Figure 17]. Choose **Change Material/Map Type** to open the **Material/Map Browser** and then choose a different type for the material or map. This option always affects the child node. The **Make Node Unique** option makes the child unique if the child node is instanced. The **Make Branch Unique** makes the child unique, as well as duplicates children of the child if the child node is instanced.

Map #2 -> Bump (Material #25)
Change Material/Map Type
Make Node Unique
Make Branch Unique

F17

Views

The active view is the main area of the **Slate Material Editor** where all action takes place. The navigating the active view is similar to the navigating a scene in 3ds Max. To pan the view, drag with the MMB. If you drag with the MMB and **Ctrl+Alt** held down, 3ds max zooms the view. You can also zoom by scrolling the wheel. The navigational tools are also available at the bottom-right corner of the editor's interface.

Table 3 summarized these controls.

Table 3: The Slate Material Editor navigational controls		
Control	Hotkey[s]	Menu
Zoom percentage drop-down list	-	
Pan Tool	Ctrl+P	View | Pan Tool
Zoom Tool	Alt+Z	View | Zoom Tool
Zoom Region Tool	Ctrl+W	View | Zoom Region Tool
Zoom Extents	Ctrl+Alt+Z	View | Zoom Extents
Zoom Extents Selected	Z	Zoom Extents Selected
Pan to Selected	Alt+P	View | Pan to Selected

If you are working on a complex scene, you might face difficulties locating nodes in the active view. You can use the search function of the editor to locate the nodes in the scene. Make a habit of renaming the nodes as you create them so that you can find the nodes using their names. To search a node, click the **Search For Nodes** button available on the bottom-left corner of the active view, 3ds Max expands the search tool. Type the name of the node in the search field and press **Enter** to locate the node and zoom on the node in the active view.

By default, the **Navigator** window appears on the upper-right corner of the **Slate Material Editor**. This window is most useful when you have lots of material trees displayed in the active view. This window shows a map of the active view. The red rectangle in the navigator shows the border of the active view. If you drag the rectangle, 3ds max changes the focus of the view.

Named Views

If you are working on a complex scene, you can create named views to organize materials in a scene. You can create any number of views in the editor and then make one of them the active view. When you open the editor in a new scene, a single view is displayed with the name **View1**. To manage views, RMB click on one of the tab and then choose the desired options from the popup menu displayed [see Figure 18].

To cycle through the tabs, use the **Ctrl+Tab** hotkeys. You can also select a view from the drop-down available above the **Navigator**. To move a tree from one view to another, RMB click on the node and then choose **Move Tree to View | Name of the View** from the popup menu.

Summary

In this unit, you have seen how you can use the **Compact Material Editor** and **Slate Material Editor** to create and organize materials and maps in the scene. I also described the **Material Explorer** that you can use to browse and manage all materials in a scene.

The unit covered the following topics:

- **Compact Material Editor**
- **Slate Material Editor**

In next unit, I will describe Standard and related materials as well as the standard maps.

Unit S2 - Standard Materials and Maps

The **Standard** material and related materials such as **Raytrace** material, **Matte/Shadow** material, **Compound** material, and **Ink 'n Paint** material are non-photometric. Do not use these materials if you plan to create physically accurate lighting models. However, these materials are suitable for games, films, and animation. In this unit, we are going to look at the standard materials and maps.

In this unit, I'll describe the following:

- Standard materials
- Standard maps

Standard Materials

The **Standard** material is a straight forward method for modeling surfaces that reflect light. You can use this material to model the reflective properties of a surface. If you don't use 2D or 3D maps with this material, it generates a single uniform color for the surface.

Let's explore the standard materials.

Standard Material

A surface having a single color reflects many other colors such as ambient, diffuse, and specular. The **Standard** materials use a four-color model to simulate the reflected colors from a surface. However, there may be variations depending on the shader you use. The **Ambient** color appears where surface is lit (the surface in the shadow) by the ambient light only. The **Diffuse** color appears on the surface when the lights falls directly on it. The term **Diffuse** is used because light is reflected in various directions. The **Specular** color appears in the highlights. Highlights are reflection of light sources on the surface.

Generally, shiny surfaces have specular highlights where the viewing angle is equal to the angle of incident. Metallic surfaces show another type of highlights called glancing highlights. The glancing highlights have a high angle of incidence. Some surfaces in the real-world are highly reflective. To model such surfaces, you can use a reflection map or use raytracing. The **Filter Color** is the color transmitted through an object. The **Filter Color** will only be visible, if **Opacity** is less than **100** percent.

The three color components blend at the edge of their respective regions. The **blend** of the **Diffuse** and **Ambient** components is controlled by the shader. However, you can control the blending by using the **Standard** material's highlight controls.

To create a **Standard** material, press **M** to open the **Slate Material Editor**. On the **Material Editor | Material |Map Browser | Materials | Standard** rollout, double-click **Standard** to add a standard material node to the active view. Figure 1 shows the **Standard** material's interface. If you double-click on the material node, its attributes appear in various rollouts on the **Parameter Editor**. The controls on these rollouts change according to the shader type chosen from the **Shader Basic Parameters** rollout [see Figure 2].

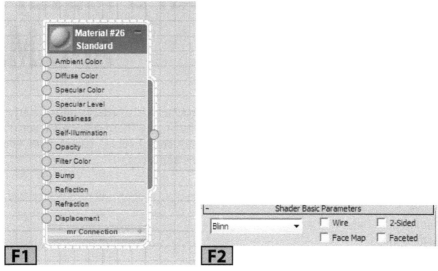

F1

F2

The controls in this rollout let you choose the type of shader to use with the **Standard** material. **Wire** lets you render the material in the wireframe mode [see Figure 3]. You can change the size of the wire using the **Size** control on the material's **Extended Parameters** rollout. Figure 4 shows the render with **Size** set to 2. **2-Sided** allows you to make a 2-sided material. When you select this option, 3ds Max applies material to the both sides of the selected faces.

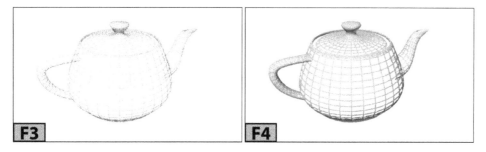

F3

F4

Note: One-sided faces
In 3ds Max, faces are one-sided. The front side is the side with the surface normals. The back side of the faces is invisible to the renderer. If you see this other side from the back, the faces will appear to be missing.

The **Face Map** control allows you to apply the material to the faces of the geometry. If material is a mapped material, it requires no mapping coordinates and automatically applied to each face. Figures 5 and 6 show the render with the **Face Map** switch is in off and on states, respectively. The **Faceted** control renders each face of the surface as if it were flat [see Figure 7].

Tip: Rendering both sides of a face
*There are two ways to render both sides of a face. Either you can turn on **Force 2-Sided** in the **Render Setup** dialog | **Common** panel | **Options** group or apply a two sided material to the faces.*

The **Shader** drop-down located at the extreme left of the rollout lets you choose a shader for the material. Here's is the quick rundown to the various material shaders:

Phong Shader

You can use this shader to produce realistic highlights for shiny, and regular surfaces. This shader produces strong circular highlights. This shader can accurately render bump, opacity, shininess, specular, and reflection maps. When you select the **Phong** shader, the **Phong Shader Parameters** rollout appears in the material's **Parameter Editor** [see Figure 8].

Phong Shader Parameters Rollout

The controls in this rollout, let you set the color of the material, shininess, and transparency of the material. The **Ambient**, **Diffuse**, and **Specular** controls let you set the colors for ambient, diffuse, and specular color components, respectively. To change a color component, click on the color swatch and then use the **Color Selector** to change the values of the color component. You can also copy one color component to another by dragging the source color swatch to the target color swatch. In the **Copy or Swap Colors** dialog that appears, click **Swap**, or **Copy** button. Click **Cancel** to cancel the operation. You can lock or unlock two color components using the **Lock** button [see Figure 9].

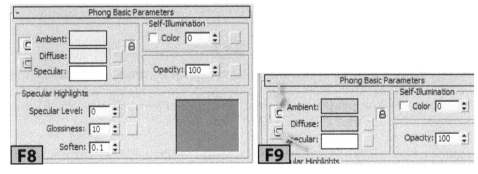

The buttons located on the right of color swatches can be used to apply texture maps to the respective color components. On clicking these buttons, the **Material/Map Browser** appears that allows you to select a map for the color component. If you want to apply different maps to the **Ambient** and **Diffuse** components, click on the **Lock** button located to the right of these components [see Figure 10].

Self-Illumination Group: You can use the controls in this group to make the material self-illuminated. The illusion of self-illumination is created by replacing shadows with the diffuse color. There are two ways to enable self-illumination in 3ds Max. Either you can turn on the switch located in this group and use a self-illumination color or use the spinner.

Note: Self-illuminated materials
Self-illuminated materials do not show shadows cast onto them. Also, they are unaffected by the lights in the scene.

Opacity Group: You can use the controls in this group, to make a material opaque, transparent, or translucent. To change the opacity of the material, change opacity to a value less than 100%. If you want to use a map for controlling opacity, click **Opacity** map button.

Specular Highlight Group: Phong, **Blinn**, and **Oren-Nayar-Blinn** shaders produce circular highlights and share same highlight controls. **Blinn** and **Oren-Nayar-Blinn** shaders produce soft and round highlights than the **Phong** shader. You can use the **Specular Level** control to increase or decrease the strength of a highlight. As you change the value for this control, the **Highlight** curve and the highlight in the preview changes. The shape of this curve affects the blending between the specular and diffuse color components of the material. If the curve is steeper, there will be less blending and the edge of the specular highlight will be sharper. To increase or decrease the size of the highlight, change the value for **Glossiness**. **Soften** softens the specular highlights especially those formed by the glancing light.

Extended Parameters Rollout

The **Extender Parameters** rollout [see Figure 11] is same for all shaders except **Strauss** and **Translucent** shaders. The controls in this rollout allow you to control the transparency and reflection settings. Also, it has controls for adjusting the wireframe rendering.

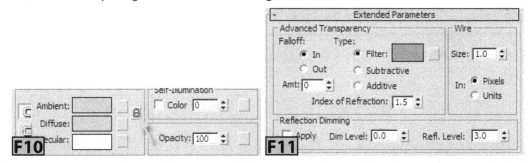

Advanced Transparency Group: These controls do not appear for the **Translucent** shader. **Falloff** allows you to set the falloff and its extent. **In** increases transparency toward the inside of the object (like glass bottle) whereas **Out** increases transparency toward the outside of the object (like clouds). **Amt** lets you adjust the amount of transparency at the outside or inside extreme.

The **Type** controls let you specify how transparency is applied. The **Filter** color swatch computes a filter color that it multiplies with the color behind the transparent surface. The **Subtractive** option subtracts from the color behind the transparent surface. The **Additive** option adds to the color behind the transparent surface.

Index of Refraction allows you to set the index of refraction used by refraction map and raytracing.

Reflection Dimming group: This group does not appear for the **Strauss** shader. These controls dim the reflection in shadow. Check **Apply** to enable reflection dimming. **Dim Level** controls the amount of dimming that takes place in shadow. **Refl. Level** affects the intensity of the reflection that is not in shadow.

SuperSampling Rollout

The **SuperSampling** rollout [see Figure 12] is used by the **Architectural**, **Raytrace**, **Standard**, and **Ink 'n Paint** materials to improve the quality of the rendered image. It performs an additional antialiasing pass on the material thus resulting in more render time. By default, a single **SuperSampling** method is applied to all materials in the scene.

Maps Rollout: The **Maps** rollout [see Figure 13] is available for all materials. The controls in this rollout allow you to assign maps to various components of the material. To assign map to a component, click a map button. Now, choose the desired map option from the **Material/Map Browser** that opens.

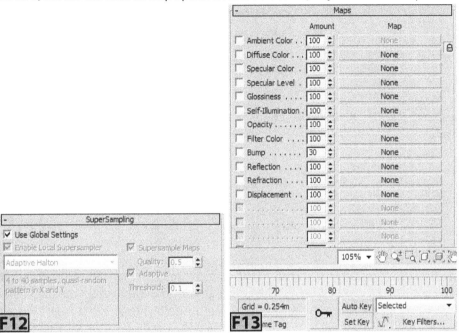

Blinn Shader

This is the default shader. It produces rounder, softer highlights than the **Phong** shader. The **Blinn** and **Phong** shaders have the same basic parameters.

Metal Shader

You can use the **Metal** shader to create realistic-looking metallic surfaces and a variety of organic-looking materials. The metal material calculates their specular color automatically. The output specular color depends on the diffuse color of the material and the color of the light.

This shader produces distinctive highlights. Like the **Phong** shader, **Specular Level** still controls intensity. However, **Glossiness** affects both the intensity and size of the specular highlights. Figure 14 shows the controls in **Metal Basic Parameters** rollout.

Oren-Nayar-Blinn Shader

This shader is a variant of the **Blinn** shader and can be used to model matte surfaces such as fabric. It has two additional controls to model a surface with the matte look: **Diffuse Level** and **Roughness**.

[Oren-Nayar-Blinn Basic Parameters rollout | Advanced Diffuse Group]: Diffuse Level controls [see Figure 15] the brightness of the diffuse component of the material. It allows you to make the material lighter or darker. **Roughness** allows you to control the rate at which the diffuse component blends into the ambient component.

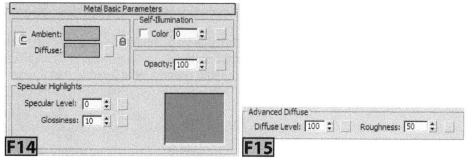

Note: The Roughness Parameter

*The **Roughness** parameter is available only with the **Oren-Nayar-Blinn** and **Multi-Level** shaders, and with the **Arch & Design** material (**mental ray**).*

Note: Diffuse Level control

*The **Blinn**, **Metal**, **Phong**, and **Strauss** shaders do not have the **Diffuse Level** control.*

Strauss Shader

This shader is a simpler version of the **Metal** shader. It can be used to model the metallic surfaces.

Strauss Basic Parameters Rollout: The **Color** control [see Figure 16] lets you specify the color of the material. The **Strauss** shader automatically calculates the ambient and specular color components. **Glossiness** controls the size and intensity of the specular highlights. On increasing the value for this control, the highlight gets smaller and the material appears shiner. The **Metalness** control adjust the metalness of the surface. The effect of this control is more prominent when you increase the **Glossiness** value. **Opacity** sets the transparency of the material.

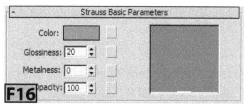

Anisotropic Shader

You can use this shader to create surfaces with elliptical, anisotropic highlights. This shader is suitable for modeling hair, glass, or brushed metal. The **Diffuse Level** controls are similar to that of the **Oren-Nayar-Blinn** shading controls, and basic parameters controls are similar to that of the **Blinn** or **Phong** shading, except the **Specular Highlights** parameters.

Anisotropic Basic Parameters Rollout | Specular Highlight Group: The **Specular Level** [Figure 17] control sets the intensity of the specular highlights. On increasing the value for this control, the highlight goes brighter. **Glossiness** controls the size of the specular highlights. The **Anisotropy** controls the anisotropy or shape of the highlight. **Orientation** controls the orientation of the highlight. This value is measured in degrees.

Multi-Layer Shader: This shader is similar to the **Anisotropic** shader. However, it allows you to layer two sets of specular highlights. The highlights are layered that allows you to create complex highlights. Figure 18 shows the two specular layers in the **Multi-Layer Basic Parameters** rollout.

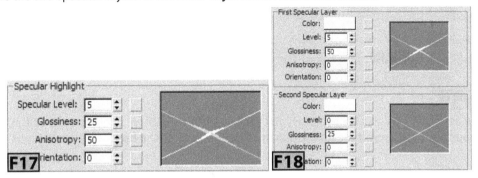

Translucent Shader: This shader is similar to the **Blinn** shader but allows you set the translucency of the material. A translucent object not only allows light to pass through but it also scatters light within.

Translucent Basic Parameters Rollout | Translucency Group

The **Translucent Clr** control [see Figure 19] sets the translucency color that is the color of the light scattered within the material. This color is different from the **Filter** color which is the color transmitted through transparent or semi-transparent material such as glass. The **Opacity** control sets the opacity or transparency of the material.

Note: The mental ray renderer
*The **mental ray** renderer is used in hands-on-exercises of this book.*

Compound Materials

Compound materials are used to combine two or more sub-materials. These materials are especially useful when you use map mask with them.

Blend Material

The **Blend** material allows you to mix two materials on a single side of the surface. You can use the **Mix Amount** parameter [see Figure 20] to control the way two materials are blended together. You can also animate this control. The **Material 1** and **Material 2** controls let you assign the two materials to be blended. You can also use the corresponding switches to turn material on or off. The **Interactive** option specifies which of the materials or mask map will be displayed in the viewport by the interactive renderer.

The **Mask** control lets you assign a map as mask. The lighter and darker areas on the mask map control the degree of blending. The lighter areas displays more of the **Material 1** whereas the darker areas show more of **Material 2**. The **Mix Amount** controls the proportion of blend in degrees. A value of **0** means only **Material 1** will be visible on the surface whereas a value of **100** means **Material 2** will be visible on the surface.

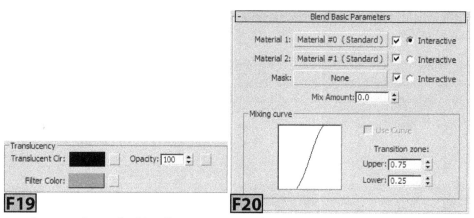

F19 **F20**

When you assign a mask map for blending, you can use the mixing curve to affect the blending. You can use the controls in the **Transition Zone** group to adjust the level of the **Upper** and **Lower** limits.

Note: Interactive renderer and Blend material
Only one map can be displayed in the viewports when using the interactive renderer.

Note: Blend Material and Noise Map
*The **Mix Amount** control is not available when you use mask to blend the material. Using a **Noise** map as mixing map can produce naturally looking surfaces.*

Double Sided Material

The **Double Sided** material lets you assign two different materials to the front and back surface of an object. The **Facing Material** and **Back Material** controls [see Figure 21] allow you to specify the material for the front and back faces, respectively. The **Translucency** control allows you to blend the two materials. There will be no blending of the materials if **Translucency** is set to **0**. At a value of **100**, the outer material will be visible on the inner faces and inner material will be visible on the outer faces.

Composite Material

This material can be used to composite up to ten materials. The materials are composited from top to bottom. The maps can be combined using additive opacity, subtractive opacity, or using an amount value. The **Base Material** control [see Figure 22] allows you to set the base material. The default base material is the **Standard** material.

The **Mat.1** to **Mat.9** controls are used to specify the material that you want to composite. Each material control has an array of buttons called **ASM** buttons. These buttons control how the material is composited. The **A** button allows you to use the additive opacity.

The colors in the materials are summed based on the opacity. The **S** button allows you to use the subtractive opacity. The **M** button is used to mix the materials using a value. You can enter the value in the spinner located next to the **M** button. When the **M** button is active, amount ranges from **0** to **100**. When amount is **0**, no compositing happens and the material below is not visible. If the amount is **100**, the material below is visible.

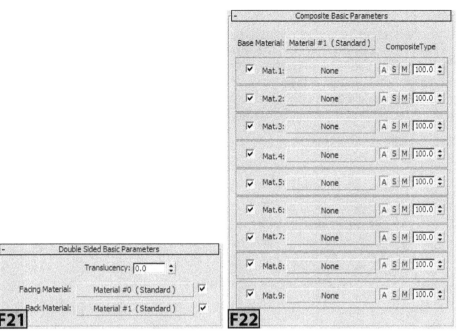

F21

F22

Tip: Composite Material v Composite Map

If you want to achieve a result by combining maps instead of combining materials, use the **Composite** *map that provides greater control.*

Note: Overloaded compositing

For additive and subtractive compositing, the amount can range from **0** *to* **200**. *When the amount is greater than* **100***, the compositing is overloaded. As a result, the transparent area of the material becomes more opaque.*

Morpher Material

The **Morpher** material is used with the **Morpher** modifier. For example, when a character raises his eyebrows, you can use this material to display wrinkles on his forehead. You can blend the materials the same way you morph the geometry using the channel spinners of the **Morpher** modifier.

Multi/Sub-Object Material

The **Multi/Sub-Object** material allows you to assign materials at the sub-object level. The number field [see Figure 23] shows the number of sub-materials contained in the **Multi/Sub-Object** material. You can use the **Set Number** button to set the number of sub-materials that make up the material. The **Add** button allows you to a new sub-material to the list. Use the **Delete** button to remove currently chosen sub-material from the list. The **ID**, **Name**, and **Sub-Material** controls allow you to sort the list based on the material id, name, and sub-material, respectively.

To assign materials to the sub-objects, select the object and assign the **Multi/sub-Object** material to it. Apply a **Mesh Select** modifier to the object. Activate the **Face** sub-object level. Now, select the faces to which you will assign the material. Apply a **Material Modifier** and then set the material ID value to the number of the sub-material you need to assign.

Shellac Material

Shellac material allows you to mix two materials by superimposing one over the other. The superimposed material is known as the **Shellac** material. The **Base Material** control [Figure 24] lets you choose or edit the base sub-material. The **Shellac Material** control lets you choose or edit the **Shellac** material. The **Shellac Color Blend** control adjusts the amount of color mixing. The default value for this control is **0**. Hence, the shellac material has no effect on the surface. There is no upper limit for this control. Higher values overload the colors of the **Shellac** material. You can also animate this parameter.

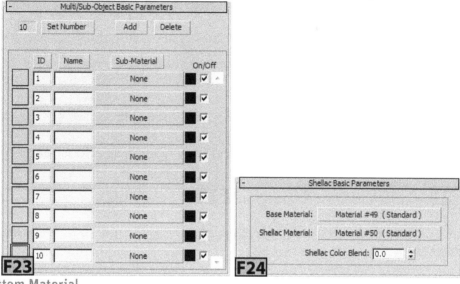

Top/Bottom Material

This material lets you assign two different materials to the top and bottom portions of an object. You can also blend the two materials. The top faces of an object are those faces whose normals point up. The bottom faces have the normals down. You can control the boundary between the top and bottom using the controls available in the **Coordinates** group [see Figure 25].

The **World** option lets you specify the direction according to the world coordinates of the scene. If you rotate the object, the boundary between the top and bottom faces remains in place. The **Local** option allows you to control the direction using the local coordinate system.

You can specify the top and bottom materials using the **Top** and **Bottom** controls, respectively. The **Swap** button allows you to swap the material. You can blend the edge between the top and bottom materials using the **Blend** control. The value for this control ranges from **0** to **1**. If you set **Blend** to **0**, there will be a sharp line between the top and bottom materials. At **100**, the two materials tint each other.

The **Position** control allows you to specify the location where the division between the two materials will occur. The value for this control ranges from **0** to **1**. If you set **Position** to **0**, only top material will be displayed. At **100**, only bottom material will be displayed.

Raytrace Material

This material is an advanced surface-shading material. It supports the same diffuse surface shading that a **Standard** material supports. However, it also supports fog, color density, translucency, fluorescence, and other special effects. This material is capable of creating fully raytraced reflections and refractions. Figure 26 shows the **Raytrace** material's interface.

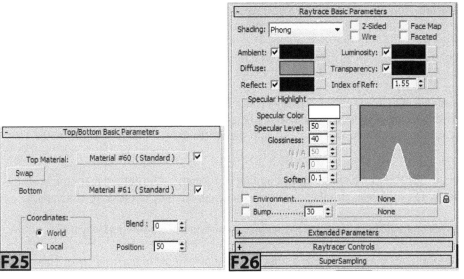

Matte/Shadow Material

The **Matte Shadow** material is used to make whole objects or any set of faces into matte objects. The matte objects reveal the background color or the environment map. A matte object is invisible but it blocks any geometry behind it however it does not block the background. The matte objects can also receive shadows. The shadows cast on the matte object are applied to the alpha channel. To properly generate shadows on a matte object, turn off **Opaque Alpha** and then turn on **Affect Alpha** [see Figure 27].

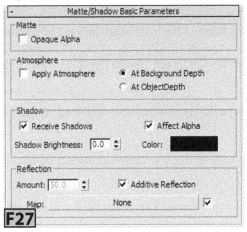

Ink 'n Paint Material

The **Ink 'n Paint** material is used to create cartoons effects. This material produces shading with inked borders.

Standard Maps

Maps allow you to improve the appearance of the materials. They also help you to enhance the realism of the materials. You can use maps in a variety of ways, you can use them to create environments, to create image planes for modeling, to create projections from light, and so forth. You can use the **Material/ Map Browser** to load a map or create a map of a particular type. A map can be used to design different elements of a material such as reflection, refraction, bump, and so forth.

Maps and Mapping Coordinates

When you apply a map to any object, the object must have mapping coordinates applied. These coordinates are specified in terms of UVW axes local to the object. Most of the objects in 3ds Max have the **Generate Mapping Coordinates** option. When on, 3ds Max generates default mapping coordinates.

UVW Mapping Coordinate Channels

Each object in 3ds Max can have **99** UVW mapping coordinates. The default mapping is always assigned the number **1**. The **UVW Map** modifier can send coordinates to any of these **99** channels.

3ds Max gives you ability to generate the mapping coordinates in different ways:

- The **Generate Mapping Coords** option is available for most of the primitives. This option provides a projection appropriate to the shape of the object type.
- Apply the **Unwrap UVW** modifier. This modifier comes with some useful tools that you can use to edit mapping coordinates.
- Apply the **UVW Map** modifier. This modifier allows you to set a projection type from several projection types it provides.

Here's the quick rundown to the projection types:

- **Box projection:** It places a duplicate of the map image on each of the six sides of a box.

- **Cylindrical projection:** This wraps the image around the sides of the object. The duplicate images are also projected onto the end caps.

- **Spherical projection:** This projection type wraps the map image around a sphere and gather the image at the top and bottom.

- **Shrink-wrap projection:** This type is like the spherical projection but creates one singularity instead of two.

- Use special mapping coordinates. For example, the **Loft** object provides built-in mapping coordinates.
- Use a **Surface Mapper** modifier. This modifier uses a map assigned to a NURBS surface and projects it onto the object(s).

Here's quick rundown to the cases when you can apply a map and you don't need mapping coordinates:

- Reflection, Refraction, and Environment maps.
- 3D Procedural maps: **Noise** and **Marble**.
- Face-mapped materials.

Tip: UVW Remove utility
*The **UVW Remove** utility removes mapping coordinates or materials from the currently selected objects. The path to the utility is as follows: **Utilities** panel | **Utilities** rollout | **More** button | **Utilities** dialog | **UVW Remove**.*

Real-World Mapping

The real-world mapping is an alternative mapping method that you can use in 3ds Max. This type of mapping considers the correct scaling of the texture mapped materials applied to the geometry in the scene.

Note: Autodesk Materials
Autodesk materials require you to use the real-world mapping.

In order to apply the real-world mapping correctly, two requirements must be met. First, the correct style of UV texture coordinates must be assigned to the geometry. In other words, the size of the UV space should correspond to the size of the geometry. To address this issue, the **Real-World Map Size** switch is added to the many rollouts in 3ds Max [see Figure 28].

The second requirement is available in the **Coordinates** rollout of the **Material Editor**. Use **Real-World Scale** is on in 3ds Max Design [see Figure 29] [3ds Max Design now discontinued by Autodesk] whereas in 3ds Max it is off [see Figure 30]. When this switch is off, **U/V** changes to **Width/Height** and **Tiling** changes to **Size**.

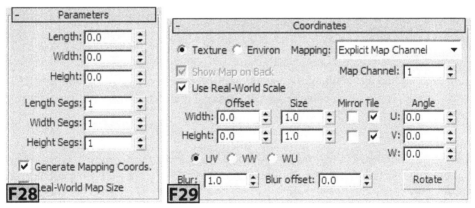

Note: Real-world Mapping
The real-world mapping is off in 3ds Max, by default.

Tip: Real-World Map Size check box
*You can turn on **Real-World Map Size** by default from the **Preferences** dialog by using the **Use Real-World Texture Coordinates** switch. This option is available in the **Texture Coordinates** section of the **General** panel.*

Output Rollout

The options in this rollout [see Figure 31] are responsible for setting the internal parameters of a map. These options can be used to determine the rendered appearance of the map. Most of the controls on this rollout are for the color output.

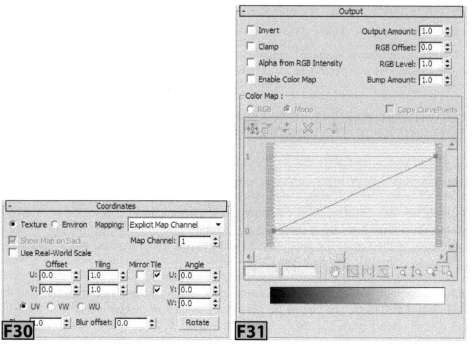

Note: Output Rollout

*These controls do not affect the bump maps except the **Invert** toggle, which reverses the direction of the bumps and bump amount.*

2D Maps

The 2D maps are two-dimensional images that are mapped to the surface of the geometric objects. You can also use them to create environment maps. The **Bitmap** is the simplest type 2D maps. 3ds Max also allows you to create 2D maps procedurally.

Coordinates Rollout

The **Coordinates** rollout shown in Figures 29 and 30 allows you to adjust coordinate parameters to move a map relative to the surface of the object. This rollout also allows you to set tiling and mirroring of the texture pattern. The repetition of the texture pattern on the surface of an object is known as tiling. The mirroring is a form of tiling in which 3ds Max repeats the map and then flips the repeated map.

In this rollout, there are two options that you can use to control the mapping type. These options are **Texture** and **Environ**. The **Texture** type applies texture as a map to the surface. The **Environ** type uses map as an environment map. For both of these options, you can select the types of coordinates from the **Mapping** drop-down.

Here's the list of options available in the **Mapping** drop-down:

- **Explicit Map Channel:** It uses any map channel from **1** to **99**. When you select this option, **Map Channel** becomes active.
- **Vertex Color Channel:** This option uses assigned vertex colors as a channel.
- **Planar from Object XYZ:** This option uses planar mapping based on the object's local coordinates.
- **Planar from World XYZ:** This option uses planar mapping based on the scene's world coordinates.
- **Spherical Environment/Cylindrical Environment/Shrink-wrap Environment:** These options project the map into the scene as if it were mapped to an invisible object in the background.
- **Screen:** This option projects a map as a flat backdrop in the scene.

Noise Rollout

You can add a random noise to the appearance of the material using the parameters available in this rollout [see Figure 32]. These parameters modify the mapping of pixels by applying a fractal noise function.

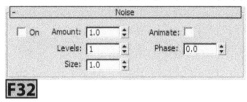

Bitmap

This map is the simplest type of map available in 3ds Max. This map is useful for creating many type of materials from wood to skin. If you want to create an animated material, you can use an animation or video file with this map. When you select this map, the **Select Bitmap Image File** dialog opens. Navigate to the location where the bitmap file is stored and then click **Open** to select the file.

Tip: Bitmap and Windows Explorer
*You can also create a bitmap node by dragging a supported bitmap file from **Windows Explorer** to the **Slate Material Editor**.*

Tip: Viewport Canvas
*The **Viewport Canvas** feature allows you create a bitmap on the fly by painting directly onto the surface of the object. To open the canvas, choose **Viewport Canvas** from the **Tools** menu.*

Checker Map

This map is a procedural texture that applies a two-color checkerboard pattern [see Figure 33]. The default colors used to produce the pattern are black and white. You can also change these colors with map and it's true for all color components of the other maps.

Camera Map Per Pixel Map

This map allows you to project a map from the direction of a particular camera. It is useful when you are working on a matte painting. Figure 34 shows the Marble map projected on the teapot using the camera [see Figure 35]. Figure 36 shows the node network.

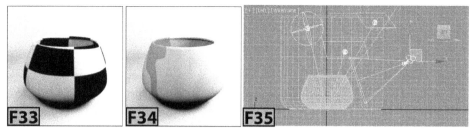

F33 **F34** **F35**

Note: Two maps with the sane name

If a map with the same name exists in two places, only one map is loaded to save the loading time. If you have two maps with different contents but with the same name, only the first map encountered by 3ds Max appears in the scene.

Tip: Swapping Colors

You can swap colors by dragging one color swatch over another and then choosing swap from the popup menu.

Warning: Camera Map Per Pixel Map

This map cannot be used with the animated objects or animated textures.

Gradient Map

This map type allows you to create a gradient that shades from one color to another. Figure 37 shows the shift from one color to another. The red, green, and blue colors are used for the gradient. Figure 38 shows the result when the fractal noise is applied to the gradient. Figure 39 shows the node network.

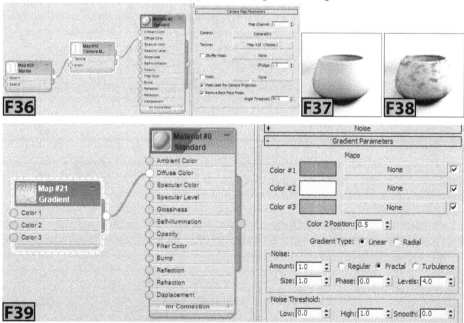

F36 **F37** **F38**

F39

Gradient Ramp Map

This map is similar to the **Gradient** map. Like the **Gradient** map, it shades from one color to another, however, you can use any number of colors [see Figure 40]. Also, you have additional controls to create a complex customized ramp. Figure 41 shows the node network used to produce the result shown in Figure 40.

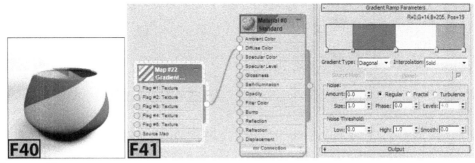

Normal Bump Map

This map allows you to connect a texture-baked normal map to a material. Figure 42 shows the bump on the surface created using the **Normal Bump** map. Figure 43 shows the node network.

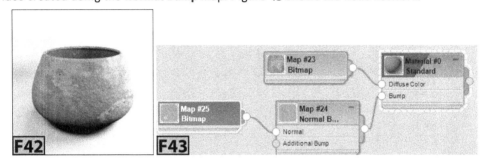

Substance Map

This map is used with the **Substance** parametric textures. These textures are resolution-independent 2D textures and use less memory. Therefore, they are useful for exporting to the game engines via the **Algorithmic Substance Air** middleware.

Swirl Map

This map is 2D procedural map that can be used to simulate swirls [see Figure 44].

Tile Map

You can use this map to create a brick or stacked tiling of colors or maps. A number of commonly used architectural brick patterns are available with this map. Figure 45 shows render with the **English Bond** type applied.

Vector Map

Using this map, you can apply a vector-based graphics, including animation as textures. You can also use **AutoCAD Pattern** (PAT) files, **Adobe Illustrator** (AI) files, **Portable Document** (PDF) files, and **Scalable Vector Graphics** (SVG) files.

Vector Displacement Map

This map allows you to displace the meshes in three directions whereas the traditional method permits displacement only along the surface normals.

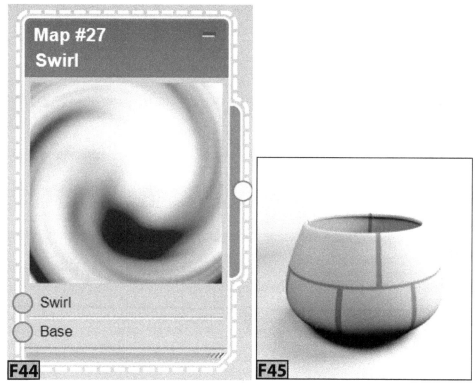

F44

F45

3D Maps

3D maps are patterns generated by 3ds Max in 3D space. Let's have a look at various 3D maps.

Cellular Map

You can use this map to generate a variety of visual effects such as mosaic tiling, pebbled surfaces, and even ocean surfaces [see Figure 46].

Dent Map

This map generated a procedural map using a fractal noise algorithm [see Figure 47]. The effect that this produces depends on the map type chosen.

Falloff Map

The **Falloff** map generates a value from white to black based on the angular falloff of the face normals. Figure 48 shows the **Falloff** map applied to the geometry with the **Falloff** type set to **Fresnel**.

F46

F47

F48

Marble Map

You can use this map to create a marble texture with the colored veins against [see Figure 49] a color background.

Noise Map

This map allows to create a noise map that creates the random perturbation of a surface based on the interaction of two colors or materials. Figure 50 shows the **Noise** map with the **Noise Type** set to **Fractal**.

Particle Age Map

This map is used with the particle systems. This map changes the color of the particles based on their age.

Particle MBlur Map

This map can be used to alter the opacity of the leading and trailing ends of particles based on their rate of motion.

Perlin Marble Map

This map is like the **Marble** map. However, it generates a marble pattern using the **Perlin Turbulence** algorithm.

Smoke Map

You can use this map [see Figure 51] to create animated opacity maps to simulate the effects of smoke in a beam of light, or other cloudy, flowing effects.

Speckle Map

This map [see Figure 52] can be used to create granite-like and other patterned surfaces.

Splat Map

This map can be used to create patterns similar to the spattered paint [see Figure 53].

Stucco Map

You can use this map [see Figure 54] as a bump to create the effect like a stuccoed surface.

Waves Map

You can use this map as both bump or diffuse map [see Figure 55]. This map is used to create watery or wavy effects.

Wood Map

This map creates a wavy grain like wood pattern [see Figure 56]. You can control the direction, thickness, and complexity of the grain.

Compositor Maps

These maps are specifically designed for compositing colors and maps. Let's have a look at these maps.

Composite Map

You can use this map to layer other maps atop each other using the alpha channel and other methods.

Mask Map

This map can be used to view one material through another on the surface.

Mix Map

With this map, you can combine two colors or materials on a single side of the surface. You can also animate the **Mix Amount** parameter to control how two maps are blended together over time.

RGB Multiply Map

This map combines two maps by multiplying their RGB values. This map is generally used as a **Bump** map.

Color Modifiers Maps

These maps change the color of the pixels in a material. Let's have a look:

Color Correction Map

This map is allows you to modify color of a map using various tools. This map uses a stack-based method.

Output Map

You can use this map to apply output settings to the procedural maps such as **Checker** or **Marble**. These maps don't have the output settings.

RGB Tint Map

This map adjusts the three color channels in an image.

Vertex Color Map

In 3ds Max, you can assign vertex colors using the **VertexPaint** modifier, the **Assign Vertex Colors** utility, or the vertex controls for an editable mesh, editable patch, or editable poly. This map makes any vertex coloring applied to an object available for rendering.

Reflection and Refraction Maps

These maps are used to create reflections and refractions. Here's is a quick rundown.

Flat Mirror Map

This map produces a material that reflects surroundings when it is applied to the co-planer faces. It is assigned to the **Reflection** map of the material.

Raytrace Map

This map allows you to create fully raytraced reflections and refractions. The reflections/refractions generated by this map are more accurate than the **Reflect/Refract** map.

Reflect/Refract Map

You can use this map to create a reflective or refractive surface. To create reflection, assign this map type to the reflection map. To create refraction, apply it to the **Refraction** map.

Thin Wall Refraction Map

This map can be used to simulate a surface as if it part of a surface through a plate of glass.

Hands-on Exercises

Complete the following hands-on exercises:

Unit Sh1-Exercise 1: Creating the Gold Material
Unit Sh1-Exercise 2: Creating the Copper Material
Unit Sh1-Exercise 3: Creating the Brass Material
Unit Sh1-Exercise 4: Creating the Chrome Material
Unit Sh1-Exercise 5: Creating the Brushed Aluminum Material
Unit Sh1-Exercise 6: Creating the Denim Fabric Material
Unit Sh1-Exercise 7: Working with the Blend Material
Unit Sh1-Exercise 8: Working with the Double-Sided Material
Unit Sh1-Exercise 9: Working with the Shellac Material
Unit Sh1-Exercise 10: Creating the Microscopic Material
Unit Sh1-Exercise 10: Creating Material for a Volleyball
Unit Sh1-Exercise 12: Creating Material for a Water Tunnel
Unit Sh1-Exercise 13: Creating Rusted Metal Texture

Summary

In this unit, you have learned about the standard and other related materials. I also explained various types of 2D and 3D maps available in 3ds Max that you can use to add realism to your models.

The unit covered the following topics:

- Standard materials
- Standard maps

In the next unit, we are going to look at the **Autodesk Materials** and mental ray's **Arch & Design** material.

Unit S3–Mental Ray and Autodesk Materials

3ds Max offers several materials that are used with the **mental ray** renderer. These materials are only visible in the **Material/Map Browser** if the active renderer is **NVIDIA mental ray** or **Quicksilver Hardware** renderer. The mental ray materials can be divided into three categories: Autodesk Materials, **Arch & Design** Material, and special-purpose mental ray materials.

Autodesk Materials are used to model commonly used surfaces in the construction, design, and the environment. These materials correspond to the materials found in other Autodesk products such as **Autodesk AutoCAD**, **Revit** and **Autodesk Inventor**. So, if you work between these applications, you can share surface and material information among them.

The mental ray **Arch & Design** material allows you improve rendering quality of the architectural renderings. This material is particularly useful when used to simulate glossy surfaces. The special-purpose mental ray materials are used to design special purpose materials such as car paint material, subsurface scattering material, and so forth.

In this unit, I'll describe the following:

- Global Illumination
- Final Gather
- Caustics
- Autodesk Materials
- Arch & Design Material

The **NVIDIA mental ray** renderer is general purpose renderer that can produce realistic and physically accurate shading and light effects including raytraced reflection and refractions, caustics, and global illumination.

Global Illumination, Final Gathering, and Caustics

Global illumination enhances realism in a scene. In 3ds Max, the **mental ray** renderer offers two methods for achieving the Global Illumination: **photon tracing** and **final gathering**. The primary difference between the two is that the photon tracing works from the light source to the ultimate illuminated target whereas final gathering works from the illuminated object to the light source. You can use these methods separately or combine them for optimal results.

In final gathering, global illumination is established for a point by either sampling a number of directions [rays] over the hemisphere over that point or by averaging a number of nearby final gather points. The orientation of the hemisphere is determined by the surface normal of the triangle on whose surface the point lies. Final gathering is useful when there is slow variations in the indirect illumination in the scene. In film production work, final gathering is the preferred method for indirect illumination. However, for accurate indoor illumination, photon mapping is the preferred method of choice.

Global Illumination

The **mental ray** renderer generates global illumination using the photon mapping technique. In this technique, the **mental ray** renderer traces photons emitted from the light. The photon is traced though the scene. In this process it is reflected and transmitted by objects in the scene. When it hits a diffuse surface, the photon is stored in the photon map. To save the system resources, you need to specify the following:

- Which lights can emit photons for the indirect illumination?
- Which objects can generate caustics or global illumination?
- Which objects can receive caustics or global illumination?

To set these properties, ensure that current renderer is set to **mental ray** and then RMB click on the object[s] in the scene and then choose **Object Properties** from the **Quad** menu. Set the options in the **Object Properties** dialog | **mental ray** panel | **Caustics and Global Illumination [GI]** section. The **mental ray** renderer saves photon maps as **PMAP** files. In order to use the global illumination in 3ds Max, the photons must bounce through two or more surfaces. When you use photon maps, you might see some artifacts in the renders such as dark corners or variations in lighting, you can eliminate those artifacts by turning on the final gathering.

Let's explore the global illumination settings:

Start 3ds Max and reset it. From the **Customize** menu, choose **Unit Setup** and then in the **Unit Setup** dialog | **Display Unit Scale** group, select **Metric**. Select **Meters** as units and then click **OK**. Create a box in the scene. Go to the **Modify** panel and set **Length** to **4**, **Width** to **4**, and **Height** to **2**. Convert box to **Editable Poly** and then delete the front face [see Figure 1].

Select all polygons and flip them. Create a **Multi-Subobject** material and assign it to the box. Create three sub-materials [**Standard** materials] and then assign them red, blue, and green colors, respectively. Connect them to the **Multi-Subobject** material. Create polygon IDs for polygons and assign the **Multi-Subobject** material to the box [see Figure 2]. Create a **Teapot** inside the box.

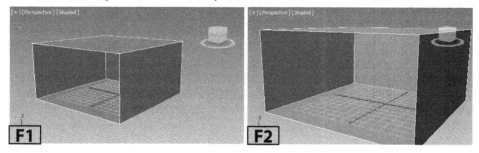

Note: Example 1 File
*You can also use the **ex1_begin.max** file.*

Open the **Render Setup** dialog. Change renderer to **mental ray**. In the **Global Illumination** panel | **Final Gathering (FG)** rollout | **Basic** section, turn off **Enable Final Gather**. Create a **mr Area Omni** light inside the box and turn on **Ray Traced Shadows**. Now, take a test render, the scene is being illuminated by the direct light coming from the **mr Area Omni** light [see Figure 3]. On the **Render Setup** dialog | **Global Illumination** panel | **Caustics & Photon Mapping (GI)** rollout | **Photon Mapping (GI)** group, turn on **Enable**. This allows the **mental ray** renderer to calculate the global illumination. Set **Maximum Num. Photons per Sample** to **1** and take a test render [see Figure 4]. You will see that effect of individual photons in the render.

This setting lets you define the number of photons used to compute the intensity of the global illumination. When you increase the value for this control, the result becomes less noisy but more blurry. The larger the sample value is, more time it will take to render.

Set **Maximum Num. Photons per Sample** to **200**. Turn on **Maximum Sample Radius**. Leave the value at **0.025** and take a test render [see Figure 5]. This value sets the size of the photons. When **Maximum Sample Radius** is **off**, each photon is calculated to be 1/10 of the radius of the full scene. Set **Maximum Sample Radius** to **0.1** and take a render [see Figure 6].

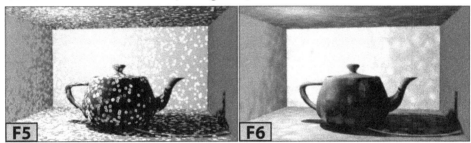

You will see that the photons are blending with each other. Generally, 1/10th of the scene produces good result. When photons overlap, **mental ray** uses sampling to smooth them. Increasing the value for **Maximum Num. Photons per Sample**, produces smooth result.

Set **Maximum Sample Radius** to **1** and take a test render [see Figure 7]. You will see that on increasing the radius the photons are blending well with each other. Set **Maximum Sample Radius** to **0.1** and turn on **Merge Nearby Photons (saves memory)** and set its spinner to **0.85** and take a test render [see Figure 8].

You will see the dots in the render. These settings allows you to set the distance threshold below which **mental ray** merges photons. It reduces the memory requirements for rendering the global illumination.

The **Optimize for Final Gather (Slower GI)** control allows photons to store additional information about how bright its neighbors are. This option is very useful when you want to combine global illumination with final gathering. It allows the final gather to quickly determine how many photons exists in a particular region. It helps in reducing the rendering time.

Turn off **Maximum Sample Radius** and **Merge Nearby Photons (saves memory)**. Set **Maximum Num. Photons per Sample** to **500**.

The controls in the **Trace Depth** group allow you to set the limits for calculating reflections and refractions. These controls refers to the photons used by caustics and global illumination. **Max Depth** control limits the combination of reflection and refraction. **Max. Reflection** controls the number of times a photon can be reflected whereas the **Max. Refractions** controls the number of times a photon can be refracted.

The options in the **Light Properties** group control how lights affect the global illumination. By default, these settings apply to all lights in the scene. You can control per light settings from the light's **mental ray Indirect Illumination** rollout. **Average Caustic Photons per Light** controls the number of photons emitted by each light for use in caustics. Increasing this setting increases the quality of caustics but it also increases the render time. **Average GI Photons per Light** allows you to specify the number of photons emitted by each light for global illumination. **Decay** controls the how the photon's energy decays as photon moves away from the source. If you set this value to **0**, the energy does not decay and photon illuminates the whole scene. A value of **1** for **Decay**, decays the energy at the linear rate proportionally to its distance from the light. A value of **2** decays the energy at inverse square rate which is how energy decays in the real world.

When **All Objects Generate & Receive GI and Caustics** is on, all objects in the scene can generate and receive caustics and global illumination, regardless of their local object properties settings. When off, **mental ray** respects the object's local properties. Select the omni light in a viewport and go to the **Modify** panel. On the **mental ray Indirect Illumination** rollout, **Automatically Calculate Energy and Photons** is on. As a result, **mental ray** uses the global light settings for indirect illumination, rather than local settings.

The **Energy, Caustic Photons**, and **GI Photon** controls are global multipliers. **Energy** multiplies the global energy value. **Caustic Photons** multiplies the global **Caustic Photons** value to increase or decrease the count of photons used to generate caustics by this particular light. **GI Photons** multiply the global **GI Photons** value to increase or decrease the count of photons used to generate global illumination by this particular light. When **Automatically Calculate Energy and Photons** is **off**, the **Manual Settings** group is active. You can use the controls in this group to set various energy and photon values.

Set **GI Photons** to **3**. On the **Render Setup** dialog | **Global Illumination** panel | **Caustics & Photon Mapping (GI)** rollout | **Photon Mapping [GI]** group, the **Multiplier** control allows you to set the intensity and color of the indirect light accumulated by global illumination. Set **Multiplier** to **1.2** and turn on **Maximum Sampling Radius**. Now, set the sampling radius to **1.5** and then take a test render [see Figure 9]. On the **Render**

Setup dialog | **Global Illumination** panel | **Caustics & Photon Mapping [GI]** rollout | **Photon Mapping [GI]** group, turn off **Enable** to switch off global illumination.

Now, let's see how the final gathering works.

Set **mr Area Omni** to its default values. On the **Render Setup** dialog | **Global Illumination** panel | **Final Gathering (FG)** rollout, turn on **Enable Final Gather** and take a test render [see Figure 10].

Multiplier controls the intensity and color of the indirect accumulated light. If you anchor the slider on the **FG Precision Presets** group to the extreme left, the final gathering will be turned off. The default presets are **Draft**, **Medium**, **High**, **Very High**, and **Custom**.

The options in the drop-down below this slider allow you to minimize flickering in the renders. The flickering may appear if you render an animation with a still or moving camera. Use the **Project FG Points From Camera Position** option when camera is not moving and **Project Points from Positions Along Camera Path** when the camera is moving. If the scene contains a fast moving camera, you might achieve better results by using the **Final Gather Map** feature. In this method, map is generated for each frame.

If you use the **Project Points from Positions Along Camera Path** option, **Divide Camera Path by Num. Segments** becomes active. This control allows you to set number of segments into which to divide the camera path. It is recommended that you set at least **1** segment per **15** or **30** frames. If you increase the number of segments, make sure that you also set the set **Initial FG Point Density** higher. The value depends on scene contents, and lighting.

Set **Initial FG Point Density** to **0.5**. **Initial FG Point Density** is a multiplier for the final gather points. It increases the number of final gather points in the scene. Set **Rays per FG Point** to **100**. **Rays per FG Point** controls how many rays are used to compute illumination in final gather. This controls helps in removing noise from the renders. Higher values increase render time.

Interpolate Over Num. FG Points defines the number of final gather points that are used for an image sample. For each final gather point, **mental ray** averages indirect light values over the nearest final gather points defined by this control. Increasing this value produces smooth results but increases the render time.

Set **Diffuse Bounces** to **2** and take a test render [see Figure 11]. You will see that there is more color bleed in the render. **Diffuse Bounces** sets the number of times **mental ray** calculates the diffuse light bounces for each diffuse ray. This control is affected by **Max Depth**. **Weight** controls the relative contribution of the diffuse bounces to the final gather solution. The value ranges from **0** [using no diffuse bounces] to **1** [use full diffuse bounces]. Set **Diffuse Bounces** to **0**.

The options in the **Noise Filtering [Speckle Reduction]** drop-down allow you to apply a median filter using the neighboring final gather points. The options are **None, Standard, High, Very High**, and **Extremely High**. The default method is **Standard**. These values make the illumination of the scene better at a cost of rendering time.

The **Max. Depth, Max. Reflections**, and **Max. Refraction** options are already discussed in the global illumination section.

Tip: Noise Filtering
*In the low light scenes, setting **Noise Filtering** to **None** can enhance the overall illumination of the scene.*

When **Use Falloff (Limits Ray Distance)** is on, you can limit the length of the light rays used for regathering using the **Start** and **Stop** controls. This feature can help in reducing the render time in those scenes which are not fully enclosed by geometry.

The controls in the **FG Point Interpolation** group provide access to the legacy method of final gather point interpolation.

FG and GI Disc Caching
Calculating final gather and photon maps required lots of time and calculations. You can save a great deal of rendering time by caching the calculations. It is very useful in situations such as adjusting the camera or re-rendering an animation. The controls in the **Reuse (FG and GI Disk Caching)** rollout are used to generate and use the final gather map [FGM] or photon map [PMAP] files. You can also use these options to reduce or eliminate flickering in the rendered animations by interpolating among the map files.

For FGM files either you can write all final gather points to a single map file or generate separate files for individual animation frames. When you have separate FGM files for each frame, you can interpolate among them to get a smooth flicker free result.

The drop-down in the **Mode** group lets you choose the method by which 3ds Max generates the cache files. There are two options available: **Single File Only (Best for Walkthrough and Stills)** and **One File Per Frame (Best for Animated Objects)**. When **Calculate FG/GI and Skip Final Rendering** is on, 3ds Max performs the final gather and global illumination calculations but does not perform the actual rendering.

The controls in the **Final Gather Map** and **Caustics and Global Illumination Photon Map** let you set the method of writing final gather or photon map cache to the files. The **Interpolate Over N Frames** control lets you set the number of FGM files before and after the current frame to use for interpolation.

Caustics

Caustics are the effects of light cast via reflection or refraction through an object. The caustics are calculated using the photon map technique. To render with caustics you need to enable **Caustics** in the **Render Setup** dialog | **Global Illumination** panel | **Caustics & Photon Mapping [GI]** rollout | **Caustics** group. The **Multiplier** control and color swatch can be used to change the intensity and color of the indirect light accumulated by caustics.

Maximum Num. Photons per Sample sets the number of photons that are used to compute the intensity of the caustics. On increasing this value, **mental ray** produces less noisy [more blurry] caustics. It is recommended that you start with a value of **20** and then increase the value later for final rendering.

Turning on Maximum Sampling Radius allows you to set the size of the photons. When this option is unchecked, each photon is calculated to be 1/100 of the radius of the full scene and this settings usually produces good results.

The **Filter** drop-down lets you choose a method for sharpening the caustics. The default method is **Box** which takes less time to render. The **Cone** method makes the caustics sharper. The **Gauss** method produces smoother results than the **Cone** method. **Filter Size** defines the sharpness of the caustics when you work with the **Cone** filter method. On decreasing this value makes caustics sharper, but also slightly noisier. When **Opaque Shadows when Caustics Are Enabled** is on, shadows are opaque, else they may appear partially transparent.

Autodesk Materials

Autodesk Materials are based on the **Arch & Design** material. These materials work best when you use them with physically accurate lights such as photometric lights in a scene, modeled in the real-world units. However, the interface of the Autodesk Materials is much simpler than the **Arch & Design** material, therefore, you can achieve good results in less time using Autodesk Materials.

Many of the Autodesk Materials use **Autodesk Bitmaps**. The **Autodesk Bitmap** is a simple bitmap type. This bitmap type always uses the real-world mapping coordinates. Therefore, if you have applied a **UVW Map** modifier to any geometry, make sure you turn on **Real-World Map Size** on the **Parameters** rollout. You can also change the default bitmap assignment.

Warning: Autodesk Bitmap compatibility
*3ds Max allows you to disconnect a bitmap, or replace it with another map. However, if you disconnect an **Autodesk Bitmap** in other application such as **Autodesk AutoCAD**, you won't be able to read the Autodesk Material. If you are using other applications, make sure that you do not replace the bitmap with a map that only 3ds Max understands.*

Warning: Autodesk Material Library
*If you uninstall or remove Autodesk material library, the materials will no longer will be available for other Autodesk products such as **AutoCAD**, **Revit**, or **Inventor**.*

You can use this material to model the glazed ceramic material including porcelain.

Open **automat_begin.max**. Open the **Slate Material Editor**. On **Material/Map Browser | Materials | mental ray**, double-click on **Autodesk Ceramic** to display the material's interface in the active view [see Figure 12]. Double-click on the material's node in the active view. In the **Material Editor | Ceramic** rollout, ensure that **Ceramic** is selected as **Type**. The **Ceramic** type produces look of earthenware.

Apply the material to teapot in the scene and take a test render [see Figure 13]. On the **Ceramic** rollout, set **Type** to **Porcelain**. Click **Color** swatch and change color to blue. **Color** sets the color of the material. The other two options available for the **Color** control are **Use Map** and **Color By Object**. The **Use Map** option allows you to assign a map to color component of the material. If you set **Color** to **Color By Object**, 3ds Max uses the object's wireframe color as the material color. The **Finish** control lets you adjust the finish and reflectivity of the material.

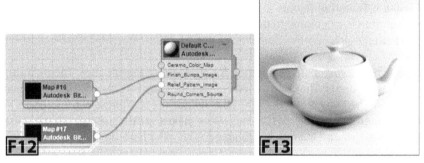

Note: Color by object
When you use this option, the color appears on rendering but not in the viewport or material previews.

Make sure **Finish** is set to **High Gloss / Glazed** and take a test render [see Figure14].

Make sure **Finish** is set to **Satin** and take a test render [see Figure 15]. Make sure **Finish** is set to **Matte** and take a test render [see Figure 16]. Now, set **Finish** to **High Gloss / Glazed**.

On the **Finish Bumps** rollout, check **Enable** and make sure **Type** is set to **Wavy** and **Amount** to **0.3**. Now, take a test render [see Figure 17]. The options in the **Finish Bumps** rollout can be used to simulate the patterns that appear in glaze during firing. You can also create custom bumps by using the **Custom** option from the **Type** drop-down. **Amount** sets the strength of the pattern to apply.

On the **Finish Bumps** rollout, turn off **Enable**. On the **Relief Pattern** rollout, turn on **Enable**. Click the **Image** button. On the **Parameters** rollout, click **Source None** button. Select **patten.jpg** from the **Select Bitmap Image File** dialog and click **Open**. On the **Relief Pattern** rollout, set **Amount** to **1.2** and take a test render [see Figure 18]. The options in the **Relief Pattern** rollout allow you to model a pattern stamped into the clay. **Amount** controls the height of the relief pattern.

Autodesk Concrete

This material allows you to model the concrete material. Figure 19 shows its interface. The **Sealant** control of the **Concrete** rollout, controls the reflectiveness of the surface. **None** [see Figure 20] does not affect the surface finish. **Epoxy** [see Figure 21] adds a reflective coating on the surface whereas **Acrylic** [see Figure 22] adds a matte reflective coating.

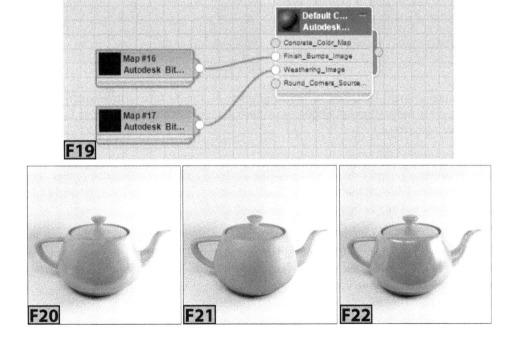

The **Type** control in the **Finish Bumps** area allows you to set the texture of the concrete. **Broom Straight** which is a default type, specifies a straight broom pattern [see Figure 23]. **Broom Curved** uses a curving broom pattern [see Figure 24]. **Smooth** creates a pattern with speckled irregularities [see Figure 25].

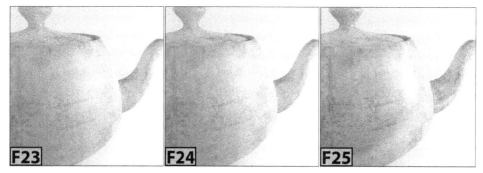

Polished uses a completely smooth pattern [see Figure 26]. **Stamped/Custom** allows you to specify a bitmap for generating the pattern [see Figure 27].

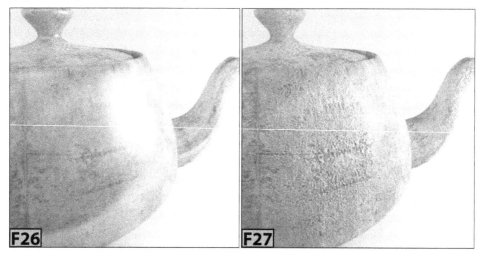

Weathering applies a slight variation in the brightness on the surface of the concrete. The default weathering method is **Automatic** that applies weathering automatically. You can use **Custom** to specify a custom weathering pattern.

Autodesk Generic

This material provides a generic interface for creating a custom appearance. You can convert an Autodesk material to the **Autodesk Generic** material by RMB clicking on the node in the **Slate Material Editor | Active View** and then choosing **Copy as Generic** from the popup menu.

Autodesk Glazing

This material allows you to model a thin and transparent material such as glazing in windows and doors. The **Color** control in the **Glazing** rollout lets you choose the color for the sheet of glass. Figure 28 shows the teapot rendered with the **Blue Green** color applied to it.

Autodesk Harwood

This material is used the model the appearance of a wood. The **Stain** control in the **Wood** rollout allows you to choose a stain to add to the base harwood pattern. Figure 29 shows the wood material with **Brown Stain** color.

The **Finish** control lets you choose the surface finish of the harwood. The **Glossy Varnish** is the default option [see Figure 29]. The other options available are: **Semi-Gloss Varnish** [see Figure 30], **Satin Varnish** [see Figure 31], and **Unfinished** [see Figure 32].

The **Used For** control lets you adjust the appearance of the wood. Flooring uses an ocean shader that adds a slight warp to the large surfaces, improving the realism. When you choose **Furniture**, the surfaces are not warped. However, you can use the **Relief Pattern** map to achieve various effects.

When you check **Enable in the Relief Pattern** rollout, **mental ray** generates a relief pattern like bump map on the wood surface. The **Type** control lets you choose the relief pattern. When you choose **Based on Wood Grain**, it generates a relief pattern based on the image map used to create the wood pattern. **Custom** allows you to choose a custom map for the relief pattern. **Amount** lets you adjust the height of the relief pattern.

Autodesk Masonry/CMU

This material can be used to model masonry or concrete masonry units [**CMUs**]. Figure 33 and 34 shows the brick and CMU material.

Autodesk Metal

You can use this material to model various metallic surfaces. The **Type** control in the **Metal** rollout lets you choose the type of material you want to create. These materials define the base color and texture of the material. Figure 35 show the brass material. The **Finish** control lets you choose the surface finish for the surface. Figures 35 and 36 show the brass material with the **Polished** and **Brushed** finish, respectively.

Autodesk Metallic Paint

This material allows you to model a metallic paint surface such as paint of a car [see Figure 37].

Autodesk Mirror

This material lets you model a mirror material [see Figure 38].

Autodesk Plastic/Vinyl

This material allows you to model the surfaces that have a synthetic appearance such as plastic or vinyl [see Figures 39 and 40].

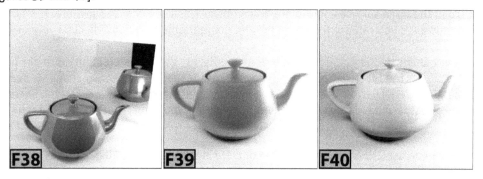

Autodesk Point Cloud Material

This is a special purpose material that is automatically applied to any point-cloud object in the scene. This material allows you to control the overall color intensity, ambient occlusion, and shadows.

Autodesk Solid Glass
This material allows you to model the appearance of the solid glass [see Figure 41].

Autodesk Stone
You can use this material to create the appearance of the stone [see Figures 42 and 43]. The **Type** control in the **Finish Bumps** rollout lets you specify the bump pattern. Available options are: **Polished Granite**, **Stone Wall**, **Glossy Marble**, and **Custom**.

Autodesk Wall Paint
This material can be used to model the appearance of a painted surface such as paint on the walls of a room [see Figures 44 and 45]. The Application control in the **Wall Paint** rollout lets you choose the texture method. In other words, you can control how paint is applied on the surface. **Roller** is the default method. Other two methods are **Brush** and **Spray**.

Autodesk Water
This material can be used to model appearance of a water surface [see Figure 46]. The **Type** control in the **Water** rollout lets you choose the scale and texture of the water.

The available options are **Swimming Pool**, **Generic Reflective Pool**, **Generic Stream/River**, **Generic Pond/Lake**, and **Generic Sea/Ocean**. The **Color** control lets you specify the color of the water. This option is only available for **Generic Stream/River**, **Pond/Lake**, and **Sea/Ocean**.

The following options are available for adjusting the color of the water: **Tropical**, **Algae/Green**, **Murky/Brown**, **Generic Reflecting Pool**, **Generic Stream/River**, **Generic Pond/Lake**, **Generic Sea/Ocean** and **Custom**.

Arch & Design Material

The mental ray **Arch & Design** material is a specialized material that allows you to create physically accurate renderings. It is designed to support most of the materials used in the architecture and product design renderings. This material includes self-illumination, ambient occlusion, and advanced options for reflectivity and transparency. It can also round off the sharp corners and edges as a render effect. It is especially fine-tuned for fast gloss reflections and refractions thus improving the workflow and performance.

The **Arch & Design** material has built-in description for all important controls. You can view the details in form of a tooltip. To view the tooltip, hover the cursor over a control's spinner, color swatch, checkbox, and so forth. The **Arch & Design** material attempts to be physically accurate and it outputs a high dynamic range. The visual appeal of the material depends on how colors inside the renderer are mapped to colors displayed on the screen. When you are using the **Arch & Design** material, it is recommended that you use an exposure control such as the **mr Photographic Exposure Control**. When using the **Arch & Design** material, make sure that you use atleast one of the two methods used with **mental ray** for indirect illumination: Final Gathering or Global Illumination. For best results, you can combine final gathering with global illumination. Also, it is recommended that you use physically accurate lights such as **Photometric** lights with the **Arch & Design** material.

To create an **Arch & Design** material, press **M** to open the **Slate Material Editor**. On the **Material/Map Browser | Materials | mental ray** rollout, double-click on **Arch & Design**. The material's interface is displayed in the active view [see Figure 47]. Figure 48 shows a render of teapot with the default **Arch & Design** material applied to it. We will explore the Arch & Design material in detail in hands-on exercises.

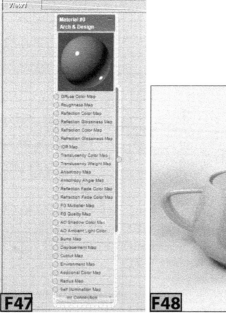

Hands-on Exercises

Complete the following hands-on exercises:

Unit Sh2-Exercise 1: *Creating the Leather Material*
Unit Sh2-Exercise 2: *Creating the Chrome Material*
Unit Sh2-Exercise 3: *Creating the Copper Material*
Unit Sh2-Exercise 4: *Creating Glass/Thin Plastic film Materials*
Unit Sh2-Exercise 5: *Creating the Water Material*
Unit Sh2-Exercise 6: *Creating the Sofa Fabric Material*
Unit Sh2-Exercise 7: *Creating the Wood Cabinet Material*
Unit Sh2-Exercise 8: *Creating the Parquet Material*

Summary

In this section, I've explained about the global illumination, final gathering, and caustics. You can use any method or both to generate indirect light in the scene. Now, you have better understanding of the indirect illumination methods used with **mental ray** in 3ds Max. This knowledge will help you, when you will complete the hands-on exercises.

The Autodesk materials give you ability to quickly model materials for any type of surface in your scene. The **Arch & Design** material is a monolithic material designed to support most of the material that you will use in the architectural and product design renderings. This material is highly tuned for modeling fast glossy reflective and refractive surfaces.

The unit covered the following topics:

- Global Illumination
- Final Gather
- Caustics
- Autodesk Materials
- **Arch & Design** Material

This page intentionally left blank

Unit SH1 - Hands-on Exercises [Shading I]

Hands-on Exercise 1: Creating the Gold Material

In this exercise, we are going to create the gold material.

The following table summarizes the exercise.

Table 1: Creating the gold material	
Topics in this section:	• Getting Ready • Creating the Gold Material
Skill Level	Beginner
Resources	**hoes1-1to13.zip**
Project Folder	**hoes1-1to13**
Start File	**hoes1-1to13-start.max**
Final Exercise File	**hoes1-1-end.max**
Time to Complete	10 Minutes

Getting Ready

Extract the content of **hoes1-1to13.zip** to a location in your HDD. This action creates a folder with the name **hoes1-1to13**. This folder contains all the subfolders and files related to this exercise. Click **Project Folder** from the **Quick Access Toolbar** to open the **Browse For Dialog**. In this dialog, navigate to the **hoes1-1to13** folder and click **OK** to set the project folder and close the dialog. Now, open the **hoes1-1to13-start.max** file in 3ds Max.

Creating the Gold Material

Press M to open the **Slate Material Editor**. On the **Material/Map Browser | Materials | Standard** rollout, drag the **Standard** material to the active view. Rename the material as **goldMat**. Apply the material to **geo1**, **geo2**, and **geo3**. Save the scene as **hoes1-1-end.max**.

On the **Parameter Editor | goldMat | Shader Basic Parameters rollout**, choose **Multi-Layer** from the drop-down. On the **Multi-Layer Basic Parameters** rollout, set **Diffuse** to **RGB [148, 70, 0]** and then set **Diffuse Level** to **25**. Take a test render [see Figure 1].

Now, we will add specularity and reflection to add the detail.

On the **First Specular Layer** section, set **Color** to **RGB [247, 227, 10]**. Set **Level** to **114**, **Glossiness** to **32**, **Anisotropy** to **82**, and **Orientation** to **90**. On the **Second Specular Layer** section, set **Color** to **RGB [192, 77, 8]**. Set **Level** to **114**, **Glossiness** to **32**, **Anisotropy** to **82**, and **Orientation** to **90**. On the **Maps** rollout, click

Reflection map button. On the **Material/Map Browser** that appears, double-click **Falloff**. On the **Parameter Editor | Falloff | Falloff Parameters rollout**, click white swatch map button. On the **Material/Map Browser** that appears, double-click **Raytrace**. Set **Falloff Type** to **Fresnel**. Take a test render [see Figure 2].

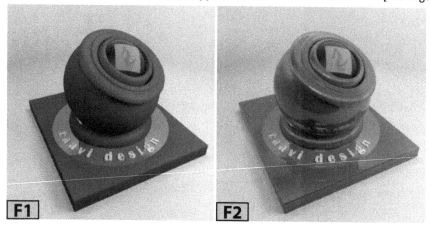

On the **Falloff | Mix Curve rollout**, RMB click on the first point and then choose **Bezier-Corner** from the contextual menu [see Figure 3]. Similarly, convert second point to **Bezier-Corner** and change the shape of the curve as shown in Figure 4. Now, take a render to view the final result [see Figure 5].

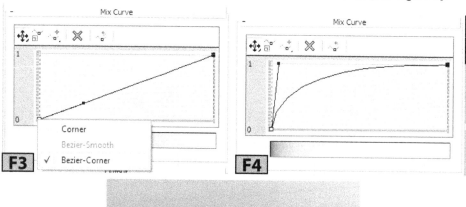

Hands-on Exercise 2: Creating the Copper Material

In this exercise, we are going to create the copper material.

The following table summarizes the exercise.

Table 2: Creating the copper material	
Topics in this section:	• Getting Ready • Creating the Copper Material
Skill Level	Beginner
Resources	**hoes1-1to13.zip**
Project Folder	**hoes1-1to13**
Start File	**hoes1-1-end.max**
Final Exercise File	**hoes1-2-end.max**
Time to Complete	10 Minutes

Getting Ready

Make sure the **hoes1-1-end.max** file that you created in Hands-on Exercise 1 is open in 3ds Max.

Creating the Copper Material

Press M to open the **Slate Material Editor**, if not already open. Create a copy of the **goldMat** node by shift dragging it [see Figure 6].

Rename the node as **copperMat** and then apply it to **geo1**, **geo2**, and **geo3**. Save the scene as **hoes1-2-end.max**.

On the **Multi-Layer Basic Parameters rollout**, set **Diffuse** to **RGB [88, 28, 9]**. On the **First Specular Layer section**, set **Color** to **RGB [177, 75, 44]**.

On the **Second Specular Layer section**, set **Color** to **RGB [255, 123, 82]**. Take the render [see Figure 7].

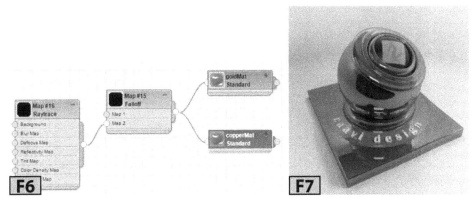

Hands-on Exercise 3: Creating the Brass Material

In this exercise, we are going to create the brass material.

The following table summarizes the exercise.

Table 3: Creating the brass material	
Topics in this section:	• Getting Ready • Creating the Brass Material
Skill Level	Beginner
Resources	**hoes1-1to13.zip**
Project Folder	**hoes1-1to13**
Start File	**hoes1-2-end.max**
Final Exercise File	**hoes1-3-end.max**
Time to Complete	10 Minutes

Getting Ready

Make sure the **hoes1-2-end.max** file that you created in Hands-on Exercise 2 is open in 3ds Max.

Creating the Brass Material

Press M to open the **Slate Material Editor**, if not already open. Create a copy of the **copperMat** node by **Shift** dragging it. Rename the node as **brassMat** and then apply it to **geo1**, **geo2**, and **geo3**. On the **Multi-Layer Basic Parameters** rollout, set **Diffuse** to **RGB [49, 38, 14]**. On the **First Specular Layer** section, set **Color** to **RGB [212, 154, 30]**. On the **Second Specular Layer** section, set **Color** to **RGB [174, 98, 61]**. Take the render [see Figure 8] and then save the file with the name **hoes1-3-end.max**.

Hands-on Exercise 4: Creating the Chrome Material

In this exercise, we are going to create the chrome material.

The following table summarizes the exercise.

Table 4: Creating the chrome material	
Topics in this section:	• Getting Ready • Creating the Chrome Material
Skill Level	Beginner
Resources	**hoes1-1to13.zip**
Project Folder	**hoes1-1to13**
Start File	**hoes1-1to13-start.max**
Final Exercise File	**hoes1-4-end.max**
Time to Complete	10 Minutes

Make sure the **hoes1-1to13-start.max** is open in 3ds Max.

Creating the Chrome Material

Load **hoes1-1to13-start.max** in 3ds Max. Press **M** to open the **Slate Material Editor**. On the **Material/ Map/Browser | Materials | Standard rollout**, drag the **Standard** material to the active view. Rename the material as **chromeMat**. Apply the material to **geo1**, **geo2**, and **geo3**. Save the scene as **chromeMat.max**. On the **Parameter Editor | chromeMat | Blinn Basic Parameters** rollout, click the **Diffuse** color swatch. On the **Color Selector : Diffuse Color** dialog, set **Value** to **12** and click **OK**. On the **Specular Highlights** section, set **Specular Level** to **150** and **Glossiness** to **80**.

On the **Maps** rollout, set **Reflection** to **90** and then click the **Reflection** map button. On the **Material Map Browser** that appears, double-click **Raytrace**. On the **Raytrace** map | **Raytracer Parameters** | **Background** section, click **None**. On the **Material/Map Browser** that appears, double-click **Bitmap**. In the **Select Bitmap Image File** dialog that appears, select **refMap.jpeg**. Render the scene [see Figure 9].

F8

F9

Hands-on Exercise 5: Creating the Brushed Aluminum Material

In this exercise, we are going to create the brushed aluminum material using Photoshop and 3ds Max.

The following table summarizes the exercise.

Table 5: Creating the brushed aluminum material	
Topics in this section:	• Getting Ready • Creating the Brushed Aluminum Material
Skill Level	Beginner
Resources	**hoes1-1to13.zip**
Project Folder	**hoes1-1to13**
Start File	**hoes1-1to13-start.max**

Final Exercise File	hoes1-5-end.max
Time to Complete	15 Minutes

Getting Ready
Make sure the **hoes1-1to13-start.max** is open in 3ds Max.

Creating the Brushed Aluminum Material

Start Photoshop. Create a **1000 x 1000 px** document and fill it with **50%** gray color. Choose **Noise | Add Noise** from the **Filter** menu and then set the parameters as shown in Figure 10 and then click **OK**.

Choose **Blur | Motion Blur** from the **Filter** menu and then set the parameters as shown in Figure 11 and then click **OK**. Choose **Adjustments | Brightness\Contrast** from the **Image** menu and then set the parameters as shown in Figure 12 and then click **OK**. Save the document as **scratch.jpg**.

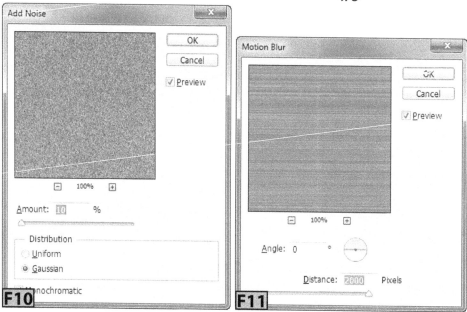

Load **hoes1-1to13-start.max** in 3ds Max, if not already loaded. Press **M** to open the **Slate Material Editor**. On the **Material/Map Browser | Materials | Standard** rollout, drag the **Standard** material to the active view. Rename the material as **balMat**. Apply the material to **geo1**, **geo2**, and **geo3**.

On the **Parameter Editor | balMat | Shader Basic Parameters** rollout, choose **Oren-Nayar-Blinn** from the drop-down. On the **Parameter Editor | balMat | Oren-Nayar-Blinn Basic Parameters** rollout, click **Ambient** color swatch. On the **Color Selector : Ambient Color** dialog, set **Value** to **84** and click **OK**. Unlock the **Ambient** and **Diffuse** components of the material.

Click the **Diffuse** map button and then on the **Material/Map Browser** that appears, double-click **Mix**. On the **Parameter Editor | Mix map**, set **Color 1** to **127** and assign **scratch.jpg** to **Color 2** using the **Bitmap** map. Set **Mix** Amount to **72%**. On the **balMat | Oren-Nayar-Blinn Basic Parameters** rollout | **Advanced Diffuse** section, set **Diffuse Level** to **81**, and **Roughness** to **80**. Now, take a test render [see Figure 13]. On the

Parameter Editor | balMat | Oren-Nayar-Blinn Basic Parameters rollout | **Specular Highlight** section, set **Specular Level** to **156**, **Glossiness** to **13**, and **Soften** to **0.48**. Now, take a test render [see Figure 14]. On the **Parameter Editor | scratch.jpg | Output rollout**, set **Output Amount** to **0.6**. Take a render [see Figure 15].

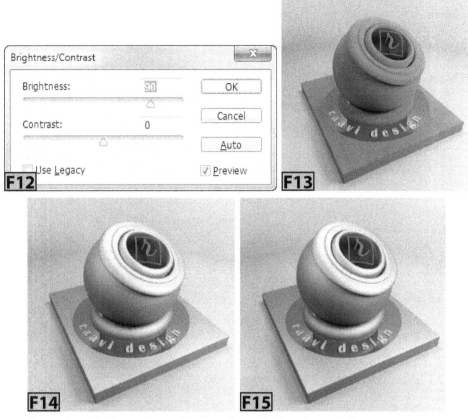

Hands-on Exercise 6: Creating the Denim Fabric Material

In this exercise, we are going to create the denim fabric material using Photoshop and 3ds Max.

The following table summarizes the exercise.

Table 6: Creating the denim fabric material	
Topics in this section:	• Getting Ready • Creating the Denim Fabric Material
Skill Level	Beginner
Resources	**hoes1-1to13.zip**
Project Folder	**hoes1-1to13**
Start File	**hoes1-1to13-start.max**
Final Exercise File	**hoes1-6-end.max**
Time to Complete	15 Minutes

Getting Ready

Make sure the **hoes1-1to13-start.max** is open in 3ds Max.

Creating the Denim Fabric Material

Start Photoshop. Create a **1000 x 1000 px** document and fill it with **RGB [41, 67, 102]** color. Create a new layer and fill it with **50%** gray. Press **D** to switch to the default colors. Choose **Filter Gallery| Sketch | Halftone Pattern** from the **Filter** menu and then set the parameters as shown in Figure 16 and then click **OK**.

Choose **Pixelate | Mezzotint** from the **Filter** menu and then set the parameters as shown in Figure 17 and then click **OK**. Duplicate the layer and rotate and scale the duplicate layer [see Figure 18]. Choose **Blur | Gaussian Blur** from the **Filter** menu and then apply a blur of radius **1**. Set blending mode to **Multiply**. Also, set the blending mode of the middle layer [Layer 1] to **Softlight** [Figure 19].

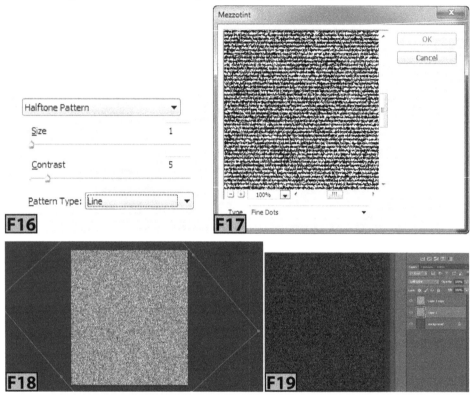

Save the file as **denimFebric.jpg**. Choose **Flatten Image** from the **Layer** menu to flatten the image. Now, press **Ctrl+Shift+U** to desaturate the image and then save it as **denimFebricBump.jpg**. In 3ds Max, press **M** to open the **Slate Material Editor**. On the **Material/Map Browser | Materials | Standard** rollout, drag the **Standard** material to the active view. Rename the material as **denimMat**. Apply the material to **geo1**, **geo2**, and **geo3**.

Save the scene as **hoes1-6-end.max**. On the **Parameter Editor | denimMat | Shader Basic Parameters** rollout, choose **Oren-Nayar-Blinn** from the drop-down. On the **Parameter Editor | denimMat | Oren-Nayar-Blinn Basic Parameters** rollout, click **Ambient** color swatch. On the **Color Selector : Ambient Color** dialog, set

RGB to **50, 53,** and **57** and click **OK**. Unlock the **Ambient** and **Diffuse** components of the material. Click the **Diffuse** map button and then on the **Material Map Browser** that appears, double-click **Bitmap**. Assign **denimFebric.jpg**. On the **denimMat | Oren-Nayar-Blinn Basic Parameters** rollout | **Advanced Diffuse** section, set **Diffuse Level** to **250**, and **Roughness** to **75**. Now, take a test render [see Figure 20].

On the **Parameter Editor | denimMat | Oren-Nayar-Blinn Basic Parameters** rollout | **Specular Highlight** section, set **Specular Level** to **7**, and **Glossiness** to **10**. Take a test render [see Figure 21]. On the **Maps** rollout, ensure **Bump** is set to **30%** and then click **Bump** map button. On the **Material/Map Browser** that appears, double-click **Bitmap**. On the **Select Bitmap Image File** dialog that appears, select **denimFebricBump.jpg**. Take a test render [see Figure 22].

Hands-on Exercise 7: Working with the Blend Material

In this exercise, we are going to create a blend material.

The following table summarizes the exercise.

Table 7: Working with the blend material	
Topics in this section:	• Getting Ready • Working with the Blend Material
Skill Level	Beginner
Resources	**hoes1-1to13.zip**
Project Folder	**hoes1-1to13**
Start File	**hoes1-1to13-start.max**
Final Exercise File	**hoes1-7-end.max**
Time to Complete	15 Minutes

Getting Ready

Make sure the **hoes1-1to13-start.max** is open in 3ds Max.

Working with the Blend Material

Save the scene as **hoes1-7-end.max**. Press **M** to open the **Slate Material Editor**. On the **Material/Map Browser | Materials | Standard** rollout, drag the **Blend** material to the active view. Rename the materials connected to the **Blend** node as **mat1** and **mat2**. Apply the **Blend** material to **geo1, geo2,** and **geo3**.

Assign **ConcreteBare.jpg** to the **mat1 | Diffuse** map and **ConcreteBare1.jpg** to the **mat2 | Diffuse** map. Take a test render [see Figure 23]. Assign a **Noise** map to the **Blend** material's **Mask** control. On the **Mixing Curve** section, turn on the **Use Curve** switch and set **Upper** to **0.78** and **Lower** to **0.3**. Take a test render [see Figure 24].

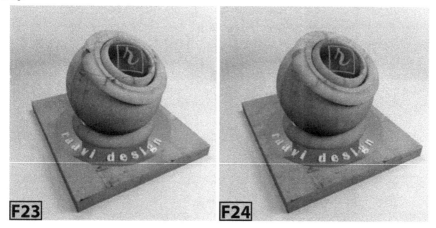

On the **Parameter Editor | Noise Parameters** rollout, set **Noise Type** to **Fractal**, **High** to **0.9**, and **Size** to **15.5**. Take a test render and press **Ctrl+S** to save the file. For the sake of clarity, I have rendered [see Figure 25] a plane with **mat1** (left image), **mat2** (middle image), and **Blend** (right image) materials applied. Figure 26 shows the node network.

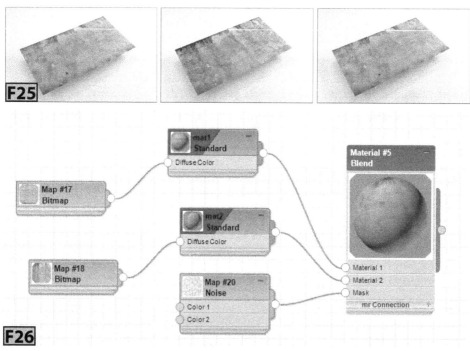

Hands-on Exercise 8: Working with the Double-Sided Material

In this exercise, we are going to create a double-sided material.

The following table summarizes the exercise.

Table 8: Working with the double-sided material	
Topics in this section:	• Getting Ready • Working with the Double-Sided Material
Skill Level	Beginner
Resources	**hoes1-1to13.zip**
Project Folder	**hoes1-1to13**
Start File	**hoes1-1to13-start.max**
Final Exercise File	**hoes1-8-end.max**
Time to Complete	15 Minutes

Getting Ready

Make sure the hoes1-1to13-start.max is open in 3ds Max.

Working with the Double Sided Material

Save the file with the name **hoes1-8-end.max**. Delete **geo4**, **geo1**, **geo6** from the scene and place a teapot at the center of **geo5**. Go to the **Modify** panel and then on the **Parameters** rollout | **Teapot Parts** section, turn off **Handle**, **Spout**, and **Lid** switches. Press **M** to open the **Slate Material Editor**. On the **Material/Map Browser** | **Materials** | **Standard** rollout, drag the **Double Sided** material to the active view. Rename the materials connected to the **DoubleSided** node as **mat1** and **mat2**. Apply the material to the teapot.

Now, we will assign maps to the back and facing materials of the **Double Sided** material. The **Facing Material** is represented by **mat1** whereas the **Back Material** is represented by **mat2**.

Assign **ConcreteBare.jpg** to the **mat1** | **Diffuse** map. Assign a **Perlin Marble** map to the **mat2** | **Diffuse** map. Set **Translucency** to **25**. Take a test render [see Figure 27] and press **Ctrl+S** to save the file. Figure 28 shows the node network.

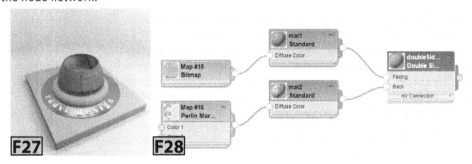

Hands-on Exercise 9: Working with the Shellac Material

In this exercise, we are going to create a **Shellac** material.

The following table summarizes the exercise.

Table 9: Working with the **Shellac** material	
Topics in this section:	• Getting Ready • Working with the **Shellac** Material
Skill Level	Beginner
Resources	**hoes1-1to13.zip**
Project Folder	**hoes1-1to13**
Start File	**hoes1-8-end.max**
Final Exercise File	**hoes1-9-end.max**
Time to Complete	15 Minutes

Getting Ready

Make sure the **hoes1-8-end.max** is open in 3ds Max.

Working with the Shellac Material

Press **M** to open the **Slate Material Editor**. On the **Material/ Map Browser | Materials | Standard** rollout, drag the **Shellac** material to the active view.

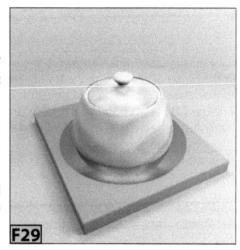

Rename the materials connected to the **Base Material** and **Shellac Mat** ports of the **Shellac** node as **mat1** and **mat2**, respectively. Apply the material to the teapot.

Assign the **Swirl** map to the **mat1 | Diffuse** map and **Wood** map to the **mat2 | Diffuse** map. Set **Shellac Color Blend** to **86**. Take a test render [see Figure 29].

Hands-on Exercise 10: Creating the Microscopic Material

In this exercise, we're going to create a microscopic material [see Figure 30]. The following material(s) and map(s) are used in this exercise: **Standard**, **Mix**, **Falloff**, and **Noise**.

The following table summarizes the exercise.

Table 10: Creating the microscopic material	
Topics in this section:	• Getting Ready • Creating the Microscopic Material
Skill Level	Beginner
Resources	**hoes1-1to13.zip**
Project Folder	**hoes1-1to13**
Start File	**hoes1-10-start.max**
Final Exercise File	**hoes1-10-end.max**
Time to Complete	15 Minutes

Getting Ready

Make sure the **hoes1-10-start.max** is open in 3ds Max.

Creating the Microscopic Material

Press **M** to open the **Slate Material Editor** and then create a new **Standard** material and assign it to the **sphGeo** in the scene. Rename the material as **msMat**. Connect a **Falloff** map to the **msMat's Diffuse** port. On the **Parameter Editor | Falloff map | Falloff Parameters** rollout | **Front:Side** section, set first color swatch to **RGB [20, 20, 20]** and second color swatch to white. Set **Falloff Type** to **Perpendicular/Parallel**. Ensure **Falloff Direction** is set to **Viewing Direction (Camera Z-Axis)** [see Figure 31]. Also, set the **Mix Curve** to as shown in Figure 32.

F30

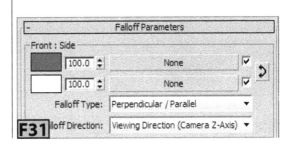
F31

Now, you will create two **Noise** maps and mix them using the **Mix** map. Connect a **Mix** map to the **msMat's Bump** port. On the **Parameter Editor | Mix** map | **Mix Parameters** rollout, set **Mix Amount** to **37.8**. On the **Slate Material Editor**, connect two **Noise** maps, one each to the **Color 1** and **Color 2** ports. For the **Color 1 | Noise** map use the settings shown in Figure 33. Figure 34 shows the **Noise** map settings connected to **Color 2**. Fig. 35 shows the node network.

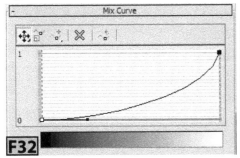
F32

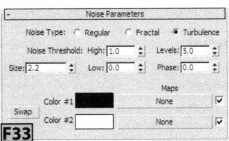
F33

Now, render the scene. Notice that the output is little bit on the darker side. To address this, on the **Parameter Editor | Falloff** map | **Falloff Parameters** rollout | **Front:Side** section, set first color swatch to **RGB [80, 80, 80]**. Render the scene [see Figure 30].

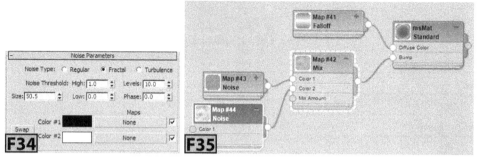

Hands-on Exercise 11: Creating Material for a Volleyball

Here, we are going to apply texture to a volleyball [see Figure 36]. Right image in Figure 36 shows the reference whereas the left image shows the rendered output. The following material(s) and map(s) are used in this exercise: **Multi/Sub-Object**, **Standard**, and **Noise**.

The following table summarizes the exercise.

Table 11: Creating material for a volleyball	
Topics in this section:	• Getting Ready • Creating Material for a Volleyball
Skill Level	Beginner
Resources	**hoes1-1to13.zip**
Project Folder	**hoes1-1to13**
Start File	**hoes1-11-start.max**
Final Exercise File	**hoes1-11-end.max**
Time to Complete	15 Minutes

Make sure the **hoes1-11-start.max** is open in 3ds Max.

Creating Material for a Volleyball

Select the **VolleyBallGeo** in any viewport and then go to the **Modify** panel. On the **Selection** rollout, click **Element** and then select the elements that make the yellow part of the volleyball [see Figure 37]. See the right image in Figure 36 for reference. On the **Modify panel | Polygon: Material IDs** rollout, set **ID** to **1** [see Figure 38]. Similarly, select the blue and white elements and assign them ID **2** and **3**, respectively.

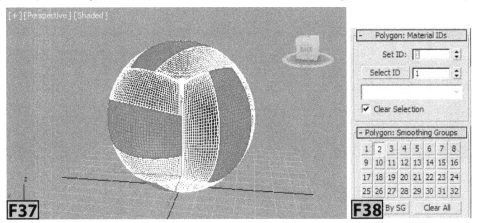

Press **M** to open the **Slate Material Editor** and then create a new **Multi/Sub-object** material and assign it to the **VolleyBallGeo** in the scene. Rename the material as **vbMat**. On the **Parameter Editor | vbMat | Multi/Sub-Object Parameters** rollout, click **Set Number** and then set **Number of Materials** to **3** in the dialog that appears. Next, click **OK**. In the **Slate Material Editor**, connect a **Standard** material to the port **1** of the **vbMat**. On the **Parameter Editor | Blinn Basic Parameter** rollout, set the **Diffuse** component to **RGB [242, 140, 8]**. On the **Specular Highlights** section, set **Specular Level** to **71** and **Glossiness** to **28**.

Connect a **Noise** map to the **Bump** port of the **Standard** material. Set **Bump** to **2%**. On the **Parameter Editor | Noise map | Noise Parameters** rollout, set **Noise Type** to **Turbulence**, **Levels** to **9**, and **Size** to **0.5**. On the **Slate Material Editor**, select the **Standard** material and **Noise** map. Now, create a copy of the selected nodes using **SHIFT**. Connect the new Standard material to the port **2** of the **vbMat**. Similarly, create another copy and connect it to port **3**. Figure 39 shows the node network. Set **Diffuse** components of the material connected to the port **2** and **3** to **RGB [11, 91, 229]** and **RGB [236, 236, 230]**, respectively. Now, press F9 to take a render.

Hands-on Exercise 12: Creating Material for a Water Tunnel

Here, we are going to apply texture to a water tunnel [see Figure 40]. The following material(s) and map(s) are used in this exercise: **Raytrace**, **Standard**, **Mix**, and **Noise**.

The following table summarizes the exercise.

Table 12: Creating material for a water tunnel	
Topics in this section:	• Getting Ready • Creating Material for a Water Tunnel

Skill Level	Beginner
Resources	**hoes1-1to13.zip**
Project Folder	**hoes1-1to13**
Start File	**hoes1-12-start.max**
Final Exercise File	**hoes1-12-end.max**
Time to Complete	15 Minutes

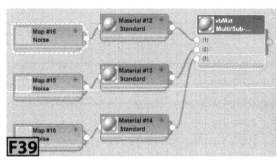
F39

F40

Getting Ready

Make sure the **hoes1-12-start.max** is open in 3ds Max.

Creating Material for a Water Tunnel

Press **M** to open the **Slate Material Editor** and then create a new **Raytrace** material and assign it to the **waterGeo** in the scene. Rename the material as **waterMat**. On the **Parameter Editor | Raytrace Basic Parameter** rollout, set **Diffuse** to black. Set **Transparency** to **RGB (146, 175, 223)**. Set **Reflect** to **RGB [178, 178, 178]**.

On the **Specular Highlight** section, set **Specular Level** to **161** and **Glossiness** to **29**. Connect a **Noise** map to the **Bump** port of the **waterMat**. Use the default values for the **Noise** map. Press **F9** to render the scene [Figure 41]. On the **Slate Material Editor**, create a new **Standard** material and assign it to the **caveGeo** in the scene. Rename the material as **caveMat**. Connect a **Mix** map to the **Diffuse** port of the **caveMat**.

Connect a **Noise** map to the **Color 1** port of the **Mix** map. On the **Noise Parameters** rollout, set **Noise Type** to **Turbulence**, **Levels** to **10**, **Size** to **31.7**. Set **Color 1** to **RGB [132, 77, 6]** and **Color 2** to **RGB [154, 100, 79]**. Connect a **Noise** map to the **Color 2** port of the **Mix** map. On the **Noise Parameters** rollout, set **Noise Type** to **Turbulence**, **Levels** to **10**, **Size** to **72**. Set **Color 1** to **RGB [212, 84, 45]** and **Color 2** to **RGB [181, 99, 54]**.

On the **Parameter Editor | Mix Parameters** rollout, set **Mix Amount** to **40**. On the **Mixing curve** section, turn on the **Use Curve** switch and then set **Upper** to **0.6** and **Lower** to **0.53**. Take a test render [Figure 42].

Connect a **Mix** map to the **Displacement** port of the **caveMat**. Set **Displacement** to **25%**. Connect a **Noise** map to the **Color 1** port of the **Mix** map. On the **Noise Parameters** rollout, set **Noise Type** to **Turbulence**, **Levels** to **8.4**, **Size** to **21.2**. Connect a **Noise** map to the **Color 2** port of the **Mix** map. On the **Noise Parameters** rollout, set **Noise Type** to **Turbulence**, **Levels** to **10**, **Size** to **81.5**. On the **Parameter Editor | Mix Parameters** rollout, set **Mix Amount** to **18.4**. Take a test render [Figure 43].

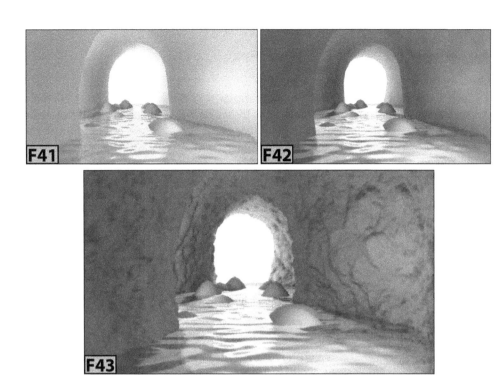

Similarly, create a material for the **floorGeo**. If you want to see the values I have used, open **hoes1-12-end.max** and check the **floorMat** material.

Hands-on Exercise 13: Creating Rusted Metal Texture

Let's now create a rusted metal texture [see Figure 44]. The following material(s) and map(s) are used in this exercise: **Standard**, **Composite**, **Bitmap**, **Color Correction**, and **Noise**.

The following table summarizes the exercise.

Table 13: Creating rusted metal texture	
Topics in this section:	• Getting Ready • Creating Rusted Metal Texture
Skill Level	Beginner
Resources	**hoes1-1to13.zip**
Project Folder	**hoes1-1to13**
Start File	**hoes1-13-start.max**
Final Exercise File	**hoes1-13-end.max**
Time to Complete	15 Minutes

Make sure the **hoes1-13-start.max** is open in 3ds Max.

Creating Rusted Metal Texture

Press **M** to open the **Slate Material Editor**. In the **Material/Map Browser | Materials | Standard** rollout, double-click on **Standard** to add a **Standard** material to the active view. Rename the material as **rustMat** and apply it to the **Teapot001**. In the **Parameter Editor | Shader Basic Parameters** rollout, turn on the **2-Sided** switch. Connect a **Composite** map to the **rustMap's Diffuse Color** port using a **Bitmap** map. Now, connect **rust.jpg** to the **Composite** map's **Layer 1** port [see Figure 45]. On the **Parameter Editor | Composite** map | **Composite Layers | Layer 1** rollout, click **Add a New Layer** button to add a new layer [see Figure 46]. Notice that a new port with the name **Layer 2** has been added to the **Composite** map node in the active view.

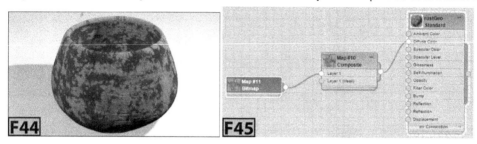

Connect **rustPaint.jpg** to the **Composite** map's **Layer 2** port. On the **Parameter Editor | Composite** map | **Composite Layers | Layer 2** rollout, set **Opacity** to **10%** and blend mode to **Color Dodge** [see Figure 47]. Now, take a test render [see Figure 48].

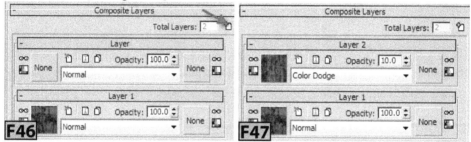

Connect **scratchesMask.jpg** to the **Composite** map's **Layer 2 (Mask)** port using a **Bitmap** map. Now, check the **Invert** checkbox from the **Bitmap's Output** rollout. Take a test render [see Figure 49]. On the **Slate Material Editor's** active view, create copy of the **Bitmap** node connected to the **Composite** map's **Layer 2 (Mask)** node using **Shift**. Connect the duplicate node to the **Bump** node of **rustMat**. On the **Parameter Editor | rustMat | Maps** rollout, set bump map's strength to **10%** and then take a test render [see Figure 50].

Connect a **Noise** map to the **rustMat's Displacement** port. On the **Parameter Editor | Noise map | Noise Parameters rollout**, set **Noise Type** to **Turbulence** and **Size** to **70**. On the **Parameter Editor | rustMat | Maps** rollout, set displacement map's strength to **19%** and then take a test render [Figure 51].

Hands-on Exercise 14: Shading an outdoor Scene

In this exercise, we are going to apply materials and textures to an outdoor scene [see Figure 52]. The rendered output of the scene after illuminating it is shown in Figure 53.

The following table summarizes the exercise.

Table 14: Shading an outdoor scene	
In this exercise, you will:	• Apply material to the objects • Use the **UVW Map** modifier • Apply textures to the material

Topics in this section:	• Getting Ready • Shading the Scene
Skill Level	Intermediate
Resources	**hoes1-14.zip**
Project Folder	**hoes1-14**
Start File	**hoes1-14-start.max**
Final Exercise File	**hoes1-14-end.max**
Time to Complete	30 Minutes

Getting Ready

Extract the content of **hoes1-14.zip** to a location in your HDD. This action creates a folder with the name **hoes1-14**. This folder contains all the subfolders and files related to this exercise. Click **Project Folder** from the **Quick Access Toolbar** to open the **Browse For Dialog**. In this dialog, navigate to the **hoes1-14** folder and click **OK** to set the project folder and close the dialog. Now, open the **hoes1-14-start.max** file in 3ds Max.

Shading the Scene

Select **wallGeo** from the **Scene Explorer** and then press **M** to open the **Slate Material Editor**. Drag **Standard** from the **Material/Map Browser | Maps | Standard** rollout to the **Active View**. Rename the material as **wallMat**. RMB click on the **wallMat** node and then choose **Assign Material to Selection**. Again, RMB click and then choose **Show Shaded Material in Viewport**.

In the **Active View**, drag the **Diffuse Color** socket onto the empty area and release the mouse button. Choose **Standard | Bitmap** from the popup menu. In the **Select Bitmap Image File** dialog that opens, select **redBrick.png** and then click **Open** to make a connection between the **Diffuse Color** socket and texture.

Double-click on the **Bitmap** node and then in the **Parameter Editor | Coordinate rollout**, set **U Tiling** and **V Tiling** to **4**. Similarly, connect the **Bump** socket to the **redBrickGray.png** and set **Tiling** to **4**. Notice in the viewport the map is displayed on the wall [see the left image in Figure 54]. Ensure **wallGeo** is selected in the **Scene Explorer** and then go to **Modify** panel and add the **UVW Map** modifier to the stack. Select the modifier's **Gizmo** and scale the texture so that the size of the bricks appear in right proportions [see the right image in Figure 54].

Select **floorGeo** from the **Scene Explorer** and then in the **Slate Material Editor**, drag **Standard** from the **Material/Map Browser | Maps | Standard** rollout to the **Active View**. Rename the material as **roadMat**. RMB click on the **roadMat** node and then choose **Assign Material to Selection**. Again, RMB click and then choose **Show Shaded Material in Viewport**.

In the **Active View**, drag the **Diffuse Color** socket onto the empty area and release the mouse button. Choose **Standard | Bitmap** from the popup menu. In the **Select Bitmap Image File** dialog that opens, select **road. jpg** and then click **Open** to make a connection between the **Diffuse Color** socket and texture. Notice in the viewport, the texture appears on the **floorGeo** [see Figure 55]. Now, we need to change the direction of the yellow line. We will do so by using the **UVW Map** modifier.

Ensure **floorGeo** is selected in the **Scene Explorer** and then go to **Modify** panel and add the **UVW Map** modifier to the stack. Select the modifier's **Gizmo** and rotate it by **90** degrees by using the **Rotate** tool. You can also use the **Move** tool to position the texture on the geometry [see Figure 56].

Now, we will apply the material to billboard. We will use the **Multi/Subobject** material. The ID **1** has been assigned to the screen component of the board whereas rest of the geometry is held by ID **2**. Select **billBoardGeo** from the **Scene Explorer** and then add a **Multi/Subobject** node to the **Active View**. Rename the material as **billboardMat**. In the **Parameter Editor**, click **Set Number**. Now, in the **Set Number of Materials** dialog, set **Number of Materials** field to **2** and click **OK**. RMB click on the **billboardMat** node and then choose **Assign Material to Selection**. Again, RMB click and then choose **Show Shaded Material in Viewport**.

Drag the **1** socket to the empty area of the view and then choose **Materials | Standard** from the popup menu. Connect the **Standard's** materials **Diffuse Color** socket to the **honda.jpg**. Connect another **Standard** material to the **2** socket of the **billboardMat**. In the **Parameter Editor | Blinn Basic Parameters rollout | Specular Highlight group** of the **Standard** material, set **Specular Level** and **Glossiness** to **92** and **33**, respectively. Also, set **Diffuse** color to **RGB [20, 20, and 20]**. The material appears on the **billBoardGeo** in the viewport [see Figure 57].

Select **ladderGeoGrp** from the **Scene Explorer** and apply a **Standard** material to it. Rename the material as **ladderMat**. Connect **wood.jpg** to the **Diffuse Color** socket of the material. Ensure **ladderGeoGrp** is selected in the **Scene Explorer** and then add a **UVW Map** modifier to the stack. In the **Modify panel | Parameters** rollout, select **Box**. In the **Alignment** group, ensure **Z** is selected and then click the **Fit** button, the texture appears on the ladder in the viewport [see Figure 58].

Create two **Standard** materials and assign dark gray and yellow colors to them. Now, apply these materials to alternate brick from the **brickGrp** group [see Figure 59].

Unit SH2 - Hands-on Exercises [Shading II]

Hands-on Exercise 1: Creating the Leather Material

Let's start by creating a leather material [see Figure 1] using the **Arch & Design** material.

The following table summarizes the exercise.

Table 1: Creating the leather material	
Topics in this section:	Getting Ready
	Creating the Leather Material
Skill Level	Intermediate
Resources	**hoes2-1to8.zip**
Project Folder	**hoes2-1to8**
Start File	**hoes2-1to8-start.max**
Final Exercise File	**hoes2-1-end.max**
Time to Complete	20 Minutes

Getting Ready

Open **hoes2-1to8-start.max**. Save the scene with the name **hoes2-1-end.max**.

Creating the Leather Material

Press **M** to open the **Slate Material Editor**. On the **Material/Map Browser | Materials | mental ray** rollout, double-click on **Arch & Design**. Apply the material to the teapot in the scene. On the **Parameter Editor | Templates** rollout, choose **Pearl Finish** from the drop-down.

Pearl Finish creates soft blurry reflections without affecting colors or maps. **Matte Finish** allows you to simulate an ideal **Lambertian** shading without affecting the colors or maps. **Glossy Finish** lets you simulate strong reflections without affecting colors or maps.

On the **Main material parameters** rollout, click **Color's** button. On the **Material/Map Browser | Maps | Standard** rollout, double-click **Bitmap**. On the **Select Bitmap Image File** dialog, choose **brownLeather. jpg**. On the **Gamma** section of the dialog, choose **Override** and set the spinner next to it to **2.2** and then click **Open**.

Tip: General Maps Rollout
*You can also assign a diffuse map on the **General Maps** rollout.*

Color controls the color of the surface in direct light. **Diffuse Level** allows you to control the brightness of the diffuse color component. **Roughness** controls the blending of the diffuse component into the ambient component. The **Roughness** values ranges from **0** to **1**. At the **0** value, classical **Lambertian** shading is used. Higher values creates more powdery look.

Tip: Gamma 2.2 Setup
*To know more about Gamma 2.2 setup in 3ds Max, visit the following link: **http://bit.ly/linear-gamma**.*

The **Arch & Design** material is energy conserving therefore the actual diffuse level used depends on the reflectivity and transparency. This material makes sure that diffuse+reflection+refraction is less than equal to **1**. The incoming light energy is properly distributed to diffuse, reflection, and refraction components so that it maintains the first law of thermodynamics. If you add reflectivity, the energy must be taken from somewhere, therefore the diffuse and transparency component will be reduced accordingly.

The rules for the energy are as follows:

- **Transparency** takes energy from the diffuse color. If you set transparency to **100%**, there will be no diffuse color.
- **Reflectivity** takes energy from diffuse and transparency, therefore, **100%** reflectivity means there is no diffuse color or transparency on the surface.
- **Translucency** is a type of transparency. The **Translucency Weight** parameter defines the percentage of transparency versus translucency.

On the **brownLeather.jpg | Coordinates** rollout, set **U** and **V** to **0.6** in the **Tiling** column. Also, set **Blur** to **0.2** and take a test render [see Figure 2].

On the **Special Purpose Maps** rollout of the material, click **Bump's None** button. On the **Material/Map Browser | Maps | Standard** rollout, double-click **Bitmap**. On the **Select Bitmap Image File** dialog, choose **brownLeather_bump.jpg**. On the **brownLeather_bump.jpg | Coordinates** rollout, set **U** and **V** to **0.6** in the **Tiling** column. Also, set **Blur** to **0.2**. On the **Special Purpose Maps** rollout of the material, set **Bump** to **0.1** and take a test render [see Figure 3].

You can use the **Bump** map button to assign a bump map. The strength of the bump can be adjusted using the spinner located on the left of the button. If you turn on **Do not apply bumps to the diffuse shading**, bumps are applied to all components except the diffuse.

On the **Main material parameters** rollout, turn off **Fast (interpolate)** to generate more accurate glossiness.

When **Fast (interpolate)** is on, a smoothing algorithm is used that allows rays to be reused and smoothed. As a result, you get faster and smoother glossy reflections at a cost of accuracy.

When **Highlight + FG only** is turned on, actual rays are not traced in the scene. Only highlights are shown. In addition to this, soft reflections are shown that are produced by final gathering. You can use this option on surfaces that are less essential in the scene. This option works well with surfaces having weak reflections and blurred glossy reflections.

Tip: Flat surfaces
This method works well with flat surfaces.

Metal material sets the color of reflection cast by the metallic materials. When **Metal material** is on, the **Color** control defines the color of reflections. The **Reflectivity** control sets the weight between the diffuse reflections and metallic reflections. When off, the Reflection **Color** control defines the color. The **Reflectivity** control plus **BRDF** settings define the intensity and color of the reflections.

Set **Glossiness** to **0.3**. **Glossiness** controls the sharpness of refraction/transparency. The values ranges from **0** [extremely diffuse or blurry transparency] to **1** [completely clear transparency].

Set **Reflectivity** to **0.2** and take a test render [see Figure 4].

Reflectivity controls the overall level of reflectivity. The reflectivity and color values, also known as specular highlight, define the level of reflections and its intensity. **Glossy Samples** specifies the number of rays [samples] **mental ray** shoots in order to calculate the glossy refraction. Higher values produce smooth result at a cost of render time.

*A value of **32** is enough for most renderings. If you set **Glossy Samples** to **1**, only one ray is shot, regardless of the actual value of **Glossiness**. It boosts the rendering performance. You can use it for your test renderings.*

On the **BRDF** rollout, make sure **Custom Reflectivity Function** is selected and then set **0 deg. refl** to **0.2** and **Curve shape** to **2**. Now, take a test render [see Figure 5].

BRDF stands for **Bidirectional Reflectance Distribution Function**. In the real world, the reflectivity of the surface is dependent on the view angle. **BRDF** function allows you to control the reflectivity of the surface based on the angle it is viewed. In real world surfaces such as glass, water, and other dielectric materials with **Fresnel** effects, the angular dependency of reflection is dependent on **IOR** or index of refraction. The **Arch & Design** material allows you to set the angular based reflectivity values using **0-degree** faces [surfaces directly facing the camera] and **90-degree** faces [surfaces 90 degrees to the camera]. **Curve Shape** controls the falloff of the BRDF curve. When you choose **By IOR [fresnel reflections]**, the reflectivity is entirely guided by the material's index of refraction.

On the **Fast Glossy Interpolation** rollout, set **Interpolation grid density** to **1** (same as rendering) and take a test render [see Figure 6].

*Interpolation can cause artifacts because it is calculated on the low res grid. It can also cause oversmoothing as it blends neighbors of the low resolution grid. **Interpolation** works with the flat surfaces. It does not work well with wavy or highly detailed surfaces that uses the bump map.*

The controls in the **Fast Glossy Interpolation** rollout can be used to interpolate reflections and refractions thus producing smooth results and improving rendering performance. The interpolation works by pre-calculating glossy reflections in a grid across the image. The number of rays shot by **mental ray** is governed by reflection **Glossy Samples** and refraction **Glossy Samples**.

Press **Ctrl+S** to save the scene.

Hands-on Exercise 2: Creating the Chrome Material

Ok, now we have some knowledge of the **Arch & Design** material. Now, let's create the chrome material [see Figure 7].

The following table summarizes the exercise.

Table 2: Creating the chrome material	
Topics in this section:	Getting Ready
	Creating the Chrome Material
Skill Level	Intermediate
Resources	**hoes2-1to8.zip**
Project Folder	**hoes2-1to8**
Start File	**hoes2-2-start.max**
Final Exercise File	**hoes2-2-end.max**
Time to Complete	10 Minutes

Open the **hoes2-2-start.max**.

Apply an **Arch & Design** material to the teapot geometry in the scene. On the **Parameter Editor | Main material parameters** rollout | **Diffuse** group, set **Color** to white. Setting color to white will create a very highly reflective surface. On the **Reflection** group, set **Reflectivity** to **1**. Also, turn on **Metal material**. Now, take a test render.

Metal material allows you to define the reflection color using the **Diffuse color** parameter. On the **Refraction** group, set **Color** to **Black** and set **IOR** to **25**.

The **Color** control on the **Refraction** group sets the color of the refraction. You can also use this control to create the colored glass.

On the **BRDF** rollout, select **By IOR (fresnel reflections)** and take a render [see Figure 7]. Save the scene with the name **hoes2-2-end.max**.

Hands-on Exercise 3: Creating the Copper Material

Now, let's create the different copper materials [see Figures 8, 12, and 19].

The following table summarizes the exercise.

Table 3: Creating the copper material	
Topics in this section:	Getting Ready
	Creating the Copper Material
Skill Level	Intermediate
Resources	**hoes2-1to8.zip**
Project Folder	**hoes2-1to8**
Start File	**hoes2-1to8-start.max**
Final Exercise File	**hoes2-3-end.max**
Time to Complete	20 Minutes

Open the **hoes2-1to8-start.max**. Save the scene with the name **hoes2-3-end.max**.

Let's start with the polished copper material.

Apply an **Arch & Design** material to the teapot geometry in the scene. On the **Parameter Editor | Main material parameters** rollout | **Diffuse** group, set **Color** to the following RGB values: **0.592, 0.278,** and **0.165**. On the **Reflection** group, set **Reflectivity** to **1** and **Glossiness** to **0.9**. Also, turn on **Metal material**.

On the **Refraction** group, set **IOR** to **45**. On the **BRDF** rollout, choose **By IOR (fresnel reflections)** and take a render [see Figure 8].

Now, let's create the copper material with satin finish.

Apply a default **Arch & Design** material to the teapot in the scene. On the **Parameter Editor | Main material parameters** rollout | **Diffuse** group, set **Color** to the following RGB values: **0.592, 0.278,** and **0.165**. On the **Reflection** group, set **Reflectivity** to **0.8** and **Glossiness** to **0.5**. Also, turn on **Metal material**. Take a test render [see Figure 9]. You will see that the material is bright. You need to reduce the brightness of the material.

Set **Diffuse Level** to **0.3** to make the material less bright and take a test render. On the **Anisotropy** rollout, set **Anisotropy** to **0.05** to change the shape of the highlights and take a test render [see Figure 10].

Anisotropy controls the shape of the highlight. At the value **1**, there will be no anisotropy and highlight will be round. At the value **0.01**, the highlight will be elongated. **Rotation** controls the orientation of the highlight. The values for **Rotation** ranges from **0** to **1**, **1** represents **360** degrees.

On the **Reflection** group, set **Glossy Samples** to **16** to increase the quality of the glossiness. On the **BRDF** rollout, set **0 deg. refl** to **0.9** and take a test render [see Figure 11]. Notice in the render that you need to reduce **Glossiness** value. On the **Reflection** group, set **Glossiness** to **0.4**. On the **Fast Glossy Interpolation** rollout, set **Neighboring points to look up** to **8** and turn on **High detail distance**. Next, set distance to **1** for High detail distance. Now, take a test render [see Figure 12].

Neighboring points to look up lets you set the number of stored grid points are looked up to smooth out the reflective glossiness. The default value for this parameter is **2**. Higher values smear the glossiness. **High detail distance** allows **mental ray** to trace second set of rays to create a clearer version of the glossiness within the specified radius defined by this parameter.

Now, let's create the brushed copper material.

Apply a default **Arch & Design** material to the teapot in the scene. On the **Parameter Editor | Main material parameters** rollout | **Diffuse** group, set **Color** to the following RGB values: **0.592, 0.278,** and **0.165**. On the **Reflection** group, set **Reflectivity** to **0.5** and **Glossiness** to **0.5** as well. Also, turn on **Metal material**. Now, take a test render [see Figure 13].

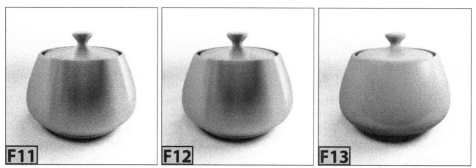

Now, we will use the **Noise** map to create brushed metal look in the reflections.

On the **Reflection** group, click **Color** button. On the **Material/Map Browser | Maps | Standard** rollout, double-click **Noise**. On the **Noise Parameters** rollout, set **Noise Type** as **Fractal** and set **Size** to **1** to create tiny dots in the noise pattern [see Figure 14]. On the **Coordinates** rollout, set **Source** to **Explicit Map Channel**. Also, set **V** and **W** to **100** in the **Tiling** column to create streaks in the noise pattern [see Figure 15].

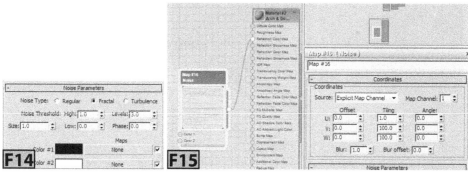

On the **Noise Parameters** rollout, set **Color #1** to medium gray and take a test render [see Figure 16]. On the material's **Refraction** group, set **IOR** to **45**. On the **BRDF** rollout, select **By IOR (fresnel reflections)** and take a test render [see Figure 17]. On the **Anisotropy** rollout, set **Anisotropy** to **0.05** to change the shape of the highlights and take a test render [see Figure 18].

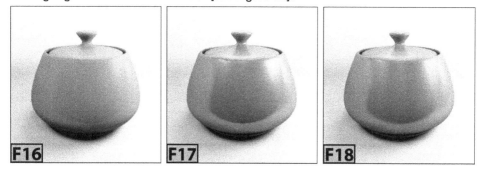

Now, I will increase the reflectivity and glossiness values of the surface.

On the material's **Reflection** group, set **Reflectivity** and **Glossiness** to **0.8**. On the **Fast Glossy Interpolation** rollout, set **Interpolation grid density** to **1/4 (quarter resolution)**, **Neighboring points to look up** to **4**, and turn on **High detail** distance. Next, set distance to **2** for **High detail distance**. Now, take a render [see Figure 19]. Press **Ctrl+S** to save the scene.

F19

Hands-on Exercise 4: Creating Glass/Thin Plastic film Materials

In this example, we're going to create different glass and thin plastic film materials [see Figures 20, 21, 23, 25, 26, and 28]. Let's start with the clear glass material. This material is suitable for solid geometries with some thickness.

The following table summarizes the exercise.

Table 4: Creating the glass/thin plastic film materials	
Topics in this section:	Getting Ready
	Creating Glass/Thin Plastic film Materials
Skill Level	Intermediate
Resources	**hoes2-1to8.zip**
Project Folder	**hoes2-1to8**
Start File	**hoes2-1to8-start.max, hoes2-4-start.max**
Final Exercise File	**hoes2-4-end.max, hoes2-4-end.max**
Time to Complete	20 Minutes

Getting Ready

Open the **hoes2-1to8-start.max**. Save the scene with the name **hoes2-4-end.max**.

Creating Glass/Thin Plastic film Materials

Here's the process:

Apply an **Arch & Design** material to the teapot geometry in the scene. On the **Parameter Editor | Main material parameters** rollout | **Diffuse** group, set **Color** to black. On the **Reflection** group, set **Reflectivity** to **1**. On the **Refraction** group, set **Transparency** to **1** and **IOR** to **1.5**. On the **BRDF** rollout, choose **By IOR** (fresnel reflections) and take a render. On the **Advanced Rendering Options** rollout, set **Max Trace Depth** to **8** in the **Reflections** and **Refraction** groups. Take a test render [see Figure 20].

When the trace depth is equal to the value specified by the **Reflections** group | **Max Trace Depth** control, **mental ray** shows only highlights and emulated reflections created using **Final Gathering**. The material behaves as if **Highlights+FG** is on in the **Main material parameters** rollout | **Reflection** group.

Cutoff Threshold sets a threshold level at which reflections are rejected. The default value for this control is **0.01**. At this value, rays that contribute less than **1%** to the final pixel are ignored.

Max Distance allows you to limit the reflections to a certain distance. It helps in speeding up the rendering as **mental ray** does not include distant objects to glossy reflections. **Fade to end color** lets you fade the reflections to this color. This is suitable for indoor scenes. When this option is turned off, reflections fade to the environment color which is suitable for outdoor scenes.

The optimization settings for the refraction are almost identical to those for reflections. When the trace depth is equal to the value specified by the **Refraction** group | **Max Trace Depth** control, the material refracts black.

Advanced Reflectivity Options group | **Visible area lights cause no Highlights** control, when on, the **mental ray** area lights with **Area Light Parameters** rollout | **Show Icon In Renderer on**, creates no specular highlights. When **Skip reflections on inside (except total internal reflection)** is on, **mental ray** retains total internal reflection [**TIR**]. Most of the reflections inside the transparent objects are very faint except few known as **TIR**. When this option is on, **mental ray** boosts the performance by ignoring the weak reflections but retaining **TIRs**. **Relative Intensity of Highlights** controls the intensity of specular highlights versus the intensity of true reflections.

Next, you will create tinted glass.

On the **Refraction** group, set **Color** to the following RGB values: **0.969**, **0.729**, and **0.659**. Now, take a test render [see Figure 21].

Next, you will create frosted glass.

On the **Refraction** group, set **Transparency** and **Glossiness** to **0.8** and take a test render [see Figure 22].

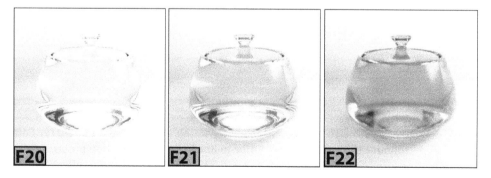

You will notice that you need to reduce the glossiness farther to make a believable frosted glass. If you reduce the **Glossiness** value, you need to increase samples to compensate. Set **Glossiness** and **Glossy Samples** to **0.5** and **16**, respectively, and take a test render [see Figure 23].

Now, the render is looking much better. Adding a little bit of translucency will make the effect much better so let's do it.

Turn on **Translucency** and set **Weight** to **0.2**. Change **Translucency Color** to the following RGB values: **0.969**, **0.729**, and **0.659** and then take a test render [see Figure 24].

Translucency is a special form of transparency. If you want a material to be translucent, there should exist some transparency in the material. The **Weight** parameter defines how much of the existing transparency is used as translucency. For example, if you set **Weight** to **0.3**, **30** percent of the transparency is used as translucency. It is best suited for thin walled objects such as windows panes or plastic films. **Color** controls the translucency color.

Note: Sub-surface Scattering
You can create sub-surface scattering effects by using the glossy transparency with the translucency. However, the effect is not as good as created using the dedicated **SSS** *shaders.*

On the **Diffuse** group, set **Diffuse Level** to **0.52** to reduce the brightness of the material. Press **Ctrl+S** to save the file.

Next, you will create a glass material that does not include any refraction. This glass is ideal for windows panes with single face.

Open **hoes2-4-start.max**. Apply an **Arch & Design** material to the plane geometry in the scene. On the **Parameter Editor | Main material parameters** rollout | **Diffuse** group, set **Color** to black. On the **Reflection** group, set **Reflectivity** to **1**. On the **Refraction** group, set **Transparency** to **1** and **IOR** to **1.5**. On the **BRDF** rollout, choose **By IOR (fresnel reflections)** and take a render.

On the **Refraction** group, set **Color** to the following RGB values: **0.737**, **0.776**, and **0.98**. On the **Advanced Rendering Options** rollout, set **Max Trace Depth** to **8** in the **Reflection** and **Refraction** groups. On the **Advanced Transparency Options** rollout, choose **Thin-walled (can use single face)** for **Glass / Translucency treat objects as**. Now, take a render [see Figure 25].

When you choose **Thin-walled (can use single face)**, the object behaves as if it is made of a very thin sheet of transparent material. On the other hand, **Solid (requires two sides on every object)** tells **mental ray** that the object is made of a solid, transparent substance.

Back Face Culling makes the surfaces invisible to the camera when seen from the reverse side. You can use this option to create magic walls. If you create walls of a room using planes with the normal facing inwards, you can render room from outside. The camera will see into the room, but the wall will still exists and behave normally. For example, they will cast shadows, photon will be bounced off them.

When you turn off **Transparency propagates Alpha channel**, the transparent objects have an opaque alpha. When on, the alpha-channel information is passed on to the background. The refraction and other transparency effects propagate the alpha of the background "through" the transparent object.

The two parameters in the **Indirect Illumination Options** group are multipliers. **FG/GI multiplier** lets you adjust the material response to the indirect light. **FG Quality** is a local multiplier for the number of final gather rays shot by the material.

Next, you will create a thin blurry plastic material.

Apply the default **Arch & Design** material to the plane geometry in the scene. On the P**arameter Editor | Main material parameters** rollout | **Diffuse** group, set **Color** to **white**. On the **Reflection** group, set **Reflectivity** to **1**. On the **Refraction** group, set **Transparency** to **0.9**, **Glossiness** to **0.6**, **Glossy Samples** to **16**, and **IOR** to **1.5**. On the **BRDF** rollout, choose **By IOR (fresnel reflections)**.

On the **Advanced Transparency Options** group, choose **Thin-walled (can use single face)** option for **Glass / Translucency treat objects as**. Also, turn on **Transparency propagates Alpha channel** and then take a render [see Figure 26].

If you want to create strong blur, adjust the values of **Transparency** and **Glossiness** in the **Refraction** group. Also, enable **Translucency**. On the **Refraction** group, set **Transparency** to **0.8**, **Glossiness** to **0.8**, and **Glossy Samples** to **16**. Check **Translucency** and set **Weight** to **0.2** and then take a render [see Figure 27].

F26

F27

Save the scene with the name **hoes2-4-end.max**.

Hands-on Exercise 5: Creating the Water Material

In this example, we are going to create the water material [see Figure 30].

The following table summarizes the exercise.

Table 5: Creating the leather material	
Topics in this section:	Getting Ready
	Creating the Water Material
Skill Level	Intermediate
Resources	**hoes2-1to8.zip**
Project Folder	**hoes2-1to8**
Start File	**hoes2-1to8-start.max**
Final Exercise File	**hoes2-5-end.max**
Time to Complete	20 Minutes

Getting Ready

Open the **hoes2-1to8-start.max**.

Creating the Water Material

Apply an **Arch & Design** material to the teapot geometry in the scene. On the **Parameter Editor | Main material parameters** rollout | **Diffuse** group, set **Color** to the following RGB values: **0.0, 0.058,** and **0.019**. On the **Reflection** group, set **Reflectivity** to **1**. On the **Refraction** group, set **IOR** to **1.3**. On the **BRDF** rollout, choose **By IOR (fresnel reflections)**. Now, take a test render [see Figure 28].

On the **Special Purpose Maps** rollout of the material, set **Bump** to **0.1** and then click **Bump's None** button. On the **Material/Map Browser | Maps | mental ray** rollout, double-click **Ocean**. Take a test render [see Figure 29].

You need to adjust the values for ocean parameters to get a nice bump.

On the **Ocean Parameters** rollout, set **Largest** to **0.5**, **Smallest** to **0.25**, **Quantity** to **3**, and **Steepness** to **1** and then take a render [see Figure 30].

Save the scene with the name **hoes2-5-end.max**.

Hands-on Exercise 6: Creating the Sofa Fabric Material

In this example, we're going to create the sofa fabric material [see Figure 31]. The following table summarizes the exercise.

Table 6: Creating the sofa fabric material	
Topics in this section:	Getting Ready
	Creating the Sofa Fabric Material
Skill Level	Intermediate
Resources	**hoes2-1to8.zip**
Project Folder	**hoes2-1to8**
Start File	**hoes2-1to8-start.max**
Final Exercise File	**hoes2-6-end.max**
Time to Complete	20 Minutes

Getting Ready

Open the **hoes2-1to8-start.max**.

Creating the Sofa Fabric Material

Apply an **Arch & Design** material to the teapot geometry in the scene. Rename the material as **sofaFabricMat**. On the **Main material parameters** rollout, click **Color's** button. On the **Material/Map Browser | Maps | Standard** rollout, double-click **Bitmap**. On the **Select Bitmap Image File** dialog, choose **sofaFabricDif.jpg**.

On the **Coordinates** rollout, set **U** and **V** to **2** in **Tiling** column. Also, set **Blur** to **0.2**. On the **Parameter Editor | Main material parameters** rollout | **Reflection** group, set **Reflectivity** to **0.08**, **Glossiness** to **0.5**, and **Glossy Samples** to **32**. On the BRDF rollout, set **0 deg. refl** to **1**. On the **Special Purpose Maps** rollout of the material, click **Bump's None** button. On the **Material/Map Browser | Maps | Standard** rollout, double-click **Bitmap**. On the **Select Bitmap Image File** dialog, choose **sofaFabricBump.jpg**.

On the **Coordinates** rollout, set **U** and **V** to **2** in **Tiling** column. Also, set **Blur** to **0.2**. On the **Special Purpose Maps** rollout of the material, set **Bump** to **0.4** and take a render [see Figure 31]. Save the scene with the name **hoes2-6-end.max**.

F31

Hands-on Exercise 7: Creating the Wooden Cabinet Material

In this example, we are going to create the wooden cabinet material [see Figure 32].

The following table summarizes the exercise.

Table 7: Creating the leather material	
Topics in this section:	Getting Ready
	Creating the Wooden Cabinet Material
Skill Level	Intermediate
Resources	**hoes2-1to8.zip**
Project Folder	**hoes2-1to8**
Start File	**hoes2-1to8-start.max**
Final Exercise File	**hoes2-7-end.max**
Time to Complete	20 Minutes

Getting Ready

Open the **hoes2-1to8-start.max**.

Creating the Wooden Cabinet Material

Apply an **Arch & Design** material to the teapot geometry in the scene. Rename the material as **woodCabinetMat**. On the **Main material parameters** rollout | **Diffuse** group, click **Color's** button. On the **Material/Map Browser** | **Maps** | **Standard** rollout, double-click **Bitmap**.

On the Select **Bitmap Image File** dialog, choose **woodCabinetDiff.png**. On the **Coordinates** rollout, set **U** and **V** to **2** in **Tiling** column. Also, set **Blur** to **0.2**. On the **Parameter Editor** | **Main material parameters** rollout | **Reflection** group, set **Reflectivity** to **0.4**, **Glossiness** to **0.7**, and **Glossy Samples** to **32**. On the **Main material parameters** rollout | **Reflection** group, click **Glossiness** button. On the **Material/Map Browser** | **Maps** | **Standard** rollout, double-click **Bitmap**.

On the **Select Bitmap Image File** dialog, choose **woodCabinetGloss.png**. On the **Coordinates** rollout, set **U** and **V** to **2** in **Tiling** column. Also, set **Blur** to **0.2**. Now, take a test render. On the **Special Purpose Maps** rollout of the material, click **Bump's None** button. On the **Material/Map Browser** | **Maps** | **Standard** rollout, double-click **Bitmap**. On the **Select Bitmap Image File** dialog, choose **woodCabinetBump.png**.

Take a render [see Figure 32]. Save the scene with the name **hoes2-7-end.max**.

Hands-on Exercise 8: Creating the Parquet Material

In this example, we're going to create parquet material for the floor [see Figure 33].

The following table summarizes the exercise.

Table 8: Creating the leather material	
Topics in this section:	Getting Ready
	Creating the Parquet Material
Skill Level	Intermediate
Resources	**hoes2-1to8.zip**
Project Folder	**hoes2-1to8**
Start File	**hoes2-1to8-start.max**
Final Exercise File	**hoes2-8-end.max**
Time to Complete	20 Minutes

Getting Ready

Open the **hoes2-1to8-start.max**.

Creating the Parquet Material

Apply an **Arch & Design** material to the teapot geometry in the scene. Rename the material as **woodParquetMat**. On the **Main material parameters** rollout | **Diffuse** group, click **Color's** button. On the **Material/Map Browser** | **Maps** | **Standard** rollout, double-click **Bitmap**. On the **Select Bitmap Image File** dialog, choose **floorParquetDiff.png**.

On the **Coordinates** rollout, set **U** and **V** to **2** in **Tiling** column. Also, set **Blur** to **0.2**. On the **Parameter Editor** | **Main material parameters** rollout | **Reflection** group, set **Reflectivity** to **0.7**, **Glossiness** to **0.7**, and **Glossy Samples** to **16**. On the **Main material parameters** rollout | **Reflection** group, click **Color's** button. On the **Material/Map Browser** | **Maps** | **Standard** rollout, double-click **Bitmap**. On the **Select Bitmap Image File** dialog, choose **floorParquetRef.png**. On the **Coordinates** rollout, set **U** and **V** to **2** in **Tiling** column. Also, set **Blur** to **0.2**.

On the **Special Purpose Maps** rollout of the material, click **Bump's None** button. On the **Material/Map Browser** | **Maps** | **Standard** rollout, double-click **Bitmap**. On the **Select Bitmap Image File** dialog, choose **floorParquetBump.png**. On the **Coordinates** rollout, turn off **Use Real-World Scale**. Set **U** and **V** to **2** in **Tiling** column. Also, set **Blur** to **0.2**. On the **Special Purpose Maps** rollout of the material, set **Bump** to **0.4** and take a render [see Figure 33]. Save the scene with the name **hoes2-8-end.max**.

F32

F33

Unit SH3 - Hands-on Exercises [Shading III]

Hands-on Exercise 1: Texturing a Cardboard Box

Let's start by texturing a cardboard box [see Figure 1] using the **UV Editor**.

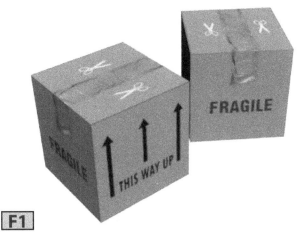

F1

The following table summarizes the exercise.

Table 1: Texturing a cardboard texture	
Topics in this section:	• Getting Ready • Texturing the Cardboard Box
Skill Level	Intermediate
Resources	**hoes3-1.zip**
Project Folder	**hoes3-1**
Final Exercise File	**hoes3-1-end.max**
Time to Complete	20 Minutes

Getting Ready

Reset 3ds Max. Set units to **Generic Units** and then create a box with the **Length**, **Height**, and **Width** set to **190**.

Texturing the Cardboard Box

Ensure the box is selected in a viewport and then go to **Modify** panel. Add the **Unwrap UVW** modifier to the stack. Click **Polygon** [ ] on the **Selection** panel and then press **Ctrl+A** to select all polygons. On the **Projection** rollout, click **Box Map** [ ] and then click again to deactivate. On the **Edit UVs** rollout, click **Open**

UV Editor to open the **Edit UVWs** window. Choose **Unfold Mapping** from the **Mapping** menu of the window. The **Unfold Mapping** dialog appears. Click **OK** to accept the default settings and unfold UVs [see Figure 2].

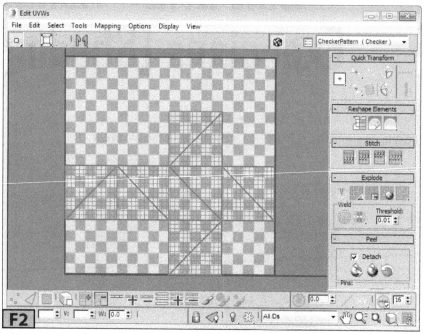

Choose **Pick Texture** from the drop-down located on the top-right corner of the window, the **Material/Map Browser** appears. In the browser, double-click on **Bitmap** from the **Maps | Standard** rollout. In the **Select Bitmap Image File** dialog, select **cardboard_texture.png** and click **Open**. The **cardboard_texture.png** appears in the **Edit UVWs** window [see Figure 3].

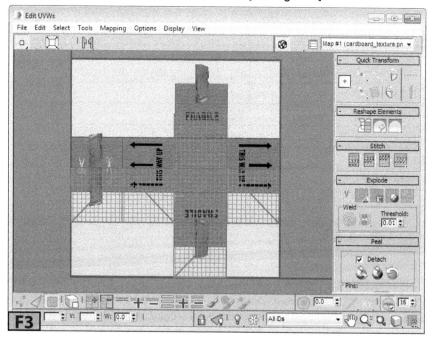

Click **Vertex** from the bottom-left corner of the window to activate the **Vertex** selection mode. All the vertices are selected. If they are not selected, press **Ctrl+A** to select them. Ensure **Move Selected Subobjects** is active from the window's toolbar and then align all UVs to the background texture [see Figure 4]. Press and hold **Shift** while dragging to constrain the movement.

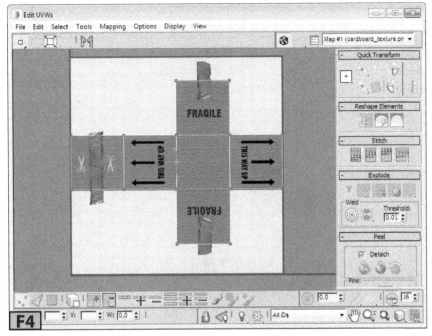

Now, select a complete column of row of the vertices and align them with the background texture [see Figure 5]. You can also select vertices in a viewport. If the UVs are not in the straight line, you can use **Align Horizontally to Pivot** and **Align Vertically to Pivot** from the **Quick Transform** rollout of the window to straighten the UVs. Close the Edit UVWs window.

Press **M** to open the **Slate Material Editor**. From the **Material/Map Browser | Material** rollout | **Standard** rollout, drag **Standard** onto the box in a viewport to apply the material to the box. Rename the material as **boxMat** on the **Scene Materials** rollout of the browser. Drag **boxMat** and the **cardboard_texture.png** map to the active view. Connect map to the **Diffuse Color** slot of the **boxMat**. RMB click on **boxMat** node and choose **Show Shaded Material in Viewport** from the menu to display the texture in the viewport.

Save the scene with the name **hoes3-1-end.max**.

Hands-on Exercise 2: Texturing a Dice

Let's start by texturing a dice [see Figure 6] using the **UV Editor**. In this hands-on exercise we will export the UVs template to the Photoshop and then use Photoshop to create the texture. We will then import the texture back into 3ds Max and will apply it to the dice geometry.

The following table summarizes the exercise.

Table 2: Texturing a dice	
Topics in this section:	Getting Ready Texturing a Dice
Skill Level	Intermediate
Resources	**hoes3-2.zip**
Project Folder	**hoes3-2**
Final Exercise File	**hoes3-2-end.max**
Time to Complete	20 Minutes

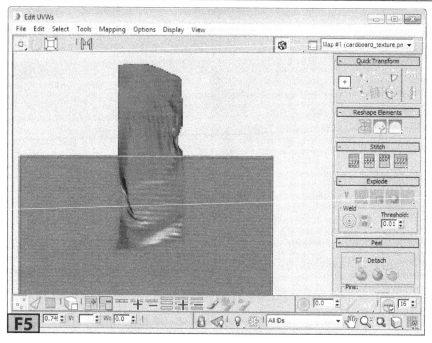

F5

F6

Reset 3ds Max. Set units to **Generic Units** and then create a box with the **Length**, **Height**, and **Width** set to **190**.

Texturing the Dice

Ensure the box is selected in a viewport and then go to **Modify** panel. Add the **Unwrap UVW** modifier to the stack. Click **Polygon** [] on the **Selection** panel and then press **Ctrl+A** to select all polygons. On the **Projection** rollout, click **Box Map** [] and then click again to deactivate. On the **Edit UVs** rollout, click **Open UV Editor** to open the **Edit UVWs** window. Choose **Unfold Mapping** from the **Mapping** menu of the window. The **Unfold Mapping** dialog appears. Click **OK** to accept the default settings and unfold UVs [see Figure 2].

Choose **Render UV Template** from the **Tools** menu to open the **Render UVs** dialog. Click **Render UV Template** on the dialog. The **Render Map** window appears. Click **Save Image** on the window's toolbar to open the **Save Image** dialog. Type **dice_template** in the **File name** field and choose **PNG Image File** from the **Save as** type drop-down. Click **Save** to save the template. Click **OK** from the **PNG Configuration** dialog. Now, close all windows and dialogs, if open.

Open **dice_template.png** in **Photoshop**. **Layer 0** appears in the **Layers** panel. Create a new layer below **Layer 0** and fill it with **black** [see Figure 7]. Now, using **Photoshop** tools and features create dice texture according to the dice template. I am putting simple numbers to identify the faces of the dice [see Figure 8]. You should go ahead and create a nice looking dice texture for your dice model.

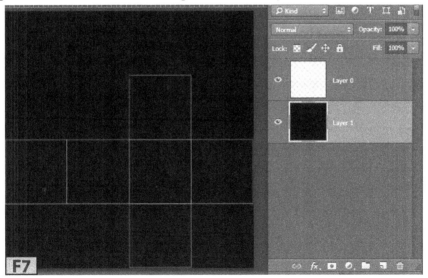

Now, switch off the **black** layer and the **template** layer. Save the **Photoshop** document as **dice_texture.png**.

In 3ds Max, apply a **Standard** material to the box. Set **Diffuse color** to **red**. Connect **dice_texture.png** to the **Diffuse Color** and **Opacity** slots of the material's node, respectively. In the **dice_texture.png** map | **Bitmap Parameters** rollout, turn off the **Premultiplied Alpha** switch. Render the scene.

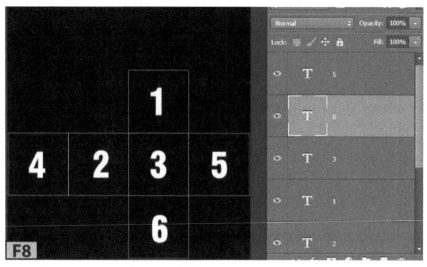

Hands-on Exercise 3: Texturing a Dice - II

In this hands-on exercise, we will use an alternate method to texture a dice. You will use six different maps for the six faces of the dice.

The following table summarizes the exercise.

Table 3: Texturing a dice - II	
Topics in this section:	Getting Ready Texturing a Dice
Skill Level	Intermediate
Resources	**hoes3-3.zip**
Project Folder	**hoes3-3**
Final Exercise File	**hoes3-3-end.max**
Time to Complete	20 Minutes

Getting Ready

Reset 3ds Max. Set units to **Generic Units** and then create a box with the **Length**, **Height**, and **Width** set to **90**.

Texturing the Dice

Ensure the box is selected in a viewport and add the **UVW Map** modifier to the stack. Select **Box** in the **Mapping** group of the **Parameters** rollout. Click **Fit** on the **Alignment** group. RMB click on the box in a viewport and then choose **Convert To : Convert to Editable Poly** from the **Quad** menu.

Press **M** to open the **Slate Material Editor** and then from the **Material/Map Browser** | **Standard** rollout | **Maps** rollout, drag **Standard** to the active view. In the **Select Bitmap Image File** dialog that appears, select **side-1.jpg** and click **Open** to load the map. Similarly, add **5** more **Standard** maps and assign **side-2.jpg** to **side-6.jpg** to them.

Drag the **Standard** material to the active view and connect its **Diffuse Color** slot with the **side-1.jpg** map.

RMB click on the **Standard** material node and then choose **Show Shaded Material in Viewport** from the menu. Similarly, connect other maps with the **Standard** material nodes. Now, add **a Multi/Sub-Object** node to the active view. In the **Parameter Editor**, click **Set Number**. Set **Number of Materials** to **6** and then click **OK**. Connect all **Standard** materials to the **Muli/Sub-Object** material. Figure 9 shows the node network. Figure 10 shows the maps in the viewport.

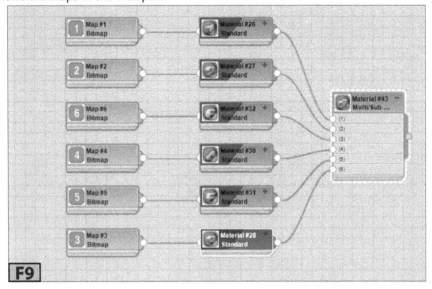

Apply the **Muli/Sub-Object** material to the box in the scene. 3ds Max assigns the maps to the faces of the box. Now, if you want to change a map for a polygon, select that polygon in a viewport and then change the **ID** of the polygon from the **Polygon: Material IDs** rollout of the **Modify** panel.

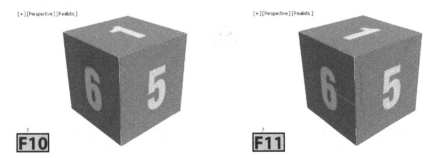

You can use the **UV Editor** to change the orientation of the map. For example, if you want to change the orientation of the top face [see Figure 11], add **Unwrap UVW** modifier to the stack and then click **Polygon** from the **Selection** rollout. Select the top polygon and click **Open UV Editor** from the **Edit UVs** rollout. Press **A** to enable angel snap and then click **Rotate Selected Subobjects** from the toolbar. Now, rotate the selected polygon by **90** degrees to change the orientation of the map.

This page intentionally left blank

Unit-L1: Standard Lighting

To achieve professional-quality, realistic renders in 3ds Max, you need to master the art of lighting. Lights play an important role in the visual process. They shape the world we see. The trick to simulate realistic looking light effects is to observe the world around us. The lights you create in a scene, illuminate other objects in the scene. The material applied to the objects simulates color and texture.

In this unit, I will describe the following:

- Basic Lighting Concepts
- Creating and placing objects
- 3ds Max Lights
- Light Linking
- Shadows
- Lighting Effects

The reasons to add the light objects to the scene are as follows:

- They improve the illumination of the scene.
- They enhance the realism of the scene through realistic lighting effects.
- They give depth to the scene by casting shadows.
- They enhance the scene by projecting maps onto the scene.
- They also help in modeling light source such as headlights of a car.
- They create lights using files from manufactures [such as IES files].

Note: IES Lights
*You can use these lights to visualize the commercially available lighting in your scene by adding **Photometric** lights to your scene.*

Standard Lights

The standard lights in 3ds Max are computer based lights that simulate lights such as lamps and bulbs. Unlike **Photometric** lights, these lights do not have the physically-based intensity values. To create a light, on the **Create** panel, click **Lights**. Choose the **Standard** from the drop-down available below **Lights** and then on the **Object Type** rollout, click the type of light you want to create. Now, click on a viewport to create the light. The creation method in the viewport depends on the type of light you have chosen. For example, if a light has a target, you need to click-drag to set the target.

Whenever you create a light in the scene, the default lighting is turned off. It will be restored when you delete all lights from the scene. Like all objects in 3ds Max, lights have a name, and color. You can set these options from the **Name and Color** rollout.

Note: The color of the light
*The color that you set for the light from the **Name and Color** rollout only changes the color of the light geometry in the scene. It has no effect on the color cast by the light.*

Note: Default Lighting

When there are no light objects in the scene, 3ds Max illuminates the scene using the default lighting. The default lighting disappears as soon as you add a light object to the scene. When you delete all light objects from the scene, the default lighting reappears.

*You can convert the default scene lighting into actual light objects. To do this, choose **Lights | Standard Lights | Add Default Lights To Scene** from the **Create** menu. The default lighting consists of a key light positioned in the front and to the left of the scene and a fill light behind the scene. This command is only available when **2 Lights** is on in the **Viewport Configuration** dialog. To open this dialog, click or RMB click on the **General Viewport Label** and then choose the **Configure Viewports | Viewport Configuration** dialog from the menu. Now, turn on **2 Lights** in the **Lighting and Shadows** area of the **Visual Style & Appearance** panel of the dialog [see Figure F1].*

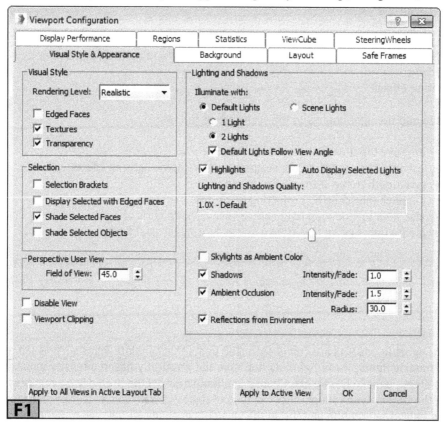

Now, let's explore the standard lights.

Target Spotlight

The target spotlight casts a focused beam of light. You can use this light to simulate flashlight, a follow spot on a stage, or the headlights of the car. To create a target spotlight, click **Target Spot** from the **Object Type** rollout. Now, drag in a viewport to place the light. The initial point of the drag defines the location of the spotlight whereas the point at which you release the mouse defines the location of the target. In Figure F2, I have marked light with 1 and its target with 2.

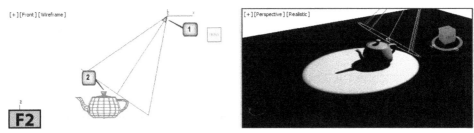

Note: Light and its target

*When you create a light that has a target, two objects will appear in the **Scene Explorer**: light object and its target. The target name has an extension **.target**. For example, if you create a spot light in the scene, the name of the light and its target will be as follows: **Spot001** and **Spot001.Target**. When you rename a light, its target object will be automatically renamed accordingly. However, remember that renaming a target object does not rename its parent light.*

Note: Free Spotlight

*The **Free Spotlight** is similar to the **Target Spotlight** except the difference that it has no target. You can move and rotate the **Free Spotlight** to aim in any direction.*

To adjust the target, select it in a viewport or from the **Scene Explorer** and then move the target using the **Select and Move** tool. The spotlight is always aimed at its target. The distance of the target from the light does not affect the attenuation or brightness of the light.

You can also change a viewport to a light view so that the viewport shows the light's point of view. This feature is immensely helpful in placing the lights correctly. To change a viewport to a light view, click or RMB click on the **POV Label**. Now, choose **Lights | Name** of the light from the menu. Figure F3 shows the point of view of the light that was shown in Figure F2.

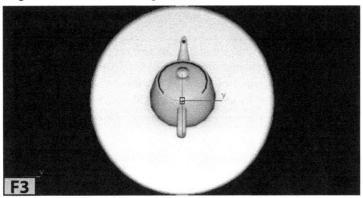

You can change the properties of the spot light from the rollouts available in the **Modify** panel. Let's explore the controls available in these rollouts.

General Parameters Rollout

This rollout is displayed for the **Standard** lights. The controls in this rollout allow you to turn light on or off, exclude or include objects in the scene, and change the type of light. You can also toggle the shadow casting from this rollout.

To turn a light on or off, toggle the **On** switch from this rollout. The drop-down on the right of the **On** switch lets you switch between the light types. When the **Targeted** switch is on, the light is targeted. When on, the distance between the light and its target is displayed on the right of this switch.

To toggle shadow casting, use the **On** switch from the **Shadows** group. Turn on the **Use Global Settings** switch to use the global settings for shadows that are cast by this light. The shadow parameters defined by the light are shared with all the lights of same class. When off, the shadow parameters are specific to that light.

The drop-down in the **Shadows** group lets you choose the algorithm to be used by the light to cast shadows. The following table summarizes various algorithms.

Table 1: The shadow generating algorithms	
Algorithm	**Description**
Shadow Map	The shadow map is a bitmap that is generated during a pre-rendering pass of the scene. This map doesn't show the color cast by transparent or translucent objects. A shadow map can produce soft-edged shadows that cannot be generated by a ray-traced shadow [see Figure F4]. Also, depth map shadows take less time to render than the ray-traced shadows. You can change the shadow map options from the **Shadows Map Parameters** rollout.
Ray-Traced Shadows/Adv. Ray-Traced Shadows	The Ray-traced shadows [see Figure F5] are more accurate than the shadow-mapped shadows and are generated by tracing the path of the rays sampled from a light source. They create better results for the transparent or translucent objects. Only ray-traced shadows can generate shadows for the wireframed objects. The Adv. Ray-Traced Shadows are same as ray-traced shadows, however they provide anti-aliasing controls to fine tune the shadows.
Area Shadows	This algorithm simulates shadows generated by a light with area of volume. You can change volume type from the drop-down available in the **Basic Options** group of the **Area Shadows** rollout. Figure F6 shows the shadows generated by using the **Box Light** volume.

Tip: Transparent and Translucent objects
If you want convincing looking shadow results for the transparent and translucent objects, use raytraced or advance raytraced shadows.

Tip: Preventing an object from casting shadows
You can prevent an object from casting shadows in the scene, to do this, select the object and then RMB click. Choose **Object Properties** *from the* **Quad** *menu and then turn off the* **Cast Shadows** *switch from the* **Rendering Control** *group of the* **Object Properties** *dialog.*

You can also exclude the selected object from the effects of the lights. This feature is very useful when you want a light to lit specific objects in the scene. Click **Exclude** to open the **Exclude/Include** dialog [see Figure F7]. Now, select the objects that you want to affect from the **Scene Objects** section of the dialog. Select **Include** or **Exclude** from the right of the dialog. Now, click **>>** to add the selected object to the right pane of the dialog. You can click **<<** to move objects from right pane to the left pane. You have three options to control the effect: **Illumination**, **Shadow Casting**, and **Both**. You can use these options to exclude/include illumination, shadows, or both. Now, click **OK** to close the dialog and include/exclude objects with the light.

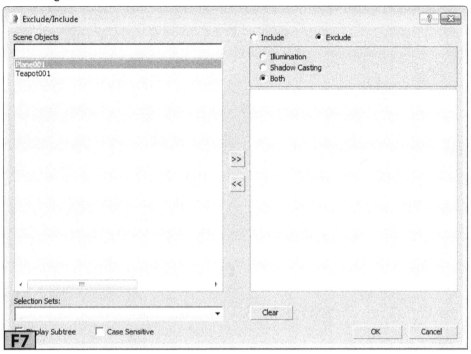

Intensity/Color/Attenuation Rollout

The controls in this rollout lets you set the color and intensity of the light. Also, you can define the attenuation of the light. The **Multiplier** control amplifies the power of the light. You can use negative values to reduce the illumination. High **Multiplier** values wash out the colors whereas the negative values darkens the objects. The color swatch next to the **Multiplier** controls lets you select a color to be casted by the light.

Tip: Flashing light on and off
*Animate the **Multiplier** value to **0** [0 and 1] in repeated keyframes and then assign step tangent to the **Multiplier's** graph.*

The controls in the **Decay** group lets you control the light's intensity over distance. The following table summarizes the options available in the **Type** drop-down.

Table 2: The decay types	
Type	**Description**
None	No decay is applied [see the left image in Figure F8]. The light retains its full strength.
Inverse	It applies inverse decay [see the middle image in Figure F8]. The formula used to calculate decay is **luminance=RO/R**. **RO** is the radial source of the light of no attenuation is used. **R** is the radial distance of the illuminated surface from **RO**.
Inverse Square	It applies inverse-square decay [see the right image in Figure F8]. The formula used is **(RO/R)2**. This decay type is used by the Photometric lights and it is the real-world decay of the light.

If you don't use the attenuation settings [discussed next], the **Start** control sets the distance at which the light begins to decay. You can use the **Show** switch to display the decay range in the viewports. For spotlights, the decay range appears as lens-shaped section of the cone [see the left image in Figure F9]. For directional light, it appears as circular section of the cone [see the middle image in Figure F9]. For omni lights and spot or directional lights with **Overshoot** turned on, the range appears as a sphere [see the right image in Figure F9].

Attenuation is the effect of the light diminishing over distance. **Far Attenuation** controls the distance at which the light drops off to zero. The **Near Attenuation** value controls the distance at which the light fades in. You can turn on the attenuation from the **Near Attenuation** and **Far Attenuation** groups of the **Intensity/Color/Attenuation** rollout by using the **Use** control. The **Start** and **End** controls in these groups define the attenuation distances.

When you set the **Far Attenuation** value, the light intensity remains at the value specified by **Multiplier** up to the distance specified by **Start** and then drops off to zero at the distance specified by the **End**. When you set the **Near Attenuation** value, the light intensity remains zero up to the distance specified by **Start** and then from the **Start** to the distance specified by the **End**, the light intensity increases. Beyond **End**, the light intensity remains at the value specified by **Multiplier**.

Spotlight Parameters Rollout
The parameters in this rollout controls the hotspot and falloff properties of the spotlight. The **Show Cone** switch displays the cone in the viewport. The cone is always visible when a light is selected. This switch allows you to show the cone even if the light is not selected. When the **Overshoot** switch is on, the light

casts light in all directions [not just within the cone] but the shadows and projections appear within the cone. The **Hotspot/Beam** and **Falloff/Field** parameters control the angle of the light's cone and light's falloff, respectively.

The **Circle** and **Rectangle** parameters define the shape of the falloff and hotspot areas. The **Aspect** parameter controls the aspect ratio of the rectangular light beam. The **Bitmap Fit** button lets you specify the aspect ratio as per the supplied bitmap.

Advanced Effects Rollout

The parameters in this rollout define how light affects the surfaces. Also, you can create projector lights. The **Contrast** parameter adjusts the ambient and diffuse areas of the surface. The default value is zero for this parameter that creates normal contrast. The **Soften Diff Edge** parameter, softens the edge between the diffuse and ambient components. The **Diffuse** switch when on, affects the **Diffuse** properties of an object's surface. Similarly, the **Specular** and **Ambient Only** switches can be used to affect the specular and ambient components, respectively.

The parameters in the **Projector Map** group let you make a light a projector. To create a projector light, open the **Material Editor** and then create a map. Drag the map from the **Material Editor** to the **None** button in the **Projector Map** group. Select **Instance** from the dialog that appears and click **OK**. The name of the map appears in as button's label. Notice in Figure F10, I have used a **Cellular** map to project it on the teapot using a spotlight.

Atmospheres and Effects Rollout

You can use this rollout to assign, delete, and edit parameters for various atmospheric and rendering effects associated with the light. For example, to create the volume fog effect, click **Add** to open the **Add Atmosphere or Effect** dialog. Select **Volume Light** from the list and then click **OK** to close the dialog. In the **Atmospheres and Effects** rollout, select **Volume Light** and then click **Setup** to open the **Environments and Effects** dialog. Now, you can adjust the parameters from the **Atmosphere** rollout. Render the scene to see the effect. Notice in Figure F11, I have projected the **Cellular** map and then added volume effect to it.

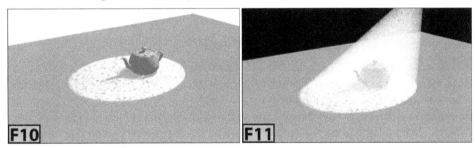

Shadow Parameters Rollout

The parameters in this rollout are displayed for all light types expect **Skylight** and **IES Sky**. You can use these parameters to define the shadow color and other general shadow properties. Use the **Color** swatch to change the color of the shadows. You can also animate the shadow color. **Dens** controls the density [darkness] of the shadows. You can also assign negative values to **Dens** that allows you to simulate the reflected light. Turn on the **Map** switch to assign a map to the shadows using the button available on its right. The process to add the map is the same as discussed with the projector light. Figure F12 shows the **Dent** map applied to the shadows. When the **Light Affects Shadow Color** switch is on, the color of the light blends with the color of the shadow.

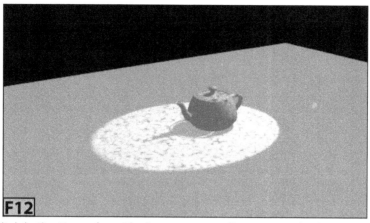

F12

Turn on the **On** switch in the **Atmosphere Shadows** group to allows atmospheric shadows to cast shadows as light passes through them. The **Opacity** parameter defines the opacity of the atmospheric shadows whereas the **Color Amount** parameter defines the amount of atmosphere color bleed into the shadows.

Shadow Map Params Rollout

This rollout is displayed when you choose the **Shadow Map** method for generating shadows. The **Bias** parameter moves the shadow toward or away from the shadow-casting objects. Figure F13 shows the render with **Bias** set to **1** and **3**, respectively. The **Size** parameter defines the size of the shadow map in square pixel computed for the light. Higher the value of Size, more detailed map will be. The **Sample Range** parameter controls how much area in the shadow is averaged. This settings effects the edges of the shadow. On increasing this value, blends the shadow edges and remove the granularity from the shadow.

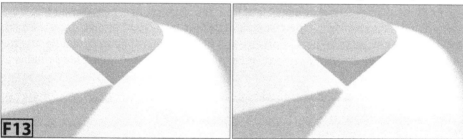

F13

The **Absolute Map Bias** switch works with the **Bias** parameter. If you specify a low value for **Bias**, the shadows can leak and if you specify a too high value, the shadow might detach from the object. Setting an extremes value in either case might result in no shadows at all. This behavior depends on the **Absolute Map Bias** switch. When off, the **Bias** is calculated based on the scene extents and then it is normalized to one. This results in similar results regardless of the size of the scene. When on, the **Bias** value is treated in 3ds Max scene units and the result is dependent on the size of the scene.

When **2 Sided Shadow** switch is on, blackfaces are not ignored when calculating shadows. Figure F14 shows the render of the teapot with the **2 Sided Shadows** switch turned on and off, respectively.

The type of renderer you choose will also affect your choice of shadow algorithm used. The **Quicksilver Hardware** renderer always casts shadow-mapped shadows whereas the **iray** renderer always casts ray-traced shadows. The following table summarizes the shadow types the **Scanline** and **mental ray** renderers support.

Table 3: The shadow types supported by the **Scanline** and **mental ray** renderers		
Type	**Scanline**	**mental ray**
Advanced Ray-Traced	Yes	No
mental ray Shadow Map	No	Yes
Area	Yes	No
Shadow Map	Yes	Yes
Ray-Traced	Yes	Yes

The following table summarizes the pro and cons of each shadow type:

Table 4: Shadow types comparison		
Type	**Pros**	**Cons**
Advanced Ray-Traced	Supports opacity and transparency. It uses less memory than the raytraced shadows. This type is recommended for complex scenes with lots of light.	It is slower than the shadow map and computed at every frame. It does not support soft shadows.
mental ray Shadow Map	Quicker than the raytraced shadows.	These shadows are not accurate as raytraced shadows.
Area	Supports opacity and transparency and uses very less RAM. It supports different format for area shadows.	It is slower than the shadow map and computed at every frame.
Shadow Map	Fastest shadow type. It produces soft shadows. It is computed once if there is no animated object present in the scene.	Uses a lot of RAM and does not support objects with transparency and opacity maps.
Ray-Traced	Supports transparency and opacity mapping. It is computed once if there is no animated object present in the scene.	It does not support soft shadows. It is slower than the shadows maps.

Ray Traced Shadow Params Rollout

This rollout is displayed when you choose **Ray Traced Shadows** method for generating shadows. The **Ray Bias** parameter moves the shadow toward or away from the shadow casting object. The **Max Quadtree Depth** parameter sets the depth of Quadtree used by the raytracer. Higher the value you specify for this parameter, more enhanced the results will be. However, you will be taxed on the render time.

Note: Quadtree

*Quadtree is the data structure used by the raytracer. It represents scene from the point of the view of the light. The root node of the **Quadtree** contains all visible objects in the scene. If there are too many objects available in the scene, four more nodes [leaf nodes] are generated to hold these objects. This process continue adaptively until each node has a small number of objects and **Quadtree depth limit** is achieved. The maximum size of a **Quadtree** is the square of two to the power of the maximum **Quadtree depth**. For example, at the depth of 7, the total number of the leaf node generated will be 27 * 27=128 * 128=16384.*

Warning: Omni Light and Quadtree

*An omni light can generate up to ten **Quadtrees** therefore, if you are using raytraced shadows with it, it will use more memory and render time.*

Tip: The raytraced shadows and renderers

*Both the **Scanline** renderer and **mental ray** renderer support raytraced shadows. If you are using the **Scanline** renderer, the **Adv Ray Traced** method gives you more control over the shadows.*

Adv. Ray Traced Params Rollout

The parameters in this rollout allow you to control the advanced raytraced shadows. These shadows are similar to the raytraced shadows, however, they give you more control over the shadows. The drop-down in the **Basic Options** group allows you to select type of raytracing. The **Simple** type casts a single ray of light toward the surface. No antialiasing is performed when you select this type.

Warning: The mental ray renderer

*This renderer does not support advanced raytraced shadows. When **mental ray** encounters a light with advanced raytraced shadows enabled, it renders the raytraced shadows. The **1-Pass Antialias** type casts a bundle of rays. The same number of rays is cast from the each illuminated surface in the scene. The **2-Pass Antialias** type casts two bundle of rays. The first batch of rays determine the point in question is fully illuminated, shadowed, or in the penumbra [soft area]. If the point is in the soft area, other set of rays are used to refine the edges.*

Shadow Integrity defines the number of rays cast from an illuminated surface. This parameter is not available if raytracing mode is simple. **Shadow Quality** defines the secondary rays cast from the illuminated surface. This parameter is not available when type is set to **Simple** or **1-Pass Antialias**. **Shadow Spread** defines the radius in pixels to blur the antialias edge. This parameter is not available when mode is set to **Simple**. **Shadow Bias** controls the minimum distance from the point being shaded that an object must be to cast a shadow. If you increase the blur value, you should also increase the bias value to compensate. The **Jitter Amount** parameters breaks the regular pattern of the rays and add randomness to the ray positions.

Area Shadows Rollout

This rollout is displayed when you choose the **Area Shadows** method for generating shadows. You need to define the dimensions of the virtual light to fake an area shadow. You can choose the type of fake light from the drop-down available in the **Basic Options** group of the rollout. The dimensions can be set from the **Area Light Dimensions** area of the rollout.

Tip: Rendering area lights
*If you are using area lights, try to match the properties of the light match the properties in the **Area Light Dimensions** group.*

Optimization Rollout

This rollout contains additional parameters for fine tuning advanced raytraced and area shadows. When the **On** switch in the **Transparent Shadows** area is on, the transparent surfaces will cast a colored shadow, otherwise, all shadows are black. **Antialiasing Threshold** defines the maximum color difference allowed between transparent object samples before the antialiasing is triggered. On increasing the value of the color, the shadow becomes less sensitive to the aliasing artifacts and rendering speed will also improve.

When the **Supersampled Material** switch is on, while shading a supersampled material only pass 1 is used during 2-pass antialiasing. When the **Reflect/Refract** switch is on, only pass 1 is used during 2-pass anti-aliasing. If these two switches are off, render time can increase without resulting in a better quality image.

The **Skip Coplanar Faces** switch in the **Coplanar Face Culling** group prevents faces from shadowing each other in curved surfaces. The angle between the adjacent faces is controlled by the **Threshold** parameter.

mental ray Shadow Map Rollout

This rollout is displayed when you choose the **mental ray Shadow map** method for generating shadows. You can set the size of the map using the **Map Size** parameter. The size of the map is square of this value. The **Sample Range** parameter can be used to soft-edged shadows. The directional light requires more **Sample Range** than the spotlights. The **Samples** parameter controls the number of samples to be removed from the shadow map to generate soft shadows. The **Use Bias** parameter is used to move shadow away from the shadow-casting object.

When the **Enable** switch in the **Transparent Shadows** group is on, shadow maps are saved with multiple Z-layers and contains transparency. When the **Color** switch is on, the color of the surface affects the color of the shadow. **Merge Dist** defines the distance between the two surfaces for them to be considered distinct. If the two surfaces are closer than the space defined by this attribute, **mental ray** treats both objects as a single object. The **Samp./Pixel** parameter controls the quality of the shadow. This value is used to generate a pixel in the shadow map. Higher values will produce a better quality result but will tax you on render time.

Target Directional Light

This light is used to simulate a distant light source [see Figure F15] that casts parallel light rays in a single direction [like Sun]. These lights are generally used to simulate sunlight. Like the **Target Spotlight**, it has a target object to aim the light. When you create a **Target Directional** light, the **Directional Parameters** appears in the **Modify** panel. You can use the parameters to define the shape of the light. These parameters are similar to the one described in the **Target Spotlight** section.

Note: Free Directional Light
*The **Free Directional** light is similar to the **Target Directional** light except the difference that it has no target. You can move and rotate the **Free Directional** to aim in any direction.*

Omni Light

An **Omni** light casts rays in all directions from a single source like a light bulb. These lights are specifically used for creating fill lighting or simulating point source lights.

Skylight

When you use this light, it models a sky as a dome above the scene. You can use this light to model daylight. You can also use a map to model the sky. When you add a **Sky** light to the scene, the **Skylight Parameters** appear in the **Modify** panel.

The **On** switch allows you to turn light on or off. The **Multiplier** parameter controls the power of the light. The parameters in the **Sky Color** group let you set the color of the sky. Select **Use Scene Environment** to color the light using the environment color set in the **Environment** panel. The **Sky Color** parameter lets you set a color tint for the sky. You can also assign a map using the **Map** switch. Use HDR files such as **OpenEXR** for best results.

Turn on the **Cast Shadow** switch in the **Render** group to cause the **Sky light** to cast shadows. Figure F16 show a teapot rendered with a skylight. The **Rays Per Sample** parameter allows you to set the number of rays used to calculate the skylight falling on a point in question. The **Ray Bias** parameter defines the closest distance at which objects can cast shadows on a given point in the scene.

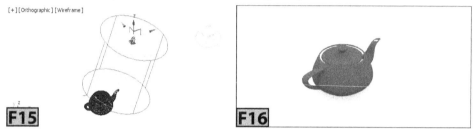

Note: Radiosity and Light Tracer
*The **Cast Shadows** switch has no effect when you are using **Radiosity** or **Light Tracer**. Also, the **Sky** light does not cast shadows in the **ActiveShader** rendering.*

Note: The Render group
*The parameters in this group are not available if you are not using the **Scanline** renderer or the **Light Tracer** is active.*

Warning: The Sky light and mental ray renderer
*If you are using a **Sky light** with the **mental ray** renderer, the objects illuminated by the **Sky** light appear dark. To improve the illumination, use **Final Gathering**.*

Tip: Sky light and Light Tracer
*There are many methods in 3ds Max to model the skylight. For best results, use the **Sky light** with **Light Tracer**.*

Note: Light Tracer
*The **Light Tracer** is a lighting plugin that is used to generate soft-edged shadows in a brightly lit scene such as outdoor scenes. It is typically used with the **Sky** light. It does not attempt to create a physically accurate lighting and it is easy to setup.*

Note: Radiosity

*It is a rendering technique used to calculate the indirect light in a scene. It calculates the inter-reflections of the diffuse light and then illuminates the scene. You can find the **Light Tracer** and **Radiosity** options in the **Advanced Lighting** panel of the **Render Setup** dialog.*

mr Area Omni Light

The area omni light emits light from a spherical and cylindrical volume instead of a point source. This light is used with the **mental ray** renderer. If you use this light with the **Scanline** renderer, it treats the area omni light like a standard omni light.

When you add the **mr Area Omni** light, the **Area Light Parameters** rollout appears in the **Modify** panel. Use the **On** switch to turn light on or off. When the **Show Icon in Renderer** switch is on, **mental ray** renders a dark shape at the location of the light. Figure F17 shows the area light in the scene and its icon in the render, respectively. Here, I have set **Type** to **Sphere** in the **Type** drop-down and then set **Radius** to **50**. Another type you can use is **Cylinder**.

The **U** and **V** parameters in the **Samples** group let you adjust the quality of the shadows. These values defines the number of samples to be taken within the light's area. Higher values can improve the rendering quality but will affect the render time.

mr Area Spotlight

This light emits light from a rectangular or disc-shaped area when you render the scene with the **mental ray** renderer. When you add the **mr Area Omni** light, the **Area Light Parameters** rollout appears in the **Modify** panel. This light offers two shapes for light emission **Rectangle** and **Disc**.

Hands-on Exercises

Complete the following exercises:

Unit LH-1, Exercise 1: Illuminating an Outdoor Scene
Unit LH-1, Exercise 2: Quickly Rendering an Architectural Plan
Unit LH-1, Exercise 3: Illuminating a Night Scene

Summary
This unit covered the following topics:

- Basic Lighting Concepts
- 3ds Max Lights
- Light Linking
- Shadows
- Lighting Effects

Unit L2: Photometric Lights

Photometric lights allow you to accurately define the lighting model for your scene. They use the light energy [**Photometric values, real-world light measurement values**] to create lights that follow the real-world scenarios. You can create lighting models using various distribution and color characteristics. You can also import photometric light files [provided by the light manufactures] into 3ds Max. In this unit, you will learn about photometric lights that 3ds Max offers.

In this unit, I will describe the following:

- Photometric light types: Target Light, and Free Light
- Color temperatures
- Shadow generating shapes
- Exposure controls

Target Light

The **Target Light** has a target sub-object that you can use to aim the light. When you create a **Target Light** in a viewport, 3ds Max automatically adds a **Look At Controller** to it. The target object of the light is assigned as the **Look At Target**. You can use the **Motion** panel of the **Command Panel** to assign any object as the **Look At Target**.

Note: Light and its target
When you create a light that has a target, two objects will appear in the Scene Explorer: light object and its target. The target name has an extension .target. For example, if you create first Target Light in the scene, the name of the light and its target will be as follows: TPhotometricLight001 and TPhotometricLight001.Target. When you rename a light, its target object will be automatically renamed accordingly. However, remember that renaming a target object does not rename its parent light.

Note: mrSky Portal
The Photometric category also include an mrSky Portal light. This light is used to gather existing sky light coming in from the external sources. This light works correctly, if the scene contains a Skylight component. This light is covered in the next Unit.

Whenever you create a photometric light, a warning box appears, recommending that the **Logarithmic Exposure Control** to be enabled. Exposure controls are plug-in components that are used to adjust the output levels and color range of a rendering as if you are adjusting the film exposure [tone mapping]. These controls are useful if you are rendering a scene with **Radiosity** or **HDR** imagery. It is especially useful for compensating the limited dynamic range of the computer displays.

The following table summarizes the exposure controls available in 3ds Max.

Table 1: Exposure Controls	
Control	**Description**
Automatic Exposure Control	This control enhances some lighting effects that would otherwise be too dim to see. It builds a histogram to give good color separation across the entire dynamic range of the rendering. Do not use this control in animation because it causes your animation to flicker. This happens because different histograms are generated for each frame. The **mental ray** renderer does not support this control.
Linear Exposure Control	It uses the average brightness of the scene to map physical values to the RGB values. This is best suitable for scene with fairly low dynamic range. The **mental ray** renderer does not support this control.
Logarithmic Exposure Control	It uses brightness, contrast, and whether the scene is outdoors in daylight to map physical values to RGB values. This control is best suitable for scenes with a very high dynamic range. Also, it is best suited for animation as it does not generate histograms. If you're rendering to texture, use the **Logarithmic Exposure Control**, not the **Automatic** or **Linear** control.
Physical Camera Exposure Control	It sets exposure for **Physical Cameras**, using an **Exposure Value** and a color-response curve.
mr Photographic Exposure Control	It allows you to modify rendered output with camera-like controls such as aperture, shutter speed, and film speed. Also, it gives you controls for adjusting highlights, midtones, and shadows. Use this control if you are rendering scene with the **mental ray** renderer, the **iray** renderer, or the **Quicksilver hardware** renderer.
Pseudo Color Exposure Control	It is a lighting analysis tool that provides an intuitive way of visualizing and evaluating the lighting levels in your scenes. You can use the **Pseudo Color** exposure control with the **mental ray** renderer.
Lighting Data Exporter Utility	It renders the active viewport to images that include luminance and illuminance data that can be used for lighting analysis. It only works if you have applied an exposure control to the scene.

To create a target light, on the **Create** panel, click **Lights** and then choose **Photometric** from the drop-down [see Figure F1]. Click **Target Light** in the **Object Type** rollout. Click **Yes** from the **Photometric Light Creation** dialog and then drag in a viewport to set the location of the light. The initial point drag of the mouse pointer defines the location of the light whereas the last drag point defines the position of the target. Now, you can use the **Move** transform to farther refine the position of the light and its target. Adjust the parameters of the light from the rollouts in the **Command Panel.**

Several of the rollouts for the photometric lights are the same as those for the standard lights but there are some key controls that are different. Let's now explore these controls.

Template Rollout

This rollout [see Figure 2] allows you to choose a light preset among a variety of preset light types. When you choose a template from this rollout, the parameters in other rollouts updated that you can use to fine-tune the settings of the light. The following presets are available in the **Template** rollout:

- (Bulb Lights)
- 40 Watt (W) Bulb
- 60W Bulb
- 75W Bulb
- 100W Bulb
- (Halogen Lights)
- Halogen Spotlight
- 21W Halogen Bulb
- 35W Halogen Bulb
- 50W Halogen Bulb
- 75W Halogen Bulb
- 80W Halogen Bulb
- 100W Halogen Bulb
- (Recessed Lights)
- Recessed 75W Lamp (web)
- Recessed 75W Wallwash (web)
- Recessed 250W Wallwash (web)
- (Fluorescent Lights)
- 4 ft. Pendant Fluorescent (web)
- 4 ft. Cove Fluorescent (web)
- (Other Lights)
- Street 400W Lamp (web)
- Stadium 1000W Lamp (web)

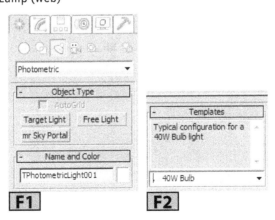

The parameters in this rollout are similar to that of the standard lights that we saw in **Unit L1** except the **Light Distribution (Type)** group. The drop-down in this group lets you choose the type of the light distribution model. The model defines the method of how a photometric light is distributed. Let's explore these types.

Uniform Spherical: This type casts lights in all directions [see Figure F3] like the standard **Omni** light. The **Uniform** distribution is represented by a small sphere in the viewports. The position of the sphere indicates whether the distribution is spherical or hemispherical.

Uniform Diffuse: This type casts diffuse light in one hemisphere [as if a light is positioned along a wall] only according to the **Lambert's** cosine law [see Figure F4].

Spotlight Distribution: This type casts a focused beam of light [see Figure F5] like a flashlight or a car's headlights. The beam angle of the light controls the main strength of the beam whereas the field angle controls the spill of the light.

Photometric Web: A photometric web is based on a geometric web that represents the light intensity distribution of a light source [see Figure 5]. The distribution information is stored in a photometric data file [that can be obtained from the light's manufacturer] in the **IES** format using the **IES LM-63-1991** standard file format.

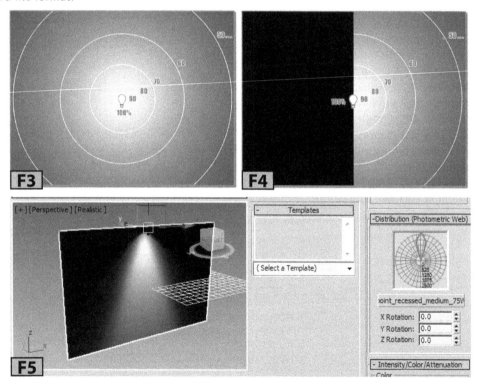

This rollout [see Figure F6] lets you set the color and intensity of the light. You can also set attenuation form this rollout.

Color Group

The first drop-down in this group allows you to pick a common lamp specification. Here're the options available:

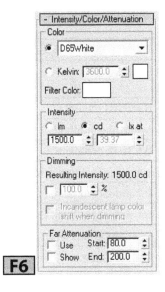

- D50 Illuminant (Reference White)
- D65 Illuminant (Reference White) (the default)
- Fluorescent (Cool White)
- Fluorescent (Daylight)
- Fluorescent (Lite White)
- Fluorescent (Warm White)
- Fluorescent (White)
- Halogen
- Halogen (Cool)
- Halogen (Warm)
- HID Ceramic Metal Halide (Cool)
- HID Ceramic Metal Halide (Warm)
- HID High Pressure Sodium
- HID Low Pressure Sodium
- HID Mercury
- HID Phosphor Mercury
- HID Quartz Metal Halide
- HID Quartz Metal Halide (Cool)
- HID Quartz Metal Halide (Warm)
- HID Xenon
- Incandescent filament lamp

Note: HID

HID *stands for high-intensity discharge.*

Note: D65 Illuminant (Reference White)

The default option in the drop-down approximates a midday sun in western or northern Europe. ***D65*** *is a white value defined by the* ***Comission Internationale de l'Éclairage (CIE)***, *the* ***International Lighting Commission***.

Figure F7 shows the render with the **D50 Illuminant (Reference White)**, **Fluorescent (Cool White)**, and **HID High Pressure Sodium**, respectively.

In addition to the list of lights, you can specify a color based on the temperature expressed in **Kelvin**. The **Kelvin** option allows you to set the color of the light by adjusting the color temperature spinners located next to it. The associated color appears on the color swatch on the right of the spinner. **Filter Color** allows you to simulate the effect of a color filter placed in front of the light source. The color temperature defines a color in terms of degree **Kelvin [K]**. The following table summarizes the color temperature for some common types of lights:

Table 2: Color Temperatures		
Light Source	**Temperature [K]**	**Hue**
Overcast daylight	6000	130
Noontime sunlight	5000	58
White fluorescent	4000	27
Tungsten/halogen lamp	3300	20
Incandescent lamp (100 to 200 W)	2900	16
Incandescent lamp (25 W)	2500	12
Sunlight at sunset or sunrise	2000	7
Candle flame	1750	5

Intensity Group

There are three controls in this group: **lm** [lumen], **cd** [candela], and **lx at** [lux]. These controls define the strength or brightness of the lights in physically based quantities. **Lumen** measures the overall output [luminous flux] power of the light. A **100 watt** bulb has about **1750 lm** luminous flux. **Candela** measures the maximum luminous intensity of the light, generally along the direction of the aim. A **100 watt** bulb has about intensity of **139 cd**. **Lux** measures the illuminate caused by the light shining on a surface at a certain distance in the direction of the source. **Lux** is the international scene unit and which is equivalent to **1 lumen per square meter**. To specify the illuminate of the light first enter the **lx** value in the first spinner and then enter **distance** in the second.

Dimming Group

The **Resulting Intensity** label shows the intensity caused by the dimming. It uses the same units that you have defined in the **Intensity** group. Turn on the **Dimming Percentage** switch to control the dimming of the light. At **100%**, the light has full intensity. When the **Incandescent lamp color shift when dimming** switch is on, the light simulate an incandescent light. The color of the light turns more yellowish as it is dimmed.

Shape/Area Shadows Rollout

You can use the parameters in this rollout [see Figure F8] to choose the light shape used for generating shadows. Let's explore the parameters.

Emit Light From (Shape) Group

The drop-down in this group allows you to choose the shadow generating shape for the light. When you choose a shadow generating shape other than **Point**, the parameters appear in the **Emit Light** group to control the dimensions of the shape. Also, the **Shadow Samples** control appears in the **Rendering** group of the rollout.

F8

The following table summarizes the shapes.

Table 3: Shadow Generating Shapes

Shape	Description
Point	Calculates shadows as if the light were emitted from a point like a light bulb. It has no other controls.
Line	Calculates shadows as if the light were emitted from a line like a fluorescent tube. This shape has a length control.
Rectangle	Calculates shadows as if the light were emitted from a rectangular area like a bank of fluorescent lights. This shape has length and width controls.
Disc	Calculates shadows as if the light were emitted from a disc like the light out of the top of a shaded lamp. This shape has radius control.
Sphere	Calculates shadows as if the light were emitted from a sphere like a Chinese lantern. This shape has radius control.
Cylinder	Calculates shadows as if the light were emitted from a cylinder. This shape has length and radius controls.

Rendering Group

When the **Light Shape Visible in Rendering** switch is on, the shape is visible in the renderings as a self-illuminated glowing shape. When switch is off, no shape is rendered. The **Shadow Samples** drop-down sets the overall quality of the shadows for the lights that have an area. If the render is grainy, increase the value for the **Shadow Samples** control. This setting does not appear for the **Point** shadow shape.

Distribution (Photometric File) Rollout

This rollout appears [see Figure F9] when you create or select a light with a photometric web distribution. You can use the controls in this rollout to select a photometric web file and adjust its parameters. After you choose a photometric file, the thumbnail [also referred to as **Web Diagram**] shows a schematic diagram of the distribution pattern of the light [see Figure F5].

The bright red outline shows the beam of the light. In some web diagrams, you will see a darker red outline that shows the field which is less bright than the beam. Click **Choose Photometric File** to select a file to use as a photometric web. The file can be in one of the following formats: **IES**, **LTLI**, or **CIBSE**. Once you select the file, this button displays the name of the file. The **X Rotation**, **Y Rotation**, and **Z Rotation** controls rotate the web about the **X**, **Y**, and **Z** axis, respectively.

Distribution (Spotlight) Rollout

This rollout appears [see Figure F10] when you select or create a photometric light with the spotlight distribution. The parameters in this rollout control hotspots and falloff of the spotlights.

Use the **Hotspot/Beam** and **Falloff/Field** spinners to increase or decrease the size of the beam angle and field angle regions. The **Cone visible in viewport when unselected** switch toggles the display of the cone on or off.

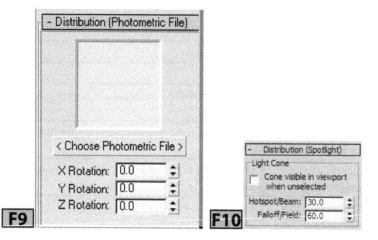

Free Light

The Free Light is similar to the Target Light except it has no target sub-object.

Summary

This units covered the following topics:

- Photometric light types: Target Light, and Free Light
- Color temperatures
- Shadow generating shapes
- Exposure controls

Unit L3: Sunlight and Daylight Systems

The **Sunlight** and **Daylight** systems are the built for simulating external lighting based on the sun. These systems follow the geographically correct angle and movement of the sun over the earth at a given location and are suitable for shadow study for proposed or existing structures. Using these systems, you can animate date and time, latitude, longitude, **North Direction** [rotational direction of the compass rose], and **Orbital Scale** [the distance of the sun from the ground plane].

In this unit, I will describe the following:

- **Sunlight** and **Daylight** Systems
- Positioning the Compass
- Choosing a location
- mr Sky Portal Light

Using the Sunlight and Daylight System

The **Sunlight** and **Daylight** are similar in how they are used [they have similar interface] but there are some differences:

- **Sunlight** uses a directional light.
- **Daylight** combines **Sunlight** and **Skylight**. The **Sunlight** component can be one of the following: **IES Sun** light, an **mr Sun** light, or a standard light (a target direct light). The **Skylight** component can be one of the following: **IES Sky** light, an **mr Sky** light, or a **Skylight**.

Note: Standard and Photometric Lights
*The **IES Sun** and **IES Sky** lights are photometric lights. You can use them if you are rendering a scene using **Radiosity** and exposure control. The **mr Sun** and **my Sky** lights are also photometric but are used with the **mental ray Sun & Sky** solution. The **Standard** light and **Skylight** are not photometric. You can use them if you are using standard lighting or you are using light tracing.*

You can access the **Sunlight** and **Daylight** systems from the **System** panel of the **Command Panel**. To create either of these systems, go to the **Create** panel and then click **Systems** [see Figure F1]. On the **Object Type** rollout, click **Sunlight** or **Daylight** and drag the mouse pointer in a viewport [should be **Top**, **Perspective**, or **Camera** view].

A compass helper object appears on the grid. Click again to create a **Direct** light representing the sun and drag to set its height above the ground plane. Figure F2 shows the compass created using the **Daylight** system.

F1

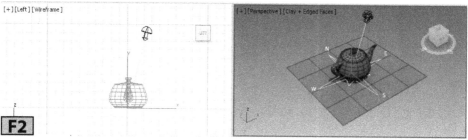

F2

When you first create a **Daylight** system, the **Daylight System Creation** warning dialog appears [see Figure F3], recommending to enable the **Logarithmic Exposure Control** for external light. Click **Yes** to enable the exposure control. If your default renderer is **mental ray**, the warning dialog recommends the **mr Photographic Exposure Control**.

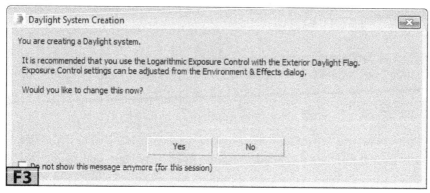

F3

Upon creation, you will have two objects in the scene. The compass rose, which is a helper object and provides the world directions for the sun. The light itself which is child of the compass is always targeted at the center of the compass rose. If you have created a **Daylight** system, you can choose the type of sunlight and skylight from the **Modify** panel. The **Sunlight** drop-down list lets you choose **IES Sun, mr Sun**, or **Standard (directional)**. The **Skylight** drop-down list lets you choose **IES Sky, mr Sky**, or **Skylight**. You can also choose **No Sunlight** or **No Skylight** from the drop-down lists.

The controls for adjusting the geographic location of the sun can be accessed from the **Motion** panel. The default time is noon whereas the default date and time is dependent on the settings of the computer you are using. The default location is **San Francisco, CA**.

Once you create a **Daylight** system, the parameters appear in the **Modify** panel. Let's explore the parameters that are unique to the **Daylight** system:

Daylight Parameters Rollout

The controls in this rollout [see Figure F4] lets you define the sun object of the **Daylight** system. You can use these controls to set the behavior of the sunlight and skylight.

The **Sunlight** drop-down lets you choose the sunlight for your scene. You can use one of the following options: **IES Sun, mr Sun, Standard**, and **No Sunlight**. The **Active** switch lets you toggle the sunlight on or off. The **Skylight** drop-down lets

F4

you choose the skylight for your scene. The available options are: **IES Sky**, **mr Sky Light**, **Skylight**, and **No Skylight**.

The controls in the **Position** group lets you define the correct geographical angle of the sun. The **Manual** control lets you manually adjust the location of the daylight. The **Date, Time and Location** control uses the geographically correct angle and movement of the sun over the earth at a given location. The **Weather Data File** control allows you to derive the angle and intensity of the sun from a weather data (**EPW**) file.

When you choose the **Weather Data File** and then click **Setup**, 3ds Max opens the **Configure Weather Data** dialog. You can choose which weather data you want the daylight system to use. When you choose the **Manual** or **Date, Time And Location** control, clicking on **Setup** button opens the **Motion** panel [see Figure F5] from where you can set the time, location, and site of your daylight system.

F5

Control Parameters Rollout
The **Azimuth** and **Altitude** controls display the azimuth and altitude of the sun. **Azimuth** is the compass direction [**North=0**, **East=90**] of the sun in degrees. **Altitude** is the height [**Sunrise/Sunset=0**] of the sun above the horizon in degrees. The controls in the **Time** group let you define the time, date, and time zone. When the **Daylight Savings Time** switch is on, 3ds Max calculates daylight savings by adjusting azimuth and altitude during the summer months.

The controls in **Location** group let you define location of your scene in the world. You can manually enter location based on the latitude and longitude. You can also specify location by using the **Geographic Location Dialog** which opens [see Figure F6] when you click **Get Location**. You can define the longitude and latitude values by selecting a location on the map or from a list of cities. The **North Direction** control sets the rotational direction of the compass rose in the scene. By default, north direction is **0**.

The **Orbital Scale** control in the **Model Scale** group lets the distance of the sun from the compass rose. The distance of sun from the compass rose has no effect on the accuracy of the sunlight.

mr Sky Portal Light
This light works with the mental ray renderer and allows you to gather existing sky light to further illuminate the scene. It effectively is an area light that derives its brightness and color from the environment. As a result, you can get good results without using high settings for final gather or global illumination.

Caution: Skylight component
*In order to **mr Sky Portal** to produce good results, make sure that the scene must contain a **Skylight** component.*

When you create a **mr Sky Portal** light, its parameter appears in the **mr Skylight Portal Parameters** and **Advanced Parameters** rollout of the **Modify** panel [see Figures F7 and F8]. Let's explore these parameters.

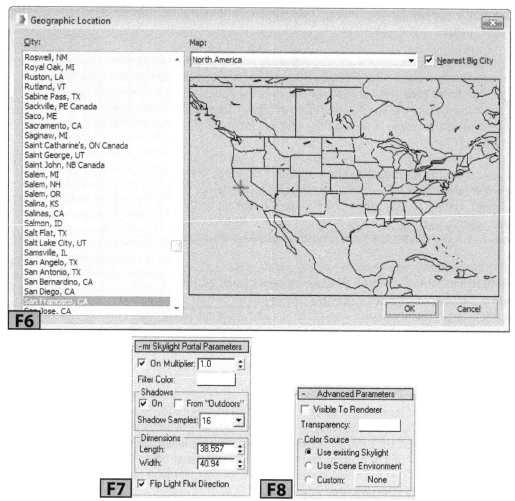

mr Skylight Portal Parameters Rollout

You already know about some of the controls available in this rollout such as the **On** switch and the **Multiplier** parameter. However, there are some parameters that are unique to this light.

The color specified using the **Filter Color** swatch tints the color gathered by the light. The **From "Outdoors"** switch casts shadows from objects on the other side [on the side away from the light's arrow] of the portal. Turning this switch on can increase the render time significantly. The **Shadows Samples** controls the overall quality of the shadows cast by the portal light. The **Length** and **Width** parameters allow you set the length and width of the portal, respectively. The **Flip Light Flux Direction** switch lets you toggle the direction of the light flow through the portal.

Advanced Parameters Rollout

When **Visible to Renderer** switch is on, the **mr Sky Portal** appears in the rendered image. The **Transparency** swatch allows you to filter the view outside the window. If you change the color of the swatch, it does not affect the light coming in, however, it makes the outside objects darker.

The parameters in the **Color Source** group allow you to specify the source of the light from which the portal drives the illumination. Here's the quick rundown:

- **Use existing Skylight**: Portal uses the skylight. By default, it uses the **mr Sky** light using the **mr Physical Sky** environment map at their default values.
- **Use Scene Environment**: Portal uses the environment map for illumination color.
- **Custom**: Portal uses the map that you specify. Click **None** to open the **Material/Map Browser** and then choose the required map.

Summary

If you are lighting an outdoor scene, the **Daylight** and **Sunlight** systems are the way to go. You can use these two systems to accurately create the lighting model using the geographical data. We have also learned about the **mr Sky Portal light** that allows you to gather existing sky light in the scene thus reducing the need of using high final gather or global illumination settings.

This unit covered the following:

- **Sunlight** and **Daylight** Systems
- Positioning the Compass
- Choosing a location
- mr Sky Portal Light

This page intentionally left blank

Unit LH1 - Hands-on Exercises [Lighting I]

Hands-on Exercise 1: Illuminating an Outdoor Scene

In this exercise, we are going to illuminate an outdoor scene using **Standard** lights. We will also use **Light Tracer** to enhance the scene [see Figure E1].

E1

The following table summarizes the exercise.

Table E1: Illuminating an outdoor scene	
In this exercise, you will:	Add lights to the scene Use the raytraced shadows Adjust the color and intensity of lights Use **Light Tracer** to enhance the scene
Topics in this section:	Getting Ready Adding Lights to the scene Enabling the **LightTracer** plugin Changing the **Scanline** renderer filter settings
Skill Level	Intermediate
Resources	**hoel1-1.zip**
Project Folder	**hoel1-1**
Start File	**hoel1-1-start.max**
Final Exercise File	**hoel1-1-end.max**
Time to Complete	45 Minutes

Getting Ready

Extract the content of **hoel1-1.zip** to a location in your HDD. This action created a folder with the name **hoel1-1**. This folder contains all the subfolders and files related to this exercise. Click **Project Folder** from the **Quick Access Toolbar** to open the **Browse For Dialog**. In this dialog, navigate to the **hoel1-1** folder and click **OK** to set the project folder and close the dialog. Now, open the **hoel1-1-start.max** file in 3ds Max.

Adding Lights to the Scene

You will first add a directional light to simulate the light coming from Sun and then the **Skylight** light to model the light coming from the sky. On the **Create** panel, click **Lights** and then select **Standard** from the drop-down available below **Lights**. On the **Object Type** rollout, click **Target Direct** and then in the **Left** viewport click on the upper-left area of the viewport to place the light and then drag toward the ladder to aim the light. Now, release the mouse button to set the aim [see Figure E2].

On the **Modify panel | General Parameters rollout**, turn on the **On** switch from the **Shadows** area and then select **Adv. Ray Traced** option from the drop-down in this area. On the **Directional Parameters rollout**, set **Hotspot/Beam** to **17.58** so that the directional light covers the whole scene [see Figure E3]. Ensure the **Perspective** view is active and then press **C** to activate the **Camera** view. Take a test render [see Figure E4].

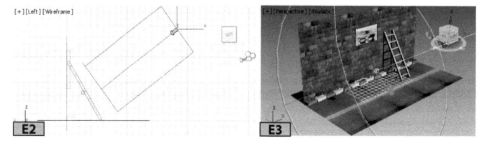

Now, you will add a **Skylight** to the scene. This light will provide the skylight and also it will create nice contact shadows. But, before we add the **Skylight**, let's turn off the directional light so that we can see what effect the **Skylight** produces. In the **General Parameters** rollout, turn off the **On** switch.

On the **Create panel | Object Type rollout**, click **Skylight** and then click anywhere in the scene to place the Skylight in the scene. The position of the **Skylight** does not affect the way it illuminates the scene therefor you can place light anywhere in the scene. Take a test render. You will notice that 3ds Max rendered a washed out image [see Figure E5]. Let's adjust some parameters to get the effect correct.

On the **Modify panel | Skylight Parameters rollout**, set **Multiplier** to **0.3**. **Sky Color** to light blue color, **RGB [189, 192, 201]**. On the **Render** group, turn on the **Cast Shadows** switch and then set **Rays per Sample** to **10**. Take a test render [see Figure E6]. Notice that now we have got the better result.

Select the directional light from the **Scene Explorer** and then turn it back on. On the **Intensity/Color/ Atteunation rollout**, set color to a warm color, **RGB [255, 234, 197]**. Take a test render [see Figure E7]; notice the render is looking much better now after both the lights in the scene illuminates the objects in in it. On the **Shadow Parameters** rollout, turn on the **Light Affects Shadow Color** switch.

Enabling Light Tracer

Open the **Render Setup** dialog and then go to **Advanced Lighting** panel. Select **Light Tracer** from the drop-down available in the **Select Advanced Lighting** rollout. Notice that the **Parameters** rollout appears in the panel. You can use the parameters available in this rollout to control the effect of the **Light Tracer** plugin.

On the **General Settings** group, set **Rays/Sample** to **500**, **Filter Size** to **0.7**, and **Bounce** to **1**. Now, take a test render to see the final render [see Figure E8 and **hoel1-1-finish.max**]. Now, save the render as a 16 bit TIF file and farther refine the render in Photoshop.

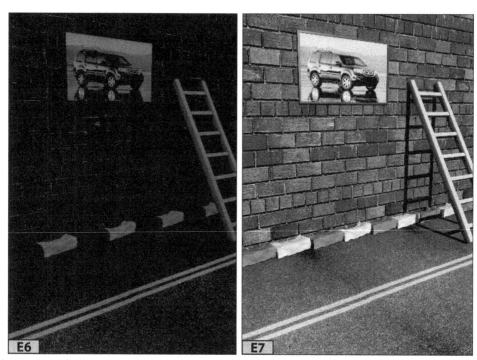

As you have seen **Light Tracer** allows you to create soft-shadows and also helps in producing a smooth render. Table 2 summarizes the **Light Tracer** parameters.

Table E1.1: The **Light Tracer** parameters	
Parameter	**Description**
Global Multiplier	It controls the overall lighting level.
Object Multi.	It controls the level of the light reflected by the objects in the scene. The effect of this parameter is more pronounced when Bounces is set to a value of 2 or higher.
Sky Lights	It scales the intensity of the skylights.
Color Bleed	Controls the color bleed that happens when light is interreflected among the scene objects.
Rays/Sample	Controls the number of rays per sample used by Light Tracer. Increasing this value produces smooth results at a cost of render time.
Color Filter	It filter all the light falling on the object. Change color to apply a tint to the scene.
Filter Size	The filter size used to reduce the noise.
Extra Ambient	The color you set for this parameter [other than black], Light Tracer adds that extra color to the ambient.
Ray Bias	It controls the position of the bounced light effects.

Bounces	Controls the number of time a ray bounces. On increasing its value, the color bleed also increases in the scene. Higher the value, more light will flow in the scene, and better result Light Tracer will produce at a cost of render time.
Cone Angle	It controls the angle used for regathering.
Volumes	When this switch is on, Light Tracer multiplies the amount of light it gathers from the volumetric lighting effects.

The parameters in the **Adaptive Undersampling** group let you speed up your renderings. These parameters allows you to specify the settings to reduce the number of light samples taken. **Light Tracer** initially takes samples from a grid superimposed on the pixels of the scene. When it finds enough contrast between the samples, it subdivide that region and takes farther samples, down to a minimum area specified by the **Subdivide Down To** parameter.

If you are rendering a complex scene, **Light Tracer** can slow down the rendering. For test renderings or a quick preview, given below are some tips:

- To generate a quick render, lower the values for the **Rays/Sample** and **Filter Size** parameters.
- Use the **Adaptive Undersampling** to create a quick preview. Set the **Initial Sample Spacing sampling** and the **Subdivide Down To** setting to the same value and then lower the **Rays/Sample** value and set **Bounced** to **0**.
- If there are some objects in the scene that have negligible impact on the scene, disable **Light Tracing** from these objects from the **Object Properties** dialog.
- To increase the amount of color bleeding, adjust the values of the **Bounces** and **Color Bleed** parameters.
- If there are glass objects in the scene, increase the number the value for the **Bounces** parameter.
- If **Skylight** is the main light in the scene and you need specular highlights, create a directional light parallel to the **Skylight**. Turn on shadows for the light and turn off the **Diffuse** switch in the **Advanced Effects** rollout of the light. In the render shown in Figure E9, I have switched off the **Diffuse** switch for the directional light to create an overcast sky like effect [see **hoel1-1-finish-overcast-sky.max**].

Tip: Using map with the Skylight
*If you are using a map for the skylight, ensure that you completely blur the image in a program like Photoshop. You can blur the map beyond recognition and **Light Tracer** will still fetch the info required for gathering light. Blurring the image helps in reducing the render time. In the render shown in Figure E10, I have completely blurred the image and then applied to the **Skylight**. I have also set the contribution of the map to **30%** using the control on the right of the **Map** switch in the **Skylight Parameters** rollout [see **hoel1-1-finish-blurred-sky.max**].*

Hands-on Exercise 2: Quickly Rendering an Architectural Plan

Sometimes, you need to send a quick draft render to your clients to check the CG assets and other related information in an architectural plan. Once approved, you can then proceed to produce the high quality render in **VRay** or **mental ray**. In this exercise, we are going to render an architectural plan using the **Standard** lights and the **Light Tracer** plugin [see Figure E11].

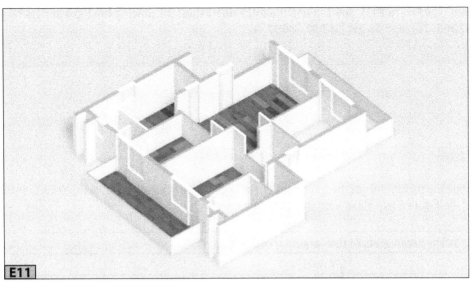

E11

Table E2 summarizes the exercise.

Table E2: Quickly rendering an architectural plan	
In this exercise, you will:	Add lights to the scene Use the advanced raytraced shadows Adjust the shadow parameters Use **Light Tracer** to enhance the scene
Topics in this section:	Getting Ready Illuminating the plan
Skill Level	Intermediate
Resources	**hoel1-2.zip**
Project Folder	**hoel1-2**
Start File	**hoel1-2-start.max**
Final Exercise File	**hoel1-2-end.max**
Time to Complete	30 Minutes

Getting Ready

Extract the content of **hoel1-2.zip** to a location in your HDD. This action created a folder with the name **hoel1-2**. This folder contains all the subfolders and files related to this exercise. Click **Project Folder** from the **Quick Access Toolbar** to open the **Browse For Dialog**. In this dialog, navigate to the **hoel1-2** folder and click **OK** to set the project folder and close the dialog. Now, open the **hoel1-2-start.max** file in 3ds Max.

Illuminating the Plan

Add a **Skylight** to the scene and then in **Modify Panel | Skylight Parameter rollout**, set **Multiplier** to **0.5** and color to **RGB [184, 184, 255]**. Turn on the **Cast Shadows** switch in the **Render** group. In the **Top** viewport, create a **Target Light** aiming toward the **Camera's** target [see Figure E12]. Now, in the **Left** viewport move the light up [see Figure E13]. You can use the following values for placing the light and its target: **Light [11825, -7069, 76]**, and **Target [11889, -7697, 0]**.

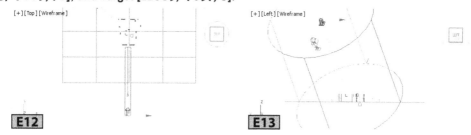

Now, change the parameters of the directional light in the **Modify** panel, refer to Table E2.1, and then take a render [see Figure E14]. Make sure the **Camera** view is active.

Table E2.1: The parameters of the **Target Light**	
Rollout	**Values**
General Parameters | Shadows	Turn on the **On** switch. Select **Adv. Ray Traced** shadows type.
Directional Parameters	Hotspot/Beam: **72**
Intensity/Color/Atteunation	Multiplier: **1.0**, Color: **RGB [255, 242, and 198]**.
Shadow Parameters	Dens: **0.5**. Turn on the **Light Affects Shadow Color** switch.
Adv. Ray Traced Params	Shadow Integrity: **10**, Shadow Quality: **5**, Shadow Spread: **20**, and Jitter Amount: **0.8**

Enable **Light Tracing** from the **Render Setup dialog | Advanced Lighting panel** and then take a test render [see Figure E15].

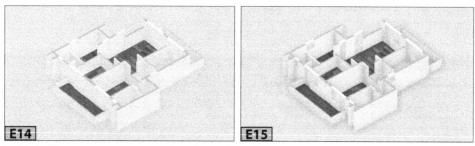

Adjust the **Light Tracer's** parameters using the values shown in Table E2.2.

Table E2.2: The parameters of the **Light Tracer**	
Rollout	**Values**
Parameters	Global Multiplier: **1.2**, Rays/Sample: **500**, Bounces: **2**
Parameters | Adaptive Undersampling	Initial Sampling Spacing: **32x32**

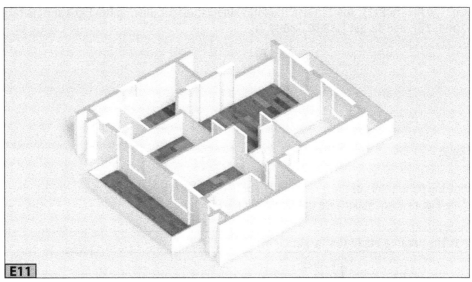
E11

Table E2 summarizes the exercise.

Table E2: Quickly rendering an architectural plan	
In this exercise, you will:	Add lights to the scene Use the advanced raytraced shadows Adjust the shadow parameters Use **Light Tracer** to enhance the scene
Topics in this section:	Getting Ready Illuminating the plan
Skill Level	Intermediate
Resources	**hoel1-2.zip**
Project Folder	**hoel1-2**
Start File	**hoel1-2-start.max**
Final Exercise File	**hoel1-2-end.max**
Time to Complete	30 Minutes

Getting Ready

Extract the content of **hoel1-2.zip** to a location in your HDD. This action created a folder with the name **hoel1-2**. This folder contains all the subfolders and files related to this exercise. Click **Project Folder** from the **Quick Access Toolbar** to open the **Browse For Dialog**. In this dialog, navigate to the **hoel1-2** folder and click **OK** to set the project folder and close the dialog. Now, open the **hoel1-2-start.max** file in 3ds Max.

Illuminating the Plan

Add a **Skylight** to the scene and then in **Modify Panel | Skylight Parameter rollout**, set **Multiplier** to **0.5** and color to **RGB [184, 184, 255]**. Turn on the **Cast Shadows** switch in the **Render** group. In the **Top** viewport, create a **Target Light** aiming toward the **Camera's** target [see Figure E12]. Now, in the **Left** viewport move the light up [see Figure E13]. You can use the following values for placing the light and its target: **Light [11825, -7069, 76]**, and **Target [11889, -7697, 0]**.

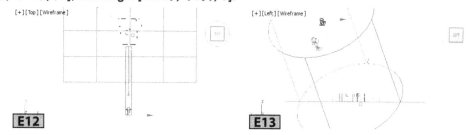

Now, change the parameters of the directional light in the **Modify** panel, refer to Table E2.1, and then take a render [see Figure E14]. Make sure the **Camera** view is active.

Table E2.1: The parameters of the Target Light	
Rollout	**Values**
General Parameters | Shadows	Turn on the **On** switch. Select **Adv. Ray Traced** shadows type.
Directional Parameters	Hotspot/Beam: **72**
Intensity/Color/Atteunation	Multiplier: **1.0**, Color: **RGB [255, 242, and 198]**.
Shadow Parameters	Dens: **0.5**. Turn on the **Light Affects Shadow Color** switch.
Adv. Ray Traced Params	Shadow Integrity: **10**, Shadow Quality: **5**, Shadow Spread: **20**, and Jitter Amount: **0.8**

Enable **Light Tracing** from the **Render Setup dialog | Advanced Lighting panel** and then take a test render [see Figure E15].

Adjust the **Light Tracer's** parameters using the values shown in Table E2.2.

Table E2.2: The parameters of the Light Tracer	
Rollout	**Values**
Parameters	Global Multiplier: **1.2**, Rays/Sample: **500**, Bounces: **2**
Parameters | Adaptive Undersampling	Initial Sampling Spacing: **32x32**

Now, take a test render [see Figure E11]. Experiment with various parameters of **Direct Light** and **Light Tracer** to achieve a different result.

Hands-on Exercise 3: Illuminating a Night Scene

Here we are going to illuminate the same scene that we used in Hands-on Exercise 1 but here we will simulate night lighting by using **Target Spot** and **Omni** lights [see Figure E16].

E16

Table E3 summarizes the exercise.

Table E3: Illuminating a night scene	
In this exercise, you will:	Add lights to the scene Use the advanced raytraced shadows Adjust the shadow parameters
Topics in this section:	Getting Ready Illuminating the Scene
Skill Level	Intermediate
Resources	**hoel1-3.zip**
Project Folder	**hoel1-3**
Start File	**hoel1-3-start.max**
Final Exercise File	**hoel1-3-end.max**
Time to Complete	30 Minutes

Extract the content of **hoel1-3.zip** to a location in your HDD. This action created a folder with the name **hoel1-3**. This folder contains all the subfolders and files related to this exercise. Click **Project Folder** from the **Quick Access Toolbar** to open the **Browse For Dialog**. In this dialog, navigate to the **hoel1-3** folder and click **OK** to set the project folder and close the dialog. Now, open the **hoel1-3-start.max** file in 3ds Max.

Illuminating the Scene

Create a **Target Spot** light in the **Front** viewport and then align it [see Figure E17]. Now, select **Spot001** from the **Scene Explorer**. In the **Front** viewport, drag the light with **Shift** held down along the X direction to the other light fixture on the left. In the **Clone Options** dialog that appears, select **Instance** from the **Object** group and then click **OK** to create a clone of the selected light. Now, align the cloned light with the fixture [see Figure E18].

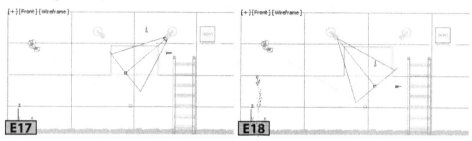

You can also use the values shown in Table E3.1 to position the spot lights.

Table E3.1: The transform values for spot lights	
Object	**XYZ Values**
Spot001	**39.991, -6.159, 116.401**
Spot001.Target	**-20.628, -6.159, 116.401**
Spot002	**-38.549, -6.159, 116.401**
Spot002.Target	**8.85, -6.159, 58.77**

Now, take a test render. You will notice [see Figure E19] that spot lights are illuminating the road as well. We need to confine the illumination to the billboard only. For that, we will use the **Atteunation** settings. Ensure a spot light is selected and then in the **Modify panel | Spotlight Parameters rollout**, set **Hotspot/Beam** to **43.7** and **Falloff/Field** to **67**. In the **Intensity/Color/Atteunation | Far Atteunation group**, turn on the **Use** and **Show** switches and then set **End** to **116**. Now, take a test render to see the area the spotlights are illuminating [see Figure E20].

Now, add an **Omni** light to the scene and place it at the following location [XYZ]: **38.169, -103.246, 117.664**.

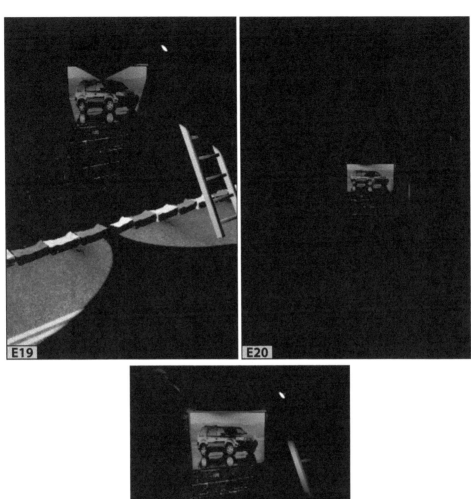

Change the parameters of the **Omni** light using the values shown in Table E3.2 and then take a test render [see Figure E21].

Table E3.2: The parameters of the Omni light	
Rollout	**Values**
General Parameters | Shadows	Turn on the **On** switch. Select **Adv. Ray Traced** shadows type.
Intensity/Color/Atteunation	Multiplier: **0.1**, Color: **RGB [173, 175,** and **208]**.
Shadow Parameters	Turn on the **Light Affects Shadow Color** switch.
Adv. Ray Traced Params	Shadow Integrity: **10,** Shadow Quality: **5,** Shadow Spread: **10,** and Jitter Amount: **0.7**

In the **Modify panel | Intensity/Color/Atteunation** rollout of a spot light, set **Multiplier** to **2** to make the area illuminated by the spot lights brighter. Render the scene to view the result.

Index

Other Books from Raavi Design

Create
Backgrounds, Textures, and Maps
In Photoshop
Using Photoshop CC 2014

Exploring
Utilities Nodes
In Maya 2016

Build Studio Light Setup
Using
3ds Max and VRay

Exploring
Standard Materials
in 3ds Max 2015

Raavi O'Connor

Beginner's Guide To
Mental Ray and Autodesk Materials
In 3ds Max 2016
raavidesign.blogspot.co.uk

Raavi O'Connor

Beginner's Guide For
Creating 3D Models
In 3ds Max 2016
raavidesign.blogspot.co.uk

Raavi O'Connor

The Tutorial Bank:
3D, VFX
& Motion Graphics
raavidesign.blogspot.co.uk

Raavi O'Connor

Exploring
Standard Materials
in 3ds Max 2016
raavidesign.blogspot.co.uk

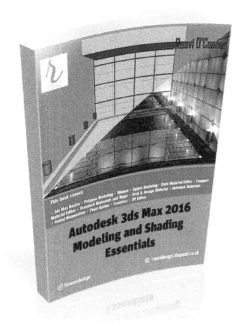

www.ingramcontent.com/pod-product-compliance
Lightning Source LLC
Chambersburg PA
CBHW080136060326
40689CB00018B/3805